BOOKS IN OUR FUTURE

PERSPECTIVES AND PROPOSALS

EDITED BY JOHN Y. COLE

LIBRARY OF CONGRESS

WASHINGTON   1987

Library of Congress Cataloging-in-Publication Data

Books in our future : perspectives and proposals.

Prepared under the auspices of the Center for the
Book.
Supplement to: Books in our future. 1984.
Bibliography: p. 375.
Includes index.
Supt. of Docs. no. : LC 1.2:B64/9
1. Books and reading—United States—Forecasting.
2. Libraries—United States—Forecasting. 3. Books in-
dustries and trade—United States—Forecasting. 4. Elec-
tronic publishing—United States—Forecasting. I. Cole,
John Young, 1940-   . II. Center for the Book.
Z1003.2.L52 1984 Suppl.   028'.9'0973   87-600047
ISBN 0-8444-0554-X

∞ The paper used in this publication meets the minimum
requirements of American National Standard for Information
Sciences—Permanence of Paper for Printed Library Materials,
ANSI Z39.48-1984.

Designed by Pat Taylor

For sale by the Superintendent of Documents, U.S. Government
Printing Office, Washington, D.C. 20402

Contents

Preface

This volume is a supplement to *Books in Our Future,* a report transmitted in 1984 to the Congress of the United States by Librarian of Congress Daniel J. Boorstin. The supplement presents the views of the advisors to the Library of Congress project on the Book in the Future, which led to the *Books in Our Future* report, and includes recommendations about the future of books and reading. Hence the subtitle of the present volume, *Perspectives and Proposals.*

The Librarian's report was the first result of the Book in the Future project. A directory of national organizations and associations promoting various aspects of book culture, *The Community of the Book,* appeared in 1986. The publication of the present volume completes the project. All these reports were prepared under the auspices of the Center for the Book in the Library of Congress.

Congress established the Center for the Book in 1977 to stimulate public interest in books and reading and to study the role of books and the printed word in society. The Center's symposia, publications, and projects are supported primarily by private contributions and occasionally by funds from other government agencies. For their support of the Book in the Future project, the Center is grateful to the following contributors: the New York Times Company Foundation, International Thomson Holdings, the McGraw-Hill Foundation, the U.S. Department of Education, the National Home Library Foundation, the Book-of-the-Month Club, Ingram Industries, and the College of Arts and Sciences at Virginia Polytechnic Institute and State University.

Many people have assisted in this undertaking. Special thanks go to Gerald Holton, chairman of the Library's Advisory Committee on the Book in the Future; to the committee members, whose views have shaped this volume; and to the other Center for the Book advisors who shared their opinions with us. Simon Michael Bessie, a director of Harper & Row and chairman of the Center for the Book's Executive Council, and Librarian of Congress Daniel J. Boorstin were constant supporters. The important contributions of project consultants Charles A. Goodrum and Helen Dalrymple include their chapters in this book. Library of Congress staff members from several divisions and, particularly, the Planning Office and the Publishing Office furnished information and guid-

vii

ance. Center for the Book consultant Joseph F. Brinley, Jr., provided valuable editorial help with this volume and prepared its bibliography, and staff member Linda Cox has assisted with the Book in the Future project since work began in November 1983. My thanks and appreciation to all.

John Y. Cole
Director, The Center for the Book
Director, Book in the Future Project
August 1986

The Book
in the Future Project

W hat is the future of the traditional book in the electronic age? How are the new technologies and other influences affecting books, reading, and learning in America? These two questions were at the heart of the Library of Congress Book in the Future project, which began in 1983, came to public attention in 1984 with the publication of *Books in Our Future: A Report from the Librarian of Congress to the Congress,* and concludes with publication of this supplementary volume. Not surprisingly, these two questions—no sure consensus answering them will be found here—are also at the heart of this book, which features the views of the project's advisors.

The Book in the Future project was authorized by Senate Concurrent Resolution 59, approved by Congress on November 18, 1983. The resolution, sponsored by Senator Charles McC. Mathias, Jr., called for a study of "the changing role of the book in the future," to be carried out under the auspices of the Center for the Book in the Library of Congress. The resolution focused, though not exclusively, on concerns that had been raised regarding the effect of new technological developments on books.

The resolution also stipulated that in conducting the study, the Librarian of Congress should "seek the advice and assistance of persons highly knowledgeable about the role of the book in civilization and the influence of new technologies on the future of the book." Such persons should include "scholars, authors, educators, publishers, librarians, scientists, and individuals in computer technology, industry, and labor." On this basis the Advisory Committee on the Book in the Future was appointed by Librarian Daniel J. Boorstin. Each advisor was interviewed by project consultants Charles A. Goodrum and Helen Dalrymple or by the project director, John Y. Cole, director of the Center for the Book. Most of the advisors also participated in a general discussion at the Library of Congress on March 7, 1984.

In transmitting his report to Congress in 1984, Librarian Daniel J. Boorstin explained that the document drew heavily on interviews and discussions with the Library's Advisory Committee on the Book in the Future and with members of the Center for the Book's National Advisory Board. On the basis of this information, published studies, and his own views of the importance of books,

Boorstin prepared the report. In the letter of transmittal he noted, "The conclusions are those of the Librarian of Congress. Some advisors do not agree with some of the conclusions." This supplementary volume, *Books in Our Future: Perspectives and Proposals,* presents the opinions and perspectives of project advisors and fulfills the promise made in the letter of transmittal to publish the advisors' views.

Much of *Books in Our Future: Perspectives and Proposals* consists of essays, studies, and reports by advisors that address the future of books and reading. Some were prepared for our study, others were first published elsewhere. To these personal views we have added excerpts from several commission reports that express important concerns of the book and educational communities. One or more of our advisors served on most of these commissions. In addition, a few articles are included that seem good presentations of views frequently encountered during the Book in the Future project.

Although not all the advisors share Librarian Boorstin's view of the future of books or his assertion of a complementary relationship between books and new technologies, most agree with his major conclusion that our "Culture of the Book...is now threatened by the twin menaces of illiteracy and aliteracy." Thus the status of reading in our culture, both in the schools and outside formal education, is a major topic in this volume. This is a difficult subject to analyze, largely because reading and its effects are difficult to measure. In some ways there seems to be more reading going on now than there was earlier in American society; the problem of illiteracy, however, persists. Moreover, a large number of people— the "aliterates"—do not read even though they know how to read. Finally, many of our advisors raise questions about *what* is being read. Professional reading, specialized hobby or avocational reading, the reading of how-to books and of genre fiction appear to be on the increase, while what many consider to be serious nonfiction and fiction reach only narrow audiences. The effects of these trends and the development of programs for teaching and motivating reading are important topics in this book.

The other emphasis in this volume is on technological change in communication. What kinds of technological developments might replace what kinds of books? What kinds of functions of books cannot be altered, improved upon, or replaced? What does the creation of expert systems—computers that can perform highly developed deductive and retrieval functions—do to or for scholarship and learning? Do such functions have anything to do with those of the traditional book? And again we must ask about the effects of these changes on the general culture.

Introduction to this Volume

The advisors are introduced in Part I through biographical information and excerpts from comments they made in the course of the project, especially at the March 1984 meeting.

Parts II, III, and IV of *Books in Our Future: Perspectives and Proposals* treat Reading and Learning, Reading and Society, and Technology and the Future of the Book. These areas obviously have some overlap, and so do the essays in the sections covering them. More important, however, is the diversity of ambitions, hopes, and fears of the authors.

In the face of change and uncertainty, the professions of the community of the book face tensions, too. Parts V and VI deal with two of these professions: publishing and librarianship. Here, too, there is a dual concern: How is the role of books changing in the general culture? and How does new technology affect the aims of each profession? Additional influences appear, as well. Publishers, for example, face the basic problem of staying in business, and research librarians are confronted with the task of preserving the books produced on highly acidic paper since the late nineteenth century.

Finally, two summary views are presented in Part VII. First, an excerpt from the recent report to the American Library Association of its Commission on the Freedom and Equality of Access to Information summarizes important issues facing the library profession and American society as a whole. Secondly, we republish the key portion of *Books in Our Future: A Report from the Librarian of Congress to the Congress.*

Freedom carries its own responsibility, perhaps a heavier one than if freedom were absent; in a democracy, all elements share in the common good, the common cause, and the common glory; publishers of books, like others whose work is with the "media of communication," are educators beyond the schools. We require much of them; they give us much.

LISTER HILL
U.S. Senator

I.
The Advisors

Advisory Committee on the Book in the Future

Gerald Holton, Chairman

Gerald Holton's unique perspective as both a scientist and a humanist made him an ideal chairman of the Advisory Committee. Since 1947 he has been on the faculty of Harvard University, where he now serves as Mallinckrodt Professor of Physics and Professor of the History of Science. In 1981 the National Council on the Humanities invited him to present the Jefferson Lecture in the Humanities. He was a member of the National Commission on Excellence in Education, which produced the report *A Nation at Risk* in 1983. His books include *Thematic Origins of Scientific Thought: Kepler to Einstein* (Harvard University Press, 1973) and, most recently, *The Advancement of Science, and its Burdens: The Jefferson Lecture and Other Essays* (Cambridge University Press, 1986).

Professor Holton's opening remarks to the committee on March 7, 1984, which follow, make clear his probing but evenhanded approach to the many questions facing the group. His statement set the tone for the discussion and, indeed, for the entire Book in the Future project.

In chairing this meeting and eliciting your contributions to the discussion, let me confess that my ears will be tuned particularly to questions such as these: How can democracy and the civilizing function of education be better served by new technological opportunities? What can be done about the large pool of illiterates, and the one and a half million adults being added to it in this country every year? Can technology help reverse the tendency toward the concentration of the news media into fewer and fewer

Unless otherwise noted, quotations are from the March 7, 1984, meeting of the advisors. During the course of the project, Harry J. Gray, Chairman and Chief Executive Officer of United Technologies Corporation, who was originally appointed to the Advisory Committee, designated Russell G. Meyerand, Jr., introduced below, to replace him on the committee.

hands? How will the young stumble across Thomas Paine or Voltaire, *The Brothers Karamazov* or Charles Darwin, Walt Whitman or, for that matter, *Winnie the Pooh,* if those are no longer conveniently and freely available on open shelves? (Perhaps it *can* be made easier.) How to rescue the scholarly monograph, which has become an endangered species? How to improve access to audiences for new talent and for the full spectrum of serious political thought? How to encourage more, and more venturesome, experimentation by a publishing industry that finds itself rather suddenly in such unfamiliar territory? These are some of the more general questions with which we and, ultimately, the Congress will have to struggle.

Let me ask that we avoid, as much as possible, confrontations between the old world of the book and the new digital world of the "chip." Just consider what might have been said at a conference like ours run in the early 1830s, when the news came that the steam engine, the long-established purveyor of energy, was threatened by the discovery of the electric generator and motor. The new motor had many things going for it. For example, you no longer had to have the energy source right nearby, but could connect to it by wires over a long distance. It could be made much more compact in relation to the amount of power delivered, and it did not tend to explode or to pollute *in situ.*

I can imagine that the manufacturers, owners, operators, and fanciers of steam engines might have called a conference against the potential threat of those new wires. But it soon became clear that the two were not natural enemies but partners in a new symbiosis. The steam engine and similar heat engines came to be so widespread and to work so well as energy sources just because they have motors and other electric devices attached to them, and also because the energy that comes over the wires to make our motors go—the average home even now has some thirty motors in appliances, clocks, fans, tape recorders, etc.—is in fact conveniently produced mostly by centralized heat engines. In short, let us here, too, seek out the symbiosis between apparent contraries. I, for one, am ready to bet that we will some day find that the book has been waiting for the chip all along.

William O. Baker

William O. Baker, in our interview in the Book in the Future project, noted that corporate managers do not read the books they should be reading. His conclusion is not, however, to demand more executive reading, but to look forward to the arrival of easily accessible databases in text and interpretive form that will provide a relatively "graceful transition" between the book and the knowledge that a person really needs.

Dr. Baker is now retired from a long career with Bell Telephone Laboratories, where he began as a research chemist in 1939. He served as President of the company from 1973 to 1979 and as Chairman of the Board, 1979-80. He received a Ph.D. from Princeton University in 1938 and now holds twenty-five honorary degrees. He also holds thirteen patents. He is Chairman of the Rockefeller University and of the Andrew W. Mellon Foundation.

Dr. Baker has served on many governmental and scientific commissions, including several that have been directly concerned with communication, education, and the future of libraries. For example, he has been a member of the National Commission on Libraries and Information Science, the Board of Regents of the National Library of Medicine, and, since 1970, of the Board of Directors of the Council on Library Resources. He also served, along with Gerald Holton, on the National Commission on Excellence in Education.

The object of computing is insight, not numbers.

New machines can now deal with combinations of symbols and the coding of words and graphics at speeds quite beyond human consideration by many, many orders of magnitude. Therefore, one sees the opportunity for combining the book, with its beauty and symmetry and serial qualities, with the capability of handling knowledge at vastly greater ranges and in vastly more intriguing combinations. For instance, a book with a plot, with a message, or with various themes going through it can easily be encoded so that the logic and memory of the composer of the book appear very clearly and simply to the reader.... This may be somewhat disillusioning in some artistic sense, but it seems very likely that the oncoming generations of people who want to learn and to enjoy and to partake of the compositions of others will also be people who have been interested in logic and memory. Perhaps this interest will be stimulated by computer experiences now, or perhaps from the learning which we believe will be widespread in the times ahead.... The report *A Nation at Risk* proposed a very strong policy of acquainting people with this way of compartmenting, or rather assembling, knowledge and examining its consistency and its interrelations, not necessarily in a critical or destructive way, but in a way to see where it hangs together, whether it is really coherent. We believe that that kind of capability from the digital processing of the content of books should be combined with the printed word.

Jacques Barzun

In his comments on the future of the book, Jacques Barzun stressed the need to make distinctions, particularly among types of books and among the various purposes of reading. His focus is on the importance to a society of citizens who read books, and he emphasizes reading rather than "looking up" and books rather than compilations of information. Reading itself is an important mental power, he argues.

Jacques Barzun is widely known as a scholar, teacher, author, and translator. He was on the faculty of Columbia University from 1927 until 1967, when he was named University Professor and Special Advisor on the Arts to the President. He resigned from Columbia in 1975 and is currently Literary Advisor at Charles Scribner's Sons. He has written more than two dozen books. The wide range of his interests can be seen in a few of his titles: *Teacher in America,* first published in 1945; *Science: The Glorious Entertainment* (1964); *Berlioz and the Romantic Century* (3d ed., 1969); and *A Stroll with William James* (1983).

Two essays by Dr. Barzun on the importance of reading books are reprinted in this volume: "The Centrality of Reading" (chap. 5), which relates to any sort of learning, and "The Future of Reading" (chap. 11), which treats trends in literature in relation to intellectual culture.

The differences between information, knowledge, and the acquisition of wisdom through reading poetry, philosophy, and so forth are perfectly obvious and should be made perfectly clear. And other distinctions exist: there is a difference between consulting a reference work to obtain a single fact, or skimming and spot-reading to grasp a point, and reading to master a whole subject or to enjoy an imaginative experience. These are different activities of the mind and correspond to different modes of using books. The mental acts and results will differ still further when we turn to the new machinery at our disposal, and so will the emotions that attend these various aims.

"The book," "a book" is by now a false abstraction. Most of the books that are published today and widely read are highly specialized. The books that publishers bring out with marked success tend to be those they can sell to groups of people already bent on buying any book on the particular subject. You would not suppose that a good novel, even when well reviewed, would sell far fewer copies than a book about types of bombers used in World War II, but that is a fact. There are "publics," not one public; the former "general reader" is a vanishing breed—or a minority in hiding. People who buy books about gardening or cookery or the Civil War buy no others, and this holds for an increasing number of "sects," each with its book club. So "the book," like the "reader of books," hardly exists as an entity that can be discussed in general terms.

Lewis M. Branscomb

Lewis M. Branscomb is Vice President and Chief Scientist of International Business Machines Corporation and a member of IBM's Corporate Management Board. Before joining IBM in 1972, he served the government as Director of the National Bureau of Standards. From 1965 to 1969 he was a member of the President's Science Advisory Committee, and from 1980 to 1984 he was Chairman of the National Science Board. He was the Chairman of the Carnegie Corporation's Task Force on Teaching as a Profession, which issued its recommendations in May 1986.

Before he was awarded M.S. and Ph.D. degrees in physics by Harvard University, Lewis Branscomb was graduated summa cum laude from Duke University. His interest in books and libraries comes naturally from his father, Harvie Branscomb, a former Director of Libraries at Duke University and the author, in 1940, of a volume titled *Teaching With Books*.

Lewis Branscomb adapted the comments below from "Video Disc Technology and the Book," a presentation he made at the 1981 meeting of the Center for the Book's National Advisory Board, which was published in *Books, Libraries, and Electronics,* edited by Efrem Sigel (White Plains, N.Y.: Knowledge Industry Publications, 1982).

McLuhan was only half right. The medium is not the message, but it can create new dimensions to the message. It's the message that matters.

From a technical perspective, the new electronic media provide capabilities going far beyond both books and motion pictures.

Clearly the potential is there for genuinely new and unique media. But will they live up to that potential, or be simply new ways to shuttle about old information?

The answer lies in how creative people use them. Who will "write" the new video books? Who will construct the electronic encyclopedias? Who will find out what is real and what is gimmick? Will new kinds of authorship evolve and survive—and should they?

We know from the hard lesson of television that the software that emerges never seems to live up to the promise of the new technology for distributing it. The same thing may happen again with computer information services and interactive video publishing, although people are working harder now to prevent it.

Can we expect libraries to play a creative role in this period of experimentation? I certainly hope so. But as my father wrote nearly fifty years ago, libraries must again become teachers and innovators—not custodians, lest the treasures in their custody become obsoleted by alternative services that fail to serve humanity as imaginatively and profoundly as they could.

Of all the artifacts of industry, the book most effectively sustains our intellectual life. And somehow, despite the temptations of commerce and the limited literacy taste of the general public, book publishers have managed to maintain a degree of social responsibility thus far unmatched by any of the new electronic media.

Ultimately these new media will stand or fall, not so much on electronics and hardware, fascinating as these may be, but on the information that goes into them. More than ever, the quality and value of that information will be the gating factor in the success of cable, direct broadcast satellite, optical fiber, videotape, videodisk, and computer information services.

John Chancellor

Now commentator on the "NBC Nightly News," John Chancellor has served NBC News in an impressive variety of posts. He has been midwestern correspondent, foreign correspondent, host of the "Today" program, Chief White House Correspondent, and, for eleven years, an anchorman on "NBC Nightly News." Mr. Chancellor has been with NBC News since 1950, except for two years (1965-67) when, as an appointee of President Lyndon B. Johnson, he was Director of the Voice of America—the first working journalist ever to hold that post. In 1967 he was the recipient of the Arthur S. Flemming Award as one of the ten outstanding young men in the federal government. He has received many important awards in broadcast journalism, including designation in 1982 by the International Radio and Television Society as Broadcaster of the Year.

I prefer to focus on the written word, not the book. The important question is not does the book have a future (because obviously it does), but how do we store writing in the future? This writing can be scientific writing, *Winnie the Pooh,* poetry, or anything, but whatever it is, there will be an avalanche in the future, and we have to find ways to store it.

Overall, it seems to me that the general base of readers in America is about where it always has been, or perhaps even a little bit higher....How many "serious book readers" can there—or *should* there—be in a society? Is it critical if most people are not serious book readers? I think not. An analogy can be made to voter turnout in elections: on one hand we bemoan the low voter turnout, but some of us wonder what the result would be if everyone did turn out....Moreover, a tremendous number of Americans read newspapers and magazines. The big, general circulation magazines have declined, perhaps because of television, but there has been an enormous increase during the past decade in specialized magazines.

Kenneth E. Dowlin

Kenneth E. Dowlin, Director of the Pikes Peak Regional Library District in Colorado Springs, Colorado, has devoted his career to increasing public access to information through the innovative uses of technology. His "Maggie's Place" in the Pikes Peak Library District is one of the most comprehensive computerized library systems in the country, and a model for systems throughout the world. In our discussions Mr. Dowlin emphasized that we are not facing an "either/or" situation in which either books or computers would be excluded; the future will be a mixture of both. He noted, for example, that the biggest use of the Pikes Peak Library computer system comes from people who want to find out about books. He is concerned about the future of reading and of libraries, however: "In this country more homes have television sets than have books. And in 1983, twice as much money was spent on home computers as was spent on public libraries."

A graduate of the Universities of Colorado and Denver, Kenneth Dowlin has been Director of the Pikes Peak Regional Library District since 1975. From 1969 to 1975 he headed the Natrona County

(Wyoming) Public Library, where he developed one of the first video reference services in the country.

An excerpt from Mr. Dowlin's book *The Electronic Library* is reprinted in chapter 13 of this volume.

The crux of the issue we are facing is how to ensure the continued creation and dissemination of *knowledge*—not information. Today we have an overload of information. How do we handle the electronic information sources in a way that will create knowledge out of all this information that constantly washes over us?

Librarians and libraries face a two-dimensional challenge. Now is the time for the library profession to develop the infrastructure (cataloging, classification, bibliographic control, facilities) needed to guarantee a minimum level of access to information and knowledge in the "Neographic Age." I do not call this the "Electronic Age," for bits, bytes, and electrons have not displaced and will not displace the print medium.

We must continue to refine methodologies for access to information and knowledge for print, yet we must recognize that the ultimate graphic knowledge instrument, the book itself, no longer has a major role in decision making in our society. This can be illustrated by contrasting the impact of John F. Kennedy's book *Profiles in Courage* on the presidential election of 1960 with the fact that the 1984 election was communicated solely by mass communications technologies and without the influence of a book.

I am strongly convinced that the book is not at risk of extinction. I am concerned, however, that as the use of the book to support decision making in society decreases, a knowledge instrument of similar power be developed.

Robert F. Erburu

Robert F. Erburu was elected Chief Executive Officer of the Times Mirror Company in 1981, and Chairman of the Board and Chief Executive Officer in 1986. A graduate of the Harvard Law School, he was an attorney for the Los Angeles firm of Gibson, Dunn & Crutcher for six years before joining the Times Mirror Company in 1961. He was elected President in 1974. He has been a director of the American Newspaper Publishers Association since 1980. His other current memberships include the

Board of Trustees of the Huntington Library, Art Gallery and Botanical Gardens; the Council on Foreign Relations; and the Board of Trustees of the Brookings Foundation.

Mr. Erburu commented on the relationships of newspapers to new technologies and to the problem of illiteracy in correspondence with the Center for the Book:

> Newspapers have benefited greatly from new technologies employed in the newsroom, the pressroom, and indeed in all aspects of their operations. When a reporter calls in a story today, it may well be his personal computer that communicates directly with the computerized editorial system in the newsroom.
>
> The threat that electronic information systems might replace newspapers entirely, or at least weaken them, seems less ominous than it did a few years ago. The disappointing results of a number of videotex trials reflect consumers' remarkably strong preference for the convenience and economy of the traditional newspaper format.
>
> What are the new problems? Economic conditions and competitive factors will result in short-term fluctuations in advertising and circulation revenues, but long-term trends in American reading habits are of greater concern. Newspapers, like books and magazines, are threatened by illiteracy and aliteracy. Both the skill and the habit of reading are essential to the health of the nation's newspapers. The newspaper industry, like its print-media brethren, is awakening to the challenge.

Warren J. Haas

Since 1978 Warren J. Haas has been President of the Council on Library Resources, a private foundation that assists libraries, particularly academic and research libraries. Under Mr. Haas's leadership, the Council on Library Resources has played a key role in funding research to improve collection development, resource sharing, and preservation activities in research libraries and in helping libraries redefine and meet their obligations in the computer age. Mr. Haas was Director of Libraries at the University of Pennsylvania from 1966 to 1969, Director of Libraries at Columbia University, 1970-72, and Vice President for Information Services and University Librarian at Columbia, 1972-77.

Warren J. Haas's essay describing issues now being faced by academic and research libraries, "New Wine, New Bottles," is reprinted in this volume (chap. 24).

As much as we are awed by what technology can do, we need still to pay attention to what it cannot do. Ink on paper offers more than comfort; it is a secure reference to information as recorded at a precise time. Computer databases can be homogenized, synthesized, and integrated. There is little assurance that a footnote to machine-stored information can be verified. Our intellectual audit trail is at risk.

Frederick G. Kilgour

In our discussions, Frederick G. Kilgour, Founder Trustee of OCLC (Online Computer Library Center) and a pioneer in applying information technology to the world of books, noted that the environment in the future will change so rapidly and extensively that he could not be confident that there always will be a printed book. He emphasized the importance of realizing that computers today still are used mostly to do old things in new ways, but in the future there will be many exciting opportunities to do new things in new ways.

Kilgour was named Founder Trustee of OCLC in 1984. He was OCLC's President and Executive Director from 1967 to 1980, and Vice Chairman of the Board of Trustees from 1981 to 1983. He has received many awards for his work, including four citations from the American Library Association and awards from the American Society for Information Science and the Medical Library Association. In 1986 he received the Governor's Award in Ohio. From 1948 to 1965 he was a Lecturer at Yale in the History of Science. His library career began as an assistant at the Harvard College Library.

The lecture "Beyond Bibliography," presented by Frederick Kilgour in 1985 at the British Library, is reprinted in this volume (chap. 23).

The Electronic Information Delivery Online System (EIDOS), for which I am the principal investigator, is based on many assumptions. One is that there will be digitized telephony before too long, maybe not in my lifetime, but in the foreseeable future. There will be digitized television; there will be extensive availability of personal computers in the home, office, and workplace, including the library; books in digital form will also be extensively available. Parallel publication of books in print and in digital form will go on for a long time. But there will be some books that will be available only in digital form, and some books that I don't think will ever be available in digital form. EIDOS is not aimed at those who *read* books, but at those who *consult* books or use small sections of books intensively. It is directed primarily at individual users, to enable them to get the information they want, and when and where they want it. In the early days of OCLC I used to say that it was my hope that in the 1990s librarians in their annual reports would be bragging about how few people came into the library. This boast is probably going to come to pass in many libraries. The libraries will have the needed information and will be acquiring it and selecting it much the way they do now, but people will not have to come into the library to use it.

Louis L'Amour

Author Louis L'Amour, whose eighty-nine novels have sold over 150 million copies, described himself in our interview as a "creature of the book," a person who educated himself entirely by reading. He now has over ten thousand volumes in his personal library, which he draws on for background in his novels and uses to answer the hundreds of specific questions he receives each year from his readers. His major concern is the increasingly high price of books: "They are too expensive and are now being priced out of the reach of many people." If people cannot afford books, he thinks, they naturally will turn to other media for entertainment and learning.

L'Amour, who was born in North Dakota, was presented the Congressional Medal in 1983. In 1984 he received the Presidential Medal of Freedom.

Our country, more than any other I know, was founded upon books. Almost every one of the founding fathers had read Plutarch, and most of them also read Locke's *Treatises on Government.* They did not have our numbers of books, but those they had they read, pondered, and discussed. In some respects they were more fortunate than we in that they were not assailed on every hand with so many social activities or things to do or be done. There was time for reading, and above all, for thinking about what they had read. This is the greatest problem of our day: how do we find the time to think? We are so busy gathering information and reading and learning that we have too little time to think about what we have learned.

F. Wilfrid Lancaster

The book, maintains F. Wilfrid Lancaster, is not the best vehicle for transmitting knowledge; in fact, he feels that the printed book in its present form will disappear. He reiterated these views in our discussions, but also clarified several points, since "there is some danger that what I have written has been misinterpreted or, in some cases, misrepresented." In particular, he emphasized that "never, at any point, have I suggested that it makes any sense to take what is already written and put it into machine-readable form." When he discusses electronics replacing the printed book, he is referring to newly conceived publications. For example, there is not, he noted, "any possible advantage in displaying the books of Jane Austen on a screen."

Mr. Lancaster is Professor of Library Science in the Graduate School of Library and Information Science at the University of Illinois at Urbana-Champaign. He has worked in the information field for over twenty-five years and has experience in the private sector, in the United States government with the National Library of Medicine, and as a consultant to governments in Europe and South America. His major publications include *Libraries and Librarians in an Age of Electronics* (Information Resources Press, 1982), *Information Retrieval Systems* (John Wiley & Company, 1979), and *Toward Paperless Information Systems* (Academic Press, 1978).

Two essays by Professor Lancaster are reprinted in this volume, "The Paperless Society Revisited" (chap. 15) and "Electronic Publishing: Its Impact on the Distribution of Information" (chap. 17).

True electronic publication comes when the author or creator of whatever it happens to be—a painting or a poem, or a novel or a scientific article—conceives from the beginning of presenting the information or the experience that he wants to present for the electronic medium. When that happens, then I think we are going to get a completely new kind of publication, which I conceive of as being much closer to the electronic game than anything that exists on the shelves of the library today. I can conceive of a children's encyclopedia in which the child actually moves an electronic analog model of a plane across the screen to learn the principles of aerodynamics. I can conceive of journals in applied mechanics in which, rather than using narrative texts and a mathematical model to describe the effects of wind loads on a structure, the author presents what are essentially data and an electronic analog model of the structure, and the reader can in fact manipulate that model.

Authorship and the effect of technology on the creative person are very important topics. What we store in the future, what we retrieve, and what we publish are very much affected by what people are creating and in what forms and for what media. There is a great deal of research and experimentation going on today in the exploitation of new technologies for the creation of new art forms and for the distribution of information in innovative ways. On the one hand, we have experimentation with electronic art, electronic painting, and electronic poetry. At the other extreme we have organizations like the National Library of Medicine producing what are essentially electronic textbooks—the hepatitis knowledge base, which is in fact an electronic textbook on a technical subject produced by consensus, arrived at by a consensus of experts, made possible by technology, readily kept up to date. So we have "a living textbook." We have a completely new way of arriving at and updating certain kinds of publications made possible by technology. I think that there should be further research and experimentation and the funding of research and experimentation on the effects of technological capabilities on the creative process. That is, to what extent can we present information and ideas through technology in ways we have never presented them before?

Sol M. Linowitz

Sol M. Linowitz has combined three careers—lawyer, businessman, and diplomat. He is Senior Counsel of the international law firm of Coudert Brothers. Previously he was Chairman of the Board of the Xerox Corporation. In 1966 he was appointed by President Lyndon B. Johnson as United States Ambassador to the Organization of American States and United States Representative on the Inter-American Committee of the Alliance for Progress. He held these posts until 1969, when he joined the Coudert law firm. He has served as Chairman of the National Urban Coalition and the Presidential Commission on World Hunger. Holding the rank of Ambassador, he was conegotiator of the Panama Canal treaties and, from 1979 to 1981, Personal Representative of the President to the peace negotiations in the Middle East. He discussed his careers in *The Making of a Public Man, A Memoir* (Little, Brown & Company, 1985).

If there is one point I would stress to our national leaders, it is the critical significance of the problem of illiteracy to the future of the United States. For if it is true that a nation cannot be both ignorant and free, and if knowledge does indeed conquer ignorance, then illiteracy is a challenge to our national security and therefore pivotal to our future as a nation.

If we are really serious about trying to preserve the future of the book, then we should be talking about the future of libraries and how to assure adequate funding for them. For clearly our libraries ought to be receiving enough support to deal not only with books, but with the new opportunities being created by the new technologies.

In furthering literacy in this country, there is a place for books which are not "classics" or "literature" or even "worthwhile." After all, learning to read includes learning to read trash, too. There is even a place for how-to-do-it and how-to-fix-it books, as well as for Jane Fonda's exercise book. The point is, however, that it must be understood that this is not all that books can be, and we must induce respect for kinds of books—of substance, of meaning, of beauty, of significance—which we are capable of producing as a reflection of the best within us.

Ruth B. Love

Educational Consultant Ruth B. Love has wide experience in teaching and public school administration. She was Superintendent of Schools in Oakland, California, from 1975 to 1981, and General Superintendent of Schools in Chicago, Illinois, from 1981 to 1984. Prior to heading the Oakland Unified School District, she was Director for four years of the Right-to-Read Office in the United States Office of Education. Her writings include articles on career education, counseling services for minority and disadvantaged youth, education in developing countries, affirmative action, and, most recently, the book *Johnny Can Read, So Can Jane* (Addison-Wesley, 1982).

The comments below are from an October 1984 letter to Librarian of Congress Daniel J. Boorstin.

The culture of the book will continue to flourish, but if we are to realize the full potential of a literate society, government funds must accompany the many and varied strategies we are developing to combat the enemies of the book. Local, state, and federal government agencies must become involved.

There is no substitute for the parental role model in stimulating a love of reading among children. The influence of the book is influenced by the model. And this influence is continued throughout early childhood education, where the activities of teachers can reinforce those of parents who began fostering a love for the book. I remain committed to a statement I made in the preface to the first edition of Jim Trelease's *The Read-Aloud Handbook:* "If we could get our parents to read to their preschool children fifteen minutes a day we could revolutionize the schools...."

Television *is* a problem. My solution is to use the threat to address the threat: many "outside-the-text" reading and verbal skills may be introduced and developed through the medium of television. Television scripts, for example, can be used during program viewing. Adults can aid students in monitoring, evaluating, and discussing television programs. Students can be encouraged to learn about and then develop their own television spot announcements and, ultimately, their own television shows. Although these activities may seem "outside the book," when efforts are made to link them to the learning experience, student esteem for books is enhanced.

Russell G. Meyerand, Jr.

Russell G. Meyerand, Jr., Vice President for Technology, United Technologies Corporation, is responsible for the corporation's programs in advanced technology. He has held this post since 1981. He joined the corporation, then called United Aircraft Research Laboratories, in 1958 as Principal Scientist of the plasma physics program. He was named Chief Research Scientist for the laboratories in 1964, became Director of Research for the United Technologies Research Center in 1967, and in 1979 was named Vice President for Research and Development, United Technologies Corporation. He is a graduate of the Massachusetts Institute of Technology, where he received degrees in electrical engineering, nuclear engineering, and plasma physics. He holds patents for twenty inventions, including patents for radar systems and lasers.

Two aspects of information will be increasingly affected by developing technologies: storage of information in very compact form, such as compact optical disks, and rapid transmission of information using such technologies as fiber optics and satellites. Obviously, rapid information handing is critical to high-technology companies like United Technologies. Decision makers *must* have the most up-to-date information to make intelligent business choices. Scientists and engineers *must* have the most recent information on technical advances to be truly productive. The new developments are exciting.

A commercially available digital optical disk, for example, holds the equivalent of more than a thirty-two–volume encyclopedia about American companies. This information is stored in a form which is compatible with widely used computer spreadsheet programs, so it is available immediately for analysis and use. Similar compendia of technical information are forthcoming and will make vast collections of data that combine text and illustration available to our scientists and engineers. Improvements in how we transmit information lower our costs. Electronic mail, for example, already a reality, may largely replace the physical movement of paper copies and transform our methods of corresponding and publishing.

Edmund D. Pellegrino

Edmund D. Pellegrino, a distinguished physician and educator, was President of Catholic University of America and Professor of Philosophy and Biology there from 1978 to 1982. In that year he became John Carroll Professor of Medicine and Medical Humanities at Georgetown University Medical Center in Washington, D.C., a position he now holds concurrently with the Directorship of the Joseph and Rose Kennedy Institute of Ethics at Georgetown University. The founding editor of *Journal of Medicine and Philosophy,* he is the author of more than 350 articles and reviews in scientific research, medical education, and philosophy and of the book *Humanism and the Physician* (University of Tennessee Press, 1979) and coauthor, with David Thomasma, of *A Philosophical Basis of Medical Practice* (Oxford University Press, 1981).

An essay, "The Computer and the Book: The Perils of Coexistence," written by Dr. Pellegrino in response to the 1984 publication of *Books in Our Future* is published below (chap. 6). The following is from that essay:

> If computers and books are to coexist—and I think this is a necessity—then we must carefully examine the kinds of illiteracy computer literacy can generate. Such an appraisal will highlight, yet again, the importance of a liberal education based in the reading of books. The antidote to computer-induced illiteracy is not to ban the computer but to reinvigorate the kind of

education that enables the computer user to remain the master of his medicine. The antidote can only be a liberal education— one based in the reading of books.

Morris Philipson

Morris Philipson combines several careers in the community of the book: novelist, short story writer, scholar, and, since 1967, Director of the University of Chicago Press. After service with the Army Signal Corps in Europe in World War II, he studied French culture at the Sorbonne for a year, then came to the University of Chicago for his B.A. degree and a master's degree in the history of philosophy. After several years of teaching, he received a Ph.D. degree in philosophy from Columbia University. Prior to joining the University of Chicago Press in 1966, he was an editor at Alfred A. Knopf's Vintage Books, Random House, Pantheon Books, and Basic Books. In 1982 he received the PEN American Center's Publisher Citation for his work at the University of Chicago Press. The next year he was the co-winner of the Society of Midland Authors annual Fiction Award for his novel *Secret Misunderstandings* (Simon & Schuster).

In our discussion, Morris Philipson reminded us that there are many different ways of defining literacy and illiteracy. For example, a scholar who specializes in a given discipline usually is, "for all practical purposes, illiterate in other areas of specialization." With regard to the future of the book, other distinctions are also necessary. For example, "the humanist and the social scientist have a psychological and aesthetic, even philosophic investment in maintaining the tradition of the physical book, which their counterparts in the sciences do not have."

An essay by Morris Philipson on publishing, technology, and the future of the book is reprinted below (chap. 18). The following remarks are from that essay:

> No invention is going to transform publishing. There is no irresistible force at work here. Purveyors of hardware and software will not transform publishing. *Publishers* will or will not transform publishing. Experiments that we are willing to undertake will be controlled by our concern for many things in addition to technological innovations. We are concerned about acceptance by our potential customers; we are wary of promises that cannot be fulfilled; we resist piracy and scorning of the responsibility to pay for use which matters mightily to both author and publisher. We are experimenting on an ad hoc

basis—the only competent way to experiment—not by a panic psychology, an either/or approach of "convert to the new techniques" or "perish." The only competent way to experiment is critically.

Gerard Piel

In our discussions Gerard Piel, Chairman of *Scientific American,* cautioned us that our main concern should not be "to preserve the book." He thought it was well to recall the eighteenth-century ideal that the function of society is to encourage and realize the fulfillment of the human potential of its members. In this context, our central concern should be "to see that the book and the new implements that technology has given to education and to communication serve their functions of making human beings out of all of us."

Gerard Piel was Science Editor for *Life* magazine and Assistant to the President of the Henry J. Kaiser Company before establishing and becoming President and Publisher of *Scientific American* in 1947. In 1984 he stepped aside as President and Publisher and became Chairman. He has won many awards for science and journalism and is the author of two books, *Science in the Cause of Man* (Knopf, 1961) and *The Acceleration of History* (Knopf, 1972). He has served on the Council on Foreign Relations, as Chairman of the Foundation for Child Development (1978-85), and as Chairman of the American Association for the Advancement of Science (1985-86).

A very large aspect of the enterprise of the increase and dissemination of knowledge goes on outside the book. The unit of reference in the natural sciences is not the book—it is the scientific paper. In traditional librarianship, the sciences are represented by the volume of the journal in which the paper is published; rarely is the paper itself represented in the library's catalog. The literature of science can be thought of as a kind of forward-moving standing wave. It is accessed through electronic data banks, most of them developed by private, profit-making enterprises, which render a service of high flexibility and responsiveness to users. The remarkable development of the citation index, for example, produces an essential window into the social process of science. The book nonetheless retains a role in the sciences. In science education the textbook organizes and brings together periodically the summation and culmination of work in each field.

Frank H. T. Rhodes

In our interview with him, Frank Rhodes, President of Cornell University, expressed the view that our survey dealt with far more than the future of an object, the book; that our true topic was "literacy as the foundation for the pyramid for existence—the character of the society we hand to our children." The books of the world, he emphasized, contain the spirit and experiences of our civilization, and if "we fail to preserve them and to use them adequately, we shortchange our future."

A geologist by training, Frank Rhodes is the ninth President of Cornell University. He took office in 1977. Before assuming the Cornell presidency, he was Vice President for Academic Affairs (1974-77), and Dean of the College of Literature, Science, and the Arts at the University of Michigan. He was born in Warwickshire, England, and holds doctor of philosophy and doctor of science degrees from the University of Birmingham, England. He is the author of over seventy major scientific articles and monographs, five books, and forty articles on education.

We must not lose sight (in our report) of the challenge of creating a love of reading. Studies show that people who do well on the Scholastic Aptitude Tests and in college tend to be people who have grown up with books in their homes. I suspect the reason they do well is that they have acquired a love of reading—not a gentle kind of idolatry for books, but the experience of books as things of explosive possibility, as things that can motivate and change a person's life. We should challenge schools and parents and others not simply to assist in the relatively easier task of increasing literacy, but to take on the much harder task of inspiring a love of reading. It isn't just the future of the book that depends on this, it is the degree of fulfillment in individual lives and ultimately the future of society.

Joan M. Ripley

Joan Ripley is the owner of Chappaqua Book Shop, which she founded in 1972 in Chappaqua, New York. She was a faculty member of the American Booksellers Association's Booksellers School from 1972 to 1980, a Director of the Board from 1977 to 1984, and President of the Association, 1980-82. From 1984 to 1986, she served as Director of Marketing for Booksellers

Order Service, an electronic order and distribution service owned by the American Booksellers Association.

The future of the book is not threatened by the computer—in fact, just the reverse might be true. For example, historically the distribution of books has been the book industry's greatest problem, and now we see that the computer is becoming a major force in streamlining book distribution throughout America. Electronic ordering systems such as the Booksellers Order Service should help to keep many independent bookstores in business. These are the types of stores that usually specialize in books as literature.

The greatest threat to the traditional book appears to be the disproportionate amount of power large-scale book buyers can exercise in the publishing industry. Although the mass merchandise bookstores now in malls around the country probably reach many people who rarely would enter a more traditional bookstore, I feel the buyers for such stores have entirely too much control over what is published and over the size of the print runs. This constitutes an alarming threat to our literary heritage. We need a future for all types of books, for literary works, first novels, poetry, and scholarly titles, not just for fast-selling and sometimes gimmicky books than can be viewed as the "fast food" of the book world.

Phyllis Steckler

Phyllis Steckler has compiled reference works, with and without computers, for the past thirty years. She is President of the Oryx Press, a small, independently owned publishing company in Phoenix, Arizona. Oryx Press uses electronic methods to compile and produce print and nonprint publications. Steckler's experience includes work for R. R. Bowker Company, Crowell Collier Macmillan Information Publishing Company, and Holt, Rinehart & Winston Information Systems.

I know of nothing that leads me to believe that the book will be extinct in twenty-five years, but I also cannot say that it will be the only medium used by publishers in twenty-five years. If I were to make any recommendation at all, it would be to encourage experimentation on the part of the publishing community to use whatever media are available to it, including the book, to publish works that are worth publishing, in whatever medium best fits. The survival of the publishing business depends on

21

how well we acclimate ourselves to uses afforded us by the new technology. We must not rely on either the book or the computer as our only delivery system, but must remain on the alert for the best combination of past and future technologies to use for the dissemination of information, knowledge, and learning.

In later correspondence with the Center for the Book Phyllis Steckler added,

The benefits and the difficulties of publishing reference works in the electronic age begin with computers. Today, in order to survive, publishers must compile, store, relate, and retrieve information electronically, using innovative production procedures and technology; the information must then be delivered to end users in the most usable and cost-effective *print or nonprint* formats.

There are three basic applications of computers in publishing. The first is to compile, relate, and retrieve information electronically that is to be delivered to end users in traditional print formats. This traditional publishing application is still continuing with as much fervor as before, with the numbers of published books steadily increasing.

The second application is to compile, store, relate, and retrieve information electronically that is to be delivered electronically online. Although the use of "online" has been in the public eye for some time, usage is still limited almost entirely to bibliographic (or secondary) databases. There are very few "full text" databases online (although there are over fifteen thousand full text databases in the humanities area alone). Limitations of this medium were apparent to users from the start: the computer is not portable in the sense that a print publication is; each time the user obtains any information from a database, an additional charge is applied; and telecommunications costs increase as usage increases, rendering it impossible to know at the outset just how much one is going to spend.

The third, and newest, application is to compile, store, relate, and retrieve information electronically that is to be delivered to the end user in a nonprint format—on tapes, floppy disks, or some sort of laser optical disk, where it is then accessed via other computers—that is, a distributed electronic format. Although there are advantages to this application, they are advantages over the online application, and are primarily in the area of ongoing cost containment. As compared to print, however, the initial cost for distributed electronic formats is still far greater than that for comparable information in print format, and the equipment needed to access (read) that information is not exactly what you'd call handy!

Robert Wedgeworth

In 1985 Robert Wedgeworth became the Dean of the School of Library Service at Columbia University, the oldest and best-known library school in the United States. Before that Wedgeworth served as Executive Director of the American Library Association from 1972 to 1985. For its first ten editions, he was Editor of the *ALA Yearbook of Library and Information Services;* he is also Editor of the *ALA World Encyclopedia of Library and Information Services* (2d ed., 1986). In his twenty-five years as a professional librarian, Mr. Wedgeworth has held posts in public, college, and university libraries.

In mid-1986, Mr. Wedgeworth made the following comments in communications with the Center for the Book:

Reading is a difficult skill to acquire and an even more difficult skill to maintain. Most functionally illiterate adults have learned how to read at some point in their lives. Like many unused skills, theirs has atrophied. Current programs to combat illiteracy quite rightly focus much of their effort on teaching or improving reading skills. However, too little emphasis is given to reading motivation and reading maintenance.

Libraries and librarians are too often left out of discussions about the literacy problem in American society. In our eagerness to teach people how to read or how to improve their reading skills, we tend to forget about one of our most familiar yet most essential institutions. The library is a built-in community resource for stimulating reading and for helping citizens stay interested in reading—and thus stay interested in the world around them.

Public awareness can stimulate the involvement of libraries, together with schools and volunteer agencies, in year-round evening and weekend programs providing reading guidance and reading materials in addition to reading instruction.

To believe in education is to believe in the future, to believe in what may be accomplished through the disciplined use of intelligence, allied with cooperation and good will. If it seems naïvely American to put so much stock in schools, colleges, universities, and the endless prospect of self-improvement and social improvement, it is an admirable, and perhaps even a noble, flaw.

DIANE RAVITCH
Professor

II.
Reading
and Learning

1. A Nation at Risk

National Commission on Excellence in Education

The 1983 report of the National Commission on Excellence in Education to the United States Secretary of Education, T. H. Bell, *A Nation at Risk* found that American education at all levels had degenerated considerably. The report attends most closely to secondary education.

We reprint here portions detailing the commission's assessment of the risk and of the resources available in the United States to meet it. The book community will be alert to the dangers to culture posed by the persistence of illiteracy, the evident substitution of minimum standards for high expectations, and the decline in textbook quality.

Reprinted from *A Nation at Risk: The Imperative for Educational Reform,* A Report to the Nation and the Secretary of Education, United States Department of Education, by the National Commission on Excellence in Education, April 1983. Washington: U.S. Government Printing Office, 1983.

Our nation is at risk. Our once unchallenged preeminence in commerce, industry, science, and technological innovation is being overtaken by competitors throughout the world. This report is concerned with only one of the many causes and dimensions of the problem, but it is the one that undergirds American prosperity, security, and civility. We report to the American people that while we can take justifiable pride in what our schools and colleges have historically accomplished and contributed to the United States and the well-being of its people, the educational foundations of our society are presently being eroded by a rising tide of mediocrity that threatens our very future as a nation and a people. What was unimaginable a generation ago has begun to occur—others are matching and surpassing our educational attainments.

If an unfriendly foreign power had attempted to impose on America the mediocre educational performance that exists today, we might well have viewed it as an act of war. As it stands, we have allowed this to happen to ourselves. We have even squandered the gains in student achievement made in the wake of the Sputnik challenge. Moreover, we have dismantled essential support systems which helped make those gains possible. We have, in effect, been committing an act of unthinking, unilateral educational disarmament.

Our society and its educational institutions seem to have lost sight of the basic purposes of schooling, and of the high expectations and disciplined effort needed to attain them. This report, the result of eighteen months of study, seeks to generate reform of our educational system in fundamental ways and to renew the nation's commitment to schools and colleges of high quality throughout the length and breadth of our land.

That we have compromised this commitment is, upon reflection, hardly surprising, given the multitude of often conflicting demands we have placed on our nation's schools and colleges. They are routinely called on to provide solutions to personal, social, and political problems that the home and other institutions either will not or cannot resolve. We must understand that these demands on our schools and colleges often exact an educational cost as well as a financial one.

On the occasion of the commission's first meeting, President Reagan noted the central importance of education in American life when he said, "Certainly there are few areas of American life as important to our society, to our people, and to our families as our schools and colleges." This report, therefore, is as much an open letter to the American people as it is a report to the Secretary of Education. We are confident that the American people, properly informed, will do what is right for their children and for the generations to come.

The Risk

History is not kind to idlers. The time is long past when America's destiny was assured simply by an abundance of natural resources and inexhaustible human enthusiasm, and by our relative isolation from the malignant problems of older civilizations. The world is indeed one global village. We live among determined, well-educated, and strongly motivated competitors. We compete with them for international standing and markets, not only with products but also with the ideas of our laboratories and neighborhood workshops. America's position in the world may once have been reasonably secure with only a few exceptionally well-trained men and women. It is no longer.

The risk is not only that the Japanese make automobiles more efficiently than Americans and have government subsidies for development and export. It is not just that the South Koreans recently built the world's most efficient steel mill, or that American machine tools, once the pride of the world, are being displaced by German products. It is also that these developments signify a redistribution of trained capability throughout the globe. Knowledge, learning, information, and skilled intelligence are the new raw materials of international commerce and are today spreading throughout the world as vigorously as miracle drugs, synthetic fertilizers, and blue jeans did earlier. If only to keep and improve on the slim competitive edge we still retain in world markets, we must dedicate ourselves to the reform of our educational system for the benefit of all—old and young alike, affluent and poor, majority and minority. Learning is the indispensable investment required for success in the "information age" we are entering.

Our concern, however, goes well beyond matters such as industry and commerce. It also includes the intellectual, moral, and spiritual strengths of our people which knit together the very fabric of our society. The people of the United States need to know that individuals in our society who do not possess the levels of skill, literacy, and training essential to this new era will be effectively disenfranchised, not simply from the material rewards that accompany competent performance, but also from the chance to participate fully in our national life. A high level of shared education is essential to a free, democratic society and to the fostering of a common culture, especially in a country that prides itself on pluralism and individual freedom.

For our country to function, citizens must be able to reach some common understanding on complex issues, often on short notice and on the basis of conflicting or incomplete evidence. Education helps form these common understandings, a point Thomas Jefferson made long ago in his justly famous dictum:

> I know no safe depository of the ultimate powers of the society but the people themselves; and if we think them not enlightened enough to exercise their control with a wholesome discretion, the remedy is not to take it from them but to inform their discretion.

Part of what is at risk is the promise first made on this continent: All, regardless of race or class or economic status, are entitled to a fair chance and to the tools for developing their individual powers of mind and spirit to the utmost. This promise means that all children by virtue of their own efforts, competently guided, can hope to attain the mature and informed judgment needed to secure gainful employment and to manage their own lives, thereby serving not only their own interests but also the progress of society itself.

Indicators of the Risk

The educational dimensions of the risk before us have been amply documented in testimony received by the commission. For example:

- International comparisons of student achievement, completed a decade ago, reveal that on nineteen academic tests American students were never first or second and, in comparison with other industrialized nations, were last seven times.
- Some 23 million American adults are functionally illiterate by the simplest tests of everyday reading, writing, and comprehension.
- About 13 percent of all seventeen-year-olds in the United States can be considered functionally illiterate. Functional illiteracy among minority youth may run as high as 40 percent.
- Average achievement of high school students on most standardized tests is now lower than twenty-six years ago when Sputnik was launched.
- Over half the population of gifted students do not match their tested ability with comparable achievement in school.
- The College Board's Scholastic Aptitude Tests (SAT) demonstrate a virtually unbroken decline from 1963 to 1980. Average verbal scores fell over 50 points and average mathematics scores dropped nearly 40 points.
- College Board achievement tests also reveal consistent declines in recent years in such subjects as physics and English.
- Both the number and proportion of students demonstrating

superior achievement on the SATs (i.e., those with scores of 650 or higher) have also dramatically declined.

- Many seventeen-year-olds do not possess the "higher order" intellectual skills we should expect of them. Nearly 40 percent cannot draw inferences from written material; only one-fifth can write a persuasive essay; and only one-third can solve a mathematics problem requiring several steps.
- There was a steady decline in science achievement scores of U.S. seventeen-year-olds as measured by national assessments of science in 1969, 1973, and 1977.
- Between 1975 and 1980, remedial mathematics courses in public four-year colleges increased by 72 percent and now constitute one-quarter of all mathematics courses taught in those institutions.
- Average tested achievement of students graduating from college is also lower.
- Business and military leaders complain that they are required to spend millions of dollars on costly remedial education and training programs in such basic skills as reading, writing, spelling, and computation. The Department of the Navy, for example, reported to the commission that one-quarter of its recent recruits cannot read at the ninth grade level, the minimum needed simply to understand written safety instructions. Without remedial work they cannot even begin, much less complete, the sophisticated training essential in much of the modern military.

These deficiencies come at a time when the demand for highly skilled workers in new fields is accelerating rapidly. For example:

- Computers and computer-controlled equipment are penetrating every aspect of our lives—homes, factories, and offices.
- One estimate indicates that by the turn of the century millions of jobs will involve laser technology and robotics.
- Technology is radically transforming a host of other occupations. They include health care, medical science, energy production, food processing, construction, and the building, repair, and maintenance of sophisticated scientific, educational, military, and industrial equipment.

Analysts examining these indicators of student performance and the demands for new skills have made some chilling observations. Educational researcher Paul Hurd concluded at the end of a thorough national survey of student achievement that within the context of the modern scientific revolution, "We are raising a new generation of Americans that is scientifically and technologically illiterate." In a similar vein, John Slaughter, a former director of the National Science Foundation, warned of a "a growing chasm between a small scientific and technological elite and a citizenry ill-informed, indeed uninformed, on issues with a science component."

But the problem does not stop there, nor do all observers see it the same way. Some worry that schools may emphasize such rudiments as reading and computation at the expense of other essential skills such as comprehension, analysis, solving problems, and drawing conclusions. Still others are concerned that an overemphasis on technical and occupational skills will leave little time for studying the arts and humanities that so enrich daily life, help maintain civility, and develop a sense of community. Knowledge of the humanities, they maintain, must be harnessed to science and technology if the latter are to remain creative and humane, just as the humanities need to be informed by science and technology if they are to remain relevant to the human condition. Another analyst, Paul Copperman, has drawn a sobering conclusion. Until now, he has noted,

> each generation of Americans has outstripped its parents in education, in literacy, and in economic attainment. For the first time in the history of our country, the educational skills of one generation will not surpass, will not equal, will not even approach, those of their parents.

It is important, of course, to recognize that *the average citizen* today is better educated and more knowledgeable than the average citizen of a generation ago—more literate, and exposed to more mathematics, literature, and science. The positive impact of this fact on the well-being of our country and the lives of our people cannot be overstated. Nevertheless, *the average graduate* of our schools and colleges today is not as well-educated as the average graduate of twenty-five or thirty-five years ago, when a much smaller proportion of our population completed high school and college. The negative impact of this fact likewise cannot be overstated.

The Learning Society

In a world of ever-accelerating competition and change in the conditions of the workplace, of ever-greater danger, and of ever-larger opportunities for those prepared to meet them, educational reform should focus on the goal of creating a *learning society*. At the heart of such a society is the commitment to a set of values and to a system of education that affords all members the opportunity to stretch their minds to full capacity, from early childhood through adulthood, learning more as the world itself changes. Such a society has as a basic foundation the idea that education is important not only because of what it contributes to one's career goals but also because of the value it adds to the general quality of one's life. Also at the heart of the learning society are educational opportunities extending far beyond the traditional institutions of learning, our schools and colleges. They extend into homes and workplaces; into libraries, art galleries, museums, and science centers; indeed, into every place where the individual can develop and mature in work and life. In our view, formal schooling in youth is the essential foundation for learning throughout one's life. But without lifelong learning, one's skills will become rapidly dated.

In contrast to the ideal of the learning society, however, we find that for too many people education means doing the minimum work necessary for the moment, then coasting through life on what may have been learned in its first quarter. But this should not surprise us, because we tend to express our educational standards and expectations largely in terms of "minimum requirements." And where there should be a coherent continuum of learning, we have none, but instead an often incoherent, outdated, patchwork quilt. Many individual, sometimes heroic, examples of schools and colleges of great merit do exist. Our findings and testimony confirm the vitality of a number of notable schools and programs, but their very distinction stands out against a vast mass shaped by tensions and pressures that inhibit systematic academic and vocational achievement for the majority of students. In some metropolitan areas basic literacy has become the goal rather than the starting point. In some colleges maintaining enrollments is of greater day-to-day concern than maintaining rigorous academic standards. And the ideal of academic excellence as the primary goal of schooling seems to be fading across the board in American education.

Thus, we issue this call to all who care about America and its future: to parents and students; to teachers, administrators, and school board members; to colleges and industry; to union members and military leaders; to governors and state legislators; to the president; to members of Congress and other public officials; to members of learned and scientific societies; to the print and electronic media; to concerned citizens everywhere. America is at risk.

We are confident that America can address this risk. If the tasks we set forth are initiated now and our recommendations are fully realized over the next several years, we can expect reform of our nation's schools, colleges, and universities. This would also reverse the current declining trend—a trend that stems more from weakness of purpose, confusion of vision, underuse of talent, and lack of leadership, than from conditions beyond our control.

The Tools at Hand

It is our conviction that the essential raw materials needed to reform our educational system are waiting to be mobilized through effective leadership:

- The natural abilities of the young that cry out to be developed and the undiminished concern of parents for the well-being of their children

- The commitment of the nation to high retention rates in schools and colleges and to full access to education for all
- The persistent and authentic American dream that superior performance can raise one's state in life and shape one's own future
- The dedication, against all odds, that keeps teachers serving in schools and colleges, even as the rewards diminish
- Our better understanding of learning and teaching, the implications of this knowledge for school practice, and the numerous examples of local success as a result of superior effort and effective dissemination
- The ingenuity of our policymakers, scientists, state and local educators, and scholars in formulating solutions once problems are better understood
- The traditional belief that paying for education is an investment in ever-renewable human resources that are more durable and flexible than capital plant and equipment, and the availability in this country of sufficient financial means to invest in education
- The equally sound tradition, from the Northwest Ordinance of 1787 until today, that the federal government should supplement state, local, and other resources to foster key national educational goals
- The voluntary efforts of individuals, businesses, and parent and civic groups to cooperate in strengthening educational programs

These raw materials, combined with the unparalleled array of educational organizations in America, offer us the possibility to create a learning society, in which public, private, and parochial schools; colleges and universities; vocational and technical schools and institutes; libraries; science centers, museums, and other cultural institutions; and corporate training and retraining programs offer opportunities and choices for all to learn throughout life.

The Public's Commitment

Of all the tools at hand, the public's support for education is the most powerful. In a message to a National Academy of Sciences meeting in May 1982, President Reagan commented on this fact when he said:

> This public awareness—and I hope public action—is long overdue....This country was built on American respect for education....Our challenge now is to create a resurgence of that thirst for education that typifies our nation's history.

The most recent (1982) Gallup Poll of the *Public's Attitudes Toward the Public Schools* strongly supported a theme heard during our hearings: People are steadfast in their belief that education is the major foundation for the future strength of this country. They even considered education more important than developing the best industrial system or the strongest military force, perhaps because they understood education as the cornerstone of both. They also held that education is "extremely important" to one's future success, and that public education should be the top priority for additional federal funds. Education occupied first place among twelve funding categories considered in the survey—above health care, welfare, and military defense, with 55 percent selecting public education as one of their first three choices. Very clearly, the public understands the primary importance of education as the foundation for a satisfying life, an enlightened and civil society, a strong economy, and a secure nation.

At the same time, the public has no patience with undemanding and superfluous high school offerings. In another survey, more than 75 percent of all those questioned believed every student planning to go to college should take four years of mathematics, English, history/United States government, and science, with more than 50 percent adding two years each of a foreign language and economics or business. The public even supports requiring much of this curriculum for students who do not plan to go to college. These standards far exceed the strictest high school graduation requirements of any state today, and they also exceed the admission standards of all but a handful of our most selective colleges and universities.

Another dimension of the public's support offers the prospect of constructive reform. The best term to characterize it may simply be the honorable word *patriotism.* Citizens know intuitively what some of the best economists have shown in their research, that education is one of the chief engines of a society's material well-being. They know, too, that education is the common bond of a pluralistic society and helps tie us to other cultures around the globe. Citizens also know in their bones that the safety of the United States depends principally on the wit, skill, and spirit of a self-confident people, today and tomorrow. It is, therefore, essential— especially in a period of long-term decline in educational achievement—for government at all levels to affirm its responsibility for nurturing the nation's intellectual capital.

And perhaps most important, citizens know and believe that the meaning of America to the rest of the world must be something better than it seems to many today. Americans like to think of this nation as the preeminent country for generating the great ideas and material benefits for all mankind. The citizen is dismayed at a steady fifteen-year decline in industrial productivity, as one great American industry after another falls to world competition. The citizen wants the country to act on the belief, expressed in our hearings and by the large majority in the Gallup Poll, that education should be at the top of the nation's agenda.

Findings

We conclude that declines in educational performance are in large part the result of disturbing inadequacies in the way the educational process itself is often conducted. The findings that follow, culled from a much more extensive list, reflect four important aspects of the educational process: content, expectations, time, and teaching.

Findings Regarding Content

By content we mean the very "stuff" of education, the curriculum. Because of our concern about the curriculum, the commission examined patterns of courses high school students took in 1964-69 compared with course patterns in 1976-81. On the basis of these analyses we conclude:

- Secondary school curricula have been homogenized, diluted, and diffused to the point that they no longer have a central purpose. In effect, we have a cafeteria-style curriculum in which the appetizers and desserts can easily be mistaken for the main courses. Students have migrated from vocational and college preparatory programs to "general track" courses in large numbers. The proportion of students taking a general program of study has increased from 12 percent in 1964 to 42 percent in 1979.
- This curricular smorgasbord, combined with extensive student choice, explains a great deal about where we find ourselves today. We offer intermediate algebra, but only 31 percent of our recent high school graduates complete it; we offer French I, but only 13 percent complete it; and we offer geography, but only 16 percent complete it. Calculus is available in schools enrolling about 60 percent of all students, but only 6 percent of all students complete it.
- Twenty-five percent of the credits earned by general track high school students are in physical and health education, work experience outside the school, remedial English and mathematics, and personal service and development courses, such as training for adulthood and marriage.

Findings Regarding Expectations

We define expectations in terms of the level of knowledge, abilities, and skills school and college graduates should possess. They also refer to the time, hard work, behavior, self-discipline, and motivation that are essential for high student achievement. Such expectations are expressed to students in several different ways:

- By grades, which reflect the degree to which students demonstrate their mastery of subject matter
- Through high school and college graduation requirements,

which tell students which subjects are most important

- By the presence or absence of rigorous examinations requiring students to demonstrate their mastery of content and skill before receiving a diploma or a degree
- By college admissions requirements, which reinforce high school standards
- By the difficulty of the subject matter students confront in their texts and assigned readings

Our analyses in each of these areas indicate notable deficiencies:

- The amount of homework for high school seniors has decreased (two-thirds report less than one hour a night), and grades have risen as average student achievement has been declining.
- In many other industrialized nations, courses in mathematics (other than arithmetic or general mathematics), biology, chemistry, physics, and geography start in grade 6 and are required of *all* students. The time spent on these subjects, based on class hours, is about three times that spent by even the most science-oriented U.S. students, i.e., those who select four years of science and mathematics in secondary school.
- A 1980 state-by-state survey of high school diploma requirements reveals that only eight states require high schools to offer foreign language instruction, but none requires students to take the courses. Thirty-five states require only one year of mathematics, and thirty-six require only one year of science for a diploma.
- In thirteen states, 50 percent or more of the units required for high school graduation may be electives chosen by the student. Given this freedom to choose the substance of half or more of their education, many students opt for less demanding personal service courses, such as bachelor living.
- "Minimum competency" examinations (now required in thirty-seven states) fall short of what is needed, as the "minimum" tends to become the "maximum," thus lowering educational standards for all.
- One-fifth of all four-year public colleges in the United States must accept every high school graduate within the state regardless of program followed or grades, thereby serving notice to high school students that they can expect to attend college even if they do not follow a demanding course of study in high school or perform well.
- About 23 percent of our more selective colleges and universities reported that their general level of selectivity declined during the 1970s, and 29 percent reported reducing the number of specific high school courses required for admission (usually by dropping foreign language requirements, which are now specified as a condition for admission by only one-fifth of our institu-

tions of higher education).

- Too few experienced teachers and scholars are involved in writing textbooks. During the past decade or so a large number of texts have been "written down" by their publishers to ever-lower reading levels in response to perceived market demands.
- A recent study by Education Products Information Exchange revealed that a majority of students were able to master 80 percent of the material in some of their subject-matter texts before they had even opened the books. Many books do not challenge the students to whom they are assigned.
- Expenditures for textbooks and other instructional materials have declined by 50 percent over the past seventeen years. While some recommend a level of spending on texts of between 5 and 10 percent of the operating costs of schools, the budgets for basal texts and related materials have been dropping during the past decade and a half to only 0.7 percent today.

Findings Regarding Time

Evidence presented to the commission demonstrates three disturbing facts about the use that American schools and students make of time: (1) compared to other nations, American students spent much less time on school work; (2) time spent in the classroom and on homework is often used ineffectively; and (3) schools are not doing enough to help students develop either the study skills required to use time well or the willingness to spend more time on school work.

- In England and other industrialized countries, it is not unusual for academic high school students to spend eight hours a day at school, 220 days per year. In the United States, by contrast, the typical school day lasts six hours and the school year is 180 days.
- In many schools, the time spent learning how to cook and drive counts as much toward a high school diploma as the time spent studying mathematics, English, chemistry, United States history, or biology.
- A study of the school week in the United States found that some schools provided students only seventeen hours of academic instruction during the week, and the average school provided about twenty-two.
- A California study of individual classrooms found that because of poor management of classroom time, some elementary students received only one-fifth of the instruction others received in reading comprehension.
- In most schools, the teaching of study skills is haphazard and unplanned. Consequently, many students complete high school and enter college without disciplined and systematic study habits.

Findings Regarding Teaching

The commission found that not enough of the academically able students are being attracted to teaching; that teacher preparation programs need substantial improvement; that the professional working life of teachers is on the whole unacceptable; and that a serious shortage of teachers exists in key fields.

- Too many teachers are being drawn from the bottom quarter of graduating high school and college students.
- The teacher preparation curriculum is weighted heavily with courses in "educational methods" at the expense of courses in subjects to be taught. A survey of 1,350 institutions training teachers indicated that 41 percent of the time of elementary school teacher candidates is spent in education courses, which reduces the amount of time available for subject matter courses.
- The average salary after twelve years of teaching is only $17,000 per year, and many teachers are required to supplement their income with part-time and summer employment. In addition, individual teachers have little influence in such critical professional decisions as, for example, textbook selection.
- Despite widespread publicity about an overpopulation of teachers, severe shortages of certain kinds of teachers exist: in the fields of mathematics, science, and foreign languages; and among specialists in education for gifted and talented, language minority, and handicapped students.
- The shortage of teachers in mathematics and science is particularly severe. A 1981 survey of forty-five states revealed shortages of mathematics teachers in forty-three states, critical shortages of earth sciences teachers in thirty-three states, and of physics teachers everywhere.
- Half of the newly employed mathematics, science, and English teachers are not qualified to teach these subjects; fewer than one-third of U.S. high schools offer physics taught by qualified teachers.

Children learn to read by being in the presence of books. The love of knowledge comes with reading and grows upon it.

HENRY WARD BEECHER

2. Illiteracy in the United States

Charles A. Goodrum and Helen Dalrymple

This article, part of a study commissioned for the Book in the Future project, summarizes opinion and statistical information on illiteracy in the United States. Beyond summarizing, it reports the meaning of functional illiteracy and the effect it has on the large minority of the population that suffers from it.

The future of the book, whether in an electronic world or a more traditional print-oriented one, is dim if millions of people are unable or unwilling to read. This chapter will look at the issues of literacy and illiteracy and the many questions being raised about the education of young people in the United States today.

Definitions

According to the measure used by the Census Bureau, 99.5 percent of the U.S. population over age fourteen is literate: they have at least a sixth-grade education, and they can read and write some English (or another language which they speak in their home).[1] Literacy, however, is neither an absolute nor a static concept; it needs to be related to the context in which it will be used. For this reason a new term, *functional literacy,* was coined in the 1940s and 1950s to describe the skills necessary to accomplish specific tasks. And functional literacy, like literacy itself, is relative; someone who could get along with a particular level of reading proficiency as an assembly line worker in 1947, for example, cannot function as well in the more technologically oriented society of the 1980s. Different levels of reading competence are required to master different tasks.

The United Nations Educational, Scientific, and Cultural Organization (Unesco) Committee on the Standardization of Education Statistics set the following definition in 1962 to describe a functionally literate individual: "A person is literate when he has acquired the essential knowledge and skills which enable him to engage in all those activities in which literacy is required for effective functioning in his group and community, and whose attainments in reading, writing, and arithmetic make it possible for him to continue to use these skills toward his own and the community's development."[2]

A 1979 study entitled *Adult Illiteracy in the United States,* by Carman St. John Hunter and David Harman, conducted for the Ford Foundation by World Education, suggests that functional literacy means "the possession of skills perceived as necessary by particular persons and groups to fulfill their own self-determined objectives as family and community members, citizens, consumers, job holders, and members of social, religious, or other associations of their choosing." Functional literates also need "the ability to obtain information and to use that information for their own and others' well-being, the ability to read and write adequately to satisfy the requirements they set for themselves as being important for their own lives, the ability to deal with demands made on them by society, and the ability to solve the problems they face in their daily lives."[3]

Illiteracy Takes Different Forms

The requirements articulated above clearly go far beyond the simple ability to read and write one's name. Regrettably, it appears that some segments of our society are not convinced that literacy is an important part of their lives until it is too late. Much has been written about the tragedy of the student who earns a high school diploma but really can't read. An English teacher in Alexandria, Virginia, Patrick Welsh, described some of his students in the *Washington Post* in this way:

> Only when you're a teacher who gets to know these kids as individuals can you appreciate the tragedy of their plight. I think of several great T. C. Williams [High School] athletes I've taught. They're some of my all-time favorite students. Charming, witty, gregarious, they were among the best-known and most popular individuals at school. There was only one hitch, a hitch no one could ever discern in a conversation with them: they could barely read. I remember one of them asking me to read him a newspaper article describing his exploits in a game.[4]

In this case, Welsh is talking about black students. He points out that he thinks the problem of low achievement has much more to do with economic class, family background, motivation, and cultural pressures than with racial factors. "There's an incredible anti-achievement ethic among a lot of kids from low-income families," writes Welsh. He quotes a black psychologist, William Carr, as saying that these young people "associate learning and achievement with whites, and they want no part of it." At the same time Carr, who counsels young prisoners at Lorton Reformatory, observed that "there were many young men in prison who had brilliant minds but read at a second- or third-grade level. Once they could face their problem without shame and saw that learning was a real value, their progress was amazing."[5]

Although students who read below grade level get some extra help all through elementary and secondary school, it clearly is not enough or is not focused sufficiently to do the job. Patrick Welsh says, "The literacy problem isn't dealt with more forcefully because it isn't the main concern of the community. The fact is that the main priority of the school system in recent years has been keeping middle-class families in the system."

At the January 1984 National Adult Literacy Conference, Jeanne Chall, director of the Harvard University Reading Laboratory, said that she was convinced that the same reading techniques that guide young readers' development can be applied to adults. "Except for changes in content, the course of development for reading is essentially the same for adults as for children." Sociologist David Harman (coauthor of the Ford Foundation study cited above) disagreed. Illiteracy is rooted in culture, not in individual abilities or instructional techniques, in his view. "If you teach skills to a culture in which written language plays no part, they will not learn to read and write. That's true across the board, even in the United States. It's not just an issue of instruction in reading. It's a matter of cultural transformation....You have to tackle simultaneously children in the schools and the environments in which they live" in order to boost literacy.

This theme was echoed in our interviews as we discussed the current wave of Asian and Hispanic immigrants entering the United States. Several of our advisors told us that while Asian cultures tended to hold the book and the printed word in high esteem, an oral tradition dominated in many Hispanic, especially Central American, societies. In some of these countries, there had never been a literate population. Those who were literate were an elite overlay constituting a small proportion of the total society. Illiterate in their own language, these Hispanic immigrants could not be expected to assimilate the English language in written form without some special support and incentives to do so. Although basic literacy and functional literacy are of unquestionable importance for the future of American society—in jobs, business transactions, even citizenship—the problem of what one writer has called "diminished literacy" may be just as important for the future of books and the printed word. Edmund Janko, a longtime high school English teacher in New York, has described how the teaching of English has changed in the past two decades. He quotes an eleventh grader who, upon receiving a copy of a novel to be read for class that term asked, "What are we going to do with this?" Janko observes that the same kinds of students who, a dozen years ago, would have come to class having read and understood the assignment and been prepared to discuss it no longer seem able to do so. "Instead of talking about the meaning of an entire poem, story, or essay, we now talk about the definitions of words and the meaning of phrases and sentences....Such a laborious, though necessary, process destroys the spontaneity that should come with a good reading experience and, when done, usually produces a confusion of new words and allusions and a weariness with the work that makes any sustained and sensible discussion of ideas unlikely." In the *New Republic* Leon Botstein expanded on this theme:

A common thread links the overt illiteracy found in the worst and most deprived schools to a more sophisticated illiteracy found among Ivy League-bound suburban grade-grubbers. The "good" students we encounter can manipulate parts of speech. They make few errors and write clean, tidy essays with topic sentences and conclusions. They hand in all the assignments and yet say nothing in their writing. For them, using language is a school-specific skill, a game to be mastered but to which they have little emotional or intellectual attachment. Writing and reading are rarely facets of out-of-school life—or of life beyond school.[6]

Many scholars and educators argue that in order to keep up in our increasingly complicated society, the nation's young people must also develop critical reading and thinking skills and the ability to interpret text and apply its meaning to other situations. Mastering the simple mechanics of reading is not enough.

Bertha Davis and Dorothy Arnof note in their recent book (in a chapter titled "Educational Malpractice in Reading") that reading test scores begin to decline after the fourth grade because the teaching of reading doesn't adapt to the changed nature of the reading task in the intermediate grades. Beginning with fourth grade and continuing on through secondary school, children must be able to read material outside their range of experience, understand its literal content, follow the author's thought from paragraph to paragraph, see the implications of what the author has written, and grasp the whole tone of the piece. "Only a tiny fraction of the pupils in our schools perform these complex intellectual tasks intuitively; most must be *taught* to do them," observe Davis and Arnof.[7] They suggest, however, that this is not being done. "The focus in the teaching of reading in those grades is skewed. Too much attention is given to the content of what is read, not enought attention to reading strategies, to *reading as a thinking process.*"[8]

Ernest Boyer, in his report on the American high school, found that in language skills many students "come to high school pathetically ill prepared."[9] He argues that "every student—not just those with problems—should learn to write more clearly, read with greater comprehension, listen with more discrimination, speak with more precision, and, through critical thinking, develop the capacity to apply old knowledge to new concepts."[10]

Dr. Edmund Pellegrino, John Carroll Professor of Medicine at Georgetown University and a member of the Advisory Committee on the Book in the Future, mentioned this same concern in an interview. He pointed out that we were coming to be a two-class society as far as verbal literacy was concerned: the intellectual elite would be those who could read books, and the second class would be those who could use computers. The intellectual elite would be the leaders; the computer-literate would only be technicians.

Any consideration of the state of literacy in the United States and how it inevitably affects books and reading must look at the whole range of literacy questions. While many millions of people literally cannot cope with the printed word in book form, millions more find books "hard" to read, not pleasurable, because they have not developed the intellectual skills required to process the information in that form.

Size of the Problem of Illiteracy

No one really knows how many functional illiterates there are in the United States today. The reason for this is that there is no one generally accepted definition of what the term means. Most of the figures cited are based on the 1975 University of Texas at Austin Adult Performance Level study.[11] The study, commissioned by the Department of Health, Education, and Welfare, used sophisticated nationwide sampling techniques to look at the adult population from the point of view of individuals' ability to function regardless of their level of academic achievement. Adult Performance Level (APL) defines literacy as communication, computation, problem-solving, and interpersonal relations skills in each of five competence areas: government and law, health and safety, occupational knowledge, consumer economics, and use of community resources. Simple examples were used to determine what skills people were capable of performing:

When given a notice posted on a cashier's desk in a store describing the check cashing policy for that store, more than one out of five respondents did not draw the correct conclusion from the notice.

Fourteen percent of the sample, when asked to fill out a check in a simulated business transaction, made an error so serious that it was unlikely that the check would have cleared the bank.

Thirteen percent of the sample did not address an envelope well enough to insure that it would reach the desired destination, and 24 percent did not place a return address on the same envelope which would insure that it would be returned to the sender if delivery were not possible. These results indicate that an estimated 28 million adults would make a serious error in addressing an envelope.[12]

Using the APL yardstick, an estimated 23 million adults were found to function with great difficulty in our society—at the first level, APL 1. Another 40 million could function, but not well. That was a total of 63 million in 1975.[13] When Secretary of Education Terrell Bell testified before the House Subcommittee on Postsecondary Education in September 1982, he estimated that because of the increase in population, those figures would have risen to 26 million people who are functionally incompetent and 46 million more who can function, but not proficiently.[14] This means that 72 million people, almost 32 percent of the population of the United States, must struggle to cope with the reading demands of everyday life.

Certain segments of the population have a greater concentration of the functionally illiterate. The Adult Performance Level study of 1975 found that illiterates are most likely to be among the 45 million adults who do not have a high school diploma. The states of Alabama, Arkansas, Georgia, Kentucky, Mississippi, North Carolina, South Carolina, Tennessee, and West Virginia have the highest concentrations of illiterates; more than half of the adults there have not completed high school. Illiteracy is typically found among the poor and members of racial or ethnic minority groups. A study by the National Institute of Education in 1980 indicated that 47 percent of black urban youth are functionally illiterate; 56 percent of Hispanic youth are in this category. The Department of Labor estimates that up to 75 percent of those who are unemployed lack the basic skills of communication, personal relations, reading, and computing capacities to enable employers to train them and use them effectively on the job. Some 60 percent of those who are in the nation's jails are functionally illiterate; 85 percent of the youngsters who appear in juvenile court are disabled readers. The wave of Asian and Hispanic immigrants in the last ten years only compounds the problem of illiteracy in the United States. Two paragraphs from the Hunter and Harman report for the Ford Foundation capture the essence of the size of the literacy problem in the United States:

One fact emerges clearly from all the statistical information available, whether the measure is competency or school completion. Despite the universal free education available in this country since early in the century, despite the fact that more and more young people of all races and ethnic groups are completing high school, and despite the recent evidence that those who do complete high school are achieving "acceptable" levels of literacy, a disproportionately large section of our adult population— well over a third—still suffers some educational disadvantage. Among these millions of adults in our society are the functionally illiterate. Their exact number is not known.

We conclude that the aggregate message of all the statistics is more important than their specific accuracy. A much larger proportion of the U.S. population than had until recently been known or assumed suffers serious disadvantage because of limited educational attainment. In this country persons with limited education are often the same persons who suffer from one or more of the other major social disadvantages—poverty, unemployment, racial or ethnic discrimination, social isolation.[15]

Can't We Do Anything About Illiteracy?

There are many programs and many dedicated people around the country working to make inroads on illiteracy. What is lacking, apparently, is a sufficiently precise understanding of the nature and extent of the problem, as well as adequate resources, to overcome it. Peter A. Waite, executive director of Laubach Literacy Action, one of the two major volunteer adult literacy organizations, has said, "We are not making any impact on the problem right now. If the American public were knowledgeable of the situation, they'd be aghast."

The major effort of the federal government in adult literacy programs comes under the Adult Education Act. These programs are providing educational services to approximately 2.2 million out-of-school adults aged sixteen years and older. Federal, state, and local funds reported in support of these programs total about $200 million. (The federal contribution amounts to about $95 million.) As Roger Thompson notes, the results have been impressive: "In 1980, approximately 90,000 participants reported they got jobs as a result of being in the program, and about 55,000 others were promoted to better jobs. In addition, 115,000 adults enrolled in other training programs at the conclusion of their adult education studies, almost 35,000 were removed from public assistance rolls, 30,000 obtained drivers' licenses, and 25,000 registered to vote for the first time." At best, however, as Thompson adds, adult education reaches only a fraction of those who need it.[16]

The national Right to Read program, initiated by the Nixon Administration in 1971, was a more ambitious program that proposed to eliminate literacy in a decade. The former director of the program, Gilbert B. Schiffman, has called Right to Read a miserable failure. "The illiteracy problem is very severe. It's a national disgrace. Right to Read was going to solve the problem by 1980. It was to be the equivalent of our commitment to go to the moon. But I think the maximum we ever got was $30 million. We had large ideas but a small budget and political clout."[17] In contrast, as Thompson has pointed out, "while the federal government channeled only a trickle of money into Right to Read, it was pouring billions into compensatory education programs in public elementary schools. The money flowed through Title I of the Elementary and Secondary Education Act, which Congress passed in 1965 specifically to improve teaching of basic skills to children from low-income homes. Between 1965 and 1981, the program pumped $29.6 *billion* into the schools."[18] And it seems to have had an impact; black nine-year-olds made by far the most significant gains in reading over the last decade, as measured by the National Assessment of Educational Progress. Despite the gains, however, the black average remains below the national average.

On September 7, 1983, President Reagan announced that the federal government was joining with many private citizen, state

47

and local government, and business and industry groups in a nationwide "Adult Literacy Initiative." Reagan addressed the need for a national effort to tackle the serious problems of adult literacy needs in stating the goal of the Adult Literacy Initiative: "...it will take a united effort by all our people to achieve our goal, the elimination of adult functional illiteracy in the United States." One of the components of this new initiative is a National Adult Literacy Project, sponsored by the Department of Education operating through the National Institute of Education.

One of the themes we heard in our interviews and at the April meeting of the Advisory Board for the Center for the Book was that the federal government must make adult literacy in the United States a high-priority national goal. As Gary Strong, State Librarian for California, put it, "We need a statement at the federal level that literacy is important. And we also need to get a commitment to put their money where their mouth is."

The two major volunteer adult literacy organizations are Laubach Literacy Action and Literacy Volunteers of America (LVA). Both are based in Syracuse, New York. Literacy Volunteers of America claims some 17,000 students in 165 programs in twenty-six states. Laubach's tutors reach about 50,000 students a year through 600 projects in forty-eight states. LVA functions mainly with a volunteer teaching staff which goes through special training. LVA volunteers may use a student's own language patterns (by transcribing a story the student tells and then teaching the student to read it), traditional reading techniques, or a variety of methods in order to come up with the combination that will work with that particular student.

Laubach Literacy stresses teaching by phonics, the breaking down of words into basic sounds and using the sounds to build new words. But Laubach volunteers also teach sight words, which are memorized. A structured series of texts developed by Laubach is used by its volunteers in teaching reading.

Many other programs are in operation around the country, some large, some small, to encourage both children and adults to read. The names are probably familiar: Reading is Fundamental, the March of Dimes Reading Olympics, Read More About It, Parents and Teachers Helping (PATH), Adopt-A-School, and many more. Corporations are joining in, in order to enable their own employees to function more effectively and are developing in-house adult tutoring programs. B. Dalton Bookseller, one of the nation's largest bookstore chains, has made literacy its top priority since 1981. In 1983 Dalton contributed a quarter of a million dollars to literacy programs around the nation.

The Business Council for Effective Literacy, created and funded by publisher Harold W. McGraw, Jr., offers a promising cooperative approach to the national adult literacy problem. The council, in McGraw's words, "is dedicated to fostering private sector involvement in effective basic literacy in American society," and its immediate priority is "to enlist the help of business and industry in attacking the problem of adult functional illiteracy." Among the goals of the council are to attract additional resources to help strengthen and expand existing programs of tutor training and to develop new approaches to tutor training and literacy provision; to help improve planning and policy-making at different levels of government; to encourage corporate support of research and policy analysis; and to create a heightened awareness, in the corporate world and the public at large, about the problem of adult literacy in the United States. Their first major grant was to help support a three-year national awareness campaign being developed by the Coalition for Literacy, the American Library Association, and the Advertising Council to present a series of public service advertisements in magazines, on radio, and on TV on the challenge of adult functional illiteracy.

The best defense against adult illiteracy is to do whatever is necessary to teach children to read, to write, and to think when they are young. With the recent spate of studies and commissions on the quality of education in America today, more attention is being focused on schools and what is being taught than at any time in the last generation. While it is apparently true that researchers have never been able to pin down exactly what makes us learn or remember, good teachers know what works with their students. And what works with one student may not work with another. Educators and psychologists are learning to diagnose specific learning problems earlier and to give children with those problems a special learning environment. Governments are recognizing that not all children can learn in the same way, but that they have a responsibility to educate them nonetheless. School administrators are acknowledging that it does no favor to the student to push him along from grade to grade whether or not he has mastered the basic skills at that level. One can argue that the most important factor in the improvement of education is that the debate continue—that the importance of education remain at the forefront of the community agenda. Only then will education be perceived as an important goal of all of society, attracting the best minds as researchers and as teachers.

Notes

1. For an account of how the Bureau of the Census derives a literacy rate from the 1970 and 1980 censuses, see Jonathan Kozol, *Illiterate America* (New York: Anchor Press/Doubleday, 1985), 37.
2. Cited by Carman St. John Hunter and David Harman in *Adult Illiteracy in the United States: A Report to the Ford Foundation* (New York: McGraw-Hill, 1979), 14.

3. Ibid., 7.
4. Patrick Welsh, "Why Don't My Poor Black Students Read Better," *Washington Post,* 27 May 1984, sec. C, 1.
5. Ibid.
6. Leon Botstein, "Why Jonathan Can't Read," *The New Republic,* 7 November 1983, 21.
7. Bertha Davis and Dorothy Arnof, *How to Fix What's Wrong with Our Schools* (New Haven: Ticknor & Fields, 1983), 15.
8. Ibid., 19
9. Ernest L. Boyer, *High School: A Report on Secondary Education in America* (New York: Harper & Row, 1983), 88.
10. Ibid., 89, citing Jeanne S. Chall, quoted by Daniel Resnick and Lauren B. Resnick, "The Nature of Literacy: An Historical Exploration," *Harvard Educational Review* 47 (1977): 383-84.
11. Hunter and Harman, *Adult Illiteracy in the United States,* 26-27. The method and results of the APL study are described in *Adult Functional Competency: A Report to the Office of Education Dissemination Review Panel* (Austin: Division of Extension, University of Texas, 1975) and *Adult Functional Competency: A Summary* (Austin: Division of Extension, University of Texas, 1975).
12. Ibid.
13. Statement of T. H. Bell, Secretary of Education, before the Subcommittee on Postsecondary Education, Committee on Education and Labor, U.S. House of Representatives, 21 September 1982.
14. Ibid.
15. Hunter and Harman, *Adult Illiteracy in the United States,* 56.
16. Roger Thompson, "Illiteracy in America," *Editorial Research Reports* 1983, vol. 1, no. 24, 485.
17. Ibid.
18. Ibid.

The man who does not read good books has no advantage over the man who can't read them.

MARK TWAIN

3. Becoming a Nation of Readers

Commission on Reading,
National Academy of Education

Becoming a Nation of Readers describes what we know about how children learn to read, moving toward a set of recommendations for improving the early education of children to improve the extent and the impact of literacy. This report focuses on early education, in contrast to *A Nation at Risk,* whose emphasis was on high school. *Becoming a Nation of Readers* works from a critical summary of research into learning to read; it avoids simplistic solutions, such as singleminded advocacy of phonics instruction, on one hand, or defense of the "sight word" method, on the other.

We reprint here the introduction, the chapter defining reading, a summary of the report that appeared originally in its foreword, and the recommendations of the report.

From *Becoming a Nation of Readers: The Report of the Commission on Reading,* prepared by Richard C. Anderson, Elfrieda H. Hiebert, Judith A. Scott, and Ian A. G. Wilkinson, with contributions from members of the Commission on Reading. Pittsburgh: National Academy of Education; Washington: National Institute of Education, U.S. Department of Education; Urbana, Ill.: Center for the Study of Reading, 1985.

Introduction

Reading is a basic life skill. It is a cornerstone for a child's success in school and, indeed, throughout life. Without the ability to read well, opportunities for personal fulfillment and job success inevitably will be lost.

Reading is important for the society as well as the individual. Economics research has established that schooling is an investment that forms human capital—that is, knowledge, skill, and problem-solving ability that have enduring value. While a country receives a good return on investment in education at all levels from nursery school and kindergarten through college, the research reveals that the returns are highest from the early years of schooling when children are first learning to read.[1] The Commission on Excellence warned of the risk for America from shortcomings in secondary education.[2] Yet the early years set the stage for later learning. Without the ability to read, excellence in high school and beyond is unattainable.[3]

How well do American children and youth read? How well do American schools teach reading? These are difficult questions to answer objectively. Partial answers can be gleaned from historical trends in achievement test data. Studies dating back to the middle of the nineteenth century usually have shown that succeeding generations of students perform better than earlier generations.[4] In one study, for example, 31,000 students in grades 2-6 representative of the United States at large were given a reading test in 1957 and the scores were compared to those of 107,000 students who had taken the same test in 1937. After adjusting for the fact that the 1937 sample was older by 4 to 6 months, because fewer children were promoted to the next grade at that time, the investigator concluded that children in 1957 had a reading ability advanced a half-year over children of the same age and intelligence twenty years before.[5]

Recent trends in test scores are mixed. With respect to basic reading skill, as gauged by ability to comprehend everyday reading material, results from the National Assessment of Educational Progress confirm that slight gains were made during the 1970s.[6] The largest gains were made by black children living in large cities. Probably these gains are attributable to the increasing aspirations and confidence of blacks and improvements in the quality of instruction that black children receive.

On the other hand, scores on tests that gauge advanced reading skill, among other abilities, showed small but steady declines from the early 1960s until the late 1970s, at which point they leveled off and started to climb slightly. Declines were sharpest on the SAT and ACT, which are taken by high school seniors hoping to enter selective colleges and universities, but there were also declines on advanced tests given to all kinds of students in junior and senior high school.[7] Reasons offered to explain the test score decline include erosion of educational standards, increases in TV viewing, changes in the size of families and spacing of children, shifts in young people's motivations and life goals, and the fact that larger numbers of youth from less advantaged families have been staying in school and taking the tests.[8]

Another approach to evaluating the level of reading proficiency attained in this country is to compare our achievement with achievement in other countries. A survey of reading performance in fifteen countries completed just over a decade ago showed that American students were never in first or second place on any test, and that on most tests they ranked at or below the international average.[9] A more recent comparison between the United States, Taiwan, and Japan showed a much wider spread of achievement among children in this country; many American children did well, but disproportionate numbers were among the poorest readers in the three countries.[10] International comparisons are tricky, depending, for instance, on the numbers of children in each age group that remain in school in different countries and the assumption that test items translated into different languages are really equivalent. Still, the figures offer no grounds for complacency.

How Americans have compared in the past is less urgent than the question of whether current generations will be literate enough to meet the demands of the future. The world is moving into a technological-information age in which full participation in educaton, science, business, industry, and the professions requires increasing levels of literacy. What was a satisfactory level of literacy in 1950 probably will be marginal by the year 2000.[11]

There is reason to be optimistic about the potential for the improvement of literacy in this country. From research supported by the National Institute of Education, and to some extent other government agencies and private foundations, the last decade has witnessed unprecedented advances in knowledge about the basic processes involved in reading, teaching, and learning. The knowledge is now available to make worthwhile improvements in reading throughout the United States. If the practices seen in the classrooms of the best teachers in the best schools could be introduced everywhere, the improvements would be dramatic.

The purpose of this report is to summarize the knowledge

acquired from research and to draw implications for reading instruction. The report is intended to reach a wide audience, including the serious layman. Thus, current practices are described in some detail, and a little is said about their history and rationale. Based on best available information, problems with current practices are identified, and the evidence and arguments for possible solutions sketched. While the report is based on research, the heavy trappings of scholarship are eschewed insofar as that is possible without diluting the message.

Based on what we now know, it is incorrect to suppose that there is a simple or single step which, if taken correctly, will immediately allow a child to read. Becoming a skilled reader is a journey that involves many steps. Similarly, it is unrealistic to anticipate that some one critical feature of instruction will be discovered which, if in place, will assure rapid progress in reading. Quality instruction involves many elements. Strengthening any one element yields small gains. For large gains, many elements must be in place.

The new knowledge about reading and schooling contains some surprises, but more often it confirms old beliefs. It answers some questions that have puzzled parents and educators, but it leaves others unanswered and sometimes furnishes conflicting answers. While there is more consensus about reading than in the past, there are still important issues about which reasonable people disagree. That knowledge about reading is incomplete is inevitable considering the marvelous complexity of the human mind and the still modest—but growing—power of social science concepts and methods.

What Is Reading?

Substantial advances in understanding the process of reading have been made in the last decade. The majority of scholars in the field now agree on the nature of reading: Reading is the process of constructing meaning from written texts. It is a complex skill requiring the coordination of a number of interrelated sources of information.

Reading can be compared to the performance of a symphony orchestra. This analogy illustrates three points. First, like the performance of a symphony, reading is a holistic act. In other words, while reading can be analyzed into subskills such as discriminating letters and identifying words, performing the subskills one at a time does not constitute reading. Reading can be said to take place only when the parts are put together in a smooth, integrated performance. Second, success in reading comes from practice over long periods of time, like skill in playing musical instruments. Indeed, it is a lifelong endeavor. Third, as with a musical score, there may be more than one interpretation of a text. The interpretation depends upon the background of the reader, the purpose for reading, and the context in which reading occurs.

How does the process of reading occur? A common view is that reading is a process in which the pronunciation of words gives access to their meanings; the meanings of the words add together to form the meanings of clauses and sentences; and the meanings of sentences combine to produce the meanings of paragraphs. In this conception, readers are viewed as always "starting at the bottom"—identifying letters—and then working up through words and sentences to higher levels until they finally understand the meaning of the text.

However, research establishes that the foregoing view of reading is only partly correct. In addition to obtaining information from the letters and words in a text, reading involves selecting and using knowledge about people, places, and things and knowledge about texts and their organization. A text is not so much a vessel containing meaning as it is a source of partial information that enables the reader to use already-possessed knowledge to determine the intended meaning.

Reading is a process in which information from the text and the knowledge possessed by the reader act together to produce meaning. Some aspects of this interaction can be illustrated with the following passage:

> When Mary arrived at the restaurant, the woman at the door greeted her and checked for her name. A few minutes later, Mary was escorted to her chair and was shown the day's menu. The attendant was helpful but brusque, almost to the point of being rude. Later, she paid the woman at the door and left.[12]

The first phrase will lead readers to expect that their existing knowledge of restaurants will be relevant. That is to say, the word "restaurant" brings to mind past associations and experiences with restaurants and the interrelations among these ideas. From there, reading is easy because of the expectations that come from this knowledge. The woman at the door is taken to be the hostess. Mary must sit at a chair at a dining table before she can eat. The "attendant" is probably the waiter or waitress, and the person referred to as leaving in the last sentence is probably Mary. These are all inferences that make use of both the information presented in the text and the knowledge the reader already has about restaurants.

Good readers skillfully integrate information in the text with what they already know. However, immature readers may depend too much on either letter-by-letter and word-by-word analysis or too much on the knowledge they already have about the topic.[13]

Some children laboriously work their way through texts word by word, or even letter by letter (e.g. m-m-M-a-r-y). They are so intent on saying the words right that they miss aspects of the meaning. In oral reading, these children tend to make nonsensical errors that look or sound like the words they are trying to read with results such as, "The woman at the door *grated* her and *locked* for her name."[14] These children sometimes fail to use the knowledge they may have about the topic to think about what they are trying to read.

Other immature readers show an overreliance on the knowledge they already have about the topic. Such children may use pictures, titles, their imagination, and only a small amount of information in the text to produce a believable story.[15] For example, "...and then Mary got to the...ah...pizza place. She went in the door and greeted her friend. Then she sat down in her chair and had a pizza." These children often do not have enough skill at word identification to make use of all of the information in the written message.

Five generalizations flow from the research of the past decade on the nature of reading. The first generalization is that *reading is a constructive process*. No text is completely self-explanatory. In interpreting a text, readers draw on their store of knowledge about the topic of the text. Readers use this prior knowledge to fill in gaps in the message and to integrate the different pieces of information in the message. That is to say, readers "construct" the meaning. In the restaurant example, the reader is able to infer that Mary sat at a table, selected her meal from the menu, and was probably served by the attendant. Yet none of this information is expressly mentioned in the text. These details are constructed from the reader's other knowledge of restaurants.

The meaning constructed from the same text can vary greatly among people because of differences in the knowledge they possess.[16] Sometimes people do not have enough knowledge to understand a text, or they may have knowledge that they do not use fully. Variations in interpretation often arise because people have different conceptions about the topic than the author supposed.

Some children may completely lack knowledge on a particular topic, others may know something, while still others may know a lot. Research shows that such differences in knowledge influence children's understanding. For example, in one study, second-grade children equivalent in overall reading ability were given a test of knowledge about spiders prior to reading a selection about spiders.[17] Then they were asked questions about the selection. Children who were more familiar with spiders were significantly better at answering the questions, particularly questions that required reasoning.

Research reveals that children are not good at drawing on their prior knowledge, especially in school settings.[18] They may know something relevant, but yet not use it when trying to understand a passage. These failures are more likely to happen when understanding the passage requires children to extend their knowledge to a somewhat different situation. Even a subtle difference between a child's interpretation and the "right" adult interpretation can give rise to the impression that the child doesn't understand the material.

The second principle is that *reading must be fluent.* The foundation of fluency is the ability to identify individual words. Since English is an alphabetic language, there is a fairly regular connection between the spelling of a word and its pronunciation. Every would-be reader must "break the code" that relates spelling to sound and meaning. Research suggests that, no matter which strategies are used to introduce them to reading, the children who earn the best scores on reading comprehension tests in the second grade are the ones who made the most progress in fast and accurate word identification in the first grade.[19]

"Decoding" a word—that is, identifying its pronunciation and meaning—involves more than letter-by-letter analysis. It has been known since late in the nineteenth century that short familiar words can be read as fast as single letters and that, under some conditions, words can be identified when the separate letters cannot be.[20] These facts would be impossible if the first step in word identification were always identification of the constituent letters and their sounds. More recently, it has been shown that a meaningful context speeds word identification.[21] For instance, *nurse* is more readily identified if it is preceded by *doctor.* Again, this is a fact that is impossible to square with the common theory that word identification consists of letter-by-letter decoding.

All of the known facts are understandable within the generally accepted current model of word identification.[22] According to this model, a possible interpretation of a word usually begins forming in the mind as soon as even partial information has been gleaned about the letters in the word. The possible interpretation reinforces the analysis of the remaining information contained in the letters. When enough evidence from the letters and the context becomes available, the possible interpretation becomes a positive identification. This all happens very quickly, within 250 milliseconds on the average, when the reader is skilled.[23]

Readers must be able to decode words quickly and accurately so that this process can coordinate fluidly with the process of constructing the meaning of the text. One piece of evidence that this is so is that good readers are consistently much faster than poor readers at pronouncing pseudowords that have regular English spellings, such as *tob* and *jate.*[24] People with more than fourth-grade reading ability make almost no mistakes with regular pseudowords. What distinguishes good and poor readers in this case is speed, not accuracy. What this fact means is that typically poor readers have barely mastered spelling-to-sound patterns, whereas good readers have a command that goes beyond simple mastery to automaticity.

Interestingly, it does not appear that skilled readers identify unfamiliar words by rapidly applying "rules" governing the relationships between letters and sounds. Instead, research suggests that they work by analogy with known words.[25] Thus, for example, the pronunciation of *tob* may be worked out from knowledge of the pronunciation of *job* plus a notion of the initial sound of words beginning with *t.* One piece of evidence in support of the decoding-by-analogy strategy is the fact that pseudowords such as *mave,* which have conflicting possible analogies, such as *have* and *wave,* are pronounced more slowly than other pseudowords, and are sometimes pronounced with a short *a* like *have* and are sometimes pronounced with a long *a* like *wave.* Notice that for the process to work the reader need not have any specific knowledge of the difference between long and short *a*'s, only an adequate vocabulary of actual words and a command of the analogy strategy.

Decoding skill must develop to the point where it is automatic and requires little conscious attention. The reader's attention must be available to interpret the text, rather than to figure out the words. Immature readers are sometimes unable to focus on meaning during reading because they have such a low level of decoding skill. They are directing most of their attention to sounding out words letter by letter or syllable by syllable.[26] Even skilled readers show much less understanding of what they read when forced to attend to the surface features of written material.[27]

Consider, for example, the way a young child might read the first sentence of the restaurant passage:

When Mary arrived at the r, ruh, ruh-es-tah, oh! restaurant!
When Mary arrived at the...rest...restaurant...

Restaurant is a difficult word for this child, and he or she requires several attempts to decode it. By this time, the child's memory for the earlier part of the phrase has faded and he or she has to reread the words to try and create a coherent meaning.

Available figures suggest that an average third grader can read an unfamiliar story aloud at the rate of about 100 words per minute.[28] The corresponding rate for poor readers at this level is 50 to 70 words per minute. According to one group of scholars, this rate is "so slow as to interfere with comprehension even of easy material, and is certainly unlikely to leave much...capacity free for developing new comprehension abilities."[29]

The third principle is that *reading must be strategic.* Skilled readers are flexible. How they read depends upon the complexity of the text, their familiarity with the topic, and their purpose for reading. Studies show that immature readers lack two strategies used by skilled readers: assessing their own knowledge relative to the demands of the task, and monitoring their comprehension and implementing fix-up strategies when comprehension fails.[30]

Skilled readers are aware that there are different purposes for reading and that they must change the way they read in response to these purposes. For instance, they know that reading for enjoyment does not require detailed understanding, while reading for a test may. In one study, third and sixth graders were asked to read two stories, one for fun and the other in preparation for a test.[31] The skilled readers adjusted their reading strategies for the two stories; the immature readers didn't. As a result, the immature readers did not remember any more of the story they were supposed to study than the one they were supposed to read for fun.

Perhaps because they frequently do not see the point of reading, poor readers often do not adequately control the way they read. One aspect of such control is being able to monitor one's own reading and notice when failures occur. To investigate this, researchers have placed inconsistent information in passages to see whether readers can detect it. Here are examples of consistent and inconsistent passages:

All the people who work on this ship get along very well. The people who make a lot of money and the people who don't make much are still friends. The officers treat me as an equal. We often eat our meals together. I guess we are just one big happy family.
All the people who work on this ship get along very well. The people who make a lot of money and the people who don't make much are still friends. The officers treat me like dirt. We often eat our meals together. I guess we are just one big happy family.[32]

Skilled readers readily detect the inconsistency in the second passage. Younger or less able readers are not as likely to notice the problem and usually say that the passage makes sense.[33]

Another aspect of control during reading is being able to take corrective action once a failure in understanding has been detected. Skilled readers know what to do if they have difficulty. There are a number of options available: keeping the problem "on hold" in the hope that it will be clarified later in the text; rereading parts of the text; looking ahead; or seeking help from outside sources. In one study, researchers asked second and sixth graders questions about their strategies for coping with failures to understand.[34] Older and better readers said that, for instance, if they did not know the meaning of a word they would ask someone else or go to a dictionary. Poorer readers were unable to say what they would do. These reports have been confirmed by actually observing children. In another study, fourth graders were asked to read and remember a story containing some difficult words.[35] They were given paper, a pencil, and a dictionary and told that they could ask questions. As expected, the good readers asked questions, took notes, and used the dictionary. The poor readers used these aids infrequently.

Throughout this report, the idea that skilled reading needs to be strategic will be emphasized. This means that the reader monitors progress in understanding, and resolves problems that prevent understanding.

The fourth principle is that *reading requires motivation.* As every teacher knows, motivation is one of the keys to learning to read. It will take most children several years to learn to read well. Somehow, their attention must be sustained during this period, and they must not lose the hope that eventually they will become successful readers.

Reading itself is fun. At least, it is for many children who are skilled readers for their age and for some children with average and below average skill. These children are, as the saying goes, "hooked on books." Increasing the proportion of children who read widely and with evident satisfaction ought to be as much a goal of reading instruction as increasing the number who are competent readers. An essential step in reaching that goal is providing children ready access to books that are interesting to them.[36]

Reading instruction can be boring. Aspects of the standard reading lesson are monotonous. Many of the tasks assigned to children in the name of reading are drudgery. Thus, it is not surprising that in one study, for instance, interviews with a sample of poor, black children reading a year above grade level indicated that most liked to read, but few liked the activities called "reading" in school.[37]

Teachers who maintain high levels of motivation conduct fast-paced and varied lessons. Tasks are introduced with enthusiasm and with explanations of why doing them will help one become a better reader. Teachers whose classes are motivated are described as businesslike but supportive and friendly. Children taught by teachers rated as having these traits make larger-than-average gains on reading achievement tests.[38]

Failure is not fun. Predictably, poor readers have unfavorable attitudes toward reading. What is not so predictable is whether lack of proficiency in reading stems from unfavorable attitudes or it is the other way around. Probably the truth can lie in either direction.

Poor readers frequently are listless and inattentive and sometimes are disruptive. They do not complete work. The give up quickly when faced with a task that is difficult for them. They become anxious when they must read aloud or take a test. A good summary description is that they act as though they were helpless to do better.[39]

The etiology of this sense of helplessness is not completely understood, but it is known that it is affected in sometimes subtle ways by teachers' behavior. It might be thought an act of kindness to express pity when students flub a test, but the hidden message may be that they lack the ability to do any better, that they are not in control of their own fate. An expression of dissatisfaction, on the other hand, may convey the message that the students could do better if they tried harder. People can control effort; people in control, even ones doing poorly, are not helpless.[40]

Effective reading teachers convey by word and deed that everyone can learn to read if they pay attention and apply themselves. In their classrooms, effort pays off. Research establishes that these teachers assign reading material on which children experience a high rate of success.[41] However, effective teachers do not offer praise indiscriminately. Praise is given in recognition of noteworthy success at a task that is difficult for *this* student. The statement of praise specifies what the student did well, attributes the success to ability and effort, and implies that similar successes are attainable in the future.[42]

Though sustained motivation is essential for learning to read, it should be cautioned that poor motivation is not the only problem, or even the most important problem, faced by poor readers. Experience indicates that even under the best of conditions some percentage of children will have difficulties in learning to read. A detailed discussion of what may be the root causes of these difficulties is beyond the scope of this report. It can be asserted with some confidence, nonetheless, that the approaches to reading outlined in this report, can help to ameliorate the difficulties faced by the very poor readers.[43]

The fifth principle is that *reading is a continuously developing skill*. Reading, like playing a musical instrument, is not something that is mastered once and for all at a certain age. Rather, it is a skill that continues to improve through practice. The process begins with a person's earliest exposure to text and a literate culture and continues throughout life.[44]

A good rule of thumb is that the most useful form of practice is doing the whole skill of reading — that is, reading meaningful text for the purpose of understanding the message it contains. This fact poses a problem for the beginner. How can a child practice reading without already being able to read?

One or more of several strategies are used to get a beginner started reading. A natural strategy is to use familiar stories that are readily understandable to the child, or maybe even partly known by heart. A common strategy is to restrict severely the vocabulary of the first selections a beginner will read. Another useful strategy is to teach the beginner something about the relationships between letters and sounds.

Like instruction in other complex skills, reading instruction most often takes the form of explanation, advice, coaching, and practice on what are judged to be the essential aspects or parts of the process. The test of the value of this instruction is whether the child's reading as a whole improves. Thus, in a well-designed reading program, mastering the parts does not become an end in itself, but a means to an end, and there is a proper balance between practice of the parts and practice of the whole.

In summary:

- *Skilled reading is constructive.* Becoming a skilled reader requires learning to reason about written material using knowledge from everyday life and from disciplined fields of study.
- *Skilled reading is fluent.* Becoming a skilled reader depends upon mastering basic processes to the point where they are automatic, so that attention is freed for the analysis of meaning.
- *Skilled reading is strategic.* Becoming a skilled reader requires learning to control one's reading in relation to one's purpose, the nature of the material, and whether one is comprehending.
- *Skilled reading is motivated.* Becoming a skilled reader requires learning to sustain attention and learning that written material can be interesting and informative.
- *Skilled reading is a lifelong pursuit.* Becoming a skilled reader is a matter of continuous practice, development, and refinement.

Summary of the
Becoming a Nation of Readers Study[45]

The Research Base

Three broad areas of inquiry have made *Becoming a Nation of Readers* possible. Studies of human cognition in the psychology of language, linguistics, child development, and behavioral science give us a clearer picture of reading as an integration of numerous learned processes. Research on environmental influences has described the impact of various settings on reading experiences. Investigations of classroom practices, especially those stemming from studies of teaching and of test use, have been interpreted in the light of the efforts to understand the reading process and to explicate factors that shape children's experience with written language. Given the scope of these inquiries, the Commission on Reading that guided the preparation of this document and the scholars who wrote it have been able to synthesize a diverse, rich body of scientific information into a systematic account of beginning reading and the comprehension of language.

The Reading Process

Research on the reading process has provided fuller understanding of how children can learn the letter patterns and associated sounds in an alphabetic language such as English, the importance of fluent word recognition, and how a text's structure influences the meaning drawn from it. It has uncovered the roots of proficient reading, and described how the development of well-practiced skills in beginning reading foster comprehension of complex texts. This research often supports accepted effective practices and removes them from unnecessary debate; the findings explain and confirm the experience and intuitions of outstanding practitioners and make their methods more widely accessible. At the same time, research findings identify practices that are less useful, are outmoded, or persist in the face of evidence to the contrary.

Knowledge about the intricacies of the reading process lay to rest once and for all some of the old debates about the roles of phonics and comprehension. We now know that learning efficient word recognition and grasping meaning are companion skills from the time a child first reads. These findings also have yielded evidence that extends early research on reading and on child development. We have learned that children bring more prior knowledge and complex mental processes to reading than was thought earlier. Reading instruction should meet the challenge of building from the knowledge that children bring to the school experience, by offering the richest texts that they are able to understand. Teaching techniques and text design can be informed by new conceptions of the potential of children's minds, and at the same time recognize individual differences in language experience and in the acquisition of reading proficiency.

Environmental Influences on Reading
Reading, comprehending, and thinking with language and the printed word are cultural phenomena. The extent of their development is affected by home and family circumstances, the encouragement of basic habits and attitudes in kindergarten and the early grades, and opportunities and social support for the development of effective skills and strategies in later life. This report addresses this complexity, understanding that too often one phase or factor of the acquisition of reading ability captures popular attention and blocks appreciation of the larger sweep of reading development.

Text comprehension depends upon a reader's prior knowledge, experience, and attitudes; meaning is constructed as a reader links what he reads to what he knows. We can think of literacy as an acquired proficiency. Like achieving high levels of competence in swimming or in playing a musical instrument, competence in reading requires appropriate conditions and long periods of training and practice. This report discusses the roles of early habits and motivation; the systematic teaching of foundation skills for decoding words, developing vocabulary, inferring meaning from sentences, and enjoying stories; and the further development of strategies for comprehending and interpreting textbooks in various subject matters.

The parent and the home environment teach the child his or her first lessons, and they are the first teacher for reading too. Acquiring sensitivity to the sounds and rhythm of words and their meanings, a love of books, and an ease of oral communication does not happen spontaneously; we can shape our homes to enable our children to become lovers of words and books. Formal school instruction takes on added value when programs in institutions out of school, like libraries, television, and museums, display attention to high standards of literacy.

Teaching Techniques, Tools, and Testing
In teaching, as in other professions, well-researched methods and tools are essential. This report makes clear the key role of teachers' professional knowledge. Research on instructional pacing and grouping and on adaptation to children's accomplishments has contributed to new ideas that can help all children master the basics and then attain levels of literacy far beyond the basic competencies. The reading teacher's repertoire must draw upon the deepening knowledge of child development, of the nature of language and linguistics, of the structure of stories that give rise to comprehension, of the art and elegance of children's literature, and of the psychology of learning. With such knowledge assisting their practices, they can best foster the acquisition of foundation skills and higher processes of comprehension. The report indicates why changes in teacher training, internship experiences, continuing education, and sabbatical periods are necessary if teachers are to learn and refine their skills for their complex task.

Becoming a Nation of Readers also draws on knowledge that has been obtained about the design of primers, workbooks, and self-study lessons; the structure of stories and texts that encourage effective habits of comprehension and thinking with language; and tests that significantly drive what is taught and learned. Fruitful directions are indicated for the designers and publishers of these materials. The report goes further and points out that our understanding of reading in the context of the subject matters of schooling, science, mathematics, social studies, and literature must be carefully researched so that texts and teaching materials can be designed for effective levels of comprehension and problem solving.

The ways in which reading achievement is tested and evaluated greatly influence what is taught and the reading skills that are valued and learned. Testing is a very useful aspect of teaching and learning, but should not emphasize only the competencies that are easy to measure and thus fix our sights below essential processes. Mastery tests must not treat reading as a set of discrete skills, when research has indicated that a closely integrated set of processes supports fluent reading. The nationally normed tests used by school systems may not accommodate the expanding view of literacy this society requires. Because of our greater understanding of reading and social influences upon it, improved forms of assessment are now feasible and can supplement strengthened instructional practices and tools in raising the national levels of literacy.

With growing recognition of the contributions of research to educational practice, educational policymaking can proceed with new vigor. Issues of educational practice, like those of health care, are of pervasive concern in this society. Where sound information on topics of national concern exists, informed policymakers, professionals, and an informed citizenry can work together to assure that high standards are observed.

Recommendations

The more elements of good parenting, good teaching, and good schooling that children experience, the greater the likelihood that they will achieve their potential as readers. The following recommendations encapsulate the information presented in this report about the conditions likely to produce citizens who read with high levels of skill and do so frequently with evident satisfaction.

Parents should read to preschool children and informally teach them about reading and writing. Reading to children, discussing stories and experiences with them, and—with a light touch—helping them learn letters and words are practices that are consistently associated with eventual success in reading.

Parents should support school-aged children's continued growth as readers. Parents of children who become successful readers monitor their children's progress in school, become involved in school programs, support homework, buy their children books or take them to libraries, encourage reading as a free-time activity, and place reasonable limits on such activities as TV viewing.

Preschool and kindergarten reading readiness programs should focus on reading, writing, and oral language. Knowledge of letters and their sounds, words, stories, and question asking and answering are related to learning to read, but there is little evidence that such activities as coloring, cutting with a scissors, or discriminating shapes (except the shapes of letters) promote reading development.

Teachers should maintain classrooms that are both stimulating and disciplined. Effective teachers of reading create a literate classroom environment. They allocate an adequate amount of time to reading and writing, sustain children's attention, maintain a brisk pace, and keep rates of success high.

Teachers of beginning reading should present well-designed phonics instruction. Though most children today are taught phonics, often this instruction is poorly conceived. Phonics is more likely to be useful when children hear the sounds associated with most letters both in isolation and in words, and when they are taught to blend together the sounds of letters to identify words. In addition, encouraging children to think of other words they know with similar spellings, when they encounter words they cannot readily identify, may help them develop the adult strategy of decoding unknown words by analogy with ones that are known. Phonics instruction should be kept simple and it should be completed by the end of the second grade for most children.

Reading primers should be interesting and comprehensible and should give children opportunities to apply phonics. There should be a close interplay between phonics instruction and reading words in meaningful selections. But most primers contain too few words that can be identified using the phonics that has already been taught. After the very earliest selections, primers should tell complete, interesting stories.

Teachers should devote more time to comprehension instruction. Teacher-led instruction in reading strategies and other aspects of comprehension promotes reading achievement, but there is very little direct comprehension instruction in most American classrooms.

Children should spend less time completing workbooks and skill sheets. Workbooks and skill sheet activities consume a large proportion of the time allocated to reading instruction in most American classrooms, despite the fact that there is little evidence that these activities are related to reading achievement. Workbook and skill sheet activities should be pared to the minimum that actually provide worthwhile practice in aspects of reading.

Children should spend more time in independent reading. Independent reading, whether in school or out of school, is associated with gains in reading achievement. By the time they are in the third or fourth grade, children should read independently a minimum of two hours per week. Children's reading should include classic and modern works of fiction and nonfiction that represent the core of our cultural heritage.

Children should spend more time writing. Opportunities to write more than a sentence or two are infrequent in most American elementary school classrooms. As well as being valuable in its own right, writing promotes ability in reading.

Textbooks should contain adequate explanations of important concepts. Textbooks in science, social studies, and other areas should be clearly written, well-organized, and contain important information and concepts. Too many of the textbooks used in American classrooms do not meet these standards.

Schools should cultivate an ethos that supports reading. Schools that are effective in teaching reading are characterized by vigorous leadership, high expectations, an emphasis on academic learning, order and discipline, uninterrupted time for learning, and staffs that work together.

Schools should maintain well-stocked and managed libraries. Access to interesting and informative books is one of the keys to a successful reading program. As important as an adequate collection of books is a librarian who encourages wide reading and helps match books to children.

Schools should introduce more comprehensive assessments of reading and writing. Standardized tests should be supplemented with assessments of reading fluency, ability to summarize and critically evaluate lengthy selections, amount of independent reading, and amount and quality of writing.

Schools should attract and hold more able teachers. The number of able people who choose teaching as a profession has declined in recent years. Reversing this trend requires higher admissions standards for teacher education programs, stronger standards for teacher certification, improved working conditions, and higher teachers' salaries.

Teacher education programs should be lengthened and improved in quality. Prospective elementary teachers do not acquire an adequate base in either the liberal arts and sciences or in pedagogy. They get only a fleeting introduction to the knowledge required for teaching reading. Teacher education programs should be extended to five years and the quality and rigor of the instruction should be increased.

Schools should provide for the continuing professional development of teachers. Schools should have programs to ease the transition of novice teachers into the profession and programs to keep veteran teachers abreast of advancing knowledge.

America will become a nation of readers when verified practices of the best teachers in the best schools can be introduced throughout the country.

Notes

1. G. Psacharopoulos, "Returns to Education: An Updated International Comparison," *Comparative Education* 17 (1982): 321-41.
2. National Commission on Excellence in Education, *A Nation at Risk: The Imperative for Educational Reform* (Washington: United States Department of Education, 1983). For extensive excerpts, see chapter 1 above.
3. There is reason to believe that instructional materials and quality of teaching in the early grades can significantly influence higher level achievement at high school and college. See J. S. Chall, "Literacy: Trends and Explanations," *Educational Researcher* 12 (1983): 3-8.
4. See R. Farr and L. Fay, "Reading Trend Data in the United States: A Mandate for Caveats and Caution," in *The Rise and Fall of National Test Scores,* ed. G. R. Austin and H. Garber (New York: Academic Press, 1982), 83-141.
5. A. I. Gates, *Attainment in Elementary Schools: 1957 and 1937* (New York: Bureau of Publications, Columbia Teachers College, 1961).
6. National Assessment of Educational Progress, *Three National Assessments of Reading: Changes in Performance, 1970-1980,* Education Commission of the States, Report 11-R-01 (Denver: the Commission, 1981).

7. Chall, "Literacy"; B. K. Eckland, "College Entrance Examination Trends," in *The Rise and Fall of National Test Scores*, ed. Austin and Garber, 9-34; Farr and Fay, "Reading Trend Data"; and A. Harnischfeger and D. E. Wiley, *Achievement Test Scores Decline: Do We Need to Worry?* (Chicago: CEMREL, 1975). Some NAEP data also tend to support the decline in more advanced reading skill. Between the 1970-71 and 1979-80 NAEP evaluations, seventeen-year-olds showed slight losses in inferential comprehension.

8. Eckland, "College Entrance Examination Trends."

9. R. L. Thorndike, *Reading Comprehension Education in Fifteen Countries: An Empirical Study* (New York: Wiley, 1973).

10. H. W. Stevenson, "Making the Grade: School Achievement in Japan, Taiwan, and the United States," in *Annual Report of the Center for Advanced Study in the Behavioral Sciences* (Stanford: the Center, 1984), 41-51.

11. Historical research shows a steady increase in the standards of literacy required to meet changing social needs and conditions. See D. P. Resnick and L. B. Resnick, "The Nature of Literacy: An Historical Exploration," *Harvard Educational Review* 47 (1977): 370-85.

12. Adapted from D. L. Schallert, "The Significance of Knowledge: A Synthesis of Research Related to Schema Theory," in *Reading Expository Material,* ed. W. Otto and S. White (New York: Academic Press, 1982), 28.

13. P. D. Pearson and R. J. Spiro, "Toward a Theory of Reading Comprehension Instruction," *Topics in Language Disorders* 1 (1980): 71-88.

14. Oral reading errors showing an overreliance on graphophonemic cues are described in J. Hood and J. R. Kendall, "Qualitative Analysis of Oral Reading Errors of Reflective and Impulsive Second Graders: Follow-up Study," *Journal of Reading Behavior* 7 (1975): 269-81; and R. M. Weber, "A Linguistic Analysis of First-Grade Reading Errors," *Reading Research Quarterly* 5 (1970): 427-51.

15. Oral reading errors showing an overreliance on contextual cues are described in A. Bienmiller, "The Development of the Use of Graphic and Contextual Information as Children Learn to Read," *Reading Research Quarterly* 6 (1970): 75-96.

16. M. S. Steffensen, C. Joag-dev, and R. C. Anderson, "A Cross-cultural Perspective on Reading Comprehension," *Reading Research Quarterly* 15 (1979): 10-29.

17. P. D. Pearson, J. Hansen, and C. Gordon, "The Effect of Background Knowledge on Young Children's Comprehension of Explicit and Implicit Information," *Journal of Reading Behavior* 11 (1979): 201-9.

18. R. A. Owings et al., "Spontaneous Monitoring and Regulation of Learning: A Comparison of Successful and Less Successful Fifth Graders," *Journal of Educational Psychology* 72 (1980): 250-56; and S. G. Paris and B. K. Lindauer, "The Role of Inference in Children's Comprehension and Memory for Sentences," *Cognitive Psychology* 8 (1976): 217-27. For implications of children's failure to draw on prior knowledge in the school setting, see I. L. Beck, "Five Problems with Children's Comprehension in the Primary Grades," in *Reading Education: Foundations for a Literate America,* ed. J. Osborn, P. T. Wilson, and R. C. Anderson (Lexington, Mass.: Lexington Books, 1985), 239-53; and P. T. Wilson and R. C. Anderson, "Reading Comprehension and School Learning," ibid., 319-28.

19. A. Lesgold, L. B. Resnick, and K. Hammond, "Learning to Read: A Longitudinal Study of Word Skill Development in Two Curricula," in *Reading Research: Advances in Theory and Practice,* ed. T. G. Waller and G. E. MacKinnon, vol. 4 (New York: Academic Press, 1985), 107-38.

20. J. M. Cattell, "The Time It Takes to See and Name Objects," *Mind* 11 (1886): 63-65.

21. D. E. Meyer and R. W. Schvaneveldt, "Facilitation in Recognizing Pairs of Words: Evidence of a Dependence between Retrieval Operations," *Journal of Experimental Psychology* 90 (1971): 227-34. This study shows facilitation effects with words presented in isolation. There is evidence to suggest that contextual constraints also facilitate processing during reading of connected

text. See D. Zola, "Redundancy and Word Perception during Reading," *Perception and Psychophysics* 36 (1984): 277-84.

22. J. L. McClelland and D. E. Rumelhart, "An Interactive Activation Model of Context Effects in Letter Perception: Part 1: An Account of Basic Findings," *Psychological Review* 88 (1981): 375-407; and D. E. Rumelhart and J. L. McClelland, "An Interactive Activation Model of Context Effects in Letter Perception: Part 2: The Contextual Enhancement Effect and Some Tests and Extensions of the Model," *Psychological Review* 89 (1982): 60-94.

23. P. B. Gough, "One Second of Reading," in *Language by Ear and by Eye,* ed. J. F. Kavanagh and I. G. Mattingly (Cambridge, Mass.: MIT Press, 1972), 331-58; and M. A. Just and P. A. Carpenter, "A Theory of Reading: From Eye Fixations to Comprehension," *Psychological Review* 87 (1980): 329-54.

24. K. E. Stanovich, "Toward an Interactive-Compensatory Model of Individual Differences in the Development of Reading Fluency," *Reading Research Quarterly* 16 (1980): 32-71.

25. R. J. Glushko, "The Organization and Activation of Orthographic Knowledge in Reading Aloud," *Journal of Experimental Psychology: Human Perception and Performance* 5 (1979): 674-91.

26. C. A. Perfetti and A. M. Lesgold, "Discourse Comprehension and Sources of Individual Differences," in *Cognitive Processes in Comprehension,* ed. M. A. Just and P. A. Carpenter (Hillsdale, N. J.: Erlbaum, 1977), 141-83.

27. R. C. Anderson and R. W. Kulhavy, "Learning Concepts from Definitions," *American Educational Research Journal* 9 (1972): 385-90; and R. C. Anderson, S. R. Goldberg, and J. L. Hidde, "Meaningful Processing of Sentences," *Journal of Educational Psychology* 62 (1971): 395-99.

28. J. V. Hoffman et al., "Guided Oral Reading and Miscue Focused Verbal Feedback in Second-Grade Classrooms," *Reading Research Quarterly* 19 (1984): 367-84.

29. Lesgold, Resnick, and Hammond, "Learning to Read."

30. See L. Baker and A. L. Brown, "Metacognitive Skills and Reading," in *Handbook of Reading Research,* ed. P. D. Pearson (New York: Longman, 1984), 353-94.

31. D. L. Forrest and T. G. Waller, "Cognitive and Metacognitive Aspects of Reading" (Paper delivered at the biennial meeting of the Society for Research in Child Development, San Francisco, March 1979).

32. From M. Grabe and S. Mann, "A Technique for the Assessment and Training of Comprehension Monitoring Skills," *Journal of Reading Behavior* 16 (1984): 136.

33. Ibid.

34. M. Myers and S. G. Paris, "Children's Metacognitive Knowledge about Reading," *Journal of Educational Psychology* 70 (1978): 680-90.

35. S. G. Paris and M. Myers, "Comprehension Monitoring, Memory, and Study Strategies of Good and Poor Readers," *Journal of Reading Behavior* 13 (1981): 5-22.

36. The full report *Becoming a Nation of Readers* discusses this in detail in the chapter "Extending Literacy."

37. D. Durkin, *A Study of Poor Black Children Who Are Successful Readers,* Center for the Study of Reading, Reading Education Report No. 33 (Urbana: Center for the Study of Reading, University of Illinois, 1982).

38. See H. J. Walberg, V. C. Hare, and C. A. Pulliam, "Social-Psychological Perceptions and Reading Comprehension," in *Comprehension and Teaching: Research Reviews,* ed. J. T. Guthrie (Newark, Del.: International Reading Association, 1981), 140-59.

39. See C. S. Dweck, "The Role of Expectations and Attributions in the Alleviation of Learned Helplessness," *Journal of Personality and Social Psychology* 31 (1975): 674-85.

40. B. Weiner, "Some Thoughts about Feelings," in *Learning and Motivation in*

the Classroom, ed. S. G. Paris, G. M. Olson, and H. W. Stevenson (Hillsdale, N.J.: Erlbaum, 1983), 165-78.

41. J. V. Hoffman et al., "Guided Oral Reading and Miscue Focused Verbal Feedback"; and B. Rosenshine and R. Stevens, "Classroom Instruction in Reading," in *Handbook of Reading Research,* ed. Pearson, 745-98.

42. J. E. Brophy, "Fostering Student Learning and Motivation in the Elementary School Classroom," in *Learning and Motivation in the Classroom,* ed. Paris, Olson, and Stevenson, 283-305.

43. An afterword in *Becoming a Nation of Readers,* not reproduced here, addresses this as well.

44. See J. S. Chall, *Stages of Reading Development* (New York: McGraw-Hill, 1983).

45. This summary is taken from the foreword of *Becoming a Nation of Readers.*

4. The London Declaration
Towards a Reading Society
Unesco World Congress on Books

The London Declaration shows the hopes of the participants in the World Congress on Books, organized by Unesco, held in 1982. The World Congress on Books aimed at comparing achievements among nations in the development of publishing industries and the dissemination of books and at making recommendations for the future.

The declaration, prepared by the International Book Committee and adopted by the congress, considers a number of themes in book culture, including the importance of books in human society, the need for national development of publishing, the importance of international book trade, and the value of self-education through books.

From *World Congress on Books, London, 7-11 June 1982: Final Report*. Paris: Unesco, 1982.

1. We, the writers, translators, publishers, printers, booksellers, librarians, educationists, government officials, and members of the general intellectual community, from 92 nations meeting in London at the World Congress on Books 1982, convened by Unesco, declare our continued support for the principles and objectives established ten years ago during International Book Year 1972.

2. Books, we believe, retain their preeminence as the carriers of knowledge, education, and cultural values in human society. They serve both national development and the enrichment of individual human life. They foster better understanding between peoples and strengthen the desire for peace in the minds of men, to which Unesco is dedicated.

3. Having reviewed the decade since International Book Year, we reaffirm the validity of the *Charter of the Book,* agreed upon by the international professional organizations in 1972, and the aim of *Books for All,*[1] yet to be achieved but still worthy of being sought. The ten principles embodied in the Charter asserted that everyone has the right to read; that books are essential to education; that society has a special obligation to enable authors to exercise their creative role; that book manufacturing facilities and a sound publishing industry are vital to national development; that booksellers and libraries provide necessary services to publishers and the reading public; that the free flow of books between countries is of fundamental importance; and that books serve and promote international understanding and peaceful cooperation.

4. Looking forward, we seek a world in which books are more readily available to more people, and in which the ability to read and the will and desire to enjoy the fruits of reading are more widely sought by all societies.

5. Men and women have a right to learn and to educate themselves. They have a right to acquire knowledge and to acquaint themselves with the wisdom and experience of other nations, of other cultures, and of previous generations. They also have a need to record their own ideas and experiences. Books are profoundly important in creating a society in which all people can play a full part and in which they can lead richer lives. Moreover, through the written and printed word, creative writers express, explore, and

develop the values and aspirations of their own societies and widen and enrich the consciousness and imagination of their readers.

6. Reading transcends national and cultural barriers. However, some potential readers are deprived of the benefits which reading might provide by lack of education, by inadequate reading abilities, and by impediments to the wide dissemination of good books. We call upon all concerned to encourage the production and dissemination of books; to encourage writers and readers, especially young readers, in schools and in the home.

7. We call upon all concerned, particularly governments, to seek the removal of restraints of all kinds on the creation, production, and publication of books and their distribution within and across national boundaries in both directions. We see the maintenance and application of national copyright laws, compatible with the international copyright conventions, as in the interest of writers, translators, publishers, teachers, and readers everywhere.

8. In pursuit of the goal of a society in which books are more readily available and more widely used, the congress has endorsed a series of objectives. These seek to create an environment in which reading is both natural and desirable and is seen as a vital activity to be stimulated by formal and conscious national book strategies and helped by cooperative international action, thus reinforcing the role of the book in the future.

9. We therefore call upon governments and upon all those professionally concerned with books to accept these guides to action. We seek a world in which there are indeed books for all, but one also in which all can read and all accept books and reading as a necessary and desirable part of daily life. We look forward, not merely to a literate world but towards a universal reading society.

Note

1. *Books for All: A Programme of Action* (Paris: Unesco, 1973).

Then occurred a miracle in man's communication with man. A few thousand years before the Christian era, the Phoenicians, on the shores of the Mediterranean, produced what we call our alphabet.

JOSEPH BLUMENTHAL
Printer

5. The Centrality of Reading

Jacques Barzun

Jacques Barzun, a member of the Advisory Committee on the Book in the Future, argues in this essay that reading itself is a power and that discipline is required to master it. He believes that we are dependent upon reading and that the sight word method of instruction in reading, among other educational practices, has irresponsibly substituted a confidence in the results of a creative haphazardness for discipline.

For further commentary from Jacques Barzun, see "The Future of Reading," chapter 11 below.

From *Michigan Quarterly Review,* vol. 9, no. 1, January 1970, pp. 7-11. Reprinted with permission from *Michigan Quarterly Review* (University of Michigan).

Anybody who has ever taught knows that the act of teaching depends upon the teacher's instantaneous and intuitive vision of the pupil's mind as it gropes and fumbles to grasp a new idea, to make a new image for a new fact.

This act is of course surrounded by other acts less intense and perhaps also less productive. From the desk, the teacher gives instructions to the group, and not all the minds present attend to it with the same force, nor can the teacher square his or her mind with each of those other minds in perfect congruence.

Moreover, as in the jury scene of *Alice in Wonderland,* there are interruptions. The king having said, like a teacher: "This is very important," the White Rabbit interrupts: "'Unimportant', your Majesty means." Just so will a child break in, from restlessness or too much zeal. All are affected: the jurymen, you remember, write down "Important," "Unimportant," as chance dictates, that is, as their degree of concentration or self-assurance or feeling for one speaker or another leads them to do. That fictional scene is a brilliantly quick glimpse not of the courtroom alone, but also of the classroom.

A good teacher, of course, does not let himself be sidetracked or confused like the poor king, but he knows that in the instant of acquiring knowledge the mind is most vulnerable to distraction, and hence to error. Its antennae are vibrating fast, swaying and searching in all directions; the mind is conscious and unconscious at once in the most extraordinary way. The least atmospheric disturbance can deflect the perceiving power from the truth of the moment.

We can all remember early misconceptions which it took years to remove because they had taken root on some occasion of King-and-rabbit excitement. That is why oral teaching, indispensable to the close fitting of mind to mind, is also difficult, delicate, dangerous— and time consuming. The state of congruence must be re-created over and over again about each aspect of the complex matters that form the branches of learning. Thanks to this repetition, there is opportunity to correct error, to refine the image of the worded idea, and most important, to establish habits of self-correction, of self-teaching—the habits we call reasoning, figuring out, catching one's mistakes before it is too late.

Now consider the only other situation in which learners also learn, the learning done from the written word.[1] Here, if what is perceived is wrong, every repetition reenforces error. Here, if what is first perceived is confused, every repetition hardens confusion. A perpetual puzzle is as bad as a protracted error, and sometimes worse; for an error can be pulled up by the roots by main strength; whereas confusion needs long and hard work to turn into order.

There is therefore no excuse for allowing the exercise of reading to be less certain in its results than the exercise of listening and remembering. To tolerate reading that proceeds by guesswork, as if at a later time someone would surely tighten the screws of the loose mental structure and make it solid and precise, is to commit an injury against the growing mind. To allow the written word to be indefinite is to undo *pro tanto* the incalculable technical advance that consisted in transfixing sounds by signs.

On this pedagogic ground alone, it could be said that no subject of study is more important than reading. In our civilization, at any rate, all the other intellectual powers depend upon it. No one can compute very far without reading correctly; no one can write decently without reading widely and well; no one can speak or listen intelligently without the mass of workaday information that comes chiefly through reading. As for acquiring some notions of history, government, hygiene, philosophy, art, religion, love-making, or the operation of a camera, they are all equally and pitifully dependent on reading. All the arguments against reading presuppose either a different culture, based on memory, myth, and physical prowess; or else a training in the interpretation of the purely visual which no one has even begun to develop and which would doubtless require extrasensory perception to make practicable.

Probably very few persons would systematically dispute these generalities. The most fanciful teachers, the laziest minds, acknowledge that several times a day they have to read the written word if life—their life—is to go on; they are willing slaves to their own writings (a shopping list) or somebody else's ("Danger: live wire"). In the longer span, they cannot earn a living, choose a career, remember obligations, stay healthy, keep friends, and avoid jail without the aid of reading. It may be deplorable, but it is so. Imagine the art of reading lost—and with it writing, study, and verbal recovery—and it is hard to see how civilized man could survive the shocks and anxieties of his state, let alone serve his multitudinous desires.

We have only to recall what impediments wisdom runs into without the written word. The fifth-century Indian philosophers who developed logic, ethics, and other means of sustaining mental balance depended entirely on memory for transmitting their achievements. "All this body of mental discipline," scholars tell us, "was taught without books. The style of the works themselves never lets us forget it, and they make shockingly bad *reading* in consequence. Often the only way to aid the burdened memory is an orderly but endless repetition of a verbal framework, wherein only one term of a series is varied at a time....yet the execution, in the absence of visible registering apparatus, [is] extraordinary. I am tempted to wonder how far the exaggeration of the Indian temperament and the temperateness of the Greek were due to the absence and presence respectively, during the florescence of each, of the fully written thought."[2]

The linguists who affect to scorn all utterance but the spoken word, the teachers' group in the midwest that has discovered the uselessness of reading and asks that it no longer be taught in the schools, the zealots who sidestep the issue but sell futures in a world where only the voice and the image will have currency—all appear deficient in imagination, the imagination they would need still more under their wayward scheme. In any case, their prophecy of the end of reading leaves me unmoved, for prophecy concerns the future, and to reach any future we must somehow get from here to there, and that will require reading.

In such an itinerary, what is in fact the here from which we start, the present situation of literacy? It is a state that does little credit to our efforts. The universal light which, according to the hopes of just a hundred years ago, when most of the great education acts were passed, was supposed to bathe the world in knowledge and reason, is not so dazzling as our generous ancestors expected. Its great source was to be literacy, and literacy is not in the ascendant. I am not qualified to judge the conflicting reports about the extent of reading-failure in the schools, nor have I firsthand knowledge of the aggravated difficulties weighing on children who come from poverty-stricken homes.[3] But what there can be no dispute about is that there are in this country some twenty-five million functional illiterates; they are so-called because in our midst they cannot function for lack of sufficient power to read and write. We know also that among the latest adult generations some two to three million such social cripples were discovered as they came up for the draft.

These calamities are everybody's concern, but they can only be repaired by teachers and other professionals adept at using the right remedies. The professionals, in turn, need the backing of parents, school boards, and interested bystanders. There must be a public opinion on the question *Where, in the matter of reading, does the public interest lie?* Certainly, it is not the parents whom I saw, in April 1968, marching toward the Chicago City Hall to protest against the lax promoting of their ill-prepared children, who are for abandoning the teaching of reading in favor of electronic telepathy. These people know what they want for their children, and they have a sound sense of what the country must require of its future citizens. Only a sophisticated mind, that is, part-educated and full of unexamined ideas, could seriously advocate the carrying on of schoolwork without schoolbooks.

Where does that sophistication come from? Why did it seem plausible and attractive, after three thousand years of teaching reading by sounding each letter, to do just the opposite and encourage guesswork about the "shapes" of words? And now that this asinine substitution has massively failed as it deserved, why does it seem advanced and (once again) sophisticated to suggest that reading is after all expendable, since we have at command so many knobs and buttons with which to circulate counterfeits of visual and vocal reality?

The reason for the second of these frauds is made up of two parts. One is, of course, the desire to hide the original blunder, as the clumsy servant whisks out of sight the fragments of the broken cup. The other is simple blindness to the truth that reading and its necessary twin, writing, constitute not merely an ability but a power. I mean by the distinction that reading is not just a device (in jargon, "a tool") by which we are reached and reach others for practical ends. It is also and far more importantly a mode of incarnating and shaping thought—as was shown in the example of the early Indian philosophers.

Now, all legitimate power is the result of a double discipline, first a discipline of the self and next a discipline of the acquired power within accepted constraints. Concretely, in order to exert the power of reading, after disciplining eye, ear, and memory, one must at each word accept the constraint of the black marks on paper. Guessing and inferring by context, and forcing these dubious egotisms upon the written text, are a refusal to accept the symbolic constraints of the written word, after failing to discipline oneself to learn their clear demands.

Here we touch the political and social causes of the whole sad odyssey that has brought America to the condition of being, in the words of Arthur Trace, "a land of semi-literates." Let us make no mistake about it: the causes are not ignorance, poverty, or barbarous instincts: they are "advanced thinking," love of liberty, and the impulse to discover and innovate. It is from on top—the action of the literate, the cultured, the philosophical, the artistic—that the common faith in the power of reading as central to western civilization has been destroyed. The target of the separate attacks and collective animus has been the very notion of power, discipline, constraint.

For it is true that none of these resembles the rival goals which sophisticated thought preferred—the free play of fancy, creativeness, and immediate enjoyment; self-expression, novelty, and untrammeled choice in pursuing one's own "thing." The intellectual elite of western society had learned the value of these meritorious pleasures in the writings of the best philosophers, artists, and political thinkers, and, with impatient contempt of school dullness and rote learning, they resolved to emancipate the child and "give" him these superior joys.

The folly consisted, not in wanting the lofty results, but in thinking they were an alternative set that could be reached directly. I have elsewhere defined this fallacy as "preposterism"[4]— seeking to obtain straight off what can only be the fruit of some effort, putting the end before the beginning. It should have been obvious that self-expression is real only after the means to it have been required. Likewise, for the other pleasant exertions there are conditions sine qua non. And these justly praised parts and privileges of a free spirit are in fact used in meeting these conditions, in learning itself; the child *is* self-expressive when he painstakingly forms the letters *a, b, c*—though he is not quite ready to "create" a poem. Nor can creativeness be the *object* of his learning, since creation is by definition unlearnable.

All this high-minded preposterism found its perfect expression in the look-and-say doctrine for the teaching of reading. The truth that practised readers recognize whole words at a glance and do not need to sound each letter with their lips was pre-post-erously made the starting point of instruction—a method which on the face of it is the quintessence of anti-method. Thanks to it the child was left free, imaginative, creative; the printed text exerted upon him no constraint whatever: he could not read. At the same time, the child was not free to start reading till some teacher decided that he was "ready"; was not free to read any book, least of all literature, but only Dick-and-Jane the Inane; was not free to connect his whole speaking vocabulary with what was given him to read, but only 400, 500, 600 words, depending on his progress in guesswork; was not free to learn spelling at any decent rate, since a blank space has no "shape" and one cannot guess how to fill it without knowing the (forbidden) sounds of the letters. In the end, the desired "development of the self" did not seen to reach very far.

Whether this well-engineered movement toward analphabetism can be reversed is what no one can predict. But before leaving the reader in suspense, like the heroine hanging from the cliff, it is, I think, useful for private and public action to mention the three or four cultural forces that encouraged and still sustain the hostility to reading, to the alphabet, to the word.

The first is the emotion of scientism, which for seventy-five years has preferred numbers to words, doing to thinking, and experiment to tradition. This perversion of true science led to calling "experiment" almost any foolish fancy and to believing in "studies" of "behavior" without a scintilla of regard to probability, logic, observation, or common sense. That it took half a century to begin admitting the error of look-and-say (through another "study," not through daily evidence of failure) shows the extent to which science has turned into superstition.

Second, the last phase of the liberalism which by 1910 had proclaimed everybody's emancipation, including the child's, took the form of total egalitarianism. Everybody was, by democratic fiat, right and just in all this actions; he was doing the best he could; he was human: we knew this by his errors, his errors were right. Q.E.D. It therefore became wrong to correct a child, to press him, push him, show him how to do better. Dialectal speech and grammatical blunders were natural and, as such, sacred; the linguists proved it by basing a profession on the dogma. Literature was a trivial surface phenomenon, the pastime of a doomed elite; why read books, why read, why teach the alphabet? Here, at least, the logic was perfect.

Third, the extension of free, public, compulsory education to all and in increasing amount (the high school dates from 1900) soon exhausted the natural supply of teachers. They had to be manufactured in large numbers, out of refractory material which could be more easily prepared in the virtues of the heart and the techniques of play than in any intellectual discipline. Themselves uneducated and often illiterate (see James Koerner's various reports), they infallibly transmitted their inadequacies, turning schoolwork into make-believe and boring their pupils into violence and scurrility.

Fourth and last, the conquest of the public imagination by the arts, by "art as a way of life," has reinforced the natural resistance of the mind to ordinary logic, order, and precision, without replacing these with any strong dose of *artistic* logic, order, and precision. The arts have simply given universal warrant for the offbeat, the unintelligible, the defiant without purpose. The schools have soaked up this heady brew. Anything new, obscure, implausible, self-willed is worth trying out, is an educational experiment. As such, it is validated by both science and art. Soon, the pupil comes to think that anything unformed, obscure, slovenly *he* may do is validated by art's contempt for tradition, correctness, and sense.

These contrasts—let us be clear about it—do *not* mean that tradition is right and innovation wrong; that artists ought not to try making all things new; that scientists may not experiment ad lib; that the imagination should not have free play; that equality is not the noblest of political ideas; that children should not be treated with courtesy and affection. The point of the contrast is this: what we have from our expensive schooling is not what we thought we were getting.

What is the lesson to be drawn? It is that no principles, however true, are any good when they are misunderstood or stupidly applied. Nothing is right by virtue of its origins, but only by virtue of its results. A stifling tradition is bad and a "great" tradition is good. Innovation that brings improvement is what we all desire: innovation that impoverishes the mind and the chances of life is damnable. Above all institutions, the school is designed for one thing only—fruits. But nowadays we despise the very word cultivation. I admit that unweeded soil grows wondrous things, which nobody can predict. And these things we have in abundance. But it would be a rash man who would call it a harvest.

Notes

1. The so-called "learning from experience," from living, is a mere name for situations in which one either listens, as in the classroom, but to fragmentary speech; or engages in work that is most likely combined with listening and reading.
2. Mrs. Rhys Davids, *Buddhism* (New York: Home University Library, 1911), 40.
3. However, the achievement of Dr. Seymour Gang and his teachers in the heart of Harlem shows what can be done by determination and judgment.
4. See my *The American University* (New York: Harper and Row, 1968), 219-23.

6. The Computer and the Book
The Perils of Coexistence

Edmund D. Pellegrino

Edmund D. Pellegrino, as a medical educator, comes from a field in which the use of computerized information, particularly computerized bibliography, is perhaps more widespread than any other. From this perspective, Pellegrino warns against a sort of "ill-literacy" that arises when preprocessed information substitutes itself for the inquisitive and personal learning that characterizes the liberal arts and the reading of books.

Dr. Pellegrino was a member of the Advisory Committee on the Book in the Future.

The report of the Library of Congress on the future of the book is certain to disappoint the zealots.[1] It does not pit computers against books or the fluorescent screen against the printed page in a struggle to the death. Nor does it match the ancients against the moderns as in Swift's *Battle of the Books.* Instead of granting victory to the bibliophiles or the computerniks, it proposes a peaceful coexistence.

This is a prudent and sensible conclusion. The choice cannot be, the book *or* the computer, anymore than it was the Dynamo *or* The Virgin in Henry Adams's day. But even as we accept the inevitability of the coexistence of computer literacy and traditional literacy, we must be wary of the dangers of confusing one with the other—of the erosion of those subtle but crucial cognitive skills which the reading of books confers.

"Computer literacy" in the sense of familiarity with the use of computers is unquestionably essential in education and scholarship today. But it cannot displace true literacy—the capacity to read the best books intelligently, creatively, and actively and to be familiar with the best models of writing and thinking the world's literature can offer.

The admirable irenic spirit of the report must not obscure the inherent differences between reading computers and reading books. Computer literacy can lead to aliteracy, and to some special forms of "ill-literacy." A quick look at these special dangers is not out of order even as we work toward peaceful coexistence.

Aliteracy—not reading books on the part of those who can read—is, as the report shows, already alarmingly on the increase among those under the age of twenty-one. Illiteracy of the grosser sort—not being able to read at all, or to do so marginally at best—has long been a problem of shameful proportions.[2] To this we must now add a special form of ill-literacy—erosion of those special cognitive skills book reading demands and cultivates.

This is not the place to dwell gloatingly on the much-discussed deficiencies of an inability to read well, or at all: the inarticulate speech, the stereotyped conversation, the distaste for abstractions, the flight from clear prose, or the mouthing of prepackaged opinions from the eleven o'clock news. Those of us who teach in college and professional schools are all too familiar with that litany. Too many commissions and committees have recently chanted that same litany and offered their remedies. Some of them have even seen computer literacy as the panacea.

I think it useful, however, to underscore for illustrative purposes one defect common to all nonbook sources of information. They all deal primarily in processed information, information that is, to varying degrees, predigested, preselected, and preordered to satisfy some special purpose. The computer is simply the most effective, efficient, and attractive form for transmittal of processed information. Added to the other nonbook devices like films, tapes, television, and the popular media, the computer accelerates the atrophy of the intellectual skills acquired for personally reading the books from which the information was extracted.

Processing, let it be said, is necessary if information is to be stored, retrieved, and used for learning and for research. To the user already educated enough to recognize its limitations, it is not a danger. This means the user knows what information he wants processed, what has been left out, when to ditch the program or the algorithm, and where to go to read it for himself. Above all, it means knowing how to frame an intelligent question, to know whether it is answerable, and to know when it is, in fact, answered.

These are the more subtle skills that come from book-based literacy. The trend to aliteracy deprives the learner of precisely the skills needed to use computer literacy wisely. Computer enthusiasts too easily forget their own education in traditional literacy in their enthusiasm for the potentialities of computer learning.

Anyone who has tried to provide the "key" words that will make his own writing computer-accessible knows the pitfalls of programmed information. If it is so difficult to process one's own thoughts, how much more perilous must it be for the programmer whose knowledge of that work is necessarily limited?

Today's scholarship already shows the results of overdependence on processed information. Bibliographies are much longer, but often obviously unread, and they bear only distant connections with a clear line of argument. The "search" rather than the question seems the object of the endeavor; finding a problem seems to have replaced framing the seminal question. Obviously no one can read intelligently all the sources the computer spits out. But to be able to select what to read calls for knowledge that only self-directed reading can supply. The paradox becomes stickier as computerized abstracts are scanned to see what should be read. We seem to be entering a state of infinite regression—key words of key words, abstracts of abstracts, summations of summations. The plethora of computerized bibliographies and computerized annotations pushes the reader further and further from the critical appraisal of a few seminal works—selected by intelligent book reading.

The perils of computer learning are equally evident. Emphasis is on the syllabus, on problem-solving, on skills acquisition, and on the completion of learning modules with limited objectives. Some kinds of learning are undoubtedly best pursued this way, especially in technical fields. But this is training and not education. It is useful in a technological society, but insufficient for a humane one. It might do for the technician, but not for the scientist and especially not for the humanist.

What is bypassed is the reader's personal perspective, his unique and self-directed dialogue with the author. Missing is the conversation with another mind. It is the seeming erratic course of reading that most often leads to the unexpected thought. It is nuances and style that so often evoke thought and imagination. The perspective of the programmer cannot be substituted for the perspective of the reader without serious damage to the purpose of true education—drawing forth the full intellectual capacities of the learner.

Processed information has all the qualities of processed cheese. It is faceless, tasteless, and without pungency. Just as a sustained diet of processed cheese obliterates the memory of the real thing, so a diet of computer literacy obliterates the memory of true literacy.

We read books for more than information. We read to learn the way of thinking of another mind. We read for the non-programmable, the gems of thought which let in light, perhaps only in us and in a unique way. We read to enter into discourse, dialectic, and dialogue with someone as obsessed with an idea or subject as we are.

One book leads to another and to a chain of bibliographies forged by a "search" not for key words, but for key thoughts—those we generate ourselves. Our search may not be complete. But it will be ordered and shaped by the questions we have framed.

The programmer eviscerates a book. He casts aside its vitals— the biases, prejudices, and flavor—to get at the "information." He discards as husks just those parts that might rescue our own thinking from conventionality.

The computer enthusiast argues that the sophisticated user also enters into dialogue with the computer, and this may be so. But it is the dialogue we associate with filling in the blanks in a vehicle registration form, a hospital admission sheet, or a survey questionnaire. Useful as such a dialogue may be, it cannot be substituted for the conversation in depth with a learned mind that self-directed book reading affords.

If computers and books are to coexist—and I think this is a necessity—then we must carefully examine the kinds of illiteracy computer literacy can generate. Such an appraisal will highlight, yet again, the importance of a liberal education. The antidote to computer-induced illiteracy is not to ban the computer but to reinvigorate the kind of education that enables the computer user to remain the master of his machine. The antidote can only be a

Edmund D. Pellegrino

liberal education—one based in the reading of books.

A true liberal education aims at making our minds free of the potential tyranny of other men's ideas. Especially, it fortifies us against any kind of programming. A liberal education in a classical sense emphasizes just what computer learning does not: independently reading, thinking, and writing, judging the good and the beautiful, knowing how to study a subject on one's own, and knowing how to enjoy the felicity of expression and stylistic peculiarities that distinguish elegant minds.

Books in Our Future is right to recommend peaceful coexistence. We must not sacrifice either the book or the computer. But in an age in which aliteracy and illiteracy are both on the increase, we must reflect on what we lose if we confuse computer with traditional literacy. Computer literacy enables us to use the unprecedented powers of the computer. We need book-based literacy if that coexistence is not to undermine the most human of our cognitive capabilities.

A technocratic society can thrive on computer literacy; a democratic society cannot, for a democratic society demands independent minds capable of critical thought. A great many citizens will undoubtedly be advantaged by computer learning. But we will always need a cadre who can rise above the program, not simply to preserve their own intellectual integrities, but to be beacons warning the rest of us when we run to close to the inhumane shoals of a programmed existence.

As usual, the poet says it more concisely:

> He ate and drank the precious Words—
> His Spirit grew robust—
> He knew no more that he was poor,
> Nor that his frame was Dust—
> He danced along the dingy Days
> And this Bequest of Wings
> Was but a Book—What Liberty
> A loosened spirit brings—[3]

The more spirits we can loosen, the more satisfying all our lives will be.

Notes

1. *Books in Our Future* (1984), most of which is reprinted below in chapter 27.
2. Jonathan Kozol, *Illiterate America* (New York: Anchor/Doubleday, 1985).
3. Emily Dickinson, *The Complete Poems,* ed. Thomas H. Johnson (London: Faber and Faber, 1970), 658.

Books and technology are symbiotic. Books and technology have been generating and regenerating each other since the beginning—and so they will, I firmly believe, until the end.

RODERICK D. STINEHOUR
Printer

To read well, that is, to read true books in a true spirit, is a noble exercise, and one that will task the reader more than any exercise which the customs of the day esteem. It requires a training such as the athletes underwent, the steady intention almost of the whole life to this object. Books must be read as deliberately and reservedly as they were written.

HENRY DAVID THOREAU

III.
Reading
and Society

7. The 1983 Consumer Research Study on Reading and Book Purchasing

A Summary

Joseph F. Brinley, Jr.

In fall 1983, two thousand Americans participated in a survey of reading and book buying habits conducted for the Book Industry Study Group by the firm of Market Facts of New York.

The survey shows that almost all Americans are readers but that a smaller proportion read books—as opposed to magazines and newspapers—than at the time of a preceding study in 1978. Mr. Brinley suggests that book reading, because it is especially reflective, is important to our culture and that efforts need to be made to attract more readers to book reading.

Joseph Brinley is a consultant to the Center for the Book.

This summary is drawn from the *1983 Consumer Research Study on Reading and Book Purchasing,* conducted by Market Facts, interpreted by Research & Forecasts, prepared for the Book Industry Study Group. 3 vols. New York: Book Industry Study Group, Inc., 1984. The summary has been reviewed by the Book Industry Study Group, Inc., and is published with its permission. For information about the availability of the full study, contact the Book Industry Study Group, 160 Fifth Avenue, New York, New York 10010.

The *1983 Consumer Research Study on Reading and Book Purchasing* gives reason for both enthusiasm and gloom in assessing the status of book culture in the United States. On the positive side, America is very much a nation of readers. According to the survey, 94 percent of Americans are readers of books, magazines, or newspapers. Fifty percent of Americans read books. Of the book readers, the large proportion who read books for leisure devote a considerable amount of time to this activity, an average of 8.7 hours per week.

Moreover, the survey shows book readers to be active, involved in many leisure activities. For example, book readers spend more time than other Americans in cultural activities, sports, physical fitness, and socializing. Television seems not to be reducing book reading in the way that is sometimes feared: book readers watch somewhat less television than those who read only magazines and newspapers, but they still devote a significant amount of time to television.

However, a number of declines in book readership appear in the *Consumer Research Study*. These declines may, in fact, threaten the future of the book. Between 1978, the time of a predecessor *Consumer Research Study,* and 1983, the proportion of the population reporting themselves to be book readers fell from 55 percent to 50 percent. This occurred in spite of overall stability in readership: in both surveys, 94 percent said they were readers, but in 1983, 5 percent more than in 1978 said that they read magazines and newspapers but not books.

The decline was greater among certain subgroups studied. Among young adults between 16 and 20 years old, the proportion of book readers fell from 75 percent in 1978 to 62 percent in 1983. Among older adults between 50 and 64 years old, book readership declined from 48 percent in 1978 to 38 percent in 1983. Among blue-collar workers, book readership fell from 50 percent in 1978 to 35 percent in 1983.

So although America is still a nation of readers, it is less a nation of book readers than it was in 1978. Reading remains a very important leisure activity: according to the survey, it is far more likely to be thought a favorite activity than television. But books seem to be losing some of their importance within the world of reading.

The meaning of this decline for the culture of the book and for the way Americans view reading is unclear. A trend away from books toward magazines and newspapers seems to be a trend away from lengthy and reflective reading and toward more specialized and information-oriented reading. Indeed, those who read only magazines and newspapers most often cite the need for general information as their most important motivation for reading, in contrast to book readers, who more often cite pleasure.

Among book readers, too, there seem to be some trends away from reflective reading, but these trends are not pervasive. Biography and history both lost readership between 1978 and 1983, and business books gained, but religious books also gained in readership. Moreover, biography and history, in spite of their losses, remain among the most popular genres of nonfiction. Similarly, historical novels and modern dramatic novels continue to be widely read fiction genres.

So books that are not simply "look-up" books are holding their own among book readers. The most disturbing question suggested by this survey, then, is whether book readers, readers who seem more likely than others to be seeking something more than information in their reading, are becoming a select few. The answer to this question, which has obvious implications for democratic culture, is not available from the results of the survey.

The summary that follows was prepared from the *1983 Consumer Research Study on Reading and Book Purchasing,* which was prepared for the Book Industry Study Group (BISG), a nonprofit research group. In the survey, roughly two thousand Americans were interviewed. There were a basic survey of adults, studying a population of about fifteen hundred, and supplemental surveys of adults 60 years old and older and of children aged 8 to 15 and their parents in order to allow for statistically sound focuses on seniors and children. The survey was designed to reflect the national situation accurately.

The summary generally follows the plan of an earlier summary that was released at the Library of Congress in April 1984 at a press conference and program sponsored by the Center for the Book. The earlier summary, however, was based on some incorrect data analysis. This revised summary is based on the final analysis. Readers of the earlier summary will find numerous changes, particularly in that the earlier report did not show the overall decline in book readership already noted, and also in the demographic characteristics of book readers found to be important.

Definitions

In order to simplify presentation of the data the following terms will be used throughout this summary. Note that a respondent did not necessarily have to have read the entire book to consider it a book read.

Book Reader   read one or more books in the previous six months

Heavy Book Reader read 26 or more books in the previous six months

Non-book Reader   did not read a book in the previous six months *but did read newspapers or magazines*

Nonreader   did not read a book, magazine, or newspaper in the previous six months

A Nation of Readers

The 1978 Consumer Research Study concluded that "America can be accurately described as a nation of readers." That description holds true today. Of the adult population, 94 percent read books, magazines, or newspapers. The remaining six percent do not read at all; this figure, however, should not be interpreted as a measure of illiteracy, which is beyond the scope of this study's design. Fifty percent read books, and almost 86 percent of these book readers also read newspapers. Thus, despite concern over the adequacy of American education and the impact of electronic forms of home entertainment, the survey results show that Americans continue to read.

Book Readers and Non-book Readers
The average American now spends 10.8 hours each week on all forms of reading material—books, magazines, and newspapers—and spends 16.8 hours watching television and 16.7 hours listening to the radio.

Book readers are not, as a rule, solitary or introverted. They are in fact, more likely than non-book readers to be involved in cultural activities, socializing, and sports. Readers devote a significant amount of time to television, though not as much time as do non-book readers. Book readers tend to see far more movies than non-book readers or nonreaders and are somewhat more likely to be involved in physical fitness activities and listening to music.

A demographic analysis of book readers reveals that they tend to be:

Women. Fifty-seven percent of women are book readers, as compared to 42 percent of men.

White. Fifty-two percent of whites are book readers, as compared to 38 percent of nonwhites.

Under 50 years old. Fifty-nine percent of those under 50 are book readers, as compared to 34 percent of those over 50; book readership declines with advancing age.

College-educated. Seventy-one percent of those with some college education are book readers, as compared to 40 percent of those with no college education.

Affluent. Book readership rises progressively with income, from 35 percent of those earing less than $15,000 per year to 70 percent of those making more than $40,000.

White-collar. Sixty-five percent of white-collar workers are book readers, as compared to 36 percent of blue-collar workers.

This profile of book readers contrasts sharply with that of non-book readers, who tend to be:

Men. Fifty-two percent of men are non-book readers, as compared to 37 percent of women.

Older. The likelihood of being a non-book reader increases with age. Sixty-one percent of those 65 and older are non-book readers, in contrast with 44 percent of the population as a whole. The decline in book reading becomes significant after age 50.

Less well educated. Fifty-three percent of those with a high school education or less are non-book readers, compared with 29 percent of those who had some college education and 24 percent of those who completed college.

At lower levels of income. Fifty-four percent of those earning less than $15,000 are non-book readers, as compared to 29 percent of those earning more than $40,000.

Blue-collar. Fifty-six percent of blue-collar workers are non-book readers, as compared to 33 percent of white-collar workers.

Further consideration to non-book readers will be given towards the end of this chapter.

Heavy Book Readers

Heavy book readers, those who read 26 books or more in the six months before they were interviewed, constitute about 34 percent of all book readers. They spend an average of 20.6 hours a week on all reading, of which 14.1 hours are devoted to reading books as a leisure activity. Heavy book readers read about as many magazines and newspapers as all readers. More often than the population as a whole, they list the following as regular activities: spending time with family, socializing, baking and cooking, and going to the theater.

The group of heavy book readers is heavily female (68 percent) and is somewhat younger, on the whole, than the general population. Half the heavy book readers did not have any formal education beyond high school, and about 30 percent had completed college.

Nonreaders

Nonreaders, those who do not read books, newspapers, or magazines, are 6 percent of the population, according to the survey. Nonreaders tend to be:

Nonwhite. Fifteen percent of nonwhites do not read, as compared to 4 percent of whites.

At low levels of education. Nearly half (47 percent) of nonreaders never went beyond eighth grade, and only 12 percent went beyond high school.

In the lowest income level. Fifty-eight percent earn less than $15,000 per year. Many of the nonreaders are not employed, mostly because they are retired.

Nonreaders are more often television watchers than the population as a whole, but they fall short in nineteen of the thirty-three activities investigated in the survey, including socializing, taking part in physical fitness activities, and participating in sports.

There have been a number of studies that seek to describe nonreaders in terms of literacy. This national sample was not designed to meet this objective and should not be used without literacy surveys in any analysis of the significant literacy problem that exists.

Trends Since 1978

The 1983 study shows that most Americans (94 percent) read, the same proportion as in 1978, and devote about the same amount of time as in 1978 to reading. But the proportion of book readers declined from 55 percent to 50 percent over those five years, which could be cause for alarm. At the same time, the proportion of non-book readers increased from 39 percent to 44 percent.

The overall demographic profile of book readers and non-book readers has remained essentially the same, indicating a relative stability in who reads what kind of material. The decline in book reading is most noticeable among the following groups, however.

Blue-collar workers. The proportion who were book readers declined from 50 percent in 1978 to 35 percent in 1983.

Those 16 to 20 years old. Declined from 75 percent to 62 percent.

Those 50 to 64 years old. Declined from 48 percent to 38 percent.

Nonwhites. Declined from 45 percent to 37 percent.

On the other hand, the findings indicate a large increase in the number of heavy book readers, from 18 percent of all book readers in 1978 to 34 percent in 1983.

Why People Read

Pleasure and Information
When asked why they read, both book readers and non-book read-

ers most often cited either pleasure or general knowledge as the most important reason.

Book readers emphasized "pleasure or recreation": 40 percent considered this to be their most important reason for reading. Their second most frequent most important reason was "general knowledge" (27 percent), followed by much lower response rates for reasons involving "work," "religion," "education," "escape," and "reading to children." This was consistent with the findings of the 1978 study. Women are more likely to cite pleasure as being among their reasons for reading (80 percent) than are men (61 percent).

Non-book readers, on the other hand, emphasized information: 50 percent considered this to be their most important reason for reading. Their second most frequent most important reason was pleasure or recreation (21 percent). This is essentially the same result as in 1978. Thus, although both groups of readers read for information, book readers stress pleasure as their primary motive.

Leisure versus Required Reading

Forty percent of the readers interviewed engage in reading specifically for their work or education. In part, this is obviously related to whether or not people are in school, so it is most prevalent among younger age groups. But such reading also increases with income, indicating that reading for work is associated with more highly paid and responsible positions; 63 percent of those earning $40,000 or more reported reading for work or school. A greater proportion of men than women reported this kind of reading, as did a greater proportion of those better educated, of people who were not married, of people with children at home, and of book readers than non-book readers.

The most commonly read materials for work or school are trade journals or newsletters, read by 58 percent of those who read for these purposes, followed closely by magazines (56 percent) and books (51 percent). Newspapers are read by four out of ten of such readers. Those who read books related to school or work spend an average of 8.1 hours per week in such reading.

Selecting Books to Read

Factors in Choosing a Book

Among the reasons for selecting a book to read, "the subject of the book" is even more important now than it was in 1978. Ninety-one percent rate it "very important" or "somewhat important," as opposed to 84 percent in the earlier study. The reputation of the book's author as a factor in book selection has declined in importance: 66 percent mention it now, as opposed to 77 percent in 1978. Other important reasons are:

Recommended by friend/relative (80 percent)
Book jacket synopsis or description (69 percent)
Review in a newspaper (62 percent) or a magazine (62 percent)
Read a few pages (63 percent)
Review in or on the book itself (60 percent)
Interview with the author on TV or radio (60 percent)
Saw movie or TV show based on book (60 percent)
Book on best-seller list (58 percent)

Fiction versus Nonfiction
Fifty-five percent of book readers read both fiction and nonfiction. Twenty-seven percent read only fiction; seventeen percent read only nonfiction. The number of fiction books read per capita is about one and one-half that of nonfiction.

Seventy-three percent of those who read only fiction are women. Ninety-two percent of those who read only fiction say one reason they read is for pleasure. Sixty-six percent of those who read only fiction have a high school education or less.

In contrast, those who read only nonfiction are mostly male (56 percent). They most often say they read for general knowledge, but 69 percent mention pleasure as among their motivations; religion, work, and education are all important as motivations among these readers, too. Forty-seven percent of those who read only nonfiction have a high school education or less, and 26 percent finished college. In comparison, 54 percent of book readers as a whole have a high school education or less, and 24 percent finished college.

Certain categories of books have become more or less popular since 1978. The biggest growth was in the frequency of reading juvenile books; in 1983, 26 percent of book readers said they had read books of this kind, but in 1978, only 10 percent had said so. Other fiction categories that gained at least 5 percent in the proportion of book readers saying they read them were action/adventure, historical novels, mysteries/detective novels, modern dramatic novels, science fiction, classics, spy novels/international intrigue, and fantasy. Gothic/historical romances lost considerably in popularity.

Among nonfiction categories, religion, business/finance/economics/management, dictionaries, and juvenile nonfiction all showed gains of 5 percent or more in the proportion of book readers who said they read them. Many categories of nonfiction showed substantial losses in popularity; current events (losing 13 percent), self help/sex (losing 12 percent), sports (losing 9 percent), geography/travel (losing 9 percent), history (losing 7 percent), politics (losing 7 percent), biographies/autobiographies, instructive/"how-to" books, anthropology/books about other cultures, and sociology. Nevertheless, the most popular categories of nonfiction books are biographies/autobiographies, religion, cookbooks/home economics, history, self-improvement, business, dictionaries, instructive/"how-to" books, and juvenile nonfiction.

Acquiring Books

Purchasing

The average book reader read 24.8 books for work or leisure (excluding school requirements) over the six-month period before the interview took place. On the average, almost half of these books, 11.9, were bought by readers for themselves. Heavy book readers bought, on average, about 46 percent of the books they read, while light book readers, those who had read only one to three books in the previous six months, bought three-quarters of the books they read.

Seventy-two percent of all book readers bought at least one book in the six months before they were interviewed. In addition, non-book readers—24 percent of them—bought books as gifts for others in the year before the interview, showing that non-book readers, too, place considerable value on books. Forty-eight percent of book readers had given books as gifts.

The people interviewed were asked a series of questions about the last book they had purchased. Forty-nine percent had last bought a work of fiction, 39 percent nonfiction, and 12 percent did not remember. About 45 percent of the last books bought were mass market paperbacks, 38 percent hardcovers, and 16 percent trade paperbacks. Of the fiction books that were the last books purchased, 59 percent were mass market paperbacks, and the average price of fiction that was the last book purchased was $5.40. In contrast, 54 percent of the nonfiction that was the last book purchased was hardcover; the average cost of nonfiction that was the last book purchased was $12.90. In general, book buyers thought that the books they had bought should have cost slightly less but said they were willing to pay considerably more for books.

Among places to buy books, chain bookstores account for the largest proportion of books bought, 18 percent, with college/school bookstores and secondhand bookstores each accounting for 13 percent, garage sales and flea markets for 9 percent, independent bookstores for 8 percent, supermarket book sections for 7 percent, the book sections of discount stores for 6 percent, drugstore book sections for 5 percent, and a variety of other outlets for the remainder. Mass market paperbacks account for 54 percent of purchases at chain bookstores and 47 percent at independents. Hardcovers constitute 39 percent of purchases at college/school bookstores and 28 percent at both chain and independent retail stores. Half of all respondents had at least visited a bookstore in the six months before being interviewed, including a majority of non-book readers. In addition it should be noted that about 16 percent of book readers belong to book clubs.

Libraries

Eighteen percent of the book readers said that the last book they read had come from a public or a school library. Forty-seven percent of book readers said they had obtained books from the public library in the previous six months, an increase of 4 percent from 1978. In addition, 20 percent cited the school library and 20 percent an employer library as a source of books in the previous six months. Groups most likely to frequent public libraries are working women, the young, those reporting increased annual family income, and the well-educated. The majority of respondents who use libraries live within one mile of a public library, and five-sixths live within three miles.

Passing Along

Borrowing, lending, and trading of books among friends constitutes a significant portion of book exchange. Twenty-one percent of book readers said that the last book they read had been borrowed from or traded for with a friend or relative. This was true for 26 percent of those who had most recently read a book of fiction, and 15 percent of those who had most recently read nonfiction. Moreover, 28 percent of book readers said they intended to pass along or trade the book they had most recently read. This happened for 33 percent of those who had most recently read fiction and 21 percent of those who had most recently read nonfiction. The pass-along phenomenon seems, then, to be broader in extent than the use of public libraries.

In addition, 8 percent of book readers said that they had received the last book they read as a gift. As was noted above, even a large proportion of non-book readers regularly give books as gifts.

Seniors

As was seen above, there is a significant decline in book reading among those older than 50, and the decline may grow with age. A special portion of the *1983 Consumer Research Study,* accordingly, focused on older Americans. In this special study, those 60 years old and older were regarded as seniors.

Reading is just about as prevalent among seniors as among the public at large: only 8 percent of seniors say they do not read. Seniors, however, are far more likely to be non-book readers than the average American. Over half (58 percent) of seniors read only magazines or newspapers, compared to 44 percent of the general public. Only about a third (34 percent) of seniors are book readers, compared to half (50 percent) of the public as a whole.

Senior book readers differ from non-book readers in ways that reflect differences found among the population as a whole. Senior book readers are more likely to socialize, attend clubs or meetings, knit or crochet, play cards, or keep physically fit than senior non-book readers. Among senior book readers, the following groups are represented at higher rates than they are represented in the senior population in general: women, whites, those aged 60 to 64 rather than 65 and above, those with at least some college education, and those with incomes higher than $15,000 per year.

As in the general population, seniors say they read for pleasure or for general information, for the most part. Again similarly to the general population, senior book readers are more likely to say that they read for pleasure, while seniors who read only magazines or newspapers are more likely to say that they read for general information.

Senior book readers are somewhat less likely than book readers as a whole to read both fiction and nonfiction. Senior fiction-only readers are heavily female and are somewhat more likely than the general population of senior book readers to have only a high school education or less and to have income of less than $15,000 per year. Fifty-two percent of the nonfiction-only readers among seniors are male, and nonfiction-only readers are slightly better educated on the whole and have higher incomes than the general population of senior book readers.

The fiction choices made by senior book readers are like those of the general population: the genres of historical novels, romances, action/adventure stories, mystery/detective novels, and modern dramatic novels are all read widely. Among nonfiction choices, 50 percent of senior nonfiction readers said that they had read at least one religious book in the six months before being interviewed; this compares to 29 percent in the general population of nonfiction readers. Seniors are less likely to have read self-improvement books. Otherwise, senior nonfiction readers seem like the population as a whole.

Seniors acquire books by purchase, from libraries, and through passing along among friends and relatives. Sixty-four percent of senior book readers report having bought a book in the six months before having been interviewed, and thirty-six percent of senior book readers say that the last book they read was then traded or passed along to a friend or relative. Fifteen percent say the last book they read was returned to the library. Seniors' rates of library use and purchase are lower than in the general population of book readers, and the rate of passing along is higher.

Juveniles

The *1983 Consumer Research Study* found a decline in book reading by young adults—those aged 16 to 20. Between 1978 and 1983, the proportion of book readers in this age group fell by about 13 percent. Accordingly, the study directed special attention at book reading among an even younger group, juveniles aged 8 to 15, to discover their reading habits and any possible reasons for the decline.

Juveniles are overwhelmingly likely to be book readers—89 percent of them reported having read a book for pleasure between

January and October 1983. Moreover, the plurality of juveniles, 43 percent, is in the group of heavy book readers, who in the juvenile study were defined as those who had read fifteen or more books in the period asked about.

But the number of books read by a child declines sharply with age. While half (53 percent) of those aged 8 to 10 are heavy readers, the proportion falls to 41 percent of those 11 or 12, and 32 percent of those 13 to 15 years old. The region in which a child lives has a strong impact—children in the west are far more likely to be heavy readers. Parental income is also a factor: the number of books read rises with income. Gender, however, does not seem to affect the amount of reading among the young.

Children acquire 70 percent of the books they read on their own, with children aged 11 to 12 acquiring the greatest number on their own. Seventy-five percent of the children said that the last book they obtained on their own was from a public library (21 percent) or school library (54 percent). Those who purchase books for children are likely to do so at chain bookstores (24 percent), discount store book sections (13 percent), book clubs (13 percent), supermarket book sections (11 percent), or independent bookstores (10 percent). It is worth noting also that parental encouragement to use the public library rises with family income: 67 percent of parents with incomes under $15,000 encouraged their children to use the library; 73 percent of those with incomes between $15,000 and $30,000; and 89 percent of those with incomes over $30,000.

Parental practices and attitudes regarding reading exert a very strong, though not decisive, influence on children's reading habits. The children of book readers are the most likely to be book readers themselves. Similarly, children who are read to regularly, either by their parents or someone else, are most likely to be heavy book readers. Children whose parents encourage them to read, have books available for them at home, and believe reading to be essential to success in school tend to read more than the children of others who do not share these views.

Watching television is the favorite and most widespread leisure activity among juveniles, but it seems to have little or no impact on the number of books they read. Children also regard playing sports and going to the movies as preferable to reading books. Children who read many books for pleasure are more likely than those who read fewer to participate in other activities, including playing sports, going to the movies, and playing at home with electronic games and computers.

Mysteries, humor or joke books, comic books, and books about outer space or the future head the list of the most popular categories of books among young people. Book selections are strongly influenced by the sex and age of the child and by family income. Girls are more likely to read mysteries, books about real people, fairy/folk tales, romances, picture books, arts and crafts books, and poetry. Boys are more likely to read comic books, books about space or the future, sports books, nature books, supernatural stories, books about the past, and spy stories. Books about real people and romances gain in popularity with age, while humor/joke books, comic books, fairy/folk tales, picture books, nature books, sports books, and religious books all lose popularity.

Who are the Non-Book Readers?

Non-book readers grew as a proportion of the population between 1978 and 1983, even as the proportion of book readers declined. It seems therefore important to summarize what the 1983 survey shows about non-book readers, with an eye towards assessing the hope of attracting them to the more reflective reading that books make possible.

Demographically, those who read only magazines or newspapers tend to be men, older, less well educated (81 percent have a high school education or less in contrast with 54 percent of book readers), at lower levels of income, and blue-collar in occupation more often than book readers. The motivation of non-book readers for reading seems different, too; they are far more likely than book readers to cite the acquisition of general information as the primary motivation for reading, while book readers are more likely to cite pleasure or recreation. Both groups frequently cite both general information and pleasure as motivations, but the difference in terms of *most* important motivation is striking.

The survey also asked non-book readers why they did not read books and whether they were likely to resume reading books. Non-book readers give the following reasons for avoiding books: not interested (39 percent), not enough time (21 percent), other leisure activities (15 percent), physical problems with reading books (15 percent), prefer reading other things (13 percent), busy with work (9 percent), busy with caring for the home (8 percent), prefer television or movies (6 percent), and busy with school (1 percent). About half of non-book readers say they used to read books, and about 57 percent of these former book readers express an interest in resuming book reading in the future. (Fewer senior former book readers expect to return to reading books, however.) Of the former book readers, 60 percent used to read books primarily for pleasure, while 22 percent read primarily for general knowledge.

The impact of improved education on the growing number of seniors in America is not entirely clear. Sixty-three percent of seniors who had completed college were book readers, as opposed to 71 percent in the general population. Thirty-three percent of seniors who had completed college were non-book readers, as compared with 24 percent in the general population. So there seems to be some drop-off in book reading even among the college-educated as they grow older.

How then to attract non-book readers to book reading? Framing a plan seems a very difficult task. To focus on just one aspect, non-book readers are overwhelmingly educated to a high school level or less. The first possible suggestion of this fact simply concerns the difficulty of the materials non-book readers might be expected to find attractive. Perhaps even more important, however, is the cultural diversity that might be found among Americans with such education. Is there enough of a common culture in the high-school education and experiences of those Americans to discover a way to "promote" book culture to them in general?

Nevertheless, two areas for encouraging book reading may be found in the different motivations of non-book readers and book readers. On one hand, non-book readers say that they read for the sake of general knowledge. Here, it would seem, the diversity of the persons to whom promotion is being made should command respect in terms of advertising to them where they already seek general information, whether that is in a cooking section, automotive page, financial page, or gossip column of a newspaper or in the general or hobby magazine.

On the other hand, book readers ascribe pleasure to their reading, and this may reveal the area of greatest promise in terms of a broadly conceived promotional effort. Many promotional efforts aimed at literacy have focused on the sad consequences of illiteracy. But a broad promotional effort aimed at book reading, perhaps, should focus on a genuinely impractical value, the pleasure involved in book reading.

8. Reading in the United States

Charles A. Goodrum and Helen Dalrymple

The survey summarized in chapter 7 reports that roughly half of Americans are book readers. Is the glass half-full or half-empty? These authors present both hopeful and pessimistic views in this essay, part of the work commissioned for the Book in the Future project. They go on to suggest some ways in which the meaning of being "a nation of readers" might be understood and describe some efforts that may contribute toward such an achievement.

T rying to get some understanding of American reading habits—how much and what kinds of materials Americans read—is as difficult as describing literacy and illiteracy in the United States. There have been many surveys, studies, and polls over the years, but they are generally not comparable because they use different parameters in defining what a book reader is. Or, they may look at a single segment of the reading public, concentrating only on newspapers or magazines. Additionally, there is a problem of interpretation of the hard data that is available. If, as *The 1983 Consumer Research Study on Reading and Book Purchasing* prepared for the Book Industry Study Group (BISG) reports, 50 percent of the adults in this country are book readers today, is that cause for celebration or alarm?[1] Contrast these two points of view, referring to the 1983 study:

> In the age of electronic entertainment and personal computers, books are thriving. Despite increased competition for Americans' leisure time, book reading has retained its unique appeal: 55 percent of the adults in this country were book readers in 1978, and 56 percent are today....And book readers are reading more today than in 1978: the proportion of heavy readers has increased from 18 percent to 35 percent of all book readers. ...Book sales are up, undisturbed by the increase in pass-along readership. The survey data reveal that 21 percent of all books read are borrowed, making book reading an even more widespread activity than book sales figures would indicate.[2]

What constitutes a "book reader?" According to the study, there are four types, ranging from "light readers" who had read one to three books in the previous six months to "heavy readers" who had read twenty-six or more. A footnote stated ominously, "Note that a respondent did not have to read the entire book to consider it a book read."...It turned out that if you had read only part of the book about Garfield the cat or a romance or "workout" book—or if as a juvenile you had read even a sentence in a *comic* book—you would qualify as a "book reader."

To me, this was appalling....There is no way I can support any claim that says "books are thriving" in the U.S. today. ..."Reading habits" have nothing to do with comic books, adult or juvenile; ... how could we say that "books are thriving" when nearly half the adult population has not even read a sentence of any kind of book, Garfield included, in the last six months?[3]

The question is, is the glass half-empty or half-full?

There is a third problem with reading surveys that needs to be taken into account: respondents may tend to tell interviewers what they think they want to hear. This is described by Al Silverman, president of the Book-of-the-Month Club:

> In its early years, the Book-of-the-Month Club commissioned the Gallup organization to conduct surveys regularly of the book reading habits of the American public. These probes were abandoned a dozen years ago, perhaps in fright. When George Gallup interviewed readers in 1937, he found that 29 percent of all adults were reading books at that time. In 1955 the percentage had fallen to 17 percent. Apparently nobody wanted to know what it was in 1970.
>
> The newer executives of the club, it appears, decided that public opinion polls of reading habits were to be trusted even less than public opinion polls on politics. It is too easy to be conned by "the reading public." There is nothing a "reader" likes better than to inflate the cultural values of America's tastemakers by offering answers to questions that bear no resemblance to reality, but that they know the questioner wants to hear. "Did I read *Gravity's Rainbow?* Well, of course. I stayed in bed all summer to read it. It's my favorite book since *Finnegan's Wake.*"[4]

While Silverman is referring principally to the *kinds* of books read, the same point may be made with regard to the *numbers* of books read. How many people, especially those with a college education, are going to admit that they haven't read a book in the last six months?

What do all the polls and surveys show? Though the figures vary widely, some generalizations can probably be drawn from them. First, let us take some specific examples. Gallup surveys taken over a period of years showed that the following percentages of their sample were "regular readers of books": in 1937, 29 percent; in 1955, 17 percent; in 1958, 21 percent; in 1964, 21 percent; in 1971, 26 percent. In 1978, in a larger study conducted for the American Library Association on "Book Reading and Library Usage: A Study of Habits and Perceptions," Gallup found that 59 percent of the sample had "read a book in the past month" and that an additional 14 percent had read a book in the past six months. This total, 73 percent, varied significantly from the 55 percent figure turned up in the same year, 1978, by Yankelovich, Skelly, and White for the Book Industry Study Group, for the proportion that had read books within the past six months. Interestingly, the interviews for the two surveys were taken within two months of each other: Gallup in July-August and BISG in May-June of 1978.[5]

Other studies have fallen within the ranges established above. Bernard Berelson reported in 1949 on a study showing that 25 to 30 percent of the American population were book readers (reading at least one book a month).[6] Philip Ennis conducted a survey for National Opinion Research Center in 1965 which estimated that 49 percent of the population were current readers.[7] And another Gallup Poll, asking the question "Did you do any book reading yesterday?" got a 14 percent positive response in 1955 (all books excluding the Bible) and a 21 percent positive response in 1984.[8]

All of the reading studies, despite the variation in definitions and specific results, indicate that the more active an individual is, the more he tends to read, and that education and economic status have a great deal to do with how much a person reads. Other factors that influence reading are one's family and social environment and the accessibility of books and reading materials. These findings seem to be true not only in the United States but in other countries as well, according to studies by the United Nations.

A Nation of Readers?

Where does all of this leave us, and what does it mean for the future of books, whether print on paper or digital on disk? Are we a "nation of readers," and if we are not, is there anything we can or should do about it? Again, it is not hard to find differing views on this question. Al Silverman has said,

> Of course no one needs a Gallup poll to know that we are not a nation of readers. That phrase, incidentally, came up a year ago when Daniel Boorstin, the Librarian of Congress, asked the Book-of-the-Month Club to cosponsor a dinner of Very Important People at the Library to kick off a book exhibit that would run through the summer of 1982. The theme was to be "A Nation of Readers."
>
> "Isn't that kind of wishful thinking?" I asked Boorstin.
>
> "Yes," he said, "but it's something to strive for, isn't it?"
>
> Most certainly, especially when we seem to be going the other way. Since the 1950s, according to a UN study, the United States has dropped from eighteenth most literate member of the 158 member nations to forty-ninth.[9]

Taking a different tack is Samuel S. Vaughan, editor-in-chief and vice president of Doubleday:

> America has a long way to go toward universal literacy. But underestimating or undervaluing what we are accomplishing is a waste of time and energy.... Despite recent declines in the unit sales of individual books, we are still doing better than we were in the fifties, and not just because of increased population. The last time I looked at a comparison of unit sales of

similarly popular novels, Herman Wouk's *Marjorie Morning-star* of 1954 and Peter Benchley's *Jaws* of 1974, the former had sold a little under two million copies in its original hardcover, paperback, and book club editions, while the latter sold, in the same three forms, around ten million....

The popular perception persists—there are not many book readers in America. By what measure can we count ourselves a "nation of readers" (in the phrase used by the Center for the Book at the Library of Congress)? One hundred percent of all Americans reading some number of books per year? Eighty percent? Anything over fifty percent? What number would you use to designate "book people?" Five million? One million? One hundred thousand?...

Yet over five million books are bought in this country *per day*. To be sure, this includes schools, libraries, book club members, paperback readers, and the rest. But institutions do not diminish the implications of this number; rather, they increase it, because an institutional copy is apt to be read by more than one person....

A *Roots,* a *Godfather,* a *Garp,* a Hailey, a Wouk, a Uris, regularly reaches readers in the millions. Instead of dismissing this fact as unrelated to serious book reading, those concerned with reading habits should ask: Why them? What does it take to rouse the reader? The evidence is not that ours is a nation of nonreaders. We appear to be a nation that can be excited by a book—but not easily.[10]

A number of the people we spoke with during the course of our interviews expressed concern about the apparent decline in reading by young adults, and the recent Book Industry Study Group survey bore this out: 62 percent of those under 21 years of age in their sample were book readers in 1983 as opposed to 75 percent in 1978. At the same time, a recent survey by the National Association of Secondary School Principals of the mood of American youth showed that reading rates second among hobbies of students aged 13 to 18. Only sports, which 90 percent of the sample said was their favorite hobby, rated higher. Reading garnered 49.1 percent of the students polled, ahead of video games (47.1 percent) and listening to music (43.8 percent). And the survey indicated that teenagers read more books (typically finishing two books and starting a third each month) than they did when asked the same questions in 1974, when they read less than one book a month. Today those books are more likely to be mysteries, romance, and science fiction novels than textbooks.

At the other end of the spectrum, the preliminary figures from the BISG study indicated that there was a greater "reader dropout" rate among those 50 years of age and older than among any other age group. Twenty-six percent of those aged 50-64 were "non-book readers" who used to be book readers; 21 percent of those in the 65 and over age bracket. Since the total population in those age ranges has increased about 8 percent since 1978, that could be a real cause for concern if the trend continues. As today's population ages, however, senior citizens will be better educated, and, with the high degree of correlation between book reading and education, it is possible that they will retain the book reading habits of their younger years.

What reasons do non-book readers give for not reading books? The BISG survey asked the question and got the following answers: books are boring (39 percent); books take too much time (21 percent); other leisure-time activities are preferable to books (15 percent); and physical problems inhibit reading books (15 percent).

Reading Promotion

While there may be some disagreement about what a "book" will look like twenty-five years from now, there is no argument about the fact that *reading* is a positive good that should be supported and nurtured in American society. And reading, at least in the short term, means reading of books. This point was stressed in many of the interviews we had, and especially in the larger meetings where there was an opportunity for an exchange of views among participants. There was a great deal of discussion of ways in which the promotion of book reading could be accomplished. To those who make up, in Samuel Vaughan's felicitous term, "the community of the book," these ideas will not sound particularly revelatory or innovative. They are basic, commonsense paths that could be taken tomorrow to move our society, with no great change in direction or expenditure of funds. For that very reason, perhaps, they deserve some thoughtful attention. Or, as Martin Levin (who has perhaps discussed these questions in as many forums on as many occasions as anyone) put it succinctly, "Just get out and *do it!* We have the ideas, the enthusiasm; many different programs have been tried and are working; we know what we have to do."

The principal ideas for the promotion of books and reading that arose in discussion during our study can be lumped into a few generalized categories.

The Passion for Reading

A number of people interviewed felt that it was most important to try to develop and nurture the "passion for reading" that seems to be absent in the younger generation today. No one felt that only "good" books should be supported, because the fun, excitement, and stretching of the imagination are the pleasures that children should derive first from reading books, whether the author is Carolyn Keene or Louisa May Alcott. They recognized that books have to capture a person's fancy if they are going to be read at all. Samuel Vaughan wrote that maybe books aren't as good as they used to be: "If book reading has slowed, it might not just be a

111

matter of Reaganomics or red-neck six-pack pleasures, but a decline of the book itself. Successful or not, some books are becoming faceless in the crowd."[11]

Jim Trelease, author of *The Read-Aloud Handbook,* makes a compelling case that children have to be turned on to books at an early age. Children have to learn through their own experience that books are fun and that reading is worthwhile. And, he argues, the way to do this is by reading aloud to them, both at home and at school—and to keep reading aloud on a regular basis up through the adolescent years. Expose children to books of all kinds. Make sure the reading teachers have the books themselves and can recommend them to the students. Make books and reading an important part of the school day, and not just through skill development and vocabulary recognition. Show children and share with them the fun, the adventure, the imaginary escapism that can be found in the world of books.

Access to Books
In order to encourage reading, both children and adults must have ready access to books. A simple enough proposition, it would seem, but eloquent statements were made by the Book in the Future advisors about Americans in rural, out-of-the-way areas of our country who are just not able to get hold of books easily. Toni Bearman, executive director of NCLIS, said that we need to make more of an effort to get books to people who want them, especially to older people who cannot get out as easily as they once did. Louis L'Amour made a strong plea for the importance of keeping books within reach (both costwise and from the point of view of availability) of the average person. One of the major aims of the Reading is Fundamental program, which now receives some support from the federal government, is to put books in the hands of children (books that they choose for themselves) who might otherwise never have the opportunity to read them.

Libraries as "Book-Sellers"
Martin Levin pointed out that with 14,000 outlets around the country, the public library system is the largest single outlet of information in the United States. It's a network that is already in place. However, libraries need to be redesigned and restructured so that they can better act as a vehicle for delivering education and information into the community. Some noted that libraries should establish linkages with other social agencies serving people who could benefit from reading or learning to read. And a solid endorsement for resurrecting the "readers' advisory" role of the library of a generation ago, when librarians took an active role in recommending particular books to their patrons, was heard from many of the participants.

Reading as a National Priority

Many of those with whom we talked expressed the view that this country needs national leadership to stress the importance of reading; or, to put it another way, "if we can go to the moon, surely we can...." In the "can do" American spirit, if we think it's important enough, we can get it done. If reading is regarded as sufficiently important to our democratic traditions and to our societal existence, then it can be accorded a higher priority in the whole scheme of American life. Julia Palmer told of the competition in Japan where children wrote essays about books that made a difference to them. They started in their local schools, with winners eventually competing from all over Japan. The final winners received prizes from the prime minister and read their essays to the emperor. In that way, she felt, a clear message was sent to all Japanese children that reading and books were important.

A "Civil Rights Movement" for Books and Reading

A "National Endowment" for the book; a "Coalition for the Book"; a professional marketing campaign to reach out and touch someone with a book: these are some of the other ideas that came out of discussions of how to promote reading and how to get books to people who don't now come in contact with them. There is no shortage of ideas on ways to proceed; the question is whether the majority of American society feels that the promotion of books and reading is important enough to deserve this kind of treatment.

Current Reading Promotion Efforts

John Chancellor noted the synergy between television and books, how one can support and extend the other. Jim Trelease and others noted this same connection. The Center for the Book has undertaken some reading promotion efforts with CBS and ABC Television: "Read More About It" trailers follow certain CBS television programs suggesting that viewers go to their local libraries and bookstores for books on the topic of the program, and a cartoon cat, Cap'n O. G. Readmore, tells children during commercial breaks in ABC Saturday morning cartoons how much fun reading a book can be.

A series on the Public Broadcasting System, "Reading Rainbow," is devoted to reading. In each half-hour episode, parts of a book are read aloud by a celebrity, accompanied by illustrations and animation, setting the theme of the show. Host LeVar Burton explores the theme—riding in a hot-air balloon, for example, or visiting the docks of Charleston, South Carolina. Finally, children comment on a number of related books. There is a community component to "Reading Rainbow" as well, with packets of information provided to libraries and PTAs.

There are many other exciting ideas, some of them already being practiced in communities across the United States, to promote books and reading. At this stage it would appear that it is not necessary to create a bureaucracy and invent a whole set of new programs to promote reading. Rather, some basic decisions must be made about whether this kind of effort is fundamental to American society and if it is, how to support the projects that are already under way.

Notes

1. *1983 Consumer Research Study on Reading and Book Purchasing,* 3 vols. (New York: Book Industry Study Group, Inc. 1984). For a summary of the study, see chapter 7 above.
2. From a summary of the *1983 Consumer Research Study* presented at the Library of Congress, 11 April 1984. Chapter 7 above is a revision of that summary and some of its statistics.
3. Patricia Holt, "Books," *San Francisco Chronicle,* 18 April 1984.
4. Al Silverman, "The Fragile Pleasure," *Daedalus,* vol. 112, no. 1, Winter 1983, 36.
5. See "Book Reading and Library Usage: A Study of Habits and Perceptions," conducted for the American Library Association by the Gallup Organization, Princeton, N.J. October 1978; and "Consumer Research Study on Reading and Book Purchasing," prepared for Book Industry Study Group by Yankelovich, Skelly and White, New York, October 1978.
6. Bernard Berelson, *The Library's Public* (New York: Columbia University Press, 1949).
7. Philip H. Ennis, *Adult Book Reading in the United States,* National Opinion Research Center Report No. 105 (Chicago: National Opinion Research Center, 1965).
8. Leonard A. Wood, "Book Reading, 1955-84: The Trend Is Up," *Publishers Weekly,* 25 May 1984, 39.
9. Silverman, "The Fragile Pleasure," 37.
10. Samuel S. Vaughan, "The Community of the Book," *Daedalus,* vol. 112, no. 1, Winter 1983, 101-3.
11. Ibid., 103.

Man's relation to written tests has always been complicated and always charged with emotions and metaphoric associations which go right back to the origins of man and to that Hebraic formula—but not exclusively Hebraic, for we find it also in other Middle Eastern languages—the Book of Life.

GEORGE STEINER
Critic

9. Reading in an Audiovisual and Electronic Era

Dan Lacy

Radio, film, and television have expanded, not constricted, our lives, according to Dan Lacy, and so far the main effect of the computer upon books is to make them easier to produce well. However, the perspective-providing distance and the formality of writing that is intended for wide distribution make books unique, and that uniqueness sometimes seems threatened.

Dan Lacy is Senior Vice-President of McGraw-Hill, Inc. His career has encompassed many different areas of the book and information worlds, including the National Archives and Records Service, the Library of Congress, the United States Information Agency, and the American Book Publishers Council. He is a member of the Executive Council for the Center for the Book in the Library of Congress. Another essay of Mr. Lacy's, "The Book and Literature in the 1980s," appears below (chap. 20), as does part of the report of the American Library Association Commission on Freedom and Equality of Access to Information, which he served as chair (chap. 26).

Reprinted by permission of *Daedalus,* Journal of the American Academy of Arts and Sciences, from "Reading: Old and New," vol. 112, no. 1, Winter 1983, Cambridge, Massachusetts.

W andering tribesmen with tales of what lay beyond the distant range or river, old men with memories of their own past and of their fathers' and grandfathers' memories, prophets who professed knowledge of the future—all have from time out of mind helped to fill the hunger of men and women to escape the narrow scope and brief moment of their lives. But the living word, fixed in no enduring form, swirled and rearranged itself in myth, and mankind emerged from a fabled and dream-haunted past to live in a world where monsters and boiling seas and magic mountains lay only a few days' journey away.

Writing, which fixed words in unchangeable order, made possible the creation of a reliable history and, within limits, a known geography. Thucydides and Tacitus, Strabo and Herodotus, were knowledge-bearers, not myth-makers. Until the invention of printing, however, this possession of real knowledge of what lay beyond men's own eyes and memories was confined to the literate few with access to precious manuscripts. The growth of science was greatly handicapped by the inability to generate and distribute uniform texts that could be relied on by investigators spread across a continent. Thus the leap of knowledge that came in the sixteenth and seventeenth centuries was both print-born and print-borne.

In the first two centuries of print, many other inventions enlarged the capacity of humans to transcend their immediate experience, among them, the telescope, the microscope, reliable timepieces, and ships adapted for transoceanic voyages. The development of a more powerful mathematics, especially the calculus in the late seventeenth century, greatly enhanced man's ability to organize newly discovered data in meaningful patterns.

Print made possible rapid, wide sharing of the new knowledge. Reports of voyages to Asia and to the newly discovered American continents, describing their geography, flora, fauna, minerals, and human inhabitants, were read avidly and became the impetus for further voyages. Equally valuable was the new ability of scientists to distribute widely, relatively quickly, and in a fixed form and uniform state the results of their observations. Man's ability to know distant lands, even distant planets, and to achieve a deeper understanding of natural processes was greatly enhanced.

So, too, was the ability to know the past. The world's documented past had existed precariously in few handwritten copies, subject to loss and decay and imperiled by errors in transcription. The enormous multiplication of copies of these works and the increased ability to compare copies made possible the technical skills of editing, verification, and textual analysis and focused attention on the past. There was a renaissance of the knowledge of antiquity that gave its name to the era. Print also facilitated not merely the preservation and dissemination of knowledge, but also its rapid accumulation, as each new student could in turn command and build on the published works of those who preceded him.

By the late nineteenth century, the processes by which verified knowledge was established and transmitted were both professionalized and institutionalized. It became possible to earn a living as a physicist or historian or philologist, and hence to devote one's full time to the discipline. Learned societies organized by discipline gave a specific focus not found in prior general academies, and created professional corps with a sense of collaboration in a shared undertaking. Universities became centers of research as well as of teaching. Learned journals multiplied, and university presses were created to provide additional means of recording and disseminating the rapidly increasing outflow of the products of research. Libraries became the centers of universities, and public libraries were created to bring the broad resources of books to the people generally.

During the same decades, a series of concurrent developments greatly widened public access to the flow of print-recorded knowledge. Steam-powered cylindrical presses, stereotype plates, and paper mass-produced from wood pulp greatly increased the output and diminished the price of printed matter. By the end of the century, several hundred times as many pages were printed per capita as at its beginning. The invention of the telegraph and the laying of the Atlantic cable enormously enhanced the speed and efficiency with which the press could convey the news; and the completion of a rail network made practical the swift nationwide distribution of magazines and books. Nearly universal elementary education and widespread literacy opened a broad public market for this enormous flow of print. With the penny newspaper and cheap magazines and books, print became a mass medium.

Indeed, during the period that in the United States extended roughly from the Civil War to the First World War, print played— as it never had before and never would again—a dominant and exclusive role. Almost all adults in the United States (as in Canada and Western Europe) could read and, moreover, had access to an abundance of print at a cost they could afford. And print was the *only* means, other than word of mouth, by which they could learn of things beyond their personal experience.

It was during this era of total print dominance that our contemporary educational system took shape, with an elementary curriculum primarily devoted to teaching children the skills of reading and writing and the comparably abstract techniques of numerical manipulation. High school and college were devoted to the use of these skills to extract knowledge from the accumulated wealth of print and, at the postgraduate level, to contribute further to it. It is no accident that a popular term for education was "book-learning."

In the decades since 1920, two major waves of change have overthrown print's dominance. The first was the audiovisual revolution. It was based on the late nineteenth-century inventions of the phonograph and the motion picture and the early twentieth-century discovery of radio, but its more important social impact came after the First World War. By the end of the postwar decade, most Americans had abundant access to all three. The speeches of political leaders could be heard rather than read; news had a visual impact through the newsreel. Films rather than novels became the major means of suggesting what life in other times and places and among other social groups and classes was like. It became possible for persons outside large cities to hear great music professionally performed. A more direct access was provided to the range of experience beyond life's daily ambit.

The power of the audiovisual revolution was enormously increased when television became widely available after the Second World War. Within an amazingly few years, television could be received in more than 90 percent of the homes in America, and the average American was spending several hours a day before the screen. Daily, hundreds of millions of hours previously spent in other ways were transferred to television watching. Probably never before in history had so massive a change in social habit been achieved in so very brief a time.

Some of the change wrought by TV may have been less important than it seemed. To a considerable degree, TV was simply a way to see movies more cheaply and without leaving home. Much of what was shown on TV did indeed consist of films previously shown in motion picture theatres, and much of what was created specifically for TV was very like the movies both in technique and in the recreational functions it served. But the amount of time devoted to the medium, even granting the similarity of the content, was so large as to be very important in itself.

Yet through its news and documentary programs, television emerged as a truly new medium. Radio had already imparted some of the instant availability of news as well as the sense of actual presence, as in Edward R. Murrow's wartime broadcasts from London or Roosevelt's fireside chats. And the newsreels and the rare filmed documentary had provided precedents for television. But the nearly universal attention to television as the principal source of news about events here and abroad, of information about politics and social conditions, about the nature of other cultures and about science, was quite extraordinary. In barely more than a decade, television replaced the newspaper as the principal source of news and, indeed, replaced print in general as the foremost means by which most Americans came to perceive reality beyond their daily experience.

In our own decade there is yet another revolution, that of the computer and its related technology of data communication. The dramatic decrease in the cost of computers has opened their use to people in general. It will probably become quite common to be able, in one's home or office, to call up almost instantly, from enormous banks of information, the particular set of data one seeks and to manipulate it and array it with extraordinary power. Texts and images as well as numerical data can be stored with incredible compactness on laser disks and recalled through the computer's extraordinary searching power, thus creating still additional possibilities. Enthusiasts for the new information technology believe that it will replace or diminish the role of a whole series of industries and institutions: the newspaper, the journal, the book, the library.

The two revolutions—audiovisual and electronic—provide a range of alternatives to communication hitherto carried by print and promise as well the possibility of many kinds of communication not achievable at all through print: the sound of speech and music, the vision of motion and color, the perception of events as they occur, the instant conveyance of constantly changing data. The average American every week spends several times as many hours with the new media as he or she does reading. The exclusive role of print to provide the reality that lies beyond personal experience has been shattered forever.

How has this affected the role of reading, and what difference does it make? The sheer production of printed matter has been affected less than one would expect. The number of newspapers has declined sharply, and urban evening newspapers have been especially affected. Few cities can any longer support more than one newspaper, very few, indeed, more than two. Television is not only a far more widely used source of news, but a more trusted one. Mass circulation magazines directly competitive with television for audience and advertisers, like the *Saturday Evening Post, Life, Look, American,* and *Colliers,* have died. Yet surviving urban newspapers and a growing number of suburban newspaper chains are highly prosperous, and the magazine industry, with it myriad journals catering for special tastes and interests, is thriving.

The total number of books published annually has approximately quadrupled since television became generally available. Sales of books as measured in copies, rather than dollars, increased rapidly in the early days of television, though they have tended to level off in recent years. Library circulation has been flat or declining in recent years, but this may be reflective more of weakened community support, declining educational enrollments, and the availability of relatively inexpensive paperbacks than of any public decline in reading.

None of these statistics gives any clear picture of the amount of reading actually done in our society, but a considerable increase—certainly no such decay as has long been prophesied—appears to have taken place. Our society is by no means ready to say, as in the title of Anthony Smith's recent book, goodbye to Gutenberg.

Yet the functions of print are changing. It is still the indispensable recorder and conveyor of research results and other scholarly activity. In fact, much of the increase in the number of books and journals published reflects the heightened level of such activity. Similarly, though there are marginal and, in some cases, growing uses of audiovisual materials and computers in the classroom, print is still the principal medium of formal education. Finally, there is a substantial increase in recreational reading of various kinds of subliterary novels, among them, romances, "Gothic" stories, suspense stories, and science fiction.

But for all these continuing strengths, reading is no longer the main, indeed almost the only, way of extending personal experience. Most people today decide whom they will vote for, what they believe about atomic weapons control or unemployment, how they perceive the issues of the Middle East, what they conceive China to be like, or how they envision the history of man much more from what they observe on television than from what they read. Beyond the bounds of our daily lives, we all react not to reality, but to an *image* of reality, created for us through the media of communication, and in the last generation, the nature of the media that create this image has changed fundamentally.

Does that matter? Is the image more clear? Less clear? Are our reactions more responsive and meaningful? Or are they being confused and made irrelevant? I suggest that it does matter, that the way we perceive external reality through the audiovisual media is a quite different process from that of perceiving it through the medium of print, and that the quality of our perception is now more important than ever before in our history.

That the quality of our perception of reality not experienced directly is important seems clear enough. In the simpler days of our national growth, the great issues we confronted were perhaps as demanding as those we face today, but they lay within the everyday experience of ordinary citizens: British versus local rule, taxation of the unrepresented, a strong or weak union, slavery or freedom, regulation of railroads or submission to their economic dominance. Issues today involve distant lands and peoples, complex economic and governmental issues, esoteric scientific questions. No ordinary citizen on the basis of personal experience alone can have a useful opinion about what our policy should be toward the Middle East—or toward Russia or China or Japan or the Caribbean—or on the control of nuclear weapons or the reduction of unemployment. The more crucial the issue to public well-being or even to national survival, the more likely its sound resolution depends on knowledge that most of us can achieve only at second hand, through one medium or another. Moreover, a consequence of the increasing involvement of the total population in the flow of the media is the near-instant stimulation and impact of public opinion. Our Constitution was evolved during weeks of secrecy by a few dozen men, unvexed by public pressures; any such effort today would be harassed into impotence by unceasing public pressures. Public opinion narrowly limits the discretion of authority in every major policy question, so that those who govern us cannot be wiser than we are.

But the demands on us for comprehension of what lies beyond the daily sweep of our eyes is not confined to the demands of public policy decision. The extraordinary enhancement of the power of human observation by instruments ranging from the electron microscope to the X-ray telescope and by techniques of chemical and physical analysis using spectrography, radioactive tracers, lasers, and other devices, plus the enormous achievements made in synthesizing intelligence, have made it possible, in the last century, to construct a perception of the universe utterly beyond anything suggested by direct experience: a universe of billions of galaxies, each composed of billions of stars and presumably of solar systems, lasting for tens of billions of years and perhaps for repeated cycles of compression and explosion, each extending over reaches so near to infinity that light itself may require billions of years to traverse them. At the same time, we have discovered that the human race is hundreds of thousands of years older than it was thought to be, and is linked with all other forms of life in a common flow of being. And our conception of the nature of the genetic and biochemical processes that determine the forms and processes of life, intelligence, and self-consciousness itself has been revolutionized.

The comprehension of all this total restructuring of the conceived reality of the universe, of life, and of man's relation to them can of course be achieved only at second hand, through the reception of messages through media of communication. In what ways, then, does it matter how—through which medium—our perception of reality beyond our direct observation is formed? To answer this, one has to begin with the function of words themselves. All words are necessarily abstractions, reaching into the swirling totality of experience and singling out a specific aspect for identification. To put a group of words together in a sentence is not merely to abstract a number of single bits of the surrounding experience, but to assert a structured relationship among them. Even the simplest sentence describing an ordinary event is an extraordinarily complex intellectual exercise, in which human meaning is imposed on a fragment of experience. This is true, of course, of speech as well as writing; but speech conveys more than the words say. Speech is a kind of action itself, bearing a freight of emotional overtone; and informal speech, in particular, may not represent a considered and digested conceptual organization of experience, but rather an instinctive reaction.

Writing distances the reader yet farther from reality than speech does the listener. An event is still described rather than experienced directly, but here the reader is removed from the writer as well as from the event. The overtones of pitch and cadence and gesture are gone; the words lie mutely on the page, stripped of their emotional penumbra.

Print lies at an even further remove. Intended for a large audience, and usually for indefinite preservation, the words are chosen and arranged with greater care. An impersonal formality takes the place of the casualness of, for example, the personal letter.

To convey meaning through print is a demanding enterprise. From an unbounded flow of reality, the author must abstract just those elements—an almost infinitely small fraction of the whole— that he will attempt to convey; must define each by selecting a particular word for each; must describe how he believes these elements relate to each other by arranging the words into sentences (and in more extended communication, such as print is commonly used for, the sentences into paragraphs, hence into chapters, and into the whole complex architecture of a treatise); and must encode all this into complex patterns of ink on paper. The reader, in turn, must decode these patterns, perceive a meaning for each of the words, and construct an image of the complex structure of conceived reality the author has created. It is simply impossible for any idea or information to be conveyed by print without both author and reader having *thought* intensively about the message.

This mode of communication—abstract, formal, and fixed—of course sacrifices much of reality as it may be conveyed through the audiovisual media. To read a description of a Mozart quartet is but a thin and desiccated experience as compared with hearing it by record or radio; to read a description of a sunset or of an El Greco painting is similarly but a poor substitute for seeing it on a slide or film, on a high-definition television screen, or in a color print (which is really an audiovisual rather than a verbal-print form). So, too, the reports of correspondents in earlier wars affected us far less directly and emotionally than the televised scenes of the Vietnam War. No description of a presidential candidate or printed text of his speech can quite convey the living sense of the man as we see and hear him deliver it on a television screen.

Yet the very distancing that separates the reader from reality described is the price paid for understanding and mastery. *Meaning* is a phenomenon created by the reduction of experience into words organized in sentences. The process of understanding is the very process involved in reducing an event to writing. A television documentary about El Salvador or Lebanon can help the viewer create an image more vivid and moving than any conveyed by print; but unless the documentary is accompanied by a spoken analysis—which is, essentially, print read aloud—the documentary will fail to give the auditor the kind of understanding, the kind of *meaning,* he would derive, say, from an article in *Foreign Affairs.* Reading is inherently a different way of constructing an image of reality than is viewing or listening. And it is an indispensable one when the purpose is to require a structured understanding, rather than an impression or an emotional experience, of reality.

There are two other rather obvious ways in which communication by reading printed matter differs from communication by watching or listening to television, radio, films, or records. One is simply the ability to present a substantial *mass* of information: the content of a single issue of the *New York Times* covers far more than a week's television news programming, and a book affords the only realistic medium for presenting an extensive, structured, and detailed treatment of a subject. The other is the almost infinitely wider range of choice of subject and treatment offered the reader as contrasted with the radio listener or the television viewer. The thrust of the broadcast media, by reason of their very technology, has been to assemble larger and larger audiences for fewer and fewer sources. A prime-time network television program with fewer than ten million simultaneous viewers can hardly be sustained. In very recent years, this situation has improved substantially, as FM radio, cable television, videocassette recordings, and videodisks have greatly increased the range of individual choice. But there are thousands of magazines, catering to every interest; and the most meager of bookstores or the smallest public library offers incomparably wider opportunities to pursue inquiries or individual tastes than the totality of audiovisual media available at any one time.

The other alternative to reading that has developed in our time is the computer with its related telecommunications facility. In fact, the computer, by increasing the efficiency of editing and printing, providing powerful bibliographic and indexing services, and simplifying library services, does far more to facilitate than to replace traditional reading. But the growing use of electronic publishing and information dissemination does give emphasis to a concept of what it is important to communicate that is widely at variance with that of traditional reading. It is customary to describe a reservoir of knowledge to be disseminated electronically as a "databank" or "database." This is significant, for it reveals the assumption that important knowledge consists of an accumulation of discrete facts, and that the function of at least this medium of information is to select out of the accumulation and deliver the individual facts or collection of facts that have been called for. It assumes that the needs and mode of thought of an inquirer are analogous to those of someone who looks up a number in a telephone directory or consults a dictionary, not those of someone who reads a novel or a biography or a poem. And the oft-expressed conviction that the computer will make the book obsolete reveals a perhaps unconscious but arid and constricted belief regarding the nature of important knowledge and important communication.

This is not to question the major and very valuable social roles in communication—roles quite beyond the power of print and reading—that the audiovisual media and computer will play. The color, vividness, and immediacy of the audiovisual media and computer have enriched the lives of all of us. And they have enormously increased the perceptive outreach of most people, for most of the time devoted to viewing or listening occupies hours that had been devoted not to reading, but to activities that did not extend beyond the daily round, perhaps to inactivity. There can be no question that the audiovisual media have extended and enlarged for untold numbers of people an awareness of other lands, other times, other ideas than their own. So, too, has the computer given us powers without which modern society could not operate, and has enhanced immeasurably the capacity of human intelligence to analyze and organize experience.

But neither provides what reading offers as a bridge to the universe of experience beyond our daily ambit. The one can bathe us directly in the unexamined flow of experience, but without the processes of abstraction and organization that give it meaning. The other can give a command over discrete facts scraped bare of penumbral meaning, but does not provide the holistic gathering of experience or endow it with a human conceptual structure.

It is well for our society that the audiovisual and electronic revolutions have complemented print, not replaced it, and that reading vigorously survives as the means of establishing a bridge of meaning, both human and thoughtful, between ourselves and the totality beyond us: a bridge between our culture and other cultures, between ourselves and the infinitely vast and infinitely microscopic worlds of science, and between our present and the past and the future. Without reading, meaning and comprehension could dissolve into "feeling" or splinter into data, the awareness and integrity of individual identity and purpose could be but ill sustained, and Burke's sense of society as an all-embracing compact of the living with the dead and those yet unborn could not be achieved.

10. The New Literacy

Benjamin M. Compaine

The new literacy—ease and habit in the use of computerized information—may not replace the old, but may take a place alongside it. Although there may be less paper, there will presumably be even more words and sentences as computerized systems are involved in more and more areas of the flow of information. "Computer literacy," then, may mean not the comprehension of digital data processing, but rather the acceptance of specialized computerized systems in most areas of work.

Benjamin M. Compaine is Executive Director of the Media and Allied Arenas at the Program on Information Resources Policy at Harvard University. He is the chief author of *Who Owns the Media?* (New York: Harmony Books, 1979).

Reprinted by permission of *Daedalus,* Journal of the American Academy of Arts and Sciences, from "Reading: Old and New," vol. 112, no. 1, Winter 1983, Cambridge, Massachusetts.

*I believe books will never disappear. It is impossible
for it to happen. Of all of mankind's diverse tools,
undoubtedly the most astonishing are his books. . . . If
books were to disappear, history would disappear. So
would men.*

—Jorge Luis Borges[1]

Reading and writing will become obsolete skills.
—Sol Cornberg[2]

On any given work day, perhaps seven million employed people are paid to spend their time in front of a television screen. They are not watching "General Hospital," but rather are reading material produced by a computer. These people are airline reservations clerks and travel agents, stockbrokers, newspaper reporters and editors, catalog showroom order-takers, and customer service representatives at telephone, utility, and other sorts of firms. Among the seven million, there are secretaries and, to a small but increasing extent, executives. They clearly have many different jobs and levels of responsibilities, but they all share one trait: more and more, they are using the computer for some portion of their information storage and retrieval. And instead of using a computer specialist as an intermediary, as they would have done only a few years ago, they are interacting directly with the computer. This means that much of what they read appears on a video display terminal—a VDT—instead of in ink on paper.

This essay is about the implications of the skills these workers are developing. It is about the possible significance of the *$8 billion* spent on video games in 1981—more than was spent on movie theater admissions and record purchases combined. It is about the phenomenon of using microcomputers in elementary and secondary schools—often at the insistence of kids and their parents, before the curriculum supervisors know what's happening. It is about computer summer camps for kids. It concerns the wired university.

My objective here is to describe several of the forces and trends at work in society—only in part a function of technology—and the

127

implications of these for traditional concepts of literacy. Central to this discussion is the role of the engine of this change, the computer, and hence "computer literacy."

In this essay, I do *not* predict the future. Nor do I advocate a course of action: I aim to neither salute nor denigrate the idea of a new literacy. But change is clearly in the wind. This essay, then, suggests what factors may impinge on future developments in reading and literacy, and that those who consider themselves to be educated and, above all, literate will want to take heed.

The Old Literacy

We cannot talk about the future of reading or the book without reference to their fellow traveler, literacy. Each generation tends to assume literacy is static, petrified, as it were, in their moment of time. Literacy, however, is dynamic, a bundle of culturally relevant skills. The appropriate skills for literacy, moreover, have changed over time. Before the written record came into wide use (in England, starting in the last half of the eleventh century), the oral tradition predominated. To be literate meant the ability to compose and recite orally. In the twelfth century, to make a "record" of something meant to bear oral witness, not to produce a document for others to read. Even if a treaty was in the form of sealed letters, "both parties also named witnesses who were to make legal record...in court if necessary." Despite the existence of written documents, "the spoken word was the legally valid record."[3]

Furthermore, at that time, to be *litteratus* meant to know Latin, rather than having only the specific ability to read and write. To be sure, the vernacular replaced Latin for discourse. But even then, because of the difficulty of writing with a quill on parchment or with a stylus on wax, writing was considered a special skill that "was not automatically coupled with the ability to read."[4] The most common way of committing words to writing in twelfth-century England was by dictating to a scribe, who was a craftsman and not necessarily himself able to compose. Thus, reading and dictating were typically paired, rather than reading and writing.

Although the basic skills of modern literacy—reading and writing—had become relatively widespread in England by the mid-nineteenth century, the literati of the period seemed to impose a greater barrier for admission to full-fledged literacy. It was not merely the ability to read, they said, but the reading of the "right" materials that separated the truly literate from the great unwashed. How, if at all, they asked, did the spread of the printed word contribute to the spiritual enrichment and intellectual enlightenment of the English nation? "More people were reading than ever before; but in the opinion of most commentators, they were reading the wrong things, for the wrong reasons, and in the wrong way."[5]

All this is grist for the notion that today's standards of literacy are rooted in the past, yet at the same time should not be presumed to be the standard for the future. For example, at a recent meeting of "experts" convened to discuss the status of books and reading, several participants indicated that when they referred to the status of "the book," they had in mind great literature and intellectual enrichment. They were not referring to the 38,000 other titles (out of about 40,000) published annually that range from cookbooks and "how-to" books to Harlequin romances. Thus they were carrying on the tradition of the nineteenth-century literati, who idealized their own past. They felt that things were far different—and infinitely better—in the old days.

Similarly, the library, today's bastion of the book and reading, has not always been held in such high regard by the literati. Free libraries for the common man in England were viciously criticized by the reading elite. Instead of encouraging "habits of study and self-improvement, they catered to the popular passion for light reading—above all, for fiction."[6] Indeed, one librarian told a meeting in 1879 that "schoolboys or students who took to novel reading to any great extent never made much progress in after life."[7] The irony of attitudes such as this should not be lost to the critics of video games as a corrupting influence on today's "schoolboys or students."

The New Literacy

"To describe our business as one that traffics in paper, ink, and type is to miss the point entirely. Our real enterprise is ideas and information." A quote from a futurist? Perhaps. This is the strategic outlook of W. Bradford Wiley, chairman of John Wiley & Sons, one of the oldest publishing houses in New York City and publisher, in the nineteenth century, of Herman Melville, Nathaniel Hawthorne, and Edgar Allen Poe and most of the first American editions of John Ruskin. Wiley adds, "Until now, our medium has been the bound book; tomorrow our medium will expand to include [computer-stored] data banks and videodisks."[8]

What evidence is there that Wiley is on to something? First, he has recognized, at least implicitly, that Marshall McLuhan was off base. The medium, by and large, is *not* the message. The message is the content, and the medium is the way it is conveyed and displayed. *Content*—the ideas, knowledge, story, information, and so on—is the work of an author, a producer, a photographer. Technology, history, and even politics play a role in how this content is processed and the format in which it is ultimately displayed. *Process* incorporates the gathering, handling, storage, and transmission of the content; it may involve typewriters, computers, file cabinets; telephone lines, broadcasting towers, printing presses; and trucks and retail stores. *Format* is the manner of display—such as ink on paper, sound from a vibrating speaker cone, images on a cathode ray tube, light projected through a film, and so on.[9] Thus the content may be quite independent of the medium.

This article, for example, has been written at a standard typewriter keyboard. But instead of paper as the format, the letters appear on a green television screen. Although you are now reading this in a conventional ink on paper format, the process for creating this bound version may be quite different from that used only ten or twenty years ago. Computerized phototypesetting equipment has substantially replaced all the old Linotype machines that used to produce lead slugs for galleys. Moreover, there is no technological or perhaps even economic reason to keep subscribers to *Daedalus* from reading this article the same way it was written—on a video screen. It may be argued that someday it will be. The major barrier to this may be cultural: most of us have been brought up to read print on paper. Many adults would today recoil in horror at the thought of losing the feel and portability of printed volumes. But, as Wiley indicated, print is no longer the only rooster in the barnyard.

There are more solid trends that support Wiley's approach. One is the pervasive and perhaps long-run impact of video games. In short order these have gone from barroom novelties to a worldwide phenomenon. In 1976 Atari's sales were $39 million; in 1981 they were $1.23 billion, and they may double in 1982 to $2.4 billion (about the size of Kellogg or Gillette). Americans may spend about $2 billion in 1982 on cartridges for home video games, and they will likely drop into video game machines in 1983 considerably more than the 22 billion quarters they did in 1981. That money is coming from somewhere, most likely from the implicit budget people have for other media and entertainment. This includes movie admissions, records, and, to some extent, books.

Even if the video game craze itself is a fad, it nonetheless may have considerable cultural significance, much as the dime novel or penny press had in earlier eras. For the first time, it has made the video tube into something other than a passive format for the masses. Heretofore, only a handful of specialists, mostly computer programmers and some designers, used VDTs as an interactive medium. The rest of the world sat back and watched on their television tube what others provided.

Moreover, while critics of video games decry the presumed ill effects of the video game parlors—much as their nineteenth-century counterparts lamented the coming of literacy for the common reader —they may well prove to be myopic regarding the nature of the games themselves. As with much great literature, which can be appreciated on several levels of understanding, video games can be viewed on one level as simply entertainment. But in his book *How to Master Home Video Games,* Harvard undergraduate Tom Hirschfeld described these games as presenting players with a challenge. He notes that those who become the best at it are those who figure out the pattern programmed into the computer. The game players are becoming, almost painlessly, computer-literate. Without becoming computer experts, they may be intuitively learning the strengths and limitations of computer logic. The U.S. army, which must train large numbers of youngsters fresh from the video game rooms, understood the implications of the games almost immediately, and has already contracted for training exercises using video game-like lessons played on microcomputers. The schools will no doubt follow.

The home video games are actually specialized personal computers. They have made consumers familiar with the concept of a computerized console that plugs into a video tube. All that a computer adds is a keyboard. Of the approximately 1.5 million personal desktop computers in use by the end of 1981, about 500,000 of these were in homes. With the Timex 1000, the retail price for a real, programmable computer has fallen to under $100. As a result, it is estimated that the number of computers in homes will triple by the end of 1982. Thus, unlike the situation in the 1960s when expensive computers in schools were imposed from the top—and computerized education failed miserably—we now see the development of grass-roots interest in having microcomputers in the schools. It is the kids and their parents who are often in the forefront of this effort, with local PTAs holding bake sales and the like to raise the money when school districts are pinched for funds. (In the past, some of that effort went to buying books for the school library.)

Thus, although educators are still concerned primarily with how students learn from print, young people today spend more time (about twenty-eight hours weekly by one study) using electronic devices like television and electronic games than with print (about twenty-five). Further, most of the discretionary time spent is with the electronic medium, while most of the time spent with printed material is involuntary.[10] Together with the video game trend, this suggests that schoolchildren of today are developing a new set of skills that may lead to a different standard for literacy.

But what about the seven million or more adults working with VDTs as part of their daily routine? How will they approach the prospect of adopting at home tools similar to those they use in the workplace? Besides home computers, there are already a few such opportunities to retrieve and manipulate content, with a great many more in prospect. Services such as those offered by Compu-Serve Information Service and Source Telecomputing have already offered portions of newspapers such as the *New York Times* and the *Los Angeles Times* via computer to home terminals, in addition to a wide range of other types of information. Houghton Mifflin has produced an interactive videodisk version of Roger Tory Peterson's venerable bird identification books.

Three "videotext"[11] services, Oracle, Ceefax, and Prestel, have been commercially available in Great Britain since 1980. Prestel, the most ambitious, has been slow to achieve much popular interest, perhaps because of its cost, its strangeness, and the method required to access its voluminous information stores. Nonetheless, several videotext services that are in the prototype stage in the United States at this time may well be made available commercially by traditional publishing firms. These include Times Mirror Company (publisher of newspapers, books, and magazines), Knight-Ridder Newspapers (publisher of newspapers and books), and CBS Inc. (which, in addition to being the largest television network, also owns the publishing company Holt, Rinehart, & Winston and many well-known magazines). While the services offered by these firms are likely to tie together home terminals with large computers by telephone lines, the country's largest book and magazine publisher, Time Inc., has also tested a text-on-the-video-screen service to be delivered via cable.

That nonpublishers are getting into the act is a fact not lost on traditional publishers. Mead Corporation, one of the largest paper manufacturers, is also one of the most successful electronic publishers. On its NEXIS Service, it offers the full text of articles from the *Washington Post, Newsweek, U.S. News & World Report, Business Week,* UPI, Associated Press, Reuters news services, *Encyclopaedia Britannica,* and scores of other publications. The company's LEXIS service is known by most lawyers and used by many. It provides nearly unlimited access to tens of thousands of laws and cases, at federal, state, and international levels, that often required days of work in a library. These services can be accessed by users who have received very little special training. Although the cost today restricts NEXIS and LEXIS to use in institutions, similar services may become as inexpensive over time as today's mainstream media.

The interest in "electronic publishing" is motivated by more than a mere fascination with technological toys. In part, there are some significant economic trends involved. The price of the paper used in book and magazine publishing has jumped substantially since the early 1970s, following years of only minimal increases. The cost of newsprint jumped 200 percent between 1970 and 1981, well over twice the rate of increase for all commodities. In large measure, these huge increases reflect the high energy component in the manufacture of paper. The physical distribution of printed material, moreover, especially newspapers, is highly energy-intensive. These cost trends contrast dramatically with the costs of computer-stored information, which have been declining at a rate of about 25 percent annually for the last thirty years. (Consider the magnitude of this decline: if the price of a Rolls Royce had decreased in proportion to that of computer storage, a Rolls Royce today would cost about $2.50.) The outlook for the foreseeable future is for continued similar decreases in cost.

As a preliminary indicator of the changing demand for a new information skills in the workplace, Carolyn Frankel, a researcher with Harvard's Program on Information Resources Policy, surveyed the help-wanted ads in the *New York Times* for the same June day in 1977 through 1982. She counted all jobs or skills in those ads that mentioned some "computer literacy" skill, such as word processing, programming, data entry, and so on. In 1977, 5.8 percent of the want ads specified those skills. The percentage increased regularly to 1982, when 10.3 percent of the jobs listed required such skills. Perhaps of equal significance is the way these jobs were described. Earlier in the period, the ads were for specific jobs that implied a computer skill, such as "Wang operator" or "word processor." By 1982 conventional job titles such as secretary specified the required skills as "experience with word processing" or "knowledge of Sabre" (a computer system for travel agents). From this apparent trend, we can conclude that, as new technology becomes more commonplace and skills in it more widespread, the skills become incorporated into traditional jobs. When the power saw was a novelty, building contractors sought out "power-saw operators." But later on, when most carpenters were expected to have some familiarity with this tool, builders again began to seek out carpenters as such, carpenters who had, among other skills, knowledge of the power saw.

In 1977 none of the help-wanted ads for travel agents in the *Times* on the day surveyed mentioned any sort of computer skill; in 1980 one-fifth mentioned a computer-related skill. By 1982, as a consequence of the implementation of computer reservations services by the industry, 71 percent required familiarity with such skills. Similarly, the number of bookkeeping jobs requiring computer-related skills doubled to 24 percent from 1977 to 1982; the proportion of secretary/typist want ads that required word processing skills went from zero in 1977 to 15 percent in 1982; and the number of jobs that were labeled "word processing" or that specified the ability to use a word processor increased eightfold in that period, despite the recession in 1982 and a lower level of help-wanted ads over all.

The impact of all this in the workplace will be visible, if not profound. About $25,000 of capital is invested for every worker in a manufacturing setting, compared to approximately $4,000 for every office—or knowledge—worker, but that may change soon. In 1980 even an information-intensive company such as Aetna Life & Casualty Company had only one video terminal for each six employees: by 1985 they expect to have one terminal for every two employees. The ubiquity of these terminals and the increased familiarity workers will have with them may result in expanded application, such as electronically transmitted and stored "mail" both within an office and from remote office sites, including overseas offices.

Other indices suggest that we are in the midst of a fundamental change in the way we receive and process information. A taxi service in Ottawa has eliminated the crackling radio heretofore used to dispatch taxis and replaced it with a video screen in the cab on which the messages flash. When the driver is called, a buzzer sounds and a fare's location is printed on the screen. Since no other driver gets that message, no one can beat him (or her) to the fare. The head of one cab company using the system likes it, he explained, because voice dispatching causes noise and confusion, not to mention slips of paper everywhere.

We now see centers of higher learning using computers in the liberal arts. Classics scholars at Princeton are studying Virgil with the help of a computer programmed to scan the text quickly, picking out passages that contain the same word used in different contexts. This reduces the drudgery, they claim, and allows them more time to study the meaning. Dartmouth applies similar analytical techniques to the Bible and Shakespeare. Apparently, students are integrating this technology into their academic lives as easily as they did the simpler calculator in the last decade.[12]

Even department stores and toy shops now carry computers so that consumers do not have to go into the threatening territory of a specialty store. At the same time, advertising campaigns by computer manufacturers are using well-known entertainers such as Bill Cosby and Dick Cavett in prime time commercials to further demystify their product.

Combining the Old and the New

Historically, the development of a literacy has gone through identifiable stages. Literacy starts with specialists, and then begins to have a wider impact on institutions, as it becomes the preferred medium of business, culture, and politics. Finally, it becomes so pervasive that even the masses are considered to be handicapped without it. We can trace modern notions of literacy from eleventh-century England, in the movement from reliance on spoken words to written records, first in the Church and then in political institutions; to the introduction of the printing press in the fifteenth century; to the development of the newspaper and mass-consumed book along with popular education in the nineteenth.

History also suggests that one need not be fully literate to participate in literacy. One measure of changing literacy in twelfth- and thirteenth-century England was possession of a seal. In the reign of Edward the Confessor, only the king possessed a seal to authenticate documents. By the reign of Edward I (1307), even serfs were required by statute to have one.[13] In colonial times in the United States, signing one's name was skill enough to be called literate.

In the thirty-five or so years since the development of modern computers, we can identify trends similar to the much slower advance of traditional literacy. At first, computers were strictly for those who could read and write in the tongue of computer machine language, a "priestly" class whom all users of computers had to depend upon. As computers became more widespread and their application more pervasive, they began to have a greater impact on business and social institutions. The languages (COBOL, FORTRAN, BASIC, etc.) evolved into something closer to the vernacular, so that more people were able to learn to read and write computer language.

Today, we are perhaps at the threshold of an era where the computer is becoming so simple to use and inexpensive that the masses can use it without having to understand how it works. They can thus participate in computer literacy without necessarily being computer-literate. That may come in time, as the computer becomes as commonplace as the book. Yet, if we look at the computer as a tool, it may be no more necessary for the mass of people to understand how a computer works in order to use it than it is to understand the mechanics of the automobile's internal combustion engine in order to drive. (This suggests a nice parallel. In the 1950s, when the automobile was king, many boys were born "with a wrench in their hand." Today, we see kids who are barely teenagers playing around with RAM chips in much the same way.)

Implications for Reading and the Book

It would be foolish, though perhaps fun, to speculate on the long-term societal impacts that may grow out of the trends I have described. As someone must surely have once said, "Predicting is a hazardous occupation, especially when it deals with the future." Moreover, while I have tried to identify some forces and trends relative to literacy and reading, there are other trends—cultural, political, and technological—that have not been included or even recognized as yet.

In the long term, it is possible, even probable, that the computer, combined with modern communications facilities, will be cited by historians of the future as a fundamental milestone for civilization, out of which many changes will be traced. What those changes will be cannot be foretold; it is difficult enough to understand the implications of our own historical antecedents. Elizabeth Eisenstein wrote: "It is one thing to describe how methods of book production changed after the mid-fifteenth century....It is another thing to decide how access to a greater abundance or variety of written records affected ways of learning, thinking, and perceiving among literate elites." [14]

In the near term, we might profitably think about computer skills as additional proficiencies in the bundle we call literacy. Note that I have referred to computer skills as additional to, not replacements for, existing skills. Reading and writing will continue to be essential; computer memory may replace some paper and file drawers; but we will still have to compose sentences for a documentary format. And although the text may appear on screen, it must still be read and, of course, understood. Thus the written word must be taught and learned. Slightly further out, however, writing—meaning composing with pen in hand or fingers on keyboard—may become less necessary. Although still far from perfected, work on voice recognition by computers is proceeding rapidly. Today, an increasing number of busy people dictate their letters, memos, and even books onto audiotape for later transcription by someone else. Ironically, this harks back to the medieval era, when the educated composed orally to scribes, who made the written record. With reliable voice recognition computers, we could return to such an era of oral literacy.

There is an even greater likelihood of computer-generated voice synthesis; that is, the output from a computer in the form of a voice —like Hal, in the movie *2001: A Space Odyssey*—rather than as text on a screen or printer. Yet it is unlikely that voice synthesis will totally replace reading, since we can assimilate information much faster with our eyes than with our ears.

Even that assertion, however, is subject to question. The current adult generations, raised on print and the book, have a close cultural identity with both. We have *learned* how to use them, how to skim, how to use an index with ease, and so on. We associate certain pleasant emotions with the tactile sensation of the book. And, as one skeptic put it, could we imagine curling up in front of a fire with a Tolstoy novel on the video screen?

But these are largely learned cultural biases. The kids today playing Pac-Man are learning to assimilate great amounts of information rapidly from a video screen. They are learning to manipulate the information on that screen at an intuitive level, using keyboards or "joysticks." If the technology results in the development of video screens with twice the resolution of today's (possible now, but prohibitively expensive), and with ever lower electronic storage costs (perhaps using a videodisk), it may not be all that farfetched to expect tomorrow's youngsters to carry their thin, high-resolution video screens with them when they travel or to sit in front of the fireplace reading from them. And, conceivably, an "oral" generation may also learn to absorb content at a faster rate from speech, with greater skill—or literacy—and with enjoyment equal to our pleasure in reading words from a book.

Such speculation should not obscure the robustness of older formats in the face of new ones. Records, film, radio, and television have successively been feared as threats to print. Yet all have survived and thrived, though sometimes having to fill somewhat different functions. General-interest mass audience magazines like *Look* and *Life* lost their national audiences to television, and as a result, magazines generally became largely a special-interest medium. Books, on the other hand, have shown remarkable resilience in the face of new informational and cultural formats. Indeed, new processes and formats frequently create opportunities for the older ones. Television spawned magazines such as *TV*

Guide and is widely credited with sparking interest in sports magazines and expanded newspaper sports pages. Cinema and television films based on books have increased sales of those books. Examples range from *Star Wars* to *The Ascent of Man.* Computer magazines are thriving. And there are now books and magazines for video game enthusiasts.

There are few fears evoked today that were not previously heard during the Victorian era. Today, the enemy of reading is television. But the doom of reading has been falsely prophesied ever since the invention of the pneumatic tire, when it was believed that the bicycle would put the whole family on wheels and thus spell the end of fireside reading.[15] On the other hand, there is a certain validity to the pessimism of Samuel Johnson—who, had he lived today, could have had in mind Atari's Pac-Man—when he wrote: "People in general do not willingly read, if they can have anything else to amuse them."[16]

It is likely that we are on the verge of yet another step in the evolution of literacy. Yet we can feel confident that whatever comes about will not replace existing skills, but supplement them. Neither the printing press nor the typewriter replaced either speech or handwriting. The electronic hand calculator has not replaced the need to understand mathematics, though it may reduce the need to memorize multiplication tables. The new literacy will likely involve a greater emphasis on the visual, but only as a continuation of the trend that has involved the improvements in photography, printing techniques, and television.

Above all, the new literacy, whatever it looks like, is not to be feared—first, because it will come about regardless of what we think about it; second, because for any threat to some existing institution or relationship, the new literacy will provide equal or greater opportunity; third, because change brought about in part by technology takes place incrementally, and adjustments by society and individuals will evolve naturally.

I remain haunted, however, by how a sixteen-year-old reporter for *Children's Express,* a newspaper published entirely by school-children, characterized the Fourth Assembly of the World Future Society in July 1982, whose theme was the new world of telecommunications: "I think the message was clear that it's really our [young people's] world. I was kind of laughing at the people here. This technology, all they talked about, they really couldn't grasp. This belongs to us."[17]

Benjamin M. Compaine

Notes

1. Quoted on the editorial page of the *Wall Street Journal,* 6 February 1982, from an article in *Horizon* about the importance of books in an era of mass communication.
2. Quoted by Alvin Toffler in *Future Shock* (New York: Random House, 1970), 144. Sol Cornberg is a communications system designer.
3. M. T. Clanchy, *From Memory to Written Record: England, 1066-1307* (Cambridge, Mass.: Harvard University Press, 1979), 56.
4. Ibid., 88.
5. Richard D. Altick, *The English Common Reader: A Social History of the Mass Reading Public, 1800-1900* (Chicago: University of Chicago Press, 1974), 368.
6. Ibid., 231.
7. Ibid., 233.
8. Jack Egan, Publishing for the Future," *New York,* 16 August 1982, 10.
9. Benjamin M. Compaine, *A New Framework for the Media Arena: Content, Process, and Format* (Cambridge, Mass.: Program on Information Resources Policy, Harvard University, 1980), 6-17.
10. Fred M. Hechinger, "About Education," *New York Times,* 15 December 1982, sec. C, p. 5.
11. "Videotext" (sometimes videotex) is a term that describes any service that provides text and graphics on a videoscreen in a "page" format; that is, material is prearranged in screenfuls to be viewed in their entirety by the user. There are several varieties of videotext, distinguished by the ways in which the user and the database of pages interact.
12. "The Wired University is on the Way," *Business Week,* 26 April 1982, 68.
13. Clanchy, *From Memory to Written Record,* 2.
14. Elizabeth L. Eisenstein, *The Printing Press as an Agent of Change* (New York: Cambridge University Press, 1979), 8.
15. Altick, *The English Common Reader,* 374.
16. Ibid., 373.
17. "Time Tripping at a Convention of World Futurists," *Boston Globe,* 4 August 1982, 55.

The author gratefully acknowledges the contribution of Harvard graduate student Carolyn Frankel for the research and analysis incorporated into this article.

To get them to read a book at all, whether they're at Eton or a Bermondsey comprehensive, is bloody difficult.

JOHN THORN
Headmaster of Winchester

11. The Future of Reading

Jacques Barzun

The invisibility of real literature in a mass of information-oriented publication, the unwillingness to teach
reading, and a decline of the quality of writing conspire
to block the future of reading, according to Jacques
Barzun. Reading becomes unattractive, no matter
whether it connotes unpleasantness or its pleasures are
hard to find for one intent upon them.

Barzun was a member of the Advisory Committee on
the Book in the Future. His essay on "The Centrality of
Reading" appeared above (chap. 5).

"The Future of Reading" by Jacques Barzun is reprinted with permission from the
February 1978 issue of *The Pennsylvania Gazette,* alumni magazine of the University of Pennsylvania. Copyright © 1978.

I t seems to me that there are in our world at least three great obstacles in the way of reading having a future at all. I mean, of course, in the way of reading *books,* as against magazines, pamphlets, and throwaways. By reading books, I mean chiefly the multiple satisfactions that come from getting to know the contents of another mind through the channel of a printed work. I attach importance, you see, to the fact of there being a mind behind a book. It helps us to mark a difference between various physical acts that look alike superficially but are essentially distinct. When you pick up the telephone directory to look up a number, you are, in one sense, reading, and, in another, you are doing nothing of the kind. Generally speaking, reading for information, indispensable as it is, is not reading in the finally important sense. It may have importance for the moment, as when you *must* have that telephone number. But it does little for your soul: it does not reshape your mind or reeducate your emotions. It provides no sustained pleasures—neither simple entertainment nor tragic joy, gaiety, serene contentment, or wisdom, all of which things a good book can do.

These are some of the matters that Charles Lamb had in mind when he wrote against books that were nonbooks, *biblia abiblia,* books in wolf's clothing. He meant all books of reference, all that is written solely to inform—guide books, digests, factual and statistical reports, tracts and polemics of all kinds—a very large class of works at any time. He felt so strongly that these tended to overshadow real books, drive them out of circulation—bury them alive —that when he came across a true book, he would kiss it.

One has the impression that if Lamb were alive today he would do precious little kissing. We publish more books than ever before —in this country, about 36,000 a year or 3,000 a month, which is about 100 a day—and, among all those volumes, there are few real books. Many are handbooks and reports that we do need, whether kissable or not. But many more have little or no excuse for being. I am not alone in thinking so. In a recent article, the editor of *Harper's* magazine, who can hardly be accused of ivory-tower estheticism, defined half a dozen large categories of pointless books, and he summed up his estimate by saying: "Of the thousands of books published every year, almost all of them (possibly as many as 95 in every 100) constitute little more than puffed up essays or articles. The author could have said what he had to say in 40 pages instead of 400."

Mr. Lewis Lapham was talking about the books he found in bookstores. That leaves out the output of the many university presses; and they are responsible for an equal and less forgivable inflation. Because of the vanities of publish-or-perish in academic life, my generation of university people has seen the footnote grow into a 20-page article and the 20-page article grow into a 400-page book.

Now what is the effect of this avalanche, this bombardment of printed books? The effect is not one thing, but many. To begin with, a helter-skelter competition. Bookstores are not big enough to put on view all that comes out. Nobody, what is more, can find his way in the confusion. Neither the bookshop managers nor the reviewers, rarely the librarians, and much less the general public can sort out what work or works might be worth the money and the time of reading. It is significant and sad that the trade magazine *Publishers Weekly* is satisfied with telling its specialized audience how much each publisher plans to spend in advertising certain books that might repay the gamble by becoming best-sellers. That appropriation is the main fact about a few of the 36,000 books just before publication. The others come out unheralded, naked, to sink or swim by themselves—and nearly all sink.

The point must not be misunderstood. There is nothing wrong with publishing being a trade or books being advertised and becoming best-sellers. The point is that, through huge production and the absence of a coherent and well-informed public, we have come to deal in books as if they were bricks—interchangeable lumps of matter of a certain size and color. And in publishing itself, as I can testify, there is more and more frequent mention of this or that acknowledged best-seller as a book that many people have bought and relatively few have read. They may have tried to read it; they may have bought it for show. In either case, they bought a brick, not a book.

In other words, we are producing books at such a rate and with so little regard for their substance that the true expressions of mind and feeling which are bound to be somewhere in the giant heap are practically invisible. Where is that book that would be congenial to our temper—really new—and worth rereading? Someone wrote it, but the reviewers overlook it—it's not their fault; the bookstores don't stock it—they can't afford to. Nobody hears of it except by chance. True enough, chance has always played a role in the fate of books—there's an old Roman proverb to prove it. But our modern system has so magnified the chances *against* any one work, that spotting the genuine books of the season is as unlikely as breaking the bank at Monte Carlo.

Compare the situation as it has been at certain times in the past.

When the sprightly daughter of Dr. Burney, the musician and scholar, published anonymously a novel called *Evelina* in 1778, the first edition of this unknown author was only 500 copies. But the town—the judgment of London—made her famous virtually overnight. That is a kind of Gallup poll we have lost.

The first result of our system of confusion, then, is neglect of good things. A corollary is the failure to see the fake and the cobbled-up for what they are. Dozens of books are not only inflated articles, they sometimes consist of articles previously written by other people and pasted together in the likeness of a book. Much popular sociology, political diagnosis, and what might be called crisis-shouting is simply a rehash of the news and the commentary that you have already read. Not long ago, one large firm in Boston gave a writer a huge advance for the biography of a gangster, which turned out to be a compilation of other people's accounts of his edifying life. And the same holds for the innumerable works now most in favor which tells us how to escape inheritance tax, avoid rape, and share fully in our wives' pregnancies.

All this would be trivial, the pages of rubbish could be written off as quickly as they've been written on if, in addition to baffling the reader's efforts to discover good work, the swamping of such work did not also affect the future; that is, the future of reading. For consider this other fact in our production of books: they are made perishable. Whether in hard covers or soft, paper and binding will not last beyond a decade or two. It follows that any book neglected or misjudged today is doomed for good. This is a new situation, born in our century.

Compare circumstances again, using once more the example of Charles Lamb. He had a highly original concern with the Elizabethan playwrights, other than Shakespeare, who in Lamb's day were largely neglected. He brought them back into favor by means of a selection of their works, thus re-endowing English literature with a good deal of dramatic poetry. Now Lamb was able to do this only because the books containing these forgotten plays had survived. Similarly, in an earlier century, Dryden reintroduced the works of Chaucer, through selection and "translation." Again, Dryden was able to do this because his patron, the Earl of Leicester, had collected early editions of Chaucer that had survived for 300 years. What poets, critics, or connoisseurs will be able to do the same for us in the next generations? Our books will not survive. Paper and binding will have turned to dust. For example, at the beginning of this century, the works of a great English historian, Frederick Maitland, were issued in a complete edition. Already those eight volumes are in fragments. In two libraries that I frequent, they have been taken off the shelf as unusable. On my own shelves is a complete edition of the works of Bernard Shaw issued in the early 1930s. Less than half a century afterwards, the edges are turning brown, and the binding is going to pieces. Next to Shaw

I have the complete Swift that Sir Walter Scott edited in 1814, and it is as solid and readable as ever.

Some among you have no doubt given rare books to a library. They were rare in part because they were old; but the great fact is they were still extant—one of a dozen or score of surviving copies, for example, the seventy-four folios of Shakespeare. They could be reprinted or microfilmed. They had survived by good paper and binding and somebody's cherishing. Where will your descendants and mine find correspondingly valuable works? Nowhere—they will have disappeared.

You may want to remind me here that there is a flourishing reprint trade. That is true, but its limitations are severe. Such publishers reissue old books by photography, on paper that they think eternal—say, 250 years. But those books are printed in editions of 100 or 200 copies, necessarily at very high prices. Only libraries can buy them, and few libraries at that. For a time, microfilm was thought to be the perfect answer to decay. It, too, was to last a couple of centuries, but it turns out to be also perishable: it develops black spots, known as measles, in 40 years or less. What is worse, microfilm, like the microcard, is ill-adapted to browsing. No one has ever pulled a microfilm box from a stack, saying to himself: "I wonder what's inside." Yet browsing is of enormous importance to scholarship, to pleasure, and to the self-education of the young. Books are not merely to fill but to feed the mind. And for this purpose, nothing can replace the book. The book has found its perfect form—like the bicycle, not to be transcended. Yet it is now an endangered species. To say so is to point to the second lion in the path of future reading.

For there are people about, full of good intentions, I may say damned by good intentions, who work for the elimination of the book, the elimination of reading. In the Midwest, one group of educators—educators, mind you—has organized on the principle that reading is obsolescent, if not obsolete. They, and others not so rash but fundamentally of like mind, are dazzled by the advent of the computer. They freely predict for it a future beyond compare. They imagine a world of tomorrow in which everybody, from the little toddler to the research scholar, will spend whatever time is left over from TV in front of another, similar screen. Seated at the console beneath it, the lover of learning of any age will only have to press buttons to formulate his questions and receive his answers on that screen. The scholar will get his answer in words spelled out as on an airline booking machine; the little tot will get pictures. How the future researcher will grow out of the tot without someone's teaching the little one how to read is not explained. The vague slogan that the world has "gone visual" is supposed to take care of all objections. And it is true that impatience with words can be felt in the cultural atmosphere. In the colleges of some great universities, it is possible for a student to "go visual" and devote himself or herself for the upper years, at least, to activities in which no book work is required.

In the lower schools, a strong argument advanced against reading is that it seems difficult to teach to some children. Three thousand years of past teaching of this art have been negated in one generation and brought to an end. The country, as a result, has a large backlog of some 25 million "functional illiterates." They are so called because they cannot function—cannot fill out an application form for a job. They can barely make out "Danger—live wire." It is inferred from this growing reserve of nonreaders that mankind has outgrown the ability to read, together with the need to do so.

This state of affairs has come about gradually, out of perfectly clear and namable causes. The abandonment of phonics in teaching reading and the substitution of "looksay," which began half a century ago, was bound to turn out nonreaders automatically. It was an early instance of "going visual." A side-effect of looksay teaching was to instill in the young the conviction that books were both difficult and dull. You remember how looksay was necessarily tied to the reading books about Dick and Jane? Those books had a carefully limited vocabulary—four or six or eight hundred words, depending on the grade, when the child could already *use* two thousand or more. The contents of those teaching books were made still more suicidal by inane repetition. "See Dick, how he runs. See Jane, how she runs. See Dick and Jane, how they run." Such was the advanced idea inculcated in the young as the quintessence of reading and its pleasures. Now, after fifty years of this idiocy, we wonder that children want to look at TV, and we blame that invention for the decline of reading. Isn't it rather that the love of TV is the *result* of our having killed reading from the start—by practicing contraception on the vocabulary and visiting extermination on good storytelling in print? One might even go farther and say that the addiction to TV among the young evinces a love of literature that has survived the horrors of school starvation in the matter of reading.

For at least the soap opera and the cops-and-robbers and even the commercials have a spark of imagination and lifelikeness in them, whereas the schoolbooks, just like the utopia by computer which the enemies of reading preach to us with their question-begging consoles and answer-ridden screens, are altogether arid and unconsoling. They are wholly concerned with information, with mere replies to the demand for facts. The new schemes involve no conceivable connection with—I won't say literature—but knowledge. Information is not knowledge. If you ask the computer what were the names of the three musketeers, it will tell you. But what you have then acquired is not knowledge, neither of the characters, nor of the book, nor of literature. And the fun has been nil. The craze for rapid reading is part and parcel of the same foolishness. Where is the fun?

It is this radical lack of common intelligence and common awareness of the real world in our utopians that constitutes a menace to reading and indeed to civilization. They have not even the sense to wonder how all this so-called knowledge they want to put up in data banks will get there. Who will do the programming? Who will do the abstracting before the programming, and the choosing of what to abstract before that? I mean: who among a generation of nonreaders—poorly taught, kept from words and from literature, and trained in the assumption that the life of the mind is merely an extension of the quiz-program and the cross-word puzzle. In truth, these project-makers are not even capable of imagining the cost of their fanciful machinery or the perpetual jam of competing demands on the system—from the trivial effort to settle an argument about the length of Brooklyn Bridge in cen-timeters, to the request for a full bibliography on the American Revolution.

To say these things is not to be "against computers" or opposed to technology. It is only to recognize what our wonderful inven-tions can do and what is still left over for the realm of intelligence—and, even more important, for the *play* of intelligence. It isn't as if we lacked all experience of computers and data banks. We have witnessed grand disasters: for example, the failure of translation by computer, which cost the taxpayer 60 million dollars, only to prove what any bilingual writer could have foreseen; namely, that even in scientific prose, the subtleties of language are too great to be foreseen and taken care of mechanically. Again, the Pittsburgh center for law research by computer retrieval has been shown to be less useful than was expected. The best legal minds distrust its rigidities and ambiguities, both; and it would be an enormously expensive as well as intellectually staggering task to make this data bank approximate the workings of a good mind. By way of illustration, I can cite an experience of my own in the use of a similar repository. I wanted to find out what articles in scientific journals had been published within the last five years on the deficiencies of scientific writing. I received a printout of nearly 250 titles. Of these, about 90 were actually on my subject. The surplus was due to such inevitable ambiguity as that in the title of one article: "The United States and Homosexuality in the Philippines—the Handwriting on the Wall." Once again, the book and its reader remain unique and untouched by their would-be competitors.

Having seen how we bury good books by overproduction and prevent their later emergence by producing them cheaply and perishably; having seen how we thoughtlessly hamper the devel-opment of reading habits and put hurdles in the path of potential and actual readers, we now come to the third and last great obstacle cutting us off from the enjoyment of literature. Before I describe it, though, let me make clear again that when I say "literature," I do not mean only great books, profound works deserving to be called masterpieces or classics. Literature has many mansions and excellence is found in many forms—some of them unassuming and even fugitive. The specifically literary qualities can grace a detective story by Dorothy Sayers or a farce by Courteline, a ghost story by M. R. James or a poem by Ogden Nash. The true reader allows himself a balanced diet and moves easily through the categories from philosophy to humor—and he is, or ought to be, equally annoyed if either of them fails to give him the *literary* thrill—the thrill of good words—on top of philosophical knowledge or hilarious entertainment.

This understood, you will not be surprised to hear that the third great blight on reading is the general decline in *writing*. Reading and writing are correlative arts, and there can be no good reader who does not possess a true feeling for the written word. Even if one's ideal of literary expression is transparency—the words letting the meaning through without drawing attention to themselves—the fit reader, when he pauses for a breathing spell, marvels at the art that produced the transparent perfection.

But there are other styles than the transparent, and their merits deserve notice. How do they get noticed? Everything today conspires and prevents both the production and the appreciation of good writing. The teaching of writing in the schools has fallen into a state of chaos and ineffectiveness that baffles characterization. Not only is little writing done, but all kinds of electives and substitutes encourage the avoidance of writing; teachers and pupils alike loathe the composition class and are happy to pretend that looking at film strips or discussing at random some piece of screenwork is composition. The traditional course in which themes were written and works of literature systematically studied is virtually extinct. It is too difficult.

Worse still is the well-established fact that in classes where writing is done, the aim is to turn out a wordy, pretentious, pseudo-intellectual kind of prose—the sort of writing that the teachers are used to from their textbooks in schools of education and that they take as proper for serious discourse. Anything simple, direct, idiomatic strikes them as too informal for schoolwork. They have, in short, totally lost any sense of the gradations of language from vulgar to colloquial to vernacular to abstract and to highfalutin. Is it any wonder that when they then turn to the reading of a book, good or bad, they are incapable of telling their pupils anything true and important about its worth as literature? They cannot analyze the means or the effects, or so much as point to the particularly artful passages. They might as well be attempting to read a cuneiform inscription.

Nor does the damage stop with omission. The books likely to be used for class reading are chosen for their so-called contemporary interest and also for their congeniality to the unstretched mind— words, tone, and sentence structure must be such as to cause no puzzlement or other distress to the average pupil; the specifications are: lots of dialogue, common clichés, and no allusions to other literature. This defines, say, the run-of-the-mill paperback western, and that is the level of literature for such results as modern schooling attains. In one school that tried to use some good specimens of science fiction, the attempt had to be given up because the vocabulary was too difficult. In another, the Sherlock Holmes stories proved unteachable because the habits and manners and occasional formality of speech bewildered the young people into rebelling against so difficult an assignment. One feels like exclaiming "Shades of *Julius Caesar!*"—I mean Shakespeare's play, which, forty years ago, used to be taught in the American high school to immigrants' children—and without causing riots.

Clearly, we are not forming readers. And outside the school, the writing we encounter does nothing to sustain our adult powers of reading, either. On the one hand, the greater part of what comes under our eyes from journalism, business, government, and cultural institutions is couched in jargon. It appeals neither to the mind, nor the ear, nor the concrete imagination, but solely to the reflex recognition of ready-made phrases. What we catch is not precise meanings, but general drift—and that is the very opposite of reading in the constructive sense.

And on the other hand, when we deliberately turn to what is offered us as literature, in novels, poems, or plays, what we find is largely a reproduction of our daily speech heightened for emotional or social significance. The tone ranges from gutter talk to the language of the commuter, and its handling often shows a special, limited sort of art. But as a material, a verbal substance, the literature of our day is not one that can expand the literary consciousness; it is indeed antiliterary and strives purposely to destroy the notion of literature, of reading. You are not supposed to be engrossed in a book but in an experience—and in one that duplicates your reality or your fantasy. Here someone may say, what about Nabokov? Wasn't he literary in the old way? True, he made great play with literary expressions, but except when he was fooling or parodying he produced—in my view—the worst possible sort of English prose. He did not handle it like a native, and it is a mass of affectations; it suggests the bad spots one finds in Conrad.

This exception of Nabokov's only sharpens the point I am making about our shrinking conception of the art of reading. Reading has all the prevailing forces of culture against it. Young and old are deterred in one way or another from exercising that freedom of choice and pursuit of pleasure one had thought guaranteed by the Declaration of Independence. The public offering of readable matter is automatically regimented by our tendency to act en masse, not burning books, perhaps, but burying them; not suppressing the word but, in and out of school, limiting the vocabulary; not controlling publication but turning our ideas over to machines and pictograms.

IV.
Technology and the Future of the Book

12. The Computer and the Book

Charles A. Goodrum and Helen Dalrymple

This chapter is part of the study commissioned for the Book in the Future project. The authors summarize the views of the project advisors on the known and anticipated effects of computers on the creation of books, the process of writing, the book industry, librarianship, and reading.

We have new information carriers and channels with which to package content and through which to distribute it. If we don't use them, others will.

—Paul Rispa,
of the Spanish publisher Salvat Editores,
addressing a convention of
international book publishers in Mexico City

The secret of the publishing world surviving—even exploiting—the electronic revolution is to be sure we're providing the word product in the format the user finds most convenient, not what's most convenient to us. That means providing some things in huge, fancy art books and others on floppy disks, while other material waits to be put into the users' own computers where they can work with it. We've got to listen to them, or we're dead. The CompuServes of the world will leave us bankrupt in five years.

—Phyllis Steckler,
President of Oryx Press

J ust what is it that the computer is supposed to do to—or for—the book? We will try to report in this chapter what we learned during the Book in the Future project about how computers are now involved in the creation, manufacture, and distribution of books; some of the ways in which it has been suggested that the electronic revolution may further change the world of books, to the point of discovering substitutes for the book as we have it physically today; the ways in which such changes will affect both reading and writing; some worries raised both by the current impact of the computer and also by the futurists' visions; and, finally, some ways in which computers may allow for very new art forms.

The Computer and the Creation of the Book

The computer can move words with great speed and accuracy straight from the author's fingers through the creative process to the cased book packed in an addressed carton. The author creates the text on a digital word processor, permitting him to work anywhere he likes; the words are sent back and forth between author and editor over a wire quickly and efficiently, speeding up the creation of the agreed-upon text. The text goes to the printer in digital form, is typeset digitally still using the original keystrokes done by the author himself, and it is printed by digitally run presses. The ease of production permits smaller but more frequent press runs, with less waste. The computerized inventory records permit more frequent catalogs to buyers, faster and more efficient ordering and billing.

Every one of the above elements is already in common use. Some interesting aspects of them:

Word Processors

The publishers with whom we talked say that two-thirds of their present manuscripts have been prepared by the authors on word processors. In 1983 most of these arrived on paper, printed by the authors on their own letter-quality (the printout looked like traditional typewriter text) digital printers. The publishers' editors do not like to work with dot matrix print ("you can't tell the difference between full colons and semicolons, and the commas aren't clear"), but increasingly the manuscripts are coming with the original floppy disks attached, and the publishers are accepting them and putting them on their own cathode ray tube screens for editing. They say they would prefer not to edit digitally, but are accepting the task in order to get the digitized text which they do prefer to use in typesetting. (It saves them from having to retype and reproofread the edited manuscript.) There is still no single, generally accepted word processing program as standard, so some authors send a copy of their own word processing program along with their floppy disk manuscripts. Interestingly, the publishers who said they are routinely accepting manuscripts on floppy disks are now abandoning them—for modems which send the text back and forth between author and editor via telephone lines.

Several of the futurists we interviewed noted that we are underestimating the impact of the word processor on the way our authors will write and think in the future. They point out first that it is not commonly recognized how many individuals are using word processors right now. Almost all of the big city newspapers are totally digitized, the copy being created by the reporter and then passed through editors to the typesetters without ever having appeared on paper. Government reports are increasingly prepared directly on the screen; almost two-thirds of all doctoral dissertations and over half of undergraduate course reports at our colleges and universities are now done on word processors. The result is that in the space of less than four years, hundreds of thousands of the people using printed words are either creating them or working with them on cathode ray tubes. The International Data Corporation estimates that in 1984 there is a digital keyboard for one out of every three white-collar workers in the United States; by 1987 this will be a ratio of one to one.

Lewis Branscomb of IBM thinks that word processors will sharpen or focus the way we write. He notes that traditionally an author decided that he had something to say—a new idea, a different concept, something he wanted to emphasize and share with a reader. He then sat down to write it serially. He rarely wrote down what was important to him first, but backed up and (1) tried to capture the reader's attention with an interesting lead, then (2) told the reader about what was known to date, who was involved, and what information he needed to understand the important part coming up, and then at last (3) the author wrote the part that had generated the idea for the piece in the first place.

With the word processor, most people write the important part immediately while it is crisp and sharp in their minds. They then begin to add parts of background or elaboration as they occur to the author, putting them into the text wherever convention requires, but the parts are actually generated in the way the author's mind moves forward and backward. Branscomb thinks that this increased logic and sharpened emphasis is so apparent that a reader can actually tell which text has been prepared on a word processor.

Curt Suplee did a startling survey of professional writers and found they fell into three clusters depending on how the author's personal creative style was comfortable with the speed and flexibility of the word processing device.[1] Among those who enthusiastically embrace the word processor are biographer Jane Howard, author of *Margaret Mead: A Life,* who said, "I used to type the same material over and over. Until I loved one page I couldn't go on to the next, now ..."; James Fallows of *The Atlantic,* who said, "It's easier to keep the train of thoughts and rhythm in mind"; President Jimmy Carter; Michael Crichton; John D. MacDonald; Stephen King; Ansel Adams; and Douglas Hofstadter.

According to Suplee, a second group still does their first draft on a traditional typewriter and then retypes it into their word processor for editing. These include Dick Francis; John Updike, who says, "Upright on a green screen, the words look quite different from the way they do flat on a piece of paper"; and Isaac Asimov, who comments, "The result is a cleaner copy, by far, and a greater willingness on my part to revise, because it's so easy."

Suplee, who himself is a strong advocate of the word processor, candidly reports that Kurt Vonnegut, Bernard Malamud, and George Will refuse to embrace the electronic shortcut. Suplee quotes Will as saying, "I write in longhand, with a fountain pen, of course. I do so not as a political statement—although a Tory could hardly do otherwise—but because writing should be a tactile pleasure."

The author Ernest Mau notes, "From an author's point of view, what I'm finding is that there's greater freedom to practice creativity as a result of using the word processor. ... A lot of writers, when they're getting down to due dates, begin to look at changes [they want to make]. But they're reluctant to look at them because of the amount of retyping required. With a word processor, it's only a matter of a few minutes or hours to change a whole manuscript."

Arielle Emmett of Hayden Publications says the word processor "makes it easier for the writer to do the hardest part of writing: getting the words right, revising, shaping the manuscript's entire form." Daniel Boorstin and Jacques Barzun firmly disagree, maintaining that with a word processor the author tends to write too fast without thinking; the mere slowness of the traditional typewriter and pencil forces writers to think ahead of their hands. Boorstin also likes to work from a single manuscript on which he makes endless changes; he likes to be able to see what stages the text passed through on the way to its final form and likes the idea of later scholars being able to see how his mind worked on the passages.

Interfacing and Digital Typesetting

The technique of using the author's own typing to "set the type," that is, drive the machine that makes the copy that will be reproduced in the photographic and mechanical printing process, is spreading quickly into routine practice. Such large presses as John Wiley and Prentice-Hall embraced it early, and at the present small university presses are finding it a great shortcut. Gerald Phillips of Pennsylvania State University says, "By some estimates, the amount of time saved by online linking of writer, editor, publisher, and typesetter is as high as 50 percent." Kent State University Press says that, in its typical runs of 1,500 or 2,000 copies, typesetting costs have been cut by half, and this ends up reducing total manufacturing costs by 25 percent.

In the long run, the opportunity to set type by using the author's own floppy disks may have the greatest impact in its application to the small, private publisher with only half a dozen titles to his list, or even to the author who publishes his own works. Michael Wiese in Westport, Connecticut, typed his own books and sent the word processing disks to a nearby printer who slipped them into its interfacing machine. The digital interfacer automatically separated the words into pre-designed pages, made the plates, and printed them in Times Roman typeface. The result was two books (now in their fourth editions) that gave the appearance of traditional publishing house format at a fraction of traditional costs.

If all the digital manufacturing is such a good idea, why isn't everyone doing it? We asked this question of a number of people and got a spectrum of answers which fell between the two following ones. One publisher of one of the nation's largest university presses pointed through his window to a building across the alley and said, "You see that press running over there? We bought that twelve years ago. It will be paid off in three more years. When that happens, we'll see what our competition is using. Until then, there's no sense of wasting time thinking about it." The other extreme was Richard Robinson of Scholastic, Inc., who is so convinced that "the computer will be a major force in the home and the school, [that] we've reshaped the company to respond to it." Scholastic has shifted so many resources into digitizing their production that *Business Week* reports it will take a $6 million loss for the year 1984 (on sales of $155 million), but Robinson says he wants his company to be at the head of the technological shift, not following it.

Bookkeeping, Marketing, and Inventories

It is obvious that the computer has made the housekeeping of the publishing industry far faster and more accurate. The chains like B. Dalton and the Book-of-the-Month Club can tell within twenty-four hours how many copies have been sold of any book in their stock; they can tell where, geographically, these copies have sold, how many copies are left in the warehouse, and what is the trend of the sales. The computer permits analysis of mailing lists to identify who is buying garden books, who would be interested in a new volume on doll houses, and who bought the previous Michener novel.

Similarly, computerized records have permitted the faster payment of bills, thus cutting down on the "float" in the business. Osborne in California has promised to put his monthly sales into the computer and pay authors royalties monthly instead of after the traditional nine- to twelve-month delay. All of these steps have introduced a precision to the dollars and cents of the publishing trade not previously known.

Theoretically, then, the computer should either have cut the costs of books or, at least by now, have retarded the increases. We saw very little evidence of this. When we asked a university press publisher how many copies of a typical volume he sold, he answered, "Between 1,500 and 4,000." The average prices of his volumes were in excess of $50. We asked whether if he sold more copies through commercial outlets or distribution channels, it wouldn't cut the cost of the individual volumes and make them available to more people? He answered, "Well, we're really getting to the people we want to read our product. We're not writing for the kind of people who go into bookstores."

When we asked a large commercial publisher if he didn't think his books were priced beyond the "ordinary" reader's budget, he replied, "To cut the jacket price of our volumes, we'd have to increase the numbers sold and reduce the unit costs. This isn't realistic unless we see we've got a real blockbuster on our hands. Otherwise, more copies pushed simply push out our own titles in bookstores. Remember, bookselling is really a zero-base game. There are so many books being published and bookstores really can handle such a limited number that if you push too many titles in, you're just shoving other titles out, and you have no way of being sure you're not shoving yourself out the door: one of your own titles has kept the owner from stocking three more of your own list. Remember, very few book buyers buy by the publisher like you'd stick with GM or Del Monte. You don't say I like Random House books or Doubleday, so you're constantly competing against yourself. We try to stick with a price across the board, and not try to sell more of any single title than the norm, unless it's clearly going to be a best-seller."

Databases, Bulletin Boards, and the Home Computer
Here is an intriguing thought from Gordon Graham, the chairman and chief executive officer of Butterworth and Company, London:

> The user is changing his habits. He is going to the shop next door. We see it in the escalating purchases of home computers and videocassettes....A database user can search for the information he needs electronically and be his own librarian. When he locates on the screen what he is seeking, he can punch a printout button and be his own publisher. Is this going to leave publishers and librarians "bare-arsed on the barren rock of truth" —Robert Burns's phrase for that blend of insecurity and discomfort so equal that each almost cancels the other?

> The electronic mode will force a clearer distinction between information and knowledge....The computer is concerned primarily with information, so far; that is to say the speedy delivery of commercially useful facts—cases to lawyers, exchange rates to bankers, share prices to brokers, timetables to travel agents, or bibliographic data to publishers and librarians. Having obtained such information, the user uses it. No pondering is required. Information is instant. Knowledge in contrast, demands deliberation and digestion for which the screen is unwilling to wait.[2]

"Electronic publishing" began with the newspaper files and the statutory codes series. Efficiency experts looked at the enormous clipping collection at the *New York Times* and decreed that the company must put it into the computer for easier, faster access and smaller storage space. Everybody looked at the federal code and the states' laws and recognized that they were constantly changing, endlessly updated, and prime candidates for computerized searches. From these early computerizations came the LEXIS-NEXISs, New York Times InfoBanks, and the Lockheed Dialogs of the world. They have become increasingly popular and moderately profitable and clearly are the way of the future for the storage and manipulation of data. (By the close of 1981 there were 1,208 ongoing database services, with over 200 million records and 199,145 paying customers.) But subscription databases have not had a major influence on the book since most of what they contain is also printed on paper and sold somewhere within the traditional publishing scene. Their greatest impact has been on the mindset, the mental approach to the printed word that they are teaching the younger users.

In our own household, the question arises: How large is the Los Angeles metropolitan area now? The father goes to his study to consult the *World Almanac,* and the son goes to his room to call up CompuServe on his computer screen. Each gets the answer in approximately the same time, but the son is surprised. It never occurred to him that something like that "might be in a book." It was a statistic, it had to be updated regularly; he thought it would only be in a computer. Each year there are more citizens like the son, fewer like the father.

Soon after the subscription databases became routine, the professional journals faced up to the computer, and here the effect on print was immediate and real. The scholarly magazines are dedicated to reporting all ongoing and completed research in their professional fields, but they are acutely aware that no one reads their publications from cover to cover when they appear. Their subscribers go back to them when a research project requires a review of knowledge and experience for the sake of new action. The American Chemical Society in America and Elsevier scientific publishers abroad began by offering their journals in three ways: (1) you could subscribe to one just like you would *Time* or *Newsweek* and get it through the mail; (2) you could subscribe to monthly or quarterly tables of contents and request just those articles you wanted to read on paper by filling out a printed order form; or (3) you could sign up for telephone access to their computerized memory banks and call up the journal on your personal computer. With the last, you then either read the piece you wanted on your CRT or printed it out on your personal printer.

Astonishingly, all three options worked, all were embraced, and all are presently expanding. The last, telephone-CRT, is working so well that the chemical society is planning to restrict some of its most specialized journals to database publishing alone—they will never appear as items printed on paper and bound. Among the many problems electronic publishing poses is what universities should do about their libraries if the material *never* arrives on paper? The University of Pittsburgh did a two-year study on journal use and found that only 2 percent of the articles in its engineering journals had been used in the past twenty years, but that no one had ever been able to guess ahead of time which ones would be in that 2 percent.

Jay Lucker, Director of Libraries at MIT, described to us the mind-boggling combination of options that he must resolve very quickly. For some examples, Does he buy print copies, bind them, and store them so he will have "complete sets" of the basic electrical, chemical, and physics journals—and then find that everyone on campus is using the computer approach since it is more flexibly indexed, and it is faster to do a literature search? Who pays for the printed paper subscription? The database subscription? The printouts and the telephone time? Are the decisions made for the standard professional journals the same decisions if the journal is published by or at MIT? What if you commit your library to database subscriptions (faster and more convenient to your users, enormously cheaper on space costs), and the journal then goes out of business, taking its computer memory with it? In the old days you still had the bound volumes on your own shelves; now...?

From the point of view of the book, the greatest impact of the database is the same as that of the legal and factual services: they are training generations of students to think in terms of words and numbers being available faster, more conveniently, and even more accurately on computer screens; they are subtly implying that printed books are more likely to be out of date, more clumsily indexed, harder to use, and even more biased than the digital. The digital data is believed to be "public, institutional, carefully checked"; a book over a single author's name is perceived as containing his personal views and data, limited, possibly already superseded, and maybe unverified.

Which brings us to the most threatening device of all, but the one still little captured in the public's attention: the computerized "bulletin boards." These are a phenomenon now primarily located on college campuses, centered within a particular professional group (for example, political scientists, doctors, engineers) or within particular computer or mainframe communities (Commodore users, people tied to a regional network or communications system).

A computer bulletin board is a block of memory in a central computer onto which anyone connected can "hang" text. In universities these boards are increasingly being used by the faculty to ask questions of other members of the staff ("Does anyone know the answer to...?") or to test theses ("I believe so-and-so; can anybody out there refute it?"). It has proved to be especially effective operating across professional disciplines, as when a pollster says he has discovered x; a psychologist, an anthropologist, and a historian tell him why his data is at variance with what their disciplines have revealed. A doctor describes unusual symptoms and asks colleagues on a medical school faculty if anyone has encountered a similar situation. Professors routinely post instructions on the boards announcing class assignments and schedule changes. Students ask questions of the professors via the boards, and the professor's reply to the querying student either can be hung so that all the members of the class can see the answer or can be made private so only the inquirer can read it.

More closely affecting the book is the growing practice among authors, poets, and satirists of hanging their short stories and poetry on the boards for responses and attention. Most of the major universities now have ongoing adventure novels growing on their university bulletin boards, some of them dozens of chapters long. They begin in the manner of the Tolkein saga; anyone on campus can add a chapter, which in turn is built upon by the next author. At some schools, wide segments of the student body wait eagerly for certain authors to make their next contributions because of their humor, their imagery, or their innovative plotting.

In all the above instances, we are educating a growing generation which expects to communicate via computer screens or printers. The computerized professional journals are now offering basic books along with their digital magazines, and "readers" can bring up single chapters and print them out much more quickly and cheaply than they can buy the complete, bound volume. Bulletin board users are "publishing"—making reputations, acquiring audiences—on their local screens. Already computer companies are offering space on their national services for innovative and popular text, promising to split the revenue with the author in the same way that Source and Dow-Jones now make profits from text in their memories. The traditional "I wonder if I can get anybody to publish my idea" is changing to "I wonder which bulletin board I should hang this on."

Videocassettes, Videodisks, and Floppy Disks
There is a form of digital publishing with which we are all familiar but which we seldom recognize as being the thin of a wedge: the futurists believe that in the long run, the greatest impact on the book will come from videocassettes, videodisks, and floppy disks.

The most popular non-movie videocassettes are presently Jane Fonda's exercise lessons and Dr. Spock's videocast baby book. The satirists have enjoyed the image of a parent holding a baby up to the television screen to see if her spots look like measles or more like chicken pox, but this is precisely what is occurring, and it is only the first of many instruction tapes entering the market. How-to books. How to paint with oils; how to fish for bass; what to do about dying house plants. In each case the traditional words of the traditional how-to books are there, but they are accompanied by motion pictures. When these first appeared the tapes were selling for $59.95 and the books for $12.95, but the videocassettes have dropped to $24.95 and the books have risen to $24.95, and the confrontation has begun.

The futurists believe that the primary role of the videocassette (and its accompanying videocassette recorder) will be to introduce the ordinary consumer to the videodisk of the future. No matter where we turned, we were told that the videodisk "is the way it's going to go." This seemed particularly strange since during the Book in the Future study the sales of the RCA videodisk player were going down and down, and by the end of the interviews the product had been taken off the market. The point, we were told, is that the RCA videodisk was not a genuine example of the technology of the future. The RCA machine could "only" play motion picture frames, and it could only play them serially.

The "true" videodisk player of the future will have every frame numbered, and frames can either be displayed one at a time like the pages of the book or run end to end like a motion picture. The player will be computer-controlled so that it can skip from one colored page to another in any sequence. It will use stereo sound: the stereo sound can be used jointly by two speakers, or the author can put a popularized text on one channel (for a tour of an art museum, for example) and a sophisticated text comprehensible only to curators and specialists on the other, with the reader choosing which channel he wishes to listen to. The videodisk will permit the user to "zoom in" on the picture, taking a space one inch square and enlarging it, up to the full size of the screen, which is said to be of help in following how-to instructions, in examining technique in reproductions of art masterpieces, and in using maps and atlases. When applied to courseware (see below), the videodisk will be tied to the computer's ability to provide text tailored to the student: if the student gives the right answer, the book moves forward down one path; if he gives the wrong answer, the book moves to restate past material in a different way with different pictures in order to try to explain what the student apparently has not grasped. Examples of every kind of videodisk application mentioned have already been demonstrated, and many of them are in routine use. Such machines will be commonly available in our stereo and TV shops by the time of the next presidential election.

Brian Aveney, of Blackwell North America, thinks that the videodisk will make the how-to book the first printed genre "to go the way of the buffalo." He points out that such skills as cooking, auto repair, sports, and crafts are ideally suited to the videodisk's ability to freeze frame, proceed at slow motion, repeat sequences, or jump directly to a particular point. Harry Gray, of United Technologies, described the great success their helicopter division had had in using the videodisk to explain repair techniques to unskilled military men in the field, as well as training the pilots themselves.

The home computer, now blanketing the same portion of the population that has traditionally been the reading segment, is making the floppy disk a matter of routine. The Book-of-the-Month Club is including floppy disks in its catalogs. McGraw-Hill offered one as an optional study aid to its traditional sociology text; to the company's astonishment it sold 10,000 copies at $14.95 on its first try. Wiley is moving its engineering and pharmaceutical data onto floppy disks and slipping them into the backs of its (therefore) much smaller annual handbooks. Houghton-Mifflin's *American Heritage Dictionary* and *Roget's Thesaurus* can be purchased on floppy disks to be used as parts of word processing programs. (An interesting footnote: Houghton-Mifflin and John Wiley and Sons, among the earliest and most vigorous of the publishers experimenting with digital publishing, are also two of the oldest publishers in the United States, having been in active business for 104 and 176 years, respectively.)

The floppy disk appears to have proven itself as a device for publishing frequently updated material; statistical material difficult to set, proof, and print; and data closely tied to desktop work, such as writing, drafting, calculations, and the like. The disk's impact on the book is both obvious and major: for this type of publishing, the digital format is simply faster, cheaper, easier to ship, and in general better for the purpose of the kind of text it contains.

Courseware

We close this listing of the various ways the computer is entering the world of the book by noting its intrusion into the textbook field. The application of technology to education has accumulated more than its share of false prophets. In very rapid succession, we have been told that microforms, filmstrips, classroom motion pictures, tape recorded lectures, and closed circuit television were going to revolutionize instruction. Each one has proved successful, but, in each case, only in a splinter, a fraction of the shimmering universe that had been promised.

When computerized educational materials arrived ("courseware"), its proponents were refreshingly restrained in their promises, but to everyone's surprise the applications have actually worked. For example, computerized reading programs for adult immigrants and older ghetto teenagers have been the most successful of any literacy programs yet tried with these age groups. Another example is the use of interactive personal computers to teach children who have been deaf from birth. Reading achievement improved greatly during the first nine months the software was used in the Pennsylvania School for the Deaf. Traditionally, sixteen-year-old deaf students read no better than nine-year-olds who can hear; new videodisks and software created by the California School for the Deaf in Riverside are closing this gap with astonishing speed.[3] The successes have been equally dramatic with children who have never spoken, with hands too uncontrolled to write; in each area the chance to touch symbols on the screen has opened a whole new world of communication.

Computers are appearing in increasing numbers in elementary school classrooms, but the educators are using this innovation as a support device, being careful not to claim it will replace the teacher (as so much audiovisual material was sold in the past). Such companies as Scholastic, Inc.; McGraw-Hill; Scott, Foresman; and Houghton-Mifflin are selling hundreds of electronic courseware diskettes, carefully designed for different grade levels, but even more carefully tied to traditional textbooks and traditional lesson plans.

The computer-tied material appears to be most effective in building information and conducting instructional drill. The computer asks questions, and the student responds. If the answers are right, the computer provides new material and then queries about it. If the answers are wrong, the computer backs up and tells the old information in a different way and asks different questions. Thus the repetition and the speed of information are tailored to the individual student.

These same advantages have appeared in military applications where computer courseware has been used with first-year military recruits. As the *Washington Post* noted, "The enormous advantage of this kind of training is that it can adjust automatically to the skill level and learning speed of each individual student, check progress automatically, and eliminate the need for expensive training machinery. Moreover the technique ensures a uniform product —each student who completes a course has mastered the same material."[4]

When McGraw-Hill moves into a school with its courseware, it starts with a series of teacher's aids: computerized records of past tests and grades and automatic programs that highlight problem areas and student learning problems. With its "Interacting Authoring System," it helps a teacher create a computerized program which will use the same material she would traditionally have distributed in worksheets or personally duplicated spot tests. The computerized programs then become richer as both the teacher and the student become more familiar with the process, at a pace comfortable to the teacher.

Most computer-specialized educators think we are now in a very short learning period which will end with three major developments. First, the present rush to provide "computer literacy" will evaporate as the programs become self-running ("you don't teach high schoolers the principles of the internal combustion engine just to get them to drive a car"). Second, the floppy disk programs now being used will disappear as soon as the interactive videodisk arrives, bringing with it the advantages of cheaper manufacture, more information per disk, faster random access, and, especially, interactivity, which gives you things like music, maps, and motion pictures, all embedded in the written text and displayed either at the author's discretion or the student's. Finally, the computer will move toward extending students' intellectual power, emphasizing how a student thinks and how he makes new connections and relates with the computer, so that it becomes an extension of his own mind and fingers, not a drill instructor asking pre-set questions.

Electronic Bulletin Boards, a New Way of Publishing
There is one aspect of the computer and the textbook which seems to have received a minimal amount of attention, yet seemed to us to have an enormous potential for changing traditional publishing. We saw it first on university campuses.

Increasingly, universities are either themselves providing personal computers in each dormitory room or expecting the students to bring them to campus. The usual applications of the devices are access to the central library catalogs and word processing, but we saw evidence of a growing use of the screens as an extension of the traditional "reserved book" assignment, in which a professor assigns a single chapter in a non-textbook volume and expects the students to visit a reserved book collection to read it. In schools with dormitory computers, we found the professors putting the assigned chapters into a central computer's memory and the students calling them up to be read in their dormitory rooms. Although we did not see it ourselves, we were told that the same thing is being done in high schools and elementary schools where a teacher has copied (typed) material from a book or short story onto a disk, so that the class reads it on computer screens, not from the traditional photocopied sheets.

Obviously this practice has a potential that is terrifying to the printing industry. The step from a single chapter to a whole book is a small one. Optical scanners are increasingly common, but most publishers have the text in digital form left over from their editorial activities, anyway. With textbooks, particularly at the college level, becoming distressingly expensive, if text were to be purchased by the university, it could put the text on its electronic bulletin boards to be accessed by the class. Most of the text could be read on students' personal screens, but if they wanted the material on paper, cheap personal printers, which will appear on the market soon, can produce 60 pages or more a minute.

The Electronic Book of the Very Near Future

The above recitation may be so dramatic as to reveal a threat to the book, or at least to the book as we have known it in our own lifetimes. We should not let ourselves be distracted by the possibilities of different formats: the book is the words, the thoughts, and facts the author is trying to communicate, and it is clear that the potential for the book's good health has never been better. The sum of the above changes in the way the book is made available to the reader adds up to the facts that it will be easier for new authors to display their talents, more people will have access to the words than ever before, the length of time between creation and distribution will be shorter, it will be easier for the author to get to his or her particular audience, and it will be easier for the audience to make its needs and interests known to the authors. The words are just as meaningful as ever, only the form of the package by which they are transmitted is changing.

Just what will these packages look like? What will they do? Barbarba Tuchman used the traditional phrase, "You can't take a computer to bed or to the beach," meaning it literally. Of course, you *can* take a computer both places, since the book the specialists are talking about can either be one of the briefcase-sized computer screens that are increasingly seen on people's laps in airplanes or the flat screens seen on designers' work benches. The latter are the size of a *Life* magazine, about three-fourths of an inch thick, with a color screen, definition so sharp you can see the serifs clearly on 10-point type. But their chief charm is that they can carry a 600-page book in their memories, the book pages are white with black letters, and you can choose whatever size of type you want. The young people use 10 or 12 point, the middle-aged use 12 or 14, and the vision-impaired can magnify the text to the point where a single word fills the entire screen. Knowing what the coming machines will be like makes considerable difference to our ability to guess with accuracy what will be done with them. Let's describe a few that were either shown or described to us during our interviews.

Cathode Ray Tube and Liquid Crystal Screens
We can start with the TV screens that will be coming on the market very soon. We all know that a present-day 19-inch color television set is sharper than the same one was only five years ago. We also know that a 9-inch TV is even sharper than the 19-inch, but you have to sit closer to get the benefit. The same is true of "monitors," the TV screens tied to computers. The original Apples and Commodores were legible, but the letters were blockish and you certainly couldn't sweep-read them as you would a book page. More recent monitors, like the IBM or the Amdeks, are much sharper. The letters look like typewriter characters, with serifs, high resolution, and crisp appearance. Very soon the screens will be as sharp as a good magazine page.

A home television set has 525 lines of resolution; the new screens from Sony and its fellow companies have 1,100 lines, and the improvement is far more than doubled. Color pictures look like magazine pictures, and print looks like type. The Sony, for example, handles 10-point type as sharply as a newspaper page.

The CrystalVision screens are barely an inch thick and their type appears in liquid crystal in a form that is a modern day extension of the early technique used in digital watches. Nowadays you can read white letters on black or black on white or have the "page" in dark green or soothing amber.

Where will the letters come from? We saw models using all sorts of storage devices. You can get a complete novel on a piece of plastic the size of a credit card which is slipped into the side of the digital page. This "Drexon Card" is laser formed, with the digital record either in pits drilled into the plastic or bubbles raised in the surface; it holds 160,000 words. Or the words can go into a silicon chip that can be screwed into the back of the flat screen. Or, if you can tolerate briefcase thickness, the text can simply be on a small, floppy disk the size of a mason jar lid slipped in a slot in the front—

here the words are magnetic charges on plastic.

Note the immediate effect of the change of the monitor screen and the computer. The Book-of-the-Month Club can send its volumes around in envelopes instead of the complicated cardboard packages it now uses; disks, chips, and plastic cards all offer cheaper postage and suffer less damage in transit. If the television screen is so sharp that it can show book print, the cable television companies can offer the best-seller of the week via a simple pager tied to the selector dial. Cable companies can also offer how-to books, probably in response to a telephone call to the local TV station.

And just to confuse things, the new Sony Mavica snapshot camera paints pictures, not with dyes or silver salts like a traditional photograph, but with digital charges like the magnetic records on a tape cassette. It was invented as a photographic device —you point the camera at the Washington Monument, it records it digitally, and when you get home you show it on your television set. But the specialists are intrigued with the thought that you can take similar pictures of book pages, put them on the plastic card, and, when you get home, read them either from your television set or from a special table-top screen. Obviously we are back to the digital page, this time by way of your home snapshot camera rather than your home computer. In all of the above instances, the present book page ends up on a screen.[5]

Printers and Paper

The screen is probably acceptable when we are dealing with facts and information; it is probably not acceptable for recreational reading, for material on which we wish to reflect, or for text we wish to change. This will require print on paper. When we try to think what the book will be like tomorrow, we must force ourselves to realize that printing on paper, at home, and on demand will be much faster and cheaper than anything we have known to date.

We first had to adjust to the fact that IBM's spinning ball typed much faster than individual keys hitting a platen when the Selectric displaced the trusty Woodstock. Next came the dot matrix printers the Japanese tied to our home computers. While the Selectric could comfortably produce 325 characters a minute, the Epson dot matrix gave us 4,800 characters a minute on a machine that cost barely half as much. The next generation of home printers will produce 120,000 characters a minute on an even cheaper machine. That is a page a second, 60 pages a minute, a 360-page novel in six minutes. These machines are already in existence, and, depending on which patents the parent companies own, will produce their product either by chisel head printers or laser ink jets. The common dot matrix printer now creates a letter by hitting the ribbon with eight tiny chisels; the next step is a single head that runs completely across the page so that 640 chisels slam out the complete line. The ink jets are even faster since they don't have to wait for the head to move in and out, but paint the characters from flying pin points in a tube.

Strangely enough, these incredibly fast machines are not very expensive. Most futurists think they will be cheap enough that the book clubs and videotext newspapers can afford to "give one free" with each subscription, while realizing savings on distribution by mailmen or newspaper carriers.

We heard applications of these inexpensive, high speed printers coming from a variety of sources. Robert Badger, editor at John Wiley, said, "The future of the book is largely entwined with laser print technology and its ability to supply quality reproductions of the printed word and graphics. People will not want to read only from screens, so the printed word will still be with us." He believes that within ten to fifteen years most journals will be on-demand, printed out only in the home or office. Elie A. Shneour's "book of the future" (Shneour is director of the Bio Systems Research Institute) pictures a cable or telephone system in which blank books are supplied to every subscriber and placed in a "black box" on top of the television set. By punching a code into a keypad, the user can request any available book to be printed by laser printer onto the blank book. The book slides out of its slot "after a few minutes... now filled with beautifully typographed text and illustrations, some in color."[6] Ithiel de Sola Pool of M.I.T. refers to such products as "editions of one."

Fred Croxton of the Library of Congress, Pool, and Tom Surprenant of Library High Technology all expressed concern about the effect of the on-demand book on libraries. All three expressed the belief that this innovation will come in the working lifetime of present library administrators and should be anticipated by present supervisors. Kenneth Dowlin of the Pikes Peak Library District thinks that home, on-demand printing holds the greatest threat/challenge to American booksellers and American libraries of all the electronic points of impact. Harry Gray of United Technologies believes that digital transmission and storage will explode into our ways of keeping and delivering words, but warns that the resulting on-demand printing will "double, treble the amount of paper that we now produce." He thinks that we will continue to read the important words on paper—but we will throw the paper away when we've finished that day's use of it, knowing we can always get it back quickly from the computer when we need it. Filing cabinets and shelves and libraries as we know them will be a thing of the past.

Books Built into the Computer Itself
When the *American Heritage* and *Random House* dictionaries were first offered as floppy disks, they were add-ons, separate miniprograms for slipping into the home computer. In just three years'

166

time, however, they have become a part of word processing programs and now are included in the computer's permanent memory when it is purchased—they are used as spelling checkers. As the user types into the computer, the memory automatically checks each word against the dictionary, and if the dictionary does not find a spelling that matches, it flashes the word on the screen until the writer either corrects it or passes the signal that that is the way he wants it. Originally intended as a device to help the author with spelling problems, they have become a device for proof reading. The programs can scan a thousand words in seconds and pick up mis-keys and transpositions as the text develops. Over 100,000 of these spelling checkers were sold in 1982, and by 1985 the figure is expected to have exceeded half a million.

Similar computerization of basic reference books has already started: thesauri, almanacs, and one-volume encyclopedias have all been included as part of the computer's built-in programs so that the writer can consult them without leaving the keyboard. Increasingly these reference books are being included "free" with the purchase of the computer, as companies attempt to get ahead of the competition in a field where most of the machines do about the same thing for the same price. Andrew Rosenheim believes that "by 1990, if not sooner, sales of electronic dictionaries will exceed sales of printed ones." As built-in memory becomes larger and larger in steady annual increases, one need not be a visionary to foresee a complete reference shelf of basic information as a standard inclusion in all computers capable of word processing.

The Optical Disk

Most of what we have discussed thus far related to the creation and distribution of the word. The preservation of the word beyond its immediate use is another area of potentially great change. The word printed on rag paper (common up to the 1860s) is holding up reasonably well. But wood pulp paper bearing print (since 1860) is in terrible shape. Major libraries are near the point of despair with the way their collections are turning, literally, to dust on their shelves. Between four and five million volumes in the Library of Congress collections have already reached a state of severe deterioration.

About fifty years ago, the libraries decided that the answer to the preservation problem was microform, whether microfilm, microcards, or microfiche—miniaturization on "chemically stable" plastic film. Since that time, most newspapers and magazines have been so preserved, and many documents and archival materials. The idea was a great success until librarians and archivists, to their horror, discovered that after thirty to forty years, microfilm begins to deteriorate. Now the libraries' reels of microfilm are crystallizing, the emulsion is separating from the base, and the impressions are being lost. Once this was discovered, the preservationists began remicrofilming, making new pictures of the old microfilms on new emulsion and new film. This has proved to be quite unsatisfactory. It has been discovered that when the first microfilms were made, the photographic process degraded the image of the letters by about 20 percent. Refilming them degrades it another 20 percent, to the extent of closing up e's, a's, and o's, filling in serifs, making manuscripts almost illegible, and, in general, defeating the purpose of the project. From the preservationists' point of view, the problem is the failure of support material, not the print itself: paper rots away, now film is splitting and falling apart.

The preservationists are trying two paths. The first is to deacidify paper so it does not deteriorate. They are now able to do this by "fumigating" books in huge vaults filled with diethyl zinc gas. The problem is that even when done in quantities of thousands of books at a time, the process costs between four and five dollars per volume. Afterwards the books must be housed in air-conditioned space forever.

The other solution is the digital way. This involves either going back up the printing chain and capturing the digital text that drove the photocomposition machines or taking a picture of the complete printed page, map, manuscript, or photograph and capturing the digital data which would traditionally be used to produce wirephotos, television pictures, or, for example, *USA Today*. Once the preservationists get the words or pictures in digital form they must then discover how to save these signals forever. Putting them on floppy disks or tapes or disks for mainframe computers is not the answer, since these develop reading errors over the years as magnetic charges fade. But putting digital signals onto optical disks appears to be the exact solution to all kinds of ills. An optical disk can be a sheet of noncorrosive metal, or it can be glass or ceramic. The bits and bytes can be physically preserved as pits are drilled into these materials by laser beam or blisters are created by heat. Preservationists, having been burned before, are pleased by the thought that even if they are wrong again and glass, gold, or silver alloy does change in a hundred years, they can hastily recapture the digital pattern on new materials without the degradation they suffer when *images* are repeatedly transferred in photographic processes.

The book, however, changes as a result of all the effort of preserving it. First, it is incredibly compressed. A single optical disk holding digitized type can preserve 15,000 pages of print. The same disk holding pictures of paintings in full color or reels of motion picture images can hold only one-fifth of this amount of information, yet a hundred-disk carousel can hold the color image of every painting in every museum in the United States.

From this great compression (with no deterioration) comes the other advantage. When such a book is used in a library, dozens of people can be reading it simultaneously. Moreover, no book is ever lost, stolen, or off the shelf, and to all intents and purposes all further library construction can cease. The old cliché that the whole Library of Congress collection can be put in a closet comes to pass.

How will people read from optical disks? Either at CRT monitors or, if they want printed text, from printouts produced on a "Xerox machine"—a copier from which the sheets come out by the page—or on a traditional digital personal printer where text is produced by the line. Where will people read this text? Anywhere you can run a telephone wire. So far as the videodisk-to-screen link is concerned, you can put the disks in the basement and the monitors in the reading room overhead—or you can put the disks in the basement and the monitors on the other side of the continent.

How close is this to reality? It is already here. The Library of Congress has disks filled with 50,000 rare photographs that are now being searched and viewed, and it is putting the text on 70 current magazines on disks so they can be viewed on computer screens.

At the present time 100 disks can be housed in a device that both looks and operates like an old-time jukebox. One of these jukeboxes can hold more than a trillion bits, which is the equivalent of ten thousand pictures or over one hundred thousand books if the text is digitized. Ithiel de Sola Pool notes that at the present time it costs about forty cents per book to get a full-sized, printed volume onto the optical disk but that projections show the cost getting down to between a nickel and a penny per volume within a decade.

Caveats and Concerns

We have looked at the devices which will carry the words of the future. If they fulfill the promises of their inventors, they will bring the author's words to his or her readers more quickly, more cheaply, and more conveniently than ever before. The words are still the point of it all, however, and everyone with whom we spoke had feelings about those words. Some were excited and could hardly wait until the new world was here to open up fascinating new forms of communication. Others were genuinely concerned that we may be opening an electronic Pandora's box which will change the way we think and the way we live together. The following concerns are a mixture of probables and possibles about which no one is sure but, many people think, someone should be brooding.

Education
There are those who believe that introducing the computer into the education process is a ticking time bomb, a potential menace. Barbara Zigli said that "computers separate children from reality and may actually interfere with learning, creativity, and intuition." Arthur Zajonc, a physics professor at Amherst, asked, "Will

the computer subvert or usurp, through its own extraordinary power, those capacities we should be seeking to cultivate in the young? . . . The learning of represented and abstract operations must be based in action, but the computer distances us from action."

John Davy, of Emerson College in England, says computer learning is "impoverished sensually, emotionally, and socially." Robert Sardello, of the Dallas Institute of Humanities and Education, agrees: "The object of computer learning is to remove the child from the actual world and to insert him into his own subjective processes where an imitation world is invented."

The Irony of Storability

F. W. Lancaster, of the University of Illinois, notes that the ability to store something easily keeps it from being used. If he is required to pass a magazine on, he reads it with care; if he can make photocopies he files the copies and never looks at them. Other research has shown that people who do not have video recording machines watch much more television than those who do; people who make VCR tapes rarely look at them once they are sure the shows are properly preserved. Given a choice of bound paper volumes and microforms, users will use the former three or four times more often; even if the paper volumes are discarded, the microform use does not rise. Once it is easy to store everything digitally, will we quit using past knowledge at all?

The Faceless Inputter

Lane Jennings, of the World Future Society, is intrigued with the labor support of the electronic book, especially of the fact and information book. Most books are tied to names of individuals, and even when the book is reporting facts instead of imagination the author gets the rewards of recognition and peer praise from peers for "having written a book." But what if more and more data and facts are simply "in the computer"? Where are we going to find these faceless providers and what will be in it for them? How will they get social rewards presently provided by by-lines and title page attributions?

Electronic Failures

What can we learn from the electronic failures? Here are some examples:

The Kurzweil machine. People working with the blind were overjoyed when Kurzweil perfected his device for reading print aloud. His unit is now very common—most major libraries have one available, and Kurzweil machines can be found in the majority of schools or rehabilitation centers for the handicapped. A blind person using one places a newspaper or a book under an automatic scanner; the machine examines each letter and word electronically and actually pronounces the words aloud in much the manner of the "automatic information operators" of the telephone directory services. It was expected that the machine would free the blind from having to find a sighted reader to help them, with their class assignments if they were students, or even to read a newspaper: the blind could do these things at their own convenience.

But Kurzweil machines have been a great disappointment. They sit gathering dust all over the country. hy? No one is certain, but the commonest explanation offered by both the blind users and the sighted owners is: No one likes the mechanical sound of the talking machine. It lacks warmth, "humanity"; it is so cold and degrading that the patron would rather not know than use one. What does this suggest for future interaction with the computer?

Telephone conferencing. We asked Kurt Cylke, the Director of the National Library for the Blind and Physically Handicapped, about the Kurzweil experience, and in the course of his discussion he pointed out the telephone conferencing situation as possibly being analogous. The ability to link simultaneously several persons or groups together by telephone has been easily available for fifty years; with the new electronic communicators, users no longer need even call an operator to make the link. But telephone conferencing has never caught on. The average person can count on one hand the number of times he has been involved in a telephone conversation involving more than two people.

Even more dramatic is the failure of the combined telephone and television screen. The ability to see the face of the person to whom you are talking has been available since the 1940s, but again, even in communities where the telephone company has promoted to the point of saturation, it has never seemed to be worth the trouble. Cylke asks if we are seeing again something about the human machine that is not satisfied simply with electronic transmittal but yearns for eye contact, "pressing the flesh," or some form of human presence. What does this mean to the theoretically unlimited reliance on the computer screen? Does it mean that all the networking and digital linkage that we hear about may reach their limits much sooner than some suggest?

Facsimile transmission. Verner Clapp, Chief Assistant Librarian of Congress in the 1950s, invested great energy and imagination in devising an improvement over interlibrary loan. Since, it was discovered, most loans sought chapters or even single pages of a work, not the whole book, Clapp decided to offer copies of pages in lieu of loaning original volumes. His pilot study was set up between the Library of Congress and the University of California at Berkeley. Two copiers were tied together by telephone. A scholar in Berkeley could ask his librarian for a book; if the California librarian discovered it was not in the library, he or she would telephone the Library of Congress in Washington, which would get the book from its shelves and place it on a facsimile machine to send a picture of each page requested over the wire. The procedures took only six minutes, but because of the coast-to-coast time difference and the time required for the Library of Congress to find the book, the turnaround time was usually overnight: the request would come in during the Washington afternoon and copies would be sent to California in the California morning. The project ran for six months, and several hundred requests and copies were transmitted. But almost two-thirds of the materials transmitted were never picked up by the requesting student or faculty member. The act of making a request for an interlibrary loan appeared to satisfy whatever the motivation for the request had been. Only one-third of the requesters appeared really to want to read what they had requested. Is there any chance that if we get our own generation's electronic inventions actually working, we may actually terminate whatever reduced research is now taking place?

Preservation for the Sake of Research.
The failure of the interlibrary loan facsimile transmission project raises the question: Should we be cautious about the value of the optical disk project? The digital revolution would seem to be on the way toward solving two of the greatest problems of the librarian and the archivist—finding the space for materials and preserving them against deterioration. It does not address the question, Why are we keeping this information anyway?

Research librarians have long known that once a book has been on their shelves for from two to five years, the chance of its ever being used again is only one in twenty. In a great university or national library, this means that an enormous amount of air-conditioned space is taken up caring for something that may never be touched again. The obvious response, Why don't you go through it and throw out what looks dated? is not as realistic as it sounds. "Looking at"—deciding—is not only risky, it is far more expensive than continuous storing. If you were to give yourself only thirty seconds per book to make the decisions, it would take you seventy-two years to go from one end of the Library of Congress to the other (during which time another 108 million more books would have arrived behind your back).

But why *are* we preserving the book so dutifully? For whom? With whose money? We kept asking people this question, and at the end of a year's interviewing we still had not heard a convincing answer. At one end of a spectrum was Mortimer Adler's reply. He told us that almost any library could be abandoned so long as you kept buying new books, because the important facts and concepts in any professional discipline are carried along by the practitioners and restated in new works. In any block of knowledge, about 90 percent is either superseded, obvious, or worthless; 10 percent is the useful, the important, the gold. The skilled and knowledgeable practitioners will select and keep the 10 percent alive and keep the subject's professionals aware of what is needed to operate. At the other end of the spectrum was Ithiel de Sola Pool (who has written some of the most passionate defenses of preservation in the literature). We asked him, If the Library of Congress burned to the ground tomorrow, what damage would be done and to whom? He laughed and said his own writings on archiving had always worried him. He said he could not think of a single profession that he could convincingly say would suffer, but that "what I'm not sure of is the thought that the *germ of an idea*—a tiny seed buried in all that old stuff—might not stimulate the innovation of today that would save us all."

The Computer and the Way We Think

David Burnham, author of *The Rise of the Computer State,* is concerned that "computers are changing our values—what we think is important—and the very process of thought."[7] Because computers compute, we are leaning ever more toward enshrining answers that are quantitative. He quotes psychologist Abram Maslow's metaphor for such a trend: "When the only tool you have is a hammer, everything begins to look like a nail."[8] Burnham says, "Society requires more than calculation, it requires intuition and wisdom."[9]

Edmund Pellegrino, past-president of Catholic University and currently professor of medicine at Georgetown Medical School, elaborates on this concern in his own field of medicine. He agrees that medicine is going into the computer, that the next generation of doctors will be overwhelmingly computer-oriented. He thinks the digital approach is splendid for diagnosis, drug reaction updates, and new procedures. But he is deeply concerned that it will become the crutch of the average (versus the top) diagnosticians. It is so easy to take the computer's recommendations without challenging them.

Pellegrino resents the path the programmer has followed to reach his conclusion. The programmer keeps it a secret to himself, and the user has no way of knowing what elements he has dropped or factored out. A physician needs values and backgrounds into which to set the computer's instructions. Where do you get these values and backgrounds? Pellegrino says in books, in the humanities and in philosophy, not in medical texts. He does not agree with Adler's assurance that the best will be brought along with each generation's writers. Pellegrino thinks some of the best will die with each generation.

He thinks the computer can be trusted for specific data; but only the book is capable of "understanding . . . involvement . . . immersion."

Jacques Barzun, a historian, author, and publisher, extrapolates this across the whole computer scene. He says that with the computer you are at the mercy of the middleman. In LEXIS, all the reader understands is how the abstractor viewed the legal case; he seldom gets back to the original and is totally dependent on the faceless scribe in between. Sol Linowitz, a lawyer and diplomat, shares this fear of the computer in law. He says the instantaneous screen looks so authoritative that it is so easy to accept it as "given truth," leaving the user unchallenging and unthinking. Linowitz also believes that words held in the hand on paper can be manipulated, thought about, challenged, while words on a cathode ray tube screen are temporary, ephemeral, and unconducive to mental reflection.

John P. Dessauer of the Book Industry Study group expresses the same concern: "When comprehensive analysis, intellectual perception, depth of understanding, keenness of vision, or profundity of grasp are sought, then the print medium in general and the book in particular are far better suited to provide them than are the computer or other electronic media....What is vital to civilized survival, to the success and meaning of civilized life, are precisely those achievements of the mind which the book is ideally suited to convey. Unless education is perceived as no more than the cramming of isolated facts into empty heads or the acquisition of skills unrelated by purpose or meaning, educators will continue to emphasize and utilize books which encourage perception, vision, and understanding."

Lane Jennings, a futurist, while less worried about this matter (he thinks the electronic change will be beneficial), still wonders, When the computer changes the form, how will it affect how we think? We now think linearly because writing is linear. When data is kept in spreadsheets having length and breadth, will it change the way we organize information in our own minds? Fred Kilgour (OCLC) wonders about the same thing, but he expresses it as "jumping around mentally...bringing up scattered facts and experiences like we bring up scattered material and files in the computer's memory."

"All of Us" and Computers
Lane Jennings noted that the statistics imply an ever-growing computerization of the nation. Some aspects of this should be built on, especially the fact that these computer-aware individuals fall into the exact group that presently contains the book readers and writers and exactly blankets the decision makers and the opinion managers. However, we should never lose sight of the fact that this "all of us" is not very many. The number of people who read or will have computers is really very small. For this reason, some of the time predictions may be quite wrong simply because a critical mass will not have been generated to achieve some things that are quite possible to do but are not yet real.

For example, Jennings believes that the potential for great strides in fiction and music is real, but not until there are "enough of us" to make it profitable to manufacture the disks or market the tapes or whatever device is used. He says, "Quality almost always is a small slice of the market. Mass marketing has to be at the point of the lowest common denominator, and if you invest a lot, even a small failure is terribly expensive." Thus many of the great potentials may take longer simply because of the risks involved. And again, while the number of people involved in the electronic revolution amounts to millions, that is only a narrow slice of many more millions who will have no direct contact with the wonders.

The Computer's Impact Like Television's

Many of the people with whom we spoke felt that our recent experience of television invading our culture ought to give us some valid analogies, but most of those who brought this up said they were still trying to figure out what the analogies were. Several people note Theodore Caplow's experience in his return to Middletown. He reported, "The amount of time Middletown's residents devoted to viewing television staggers the imagination. We might expect that reading would have been swamped by the audiovisual deluge but the reverse seems to have occurred.... There is much more recreational reading in Middletown today than in 1925, and its content is not noticeably less serious."[10] Others noted that although the Caplow report was published in 1982, the research had been done in 1976, and they wondered what the increases in having two working breadwinners, getting cable TV, and having a computer might be having now.

For what it is worth, Unesco discovered that when television is introduced to a new country, reading drops by 25 percent. At the other extreme, Pool points out wryly that there really are a surprising number of printed words in any 30-minute sequence on the television screen, and therefore, "We will never lose literacy totally. They couldn't understand their television!"

The Timetables are Wrong

Ithiel de Sola Pool thinks that all the timetables (including his own) may be wrong. He pointed out that all innovations take much longer than is expected. He noted that everything necessary for television was understood in 1912; the leading futurist of the time said it would come in 1935. In fact, it came in 1951. He thinks that the great flood of digital insertion into all aspects of Western life may not be seen before 2000, but "then it will come in a rush."

Daniel J. Boorstin, Librarian of Congress, doubts the extent or the nearness of the computer's impact even more strongly. He calls this the "displacive fallacy." He says, "our faith in progress leads us to assume that the bad is always, if gradually, being displaced by the good, and the good is being displaced by the better." He points out that the mistake is made "both by the unimaginative opponents of the new, and by the fanatical champions of the new."

He believes the book as a paper, bound, shelf-stored artifact is immune to attack from television or the computer or any other presently known device. He believes the book's defenses are the strongest because of the "book's independence from external (artificial) sources of energy, unlike a motion picture machine, a radio, or a television set. The energy that makes a book communicate is natural energy and is within the reader himself....So long as there are new and unique messages which can be put into books, and so long as there are people who do not possess the books containing the old messages,' the market for books has not been saturated. And since the market for books can probably never be saturated, the device itself cannot be displaced."

Computers for Creativity

To conclude this chapter, we mention some of the more futuristic suggestions about how books will change human creativity. We have already noted some fears and hopes about how machines may affect people's active responsibility in thinking or may move us out of linear thinking into thinking of a broader sort. Here we focus more on creativity in terms of art.

Lane Jennings, of the World Future Society, thinks that in another generation people will use paper mainly for preserving data when the situation demands the kind of convenience paper gives, and they will use the computer for creative activities involving speculation or emotional involvement. He thinks that when we grope for the answer to the question, How will things be different in the future world of the computer? we should use the phenomena we can observe in the video arcade as the analogue and guide. Here we see young people of high energy, both physical and mental, captured by the sense of personal involvement. The very complex adventure games, at different levels, with different screens, let the user create characters, manipulate them, and relate to them. Essentially what the players are doing is what their parents did in books: building characters and scenes in their own minds as "surrogate memory experience." But in many cases when these young people grow older, they are "turned off" by books because reading a book seems passive: the reader can't do anything different with the characters.

Some speculators think that this is one way the computer may direct the energy now invested in fiction. Books were descriptive and philosophical until the invention of the novel in the mid-eighteenth century. At that point, made-up characters like Tom Jones and Pamela *did* things and *had things happen to them* in places and times that the reader could imagine. Using the arcade analogy from above, instead of playing dungeons and dragons in mystical kingdoms, it is possible that future videodisk novels will provide scenes of historic crisis, fantasy castles, or exotic modern locales which the "readers" will people, both visually and imaginatively, with characters of their own choosing.

Several people with whom we spoke believe that the present preoccupation with laser painting and electronic music may be a hint of the way art and music will go. Walt Disney's early mixture of graphic images with music by Bach and Stravinsky in *Fantasia* has spoken to large audiences and stood the test of time. Such mixtures now seem to be appearing in the video music pieces, which again attempt to project sound and rhythm visually. What does a Chopin prelude "look" like? How about a Beethoven quartet? Can the electronically produced *visual* image of a computer give us a new way of expanding our appreciation of the creative genius of the *sound* of music? Jennings see these less as examples of the way the next creative step will go than as indications of the fact that the computer is going to bring us something new. Frederick Kilgour, of OCLC, expressed the same thought when he told us, "The computer is not going to do old things in new ways; it is going to do entirely new things in new ways and we should be ready to recognize them when they appear."

How we get from here to there is intriguing writers and artists across the literary spectrum. At one extreme we find Arthur C. Clarke and Byron Preiss making "electronic books" out of their *Rendezvous with Rama* and *Dragonworld* novels. Joanne Davis of *Publishers Weekly* describes the technique: the reader, "(who is transmogrified into Amsel, the hero of *Dragonworld)* is presented with one or two pictures at the top of the screen and a body of text at the bottom describing the situation. He or she then types in commands to travel through the network of screens that comprise the simulated Dragonworld, encountering various adventures and characters (who can be spoken to and asked questions) in the process."

At the other extreme we have children's book illustrator and writer Mercer Mayer of the *Little Critters* and *Little Monster* series, who is creating digital children's books called TinkTonks. "These colorful, robot-like characters live deep inside your computer on little disks that float above the CrissCross Sea." When the child turns on his computer the characters are in their home at the start of a new day, and the "reader" determines which way they go and who they meet at "crossroads" in the story. The story, accordingly, follows a new path each time. The endlessly changing stories are reputed to be totally engrossing—to children four to eight. Mayer is internationally known for his Little Golden books. He describes his present explorations in the same metaphor we heard so often: "The appeal is that it is the next quantum leap from a communications standpoint. What the printing press was back in the 1400s is what the computer is today. It's going to radically change everybody's way of communicating."

Of the one hundred people we interviewed, the overwhelming majority looked at the future of the book with eager, optimistic anticipation. The world of the word was perceived to be at the threshold of its most triumphant period. A small fraction, however, were not so sure. There were simply too many unknowns and variables, too many untested assumptions floating around to make them as comfortable as their neighbors.

Notes

1. Curt Suplee, "Word Processing Changing the Art of Writing," *PC Magazine,* 29 May 1984, 248ff.
2. Gordon Graham, "Adversaries or Allies?" *Scholarly Publishing* 14 (1983): 291-97.
3. For some information on the program at Pennsylvania School for the Deaf, see "Early Reading in Young Deaf Children Using Microcomputer Technology," *American Annals of the Deaf* 127 (1982): 529-35. For a preliminary account of the program at California School for the Deaf-Riverside, see Rod J. Brawley and Barbara A. Peterson, "Interactive Videodisc: An Innovative Instructional System," *American Annals of the Deaf* 128 (1983): 685-700.
4. "Space Age Training" (editorial), *Washington Post,* 26 November 1983, sec. A, 20.
5. William Saffady, in *Video-Based Information Systems: A Guide for Educational, Business, Library, and Home Use* (Chicago: American Library Association, 1985), describes many information uses of current and future systems that display their results on screens.
6. Elie A. Shneour, "A Look into the Book of the Future," *Publishers Weekly,* 21 January 1983, 48.
7. David Burnham, *The Rise of the Computer State* (New York: Vintage Books, 1984), 147.
8. Ibid., 151.
9. Ibid.
10. Theodore Caplow and Howard M. Bahr, and others, *Middletown Families: Fifty Years of Change and Continuity* (Minneapolis: University of Minnesota Press, 1982).

Television extends human sight, computers extend memory and ability for calculation. Books extend wisdom. It is now our task to fit together these tools, the new ones with the old.

ERNEST L. BOYER
Educator

13. The Electronic Library

Kenneth E. Dowlin

This chapter characterizes the role of the library—particularly the public library—in a society in which home computers and everyday use of electronic information media are commonplace. The library may become focal, not only by providing electronic access to its own resources, but even more by providing a community center for transfer of information and by acting as a guide and intermediary to the world of information.

The author, director of the Pikes Peak Library District in Colorado, was introduced above as one of the advisors to the Book in the Future project.

The "information explosion" has been documented in many sources and is receiving considerable press. The U.S. federal government may alone spend more than $1 billion a year on information-related activities. A mechanism for organizing and providing access to this information is essential. The controller of information—in terms of its communication and availability—will be in control of this country. We must ensure a variety of sources for information, and we must also ensure access to this information by everyone. Our society is founded on the premise that individual needs should be met by the marketplace. Yet, the provision of services that contribute to society as a whole is considered to be a valid government function. Since access to information is required for the preservation of our marketplace economy, it therefore must be considered a public good to be financed through the political process, rather than the marketplace.

Even though precise predictions of societal trends are difficult, general conclusions can be reached with a degree of accuracy. There is little doubt that technology will continue to impact lifestyles, and that access to information will be a key variable in people's ability to solve problems, to form a better society, and, in some cases, to exist. Because of the importance of information in future societies, it is important that we assess the role of information and implement strategies that can enhance society's abilities to use information for positive purposes. An understanding of what the role of information will be in the future requires a look at the changes in characteristics that have already taken place.

Changes in Personal Familiarity

Growing up in a small rural town was far different from my present life in an urban area. My father knew the people with whom he dealt for goods and services. He always bought his cars from the same dealer. The grocery store owner knew our family and extended credit. If my father bought something that did not work, he took it back, and it was fixed. Most communication was face to face between people who knew each other.

The increasing number of people, the breaking down of personal ties, and the greater mobility of individuals in the last thirty years have created an environment that is extremely impersonal. This environment places a premium on communication, for there is little time to establish personal ties, and the need for information has become too great to be limited to personal ties. All present indications show that the depersonalization of communication will increase.

Geographic Distances Involved

Technology has removed geographic barriers to communication: satellites can broadcast to an entire continent, and the telephone allows instantaneous communication throughout the free world. This ability to communicate has created a marketplace not limited to countries or continents. In fact, the need for new markets for manufactured books spurred the development of long-distance communication.

However, distance between the sender and receiver does change the parameters of the communication. Since few common experiences may be shared by the sender and receiver separated by an ocean, the communication must be more precise, less subject to interpretation. And there is a cost associated with distance—the further the communication, the greater its cost.

An example of the increased ability to communicate over distance is the use travel agencies have made of information technology. For decades they operated using published airline schedules. But with the deregulation of the airline industry, the old methods are no longer viable. Agencies now either use the telephone to call an airline directly or have terminals connected into a centralized database of airline schedules. These terminals provide much more current information and indicate the occupancy level of individual flights. Having completed seventy thousand miles of travel in eighteen months, including a tour of Australia and New Zealand, I can appreciate the power that a modern communication system gives to my travel agent. Distance is no longer bound by technology; it is constrained only by governments.

Style of Information Transmission

F.W. Lancaster states that society is in the process of evolving away from formal communications patterns, which for centuries have been based almost exclusively on printed paper, to a communication system which will be largely paperless—electronic. We are currently in an interim stage in this evolutionary process since the computer is still primarily used to produce print for paper publications.[1] Even though the distribution of transient information is achieved through traditional methods, we are seeing increased availability of this information electronically. The information that is not volatile and is perhaps more permanent in nature will still be published and distributed in a traditional mode, but greater amounts of transient or volatile information are becoming available only by electronic means.

Complexity of Information

Chris Burns, associate publisher of the *Minneapolis Star/Tribune,* has been credited with coining the term "information complexity." Information complexity is the totality of all information, including good information, bad information, incomplete information, too much information, falsehoods, assumptions, and inferences. This complexity of information creates an environment in which the individual who has not developed the skills of critical analysis may find survival difficult. A survey of the information industry found that there were sales of $9.6 billion in 1979 and forecasted an annual growth rate of 20 to 22 percent.[2] The growth of this industry will contribute to the complexity of information and to the confusion of the information seeker.

Little work has been done to provide standard modes of access, indexing, and retrieval of information provided by the information industry. I do not recommend that such standards be arbitrarily forced on the industry. Yet it must be recognized that standard technology and methodology are important for growth of a networked information system. Complexity will increase as technology continues to accelerate the number of channels for communication.

In the late 1700s, there were barely a dozen channels or products related to information and communication. Today there are nearly one hundred channels. This proliferation requires the ability to locate information sources, to discriminate their appropriateness, and to have access to them. In his book, *How to Harness Information Resources,* Forest W. Horton, Jr., claims that we must be concerned with the "information imperative," which is the establishment of mechanisms for the recognition and use of existing and new sources of information. He feels that in an age of proliferating information sources we must develop early-warning systems to recognize emerging sources of information. Networks already developed must be capable of recognizing new sources and including information from them.[3] Channel selection will be much more complicated than just switching the selector on the television set.

Length and Permanency of Information

In analyzing the differences between messages of our past and those of today, one characteristic that has changed is length. Communication takes place in increasingly shorter bursts. Commercials on television provide a microcosm of our overall communication patterns. Network television routinely squeezes four or more commercials into ninety seconds. News is presented as bits of information completely unrelated to a context. A one-hour program on television compresses a story to only a fraction of the time that would be required in real life. A story that covers many life spans can be presented on television in a matter of hours. World War II has been shortened to one evening of television viewing innumerable times. The pace of life, itself, seems to have been accelerated. Some day we may look at the ninety-second commercial as a nostalgic feature of today's communications.

Information has reached the stage where a significant proportion of what is produced is throw-away. Scientific theories have a much shorter period of relevance than they once did. The bumper sticker is the epitome of communication today. A premium is placed on one's ability to communicate in short bursts. Celebrities rise to prominence and then disappear very quickly. In sports it is difficult to remember the teams, let alone the players. The disposable syndrome has moved from paper plates, diapers, and clothes to information.

Technology has been the major contributor to our ability to throw away images or information. The Polaroid camera is to permanent photography as the copying machine is to publishing. Audio and video information are easily copied, and just as easily discarded.

Audience Fragmentation

The drive for mass audiences has reached its peak. Cable television technology is forcing providers of programs into narrowcasting. (Where broadcasting aims at the largest audience possible, narrowcasting directs programming at a more precise audience.) Magazines have moved away from general interest publications into highly specialized areas. The Federal Communications Commission has recently opened the door for low-power television stations. There is a backlog of thousands of applications. Television may follow magazines into the arena of communicating with special interest audiences.

The unwrapping of the citizen's band broadcast frequency for the general public has created a communications revolution. It is no longer necessary to go through the arduous licensing process that is required of ham radio operators. It is even possible to broadcast on a new "CB" radio even before the license is formally issued. The government cannot monitor the communication on that frequency due to the number of channels available and the number of transmitter/receivers that are in use. Broadcasting will not disappear, but it will not continue as the dominant communication medium.

Focus of Communication

In previous generations, institutions and communication channels reinforced messages that were common to our communities. The local "moral code" was reinforced on a daily basis by the churches, schools, and media. Parents reigned supreme and the institutions of society reinforced the values that the parents communicated to their children. Today, the messages are mixed as to direction and very scattered in focus. The media, schools, and churches are part of a communications environment that fragments moral codes. Today's youth must have the ability to sift through conflicting messages and determine those which have relevance and reinforcement.

It is important for us to examine the issues that have arisen in the use of information within the electronic society. These issues revolve around several questions:

1. Will the individual be able to control the use or misuse of information concerning himself or herself?
2. Will competition between the free-market information providers increase the utility of information, or will it hamper society's ability to advance?
3. Who is responsible for the creation of information that is important to society or a particular community?
4. How is the information creator able to protect his or her rights of ownership in a time when copying information, regardless of format, can be accomplished quickly and cheaply?

Privacy of Personal Information

The rapid acceptance of the microcomputer in business and the home is mitigating one of the major fears that surfaced with the introduction of computers. Although the computer has certainly increased the ability of the government and others to collect and disseminate information about individuals and organizations, the specter of the gigantic all-seeing computer that spies on the citizen is becoming less real. As the microtechnology for electronic data processing spreads throughout the country, it will become less possible to centralize information banks. This is a positive trend. But a philosophical stand must be taken that balances the right to privacy with the need for information for societal purposes.

An example of the issues concerning privacy is the use of library borrower registration files. There are very few centralized files of borrower records which cross political jurisdictions. As a consequence, it is possible for a determined individual not to return books to libraries all over the United States, with the utmost confidence that one library will not notify another of the transgressions.

The implementation of computerized circulation systems and their linkage among libraries reduces losses; this also creates one more master file of information on individuals. However, the automated circulation system can actually increase the privacy of individuals who check out books. Once a book is returned, all physical evidence of the reader's choice is deleted. The implementation of microcomputer circulation systems therefore decreases the ability of libraries to provide a centralized file on persons who check out books and do not return them. The technology does not make the decision to acquire and store information on an individual. This is determined by those making the policies on the use of the technology. A policy on the use of information about people requires serious thought and conscious concern.

Information in a Free-Market Economy

The United States is philosophically committed to a free-market economy. Yet we see examples in most industries that belie that philosophy. The role of information in our society must be determined and articulated. Governmental control is exercised in radio, television, transportation, and publishing. Should not the creation of information and access to it also be an area of societal concern? The marketplace will determine the success or the failure of any particular company for the private information providers.

Some private information providers oppose government-supported efforts for increasing public access. These companies contend that such efforts are undermining their right to charge for the dissemination of information. In some cases, this is a valid complaint, yet there are a number of companies that provide increased access to information that was funded by government entities. In fact, even the most diehard free-market advocate would be aghast at the thought of the government doing away with patents, copyrights, and legal titles to property. These three government activities are desired more by business than by the consumer. They certainly provide added value to the information by indexing it and providing online access to the user. It is of concern, however, when they act in a proprietary manner towards the information and try to corner the market. For example, in a recent discussion with a representative of one of the companies that provides dial-up access to scientific information, I countered his complaint that libraries were giving away information that such companies were trying to sell by pointing out that the majority of the data that his company was brokering was originally funded by the federal government, and thus by the people who were paying for access through the company. This is an issue that must be explored publicly. Policy changes by the federal government to charge individuals for access to information, or for the distribution of information, must be monitored, and fees that seriously hamper access to the information must be resisted. There is a level of fee that provides funding for an agency that will enhance the ability of information gatherers and disseminators, but care should be taken that the fees are never of such magnitude that they inhibit access.

Private enterprise has shown itself remarkably capable of adjusting to the times. For example, it was feared that the increase in the popularity of television would reduce the revenues of radio. This may have occurred for a short period of time, but radio is now extremely healthy. Today there are more radio stations than before the advent of television. They have made changes in their format to attract different audiences and have focused their efforts to times when people are driving automobiles.

Because of the free-market philosophy in the United States, information is often viewed as a commodity; yet it does not fit the classic definition of a commodity. Its use by one person does not prohibit another person from using the same information. On the other hand, its intangible nature complicates the legal aspects of transfer and use.[4] Even though the content is increasing at a rapid rate, its growth is being far surpassed by the increasing number of different conduits and methods of access that are becoming available. This increase in the number of choices is desirable for a society. Yet, it also makes access by an individual more complicated and increases the task of protecting ownership. The property of sharing leads to the concept of networking.

Information has four properties that make self-multiplication possible but that create difficulties when theorists attempt to treat information as a commodity:

1. Information is inconsumable. A commodity can be used up, whereas information is not depleted by use.
2. Information is untransferable. The use of information can be given to another person without the originator losing possession.
3. Information is indivisible. Information is an accumulation and interpretation of data. One component of information has little value, the whole must be present for it to have value.
4. Information is accumulative. Money and other goods can only be accumulated through non-use. Use of information does not detract from the collection.[5]

Perhaps the consideration of the role of information would be further advanced if, rather than considering information as a commodity, *access* to information be held up to the test as a commodity. When the number of channels to information (technology) or the number of units (books, recordings, etc.) are limited, then possession of the channels or vessels is tantamount to ownership of the information. The increase in either channels or vessels compounds the question of ownership. For example, it is assumed that the commodity involved in commercial television broadcasting is the information or entertainment being broadcast. In fact, the commodity is the audience.

Competition is growing among large corporations that supply computer equipment, communications equipment, and office equipment. There is also intense competition among the different segments of the information providers. Newspapers are confronting the telephone system over AT&T's right to provide terminals in the home and to supply information services. The newspapers contend that the monopoly position of the telephone company will be further strengthened by the supply of information and communications by the same company. The lawsuit over a proposed information system by AT&T in Austin, Texas, may provide a landmark legal case. The newspapers have been joined in their suit by two computer manufacturers. The American Library Association has adopted the position that the communicator should not be the same company as the creator or supplier of the information and is actively advocating this position to Congress. Initially, this position was proposed for the library community by a resolution adopted by the White House Conference on Library and Information Service in 1980.

Responsibility for Sharing

The ability to share information (networking) does not develop in a vacuum; it must by nurtured by a responsible entity. Information seldom occurs spontaneously. It must be located, codified, and validated. It is likely that the network may take longer to develop than did the location, codification, and validation of the information itself. Most networks, by definition, cross traditional governmental jurisdictions and also generally require cooperation for their implementation and development. The creation of networks is further complicated by the fact that boundaries or components are constantly shifting.[6]

Knowledge has always been the key to power. The new information technologies may change power relationships by accelerating society's reaction time and decreasing the dependence of lower income people on those of higher income for information (power based on initial possession is destroyed). It may be difficult for leadership and institutions to react fast enough to suit the public.[7] The control of knowledge is an awesome responsibility and must be considered carefully.

Technological advances have improved communications, causing a fusing or crossover between traditional uses of a single medium. For example, the laser videodisk can be accessed via an index provided online by a microcomputer. Cable television companies will be using computers as a source of information for subscribers, and the use of videodisk for information storage is within the possibility of existing technology. The content is not necessarily changing; in fact, no matter how many new technologies are implemented, the information may change little. The fusing or linking of technologies opens new channels for access and can enhance the ability of any single medium. It is cumbersome to index microfilm or videodisks without the computer. This fusing provides greater capacity and greater access and reduces barriers of time and distance. It also increases the knowledge needed by entities dedicated to the promotion of communications as a societal good.

Responsibility must be assumed for information at all of the levels of government in the United States. A concern that has not been addressed in the policy discussions surrounding communication—one I feel may be critical for the quality of life in our communities—is lack of access to communication media on a local level. It is difficult for individuals or organizations to gain access to mass media for community information purposes. The FCC has been deregulating the airwaves through such actions as the extension of the time period for license ownership, the deletion of public input for license renewal, and the weakening or elimination of required public service time. In the 1981 session of Congress, serious attempts were made to take control of cable television completely out of the hands of local governments. It may be unfair to single out cable television as the only mass medium to be controlled locally. However, it is the only medium that has identifiable boundaries that correlate to governmental boundaries. If this control is removed, there would be no local mass medium that a community could encourage to provide local communications. Commercial television reached the point some time ago where it is more profitable to show network programming than to produce and broadcast local programs.

A community communication system is vital for the survival of our communities in the future. A "sense of community" is important to initiate newcomers into the mores, traditions, and heritage of a community. In a highly transient community, such as Colorado Springs, the high rates of suicide, alcoholism, and crime could be attributable to the absence of a process for orientation and involvement of newcomers into the life of the community. If the electronic age eliminates the barriers of time and distance, we could see the decline of geographically based communities. "Communities" of the future may consist of networks of like-minded people. It is important to have a communication system in a community that can enhance the sense of belonging to the community.

The discussion of responsibility for information must concern itself with access to the information. The fragmentation of the channels for information, the multiplication of techniques for access, and the proliferation of information compound the problem of access for individuals. Information and referral services provide an example of too much of a good thing in some communities and not enough in others. The federal government started encouraging programs that supply information to a variety of constituencies in the 1970s and required information and referral components in several federally funded programs. For example, Colorado Springs, a metropolitan area of over 300,000 people, currently has fourteen information and referral centers. Citizens need a guide to determine which service or services can meet their need for information. I am sure that in larger metropolitan areas, the multiplicity of information sources creates an even greater problem. The linking of the channels and the networking of the components must occur for the full benefit of the information systems to be realized.

We know that information will continue to proliferate and that the number of channels for access and transmission will also continue to grow. The relevant questions are, Who will have access to what information? and How will its creation, storage, and transmission be funded? There is very little precise data on the value of information. Value can often be assigned to information in certain instances, but its value to society at large is yet unknown. Many commercial organizations have determined that information is the fabric that holds the organization together.[8] Unless information access for society is costed out and decisions made establishing access to information for society, it will be left to the marketplace to determine the access by individuals. The marketplace may not provide access to information to those who cannot pay, or to those to whom the cost will be prohibitive because of distance or sparsity of population.

Ownership of Information

It has been the policy of our government to protect the rights of the originator or creator to possession of his or her ideas. This has been patterned after property rights. However, ideas are less tangible than land. The rapid growth of technology that allows the easy and inexpensive copying of content has made it very difficult to protect the rights of the originator, and the ability to transfer those rights for a consideration. Today's technology will continue to impact these rights, and the technology of tomorrow may obliterate them. Yet without this protection, the flower of creativity will die. A balance must be sought that encourages the arts, science, and engineering necessary to advance society. Ownership is the driving force behind the marketplace and must be a societal priority.

We know that information and access to information are vital policy issues. I would argue that the public and the private sector must reach a balance for the provision of access to information and that this must happen soon. Partnerships should be formed that allow the private information provider the right to entrepreneurship, but at the same time provide a clearinghouse to the information with some politically determined level of access by all. As James Madison stated, "A popular government without popular information or the means of acquiring it is but a prologue to a farce or a tragedy, or perhaps both. Knowledge will forever govern ignorance and a people who mean to be their own governors must arm themselves with the power knowledge gives."[9]

The Role of Libraries and Librarians in the Electronic Age

It is significant that the index to the book *The Third Wave* contains only one reference to libraries. Alvin Toffler states there that libraries are a second wave phenomenon and implies that they will have only a minor role, if any, in the electronic age. Although it is interesting to assess the impact that technology will have on our society in the future, the relevant point for librarians is the impact technology will have on Library and Information Service (LIS) organizations and its impact on their relationship with their communities.

The Role of the Public Library

The public library is the only institution that provides information on any question needed by any person during convenient times. The term "public" mandates that library resources be equally available to all citizens of the community and that the collections attempt to represent the widest possible number of viewpoints. Virtually every community in this country has a public library that can serve as an access mechanism to the "national" information networks of informational resources.

Access to information requires attention to all of its elements (1) legal access; (2) physical access; (3) affordable access; and (4) organized access. All elements must exist for total access and the absence of any one element may serve to deny access. Legal access means that one has the right to the information, whether established through laws such as the "sunshine laws" and the Freedom of Information Act, or by a transaction with the owner. Physical access means the ability to get to the information in whatever form is useful. Affordable access means that the cost of obtaining the information is not greater than the value of the information. Organized access means that the information and the sources of information are arranged in such a manner that finding the information does not make the cost prohibitive or the time excessive.

In the same way that libraries have provided publicly subsidized access to knowledge in the past, so should they continue to provide publicly subsidized access to information now and in the future. The political process for establishing the library's budget determines the level of publicly funded access. Borrowing from current management terminology, the public library should be the "decision support system" for all members of the community. This means providing the information needed for individual decisions and for community-wide decisions.

Access node. Today's technology offers the opportunity to increase access far beyond that which has been achieved thus far. At the same time, however, technology also increases the ability and means to control access to information, thus requiring our society to maintain a certain level of access for everyone. The increased use of the computer and telecommunications is changing the capabilities which we have in our libraries, and a new paradigm must be constructed that provides a reference for evaluating these tools that are available to libraries and librarians. It is not possible for any one library to have all of the published material and informational resources that are needed by the community. Commitment should be made to consider each library as a node in state, regional, and national networks. The library of the future must be a member of an electronic network that embraces the informational resources of the entire nation. Networking has occurred all over the country and there are few libraries that are not already participating. There has been, however, less effort toward linking existing networks. Perhaps one day we will see all libraries connected through some general-purpose automated network.

Local information source. If we consider the first role of the library as an access point to a national informational network, then the second role of the library must be to mitigate the forces that are turning us into a national information community. Today, all of the online information utilities are designed for a national audience. Although there is certainly a need for such utilities, a system that strives to serve a national audience will not have the resources to meet the needs of each local community. A national information system must be viewed not as a huge database on a gigantic computer, but as a series of interlinked databases with many access points and with the capability of providing databases which have only local relevance. Just as the trend in computers is toward distributed networks, in contrast to the initial development of large centralized systems, so must the development of our national information system be directed equally to localized information and communications systems.

It is my view that a policy of benign neglect for community information has wreaked havoc on the complex societal systems that have developed. Because of librarians' penchant for published material, we have allowed other entities to provide community information. As a result, there are a multitude of information sources in each community, much duplication of effort, and some major gaps in coverage.

The local public library could provide leadership in the effort for effective local information systems. The library staff has a head start over most of the other agencies: it has been acquiring and organizing information for decades, and has mastered a very sophisticated schema for the organization of information materials. If a library staff can master the Dewey Decimal system or the Library of Congress system for classification, it can file anything. There is still a need to develop skills for acquiring, organizing, and storing unpublished information. Librarians should be directing attention toward local information sources and should be mastering the new technology that can provide more accurate and more responsive information.

Libraries have a highly visible physical facility which can serve as a focal point for information on the community. An active local information component can provide a library with increased leverage for funding, as can the ability to provide leadership and assistance with the new information technology. While Director of the Natrona County Public Library in Casper, Wyoming, I volunteered the library to design and implement a county records system in the county offices. The county commissioners accepted the offer and funded the training of the design team, purchased not only the hardware for the county records system but a great deal of equipment for the library, and funded the operation of the program. The staff for the project analyzed the information needs for the county clerk, treasurer, sheriff, assessor, and the commissioner's office. Based on the analysis, a comprehensive system was designed which not only considered the needs of each individual office but the county as a whole. The system uses microforms for the basic storage and a computer to provide the indexing. Archival records are stored on 16-millimeter reel microfilm, and more current information is stored on automated microfiche units, with their index from the computer stored on the first fiche.

During the time that the library operated the records system, the funding for the library from the county increased significantly. The reason was twofold: (1). The county officials could see that the library had a valid purpose in the community by functioning not only as a place for books, but as an information systems resource, and (2), a healthy and happy library ensured a well-operated county information system. The ability of the library and the librarians to provide information services and information system services placed the library on a significant level of status in the political arena.

Conceptual Model of an Electronic Library

It should be stressed that the electronic library is an institution that is committed to two basic principles: the widest possible access to information and the use of electronic technology to increase and manage information resources. A visualization or model of the electronic library is important to the process of communication. This model can be used for communication within the organization and for communication with the environment. Figure 1 portrays my visualization of the electronic library. The model is based on the assumption that the user will use electronic communication to select the information needed and that the information will then be transmitted to the user. The initial function encountered by the user is the directory system which provides the choice of services. The directory system includes substantial explanation of the services and how to use them. The intervention function provides the user electronic access to an information specialist. This information specialist is trained in the use of the different electronic information systems and has the ability to bridge the transactions of the user. For example, if the user is linked with an online bibliographic utility and has problems in the search, the

Kenneth E. Dowlin

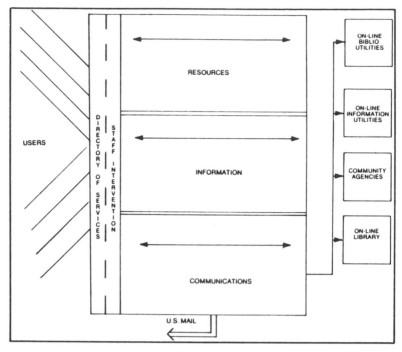

Figure 1

The model of the electronic library is depicted as an organization that uses electronic communication to provide access to information resources contained in the organization, to other organizations in the community, and to regional or national online information sources. The information specialists have the ability to intervene in the communication process to assist the user. The electronic library uses online technology to maintain the catalog of printed resources, as well as provide access to the system from the home.

user can request assistance from the information specialist without disrupting the search. The system monitors the activity which has already occurred and reports the status of the search to the information specialist. The process is analogous to bridging a

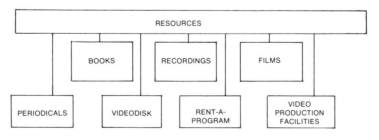

Figure 2

A major function of the electronic library is to serve as the community resource center for published materials. Types of materials are depicted here.

two-party telephone conversation to allow the addition of another person.

There are three major functions of the electronic library: resources, information, and communication. Figures 2, 3, and 4 provide a detailed look.

Resources is the function that allows the user to search the catalog for published materials in a nonelectronic format (figure 2). Entries for materials in the library are contained in the catalog and are searchable by the standard accesses (author, title, subject, LCCN, call number). The "transmission" of these materials to the requester is manual (that is, nonelectronic). There is little question in my mind that LIS organizations will need to deal with nonelectronic information forever. Periodicals, books, recordings, and films are published materials collected by libraries. Many libraries also have video production facilities and some have videodisks.

The *information* function includes all of the data, information, and knowledge that can be accessed and transmitted in electronic form (figure 3). It may be on video or computerized. This is also

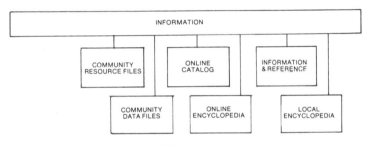

Figure 3

Another major function of the electronic library is to serve as the community information center. This figure illustrates some of the databases that are necessary to provide a broad-based information center.

information contained within the confines of the electronic library. The electronic files that are available are:

- The community information files that are generated by the community information system
- The online catalog of all nonelectronic forms of information
- The electronic messaging system, which enables one to ask information and reference questions and to receive the answers via the same mode
- Files of data about the community, for example, demographic or consumer files
- Various electronic encyclopedias provided by commercial vendors
- A local online encyclopedia which organizes and indexes the questions asked and answered through the computer

The *communication* function allows the user to use the electronic library as a node to enter a network of other electronic libraries or database providers (figure 4). In this function, the library provides the directory function, the linking function, and the staff intervention function. These services are:

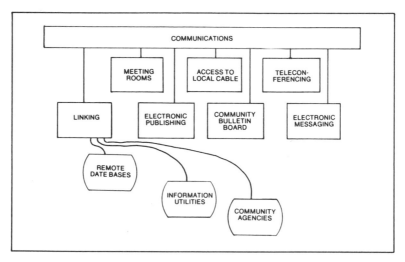

Figure 4

The key to the communication function is the linking of the user to other users, to organizations, and to information utilities.

- Meeting rooms in the library facilities with scheduling done through the computer. The individual may schedule a meeting by dialing into the computer.
- Access to local cable television. The library may house a local origination or public access studio for the local cable television system.
- Facilities for teleconferencing for library or public groups
- A linking facility for online bibliographic utilities, online information utilities, community agencies, and online library networks
- Online publishing on the library communication system for local newspapers or periodicals
- An electronic community bulletin board for the entire community
- Electronic messaging between the library and the user and electronic messaging among the members of the community with other governmental agencies

Characteristics of an Electronic Library

An electronic library does not have to provide all of the services.

Some may not be feasible or desired by the community. But there are four attributes that characterize an electronic library:

- Management of resources with a computer
- The ability to link the information provider with the information seeker via electronic channels
- The ability for staff to intervene in the electronic transaction when requested by the information seeker
- The ability to store, organize, and transmit information to the information seeker via electronic channels

Thus, an electronic library is an information organization that incorporates the new technology available in the electronic age to enhance its ability to provide service. It investigates each technology that appears to possess the ability to improve existing services and to provide new services within its mission. The tools available to us (hardware, systems, and skills) provide new opportunities that have not existed until this time.

An electronic library is also one that has incorporated the electronic information technologies into its organization for purposes of increasing efficiency and effectiveness. These are all online and include bibliographic searching, acquisitions, cataloging, circulation, a public catalog, community resource files, networking, budgeting and other administrative functions, periodical and serials control, word processing, electronic mail, and a decision-support system. The resource files are available directly to the home through a general purpose communications system, such as the telephone or cable television, twenty-four hours a day, every day of the year.

In addition to the automated resource management system and online access from the home, the electronic library has the ability to use video, videodisk, and microforms to capture, store, and retrieve information, events, and text. An electronic library should have a satellite receiver to receive programs that are of interest to the community that would not be available through commercial channels. This receiver feeds a large screen projection system in the public meeting rooms and could also be used for continuing education programs available via satellite.

The model, even the vision, of the electronic library is just becoming a reality. Its actual shape may be far different from that presented here. It is hoped that LIS professionals will add to the model, even redraw it, in a way that promotes consideration and discussion within the profession. All of the functions outlined here can be implemented using today's technology.

The Role of the Librarian

Value added. The role of the librarian is to provide "value added" to the data, information, or knowledge by collecting, storing, and retrieving it within a framework that guarantees and enhances access and retention and tailors the collection to the community that the library serves. The librarian has traditionally added to the value of books by collecting, storing, and retrieving them in a manner that reduces the time and effort required for their identification and use. In the electronic age, this added value may spell the difference between survival and extinction. The ability of the librarian combined with information technology provides a powerful tool for the community. As information technology increases its scope it also increases in complexity. This complexity ensures a role for the individual or institution that has the ability to provide a framework for or interface between the channels and the individual who does not have the skills, or awareness, to use the mechanism to meet his or her needs.

The concept "value added" assumes that the individual has access to an electronic mail system that is operated by the library or that the library is on a mutual electronic mail system with the user. The individual who needs the information sends the request to the information services or reference department of the library, which then processes the request for information (RFI) by using printed material, the bibliographic utilities, the information utilities, or the interlibrary loan system. The response is sent to the information seeker's electronic mailbox. If necessary, the information seeker could be requested to provide additional information concerning the request. If the library resources are online and are available for searching by the information seeker, he or she can select the items that are wanted or indicate similar items.

In addition, if the information seeker has the sophistication to search online bibliographic or information databases, he or she may use the communication link in a "real time" mode to enter into a dialog with the information specialist, or may access the remote utilities without help. At some point, it may be possible for the information specialist to enter into the searching transaction that is occurring to provide assistance. It would be possible for the communications interface to provide not only "help" messages to the information seeker that are generated by the computer systems involved, but to allow the information specialist to respond to "help" indications from the searcher. This human intervention is very important to allow the remote reference system to reach its greatest potential.

There will always be information seekers who need assistance, regardless of the sophistication of the computer-supplied systems. Therefore, all automated systems must supply the opportunity for this. A comprehensive information system design would be faulty if there were no avenues for intervention by humans. We do not have the ability to design the perfect system for machines. Not only is it difficult to be comprehensive in our system design; the fact is that the changing technology forces us into the mode of building sand castles that are eroded by the changing technology. We must develop the system to provide for the adaptation and rebuilding of the sand castles, or to build new sand castles in more secure portions of the beach. As LIS professionals, we must concentrate on the system and use the skills of the technicians to provide the elements in the system. A librarian is not essential for the writing of the computer program for a circulation system. Librarians should, however, be involved in determining the goals of such a system.

Gatekeeper. Another way to view the role of the LIS professional is as a gatekeeper. This concept is widely discussed in management literature. It is a crucial role in organizations. The gatekeeper is an individual who controls the flow of communication to other people. Because of their authority and skills, gatekeepers are in a position to influence others through the amount of correct or incorrect information that they allow through. The gatekeeper is often viewed in the negative context of restricting access to information. However, without some targeting of the information flow, it is easy for the information seeker to become overloaded. In a public library this role should be viewed as positive, since a library's purpose is to increase the width of the "gate" or to increase the number of people who can receive information through it.

Guide. Librarians have always served as guides to information resources. If the philosophy of service is to find the vehicle carrying the information, it needs to be expanded. If the librarian's concern is for supplying the information, regardless of the container, one has already made major progress towards the electronic library. Whereas the current criterion for success of a librarian is to find the container of the information, the new criterion must be based on finding the information.

The librarian who possesses the skills to provide access to a macro database which has integrated multiple formats is a valued part in a community. The librarian can also be viewed as an information transfer agent and should serve as an advocate for access to information.[10] Our passive acceptance of the material that is published, our lack of ability to influence the design of technologies that we use, and our lack of concern for information that is not published all tend to reinforce the image of the library as a poor source for current, unpublished information. In turn, librarians are viewed as being more interested in the past than the present or future.

The roles of LIS professionals and of the institutions which provide LIS must be defined and articulated, communicated to those within the profession, and communicated to the individuals and organizations in our society. Advocacy of the essential nature of access to information must take place.

Kenneth E. Dowlin

Notes

1. F. W. Lancaster and Linda Smith, "Science, Scholarship and the Communication of Knowledge," *Library Trends* 27 (1979): 367-88, p. 384.
2. Paul G. Zurkowski, "The Library Context and the Information Context: Bridging the Theoretical Gap," *Library Journal* 106 (1981): 1381-84, p. 1383.
3. Forest W. Horton, Jr., *How to Harness Information Resources: A Systems Approach* (Cleveland: Cleveland Association for Systems Management, 1974), 42.
4. Benjamin M. Compaine, "Shifting Boundaries in the Information Marketplace," *Journal of Communication* 31, no. 1 (Winter 1981): 132-42, p. 133.
5. Barry O. Jones, "Social Implications of an Information-Based Economy: The Role of Libraries and Librarians," in *Meeting the Challenge of Technology,* Proceedings of the VALA National Conference on Library Automation, vol. 1 (Melbourne, Victoria: Victorian Association for Library Automation, 1982), 3-4.
6. Douglas Cater, "Human Values in the Information Society," in *An Information Agenda for the 1980s: Proceedings of a Colloquium, June 17-18, 1980,* ed. Carlton C. Rochelle (Chicago: American Library Association, 1981), 55-64, p. 57.
7. Ben H. Bagdikian, *The Information Machines: Their Impact on Men and the Media* (New York: Harper and Row, 1971), 1.
8. Charles G. Schoderbek, Peter P. Schoderbek, and Asterios G. Kefalas, *Management Systems: Conceptual Considerations,* rev. ed. (Dallas: Business Publications, Inc., 1980), 139.
9. Cited by Jones, "Social Implications of an Information-Based Economy," 13.
10. Gerald R. Shields, "The New Role of the Librarian in the Information Age," in *The Information Society: Issues and Answers,* ed. E. J. Josey (Phoenix: Oryx Press, 1978), 75.

We librarians invented information management, but we are losing our birthright. The unfortunately all too common misperceptions about librarians stem from a sometimes undeserved bad press and from some of our own self-inflicted bibliomysticism, myopia, and technophobia.

HERBERT B. LANDAU
Librarian

14. The Human Side of the Technological Revolution

James R. Squire

James R. Squire suggests three broad ways in which the computerization of our information activities may affect human interaction: (1) an aggravation of the generation gap as younger people eagerly embrace new technologies, (2) changes in the kinds of competencies needed to function effectively in the new environment, and (3) exaggeration of social inequalities between those with access to the new technologies and those without.

James R. Squire, a senior vice-president at Ginn and Company and an early member of the Center for the Book's National Advisory Board, brings to this discussion long experience in textbook publishing and awareness of the impact of technological changes on education. This essay was prepared originally for a 1984 conference on "The Book in the Electronic Age," sponsored by the Center for Book Research.

Published by permission of Transaction, Inc., from *Book Research Quarterly,* vol. 1, no. 1, Spring 1985, copyright © 1985 by Transaction, Inc.

However impressive the new technologies, however accelerated the rate of their acceptance, however revolutionary their long-range consequences for our society, we cannot ignore the impact of evolutionary change on human behavior. For better or for worse, the effects are legion, and here I discuss three that seem likely to affect particularly the warp and woof of the book industry:

- The intensification of the generation gap in individual perception of and response to life
- The enhancement of the competencies and processes required to cope with changing communication in our society
- The threatened increase in inequities among various strata of society

For the past three decades at least, serious analysts of change in communication, most notably Marshall McLuhan and his followers, have observed how the shift from a print-oriented to an oral and audiovisual culture, and thence to a full electronic culture, has begun to change patterns of knowing, feeling, and learning. Celebrated value conflicts between parent and child—in experience vicarious and otherwise and in exposure to the crude realities of our society as well as to some of its more sensitive achievements—have materially altered points of view and basic perceptions from one generation to the next. The shift for large numbers of individuals from print to television as a major vehicle for transmitting information has created well-documented changes.

These changes have included new developments in how and where children learn, dislocations affecting the values of successive generations, increasingly holistic rather than linear responses to ideas, and conflicts between the traditional cultural heritage that schools and colleges were expected to teach and the content that has interested youth. The protests of the fifties, the street front schools of the sixties in which romantic reformers attempted to achieve relevance, and the bitter school censorship struggles of the seventies in such celebrated instances as that of Kanawha County, West Virginia, can now be viewed in large measure as reflections of cultural change in communication and perception.

James R. Squire

Today's increased reliance on electronic transmission of ideas seems likely to intensify earlier dislocations. No one who has observed young people, from preschool to late adolescence, can fail to be impressed by their spontaneous, even joyful embrace of each new computer or video game, particularly in comparison to their parents and teachers. The Nancy Drew/Tom Swift folk myth of the superbright adolescent capable of outmaneuvering stolid adults in critical situations is reborn in tales of computer whiz kids engaged in electronic espionage who tap into top secret military computer networks and engage in serious "war games." We cannot dismiss the myth too lightly. Newspaper accounts, to say nothing of congressional hearings, suggest that such youth activity may be all too real.

Modern computer technology is not more than forty years old. Most parents, teachers, editors, writers, readers, and publishers attended schools and colleges untouched by computer technology. Small wonder that all but a few lack any proprietary feeling for electronic transmission of ideas, word processing, or computer-based education. Nor can they boast of much knowledge about or insight into present and proposed developments in the power, size, and reliability of computers or their future potential for graphics and sound generation. Yet the human consequences of these developments for the book industry are enormous. Three of them seem particularly worthy of comment.

First, the youth generation itself brought computers into the family, creating a home market and generating the conviction among adults that computer literacy is an essential requirement in preparing for tomorrow's technological age. The clamor for computer literacy has sometimes approached a kind of lunacy. Witness the inability of educators to formulate adequate definitions of the content and objective of the new literacy. Witness, too, the spectacle two or three years ago of parents in the bankrupt schools of Michigan holding bake sales to raise funds for installing microcomputers in schools that were unable to purchase urgently needed textbooks or to remain open for the full academic year. Witness the associate superintendent of the state of Maryland reporting to the conference of school reform that schools and libraries in his state have been permitted to atrophy and decline even as technological centers were being opened. Clearly the older generation recognizes the impact of technology on our society even if it doesn't fully understand it. But lacking understanding, it can make unfortunate decisions.

Secondly, the tensions, concerns, and urgent need for knowledge about technology has spawned a whole new industry. Newsletters, journals, and handy guides on how to live with the electronic revolution vie for attention with workshops, conferences, and academic courses. Is there no end to the print and talk to emerge from the current morass? Ten percent of quality paperback publishing in 1984 deals with the computer. Ten percent! Thus, one curious development during the first phase of the computer age is the generation of more print, more verbal interchange, not less— despite warnings that our reliance on computers will lead to the decline of the print medium. The decline, if there is to be one, will apparently be in the book as a form of idea transmission and storage, not in reading and writing, which promise to become more important.

Not the least aspect of the massive need to know is the requirement to retrain the entire present generation of teachers, editors, and publishers, and to do so *now*. A recent estimate by the Center for Education Statistics reports that only 214,000 of our 3 million teachers have had even minimal training in computer literacy, and that only 37,000 are highly trained. Thirty-seven thousand out of 3 million! Far fewer than one per school or college. Not many more than one per school district. Parallel data on editors and publishers are not readily available, but inadequacies must be at least as great. One wonders whether the nation has the resources to bell the cat or even to define the task.

Thirdly, due to past experiences, many teachers and editors have an irrational fear of technology that they must still overcome. A distrust even of simple audiovisual aids has long been common among elementary and secondary school teachers, except those teaching science and mathematics. Few teaching machines, video- or audiocassette players, and motion picture and overhead projectors have made their way into elementary school classrooms when teachers were allowed to supervise their own program. A recent study revealed that elementary school teachers were the least likely of twenty occupational groups to use even hand-held calculators. A bias against machines has been endemic to the profession. When I first entered educational publishing, I was advised that any school program utilizing equipment that required more than two simple steps to operate was doomed to failure. I find little even now to disprove that observation.

The reasons for this bias are legion. They relate, I think, to the personal characteristics of individuals motivated to interact with young people. Machines are too frequently seen as interrupting the teaching/learning process, as injecting themselves into the personal relationship between teachers and students. When the programmed learning specialists of the sixties developed "teacher-proof" materials, they created suspicions of hardware that will not easily die. Individuals who choose teaching look forward to a lifetime of interaction with youth and will not readily give up this dimension of their careers.

Furthermore, the faith that education and industry placed in audiovisual equipment to solve teaching and learning problems was seriously disappointed in the sixties. Teachers and administrators, once sold on the promise of technological revolution, now contemplate closets filled with dusty, unused equipment. If today's pied pipers of technological change are encountering a reluctance by school people to dance to their tune, it is because this second coming of technology often seems to them too much like the first.

In addition, the analytical nature of computerized learning is associated in the minds of many with mathematics and hard science, subjects little studied, scarcely understood, and widely feared by most of today's teachers. Note the severely depleted numbers of informed teaching specialists in these subject areas reported by the Task Force on Pre-College Mathematics and Science. Here, too, we have nameless fears to overcome.

Most computer installations in schools—save again in high school science and math—have been initiated by administrators. Lured by the promise of administrative applications and responsive to pressures from parents, administrators have often purchased equipment first and only then raised questions about its purpose and use. Such "top down" imposition inevitably breeds resistance from teachers and supervisors who are at a loss to determine how the hardware should be employed when the reason why it is in the classroom is not clear.

Inevitably attitudes are shifting. Educators with memories of unfulfilled promises long ago are gradually retiring from the schools; the new generation is more willing to begin anew. As teachers get their hands on hardware and software, present fears and past resentments begin to subside. The editor of *Instructor* magazine now sees the growing market as teacher-driven with more and more individuals developing programming skills. In publishing houses, the one or two adventurous editors who five years ago pioneered the use of word processors have been joined by an overwhelming majority of their colleagues. Teachers with children at home find that they must adapt to the new equipment. The bandwagon effect has been enormous.

This leads me to the second challenge I wish to discuss: that the technological revolution is redefining the competencies and processes required for thought and communication. Our reliance on the microcomputer seems sufficently established that we can begin to speculate on the impact the technology will have on educated society. If we once thought that the new technology would lead to the creation of new employment opportunities in high-tech industries, the recent, well-publicized study by Lewin and Rumberger should make us think again. The study suggests that the growth of technology may decrease the skill level of many workers and result in a lesser demand for highly trained computer specialists than our futurists once supposed. Of the twenty new occupations predicted to provide the greatest increases in employment over the next decade, none apparently will be related to high technology. Job displacement will not be the most significant result of the technological revolution. What, then, will be?

Probably the most basic and far-reaching impact will be on ways of learning and communicating:

- More important than new job opportunities will be the transformation of requirements for existing positions.
- While computers can be used to replace people in routine communication roles, a far more vital consequence will result from the fact that they require higher proficiency in composing, comprehending, and cognitive processing.
- In education, while computers can be used to teach old skills more effectively, their more significant use will come with the introduction of greater procedural learning in the curriculum.

Let me suggest some possibilities. Innovators like Seymour Papert have demonstrated that children learn to think when they respond to and are responded to by a rich learning environment, such as can be provided by Logo. By sharing, discussing, and playing with rich mathematical ideas, they begin to process concepts and develop ownership of these ideas. John Henry Martin, in his "writing into reading" approach in early childhood education, utilizes word processors and typewriters to stimulate early communication. Now in experimental use with close to 10,000 children in American classrooms, the program has demonstrated its effectiveness. In one Florida school I visited, authorities were wondering what to offer in the second grade to first graders who were writing extensively after completing Martin's short-term program. The conventional second- and third-grade curriculum is now viewed as an obstacle to children's progress in writing and reading. Indeed, as a result of this program alone, that school will never be the same again.

As children learn language, they learn to think, for thinking and language, if not identical, are closely associated in our culture. More than motivation is involved in early interactive uses of technology. Basic transformations in the processes of learning will lead in time from composing and comprehending language—actively and interactively—to experiences with and through the computer in graphing, linearization, background removal, signal averaging, and converting printed data into graphic displays. All these processes require cognitive skills and enhance human perception. In short, the impact of the computer on the psychological growth of the child will be active and productive in enhancing learning.

This bodes well, because the standards demanded of tomorrow's society are likely to exceed the present minimum standards for literacy. Electronic mail, networking, and various other forms of instantaneous transmission of ideas will require that more prose be read and more be written. And the ability to receive and respond quickly to such transmissions will be highly valued and in great demand. Teachers of reading and writing and publishers of books and software need to reflect on how these competencies are to be developed as we create new programs for teaching reading, composing, and comprehending. Theodore Sizer is correct in suggesting in his new analysis of the ills of education that we must greatly enhance attainment in reading and writing by the end of the eighth grade.

The changes in education will not be restricted solely to enhancing goals. As uses of technology expand, basic changes can be expected in the classroom social structure. The educational power of the computer lies in providing students with the means of manipulating numerical and verbal symbols. As Bertram Bruce has recently pointed out, that use inevitably changes interaction in the classroom. Through "milling around," waiting for a turn on the computer, reading one another's writing, discussing ideas, and providing an audience for each act of symbol manipulation, children create a dynamic communication atmosphere that has not been easily obtainable in the past. The very shortage of word processors feeds this phenomenon. As one computer specialist has suggested, when you throw one steak to twelve dogs you create interaction.

It seems clear that computers can change the ways individuals write as well. Rhetorician William Zinsser believes that word processors are helping individuals to achieve unity, coherence, and emphasis in their writing, to eliminate clutter, enhance sentence structure, and improve word choices. A word processor, he says, is far from a glorified typewriter. Rather it is a tool enabling a writer not only to create a text but to revise, print, control, distribute, and file it. The full utilization of word processors as mind tools for writers deserves to be carefully explored.

The third challenge I am addressing regards the social dislocations already disrupting our society, which the technological revolution is likely to intensify. Computers are moving into our homes and schools and into all segments of our society whether or not we insure their effective use. Because they are entering our lives through the home and business more than through the schools, they seem likely to increase the disparity between rich and poor, the advantaged and disadvantaged, the haves and the have-nots. Here are some ominous examples illustrating the lack of equal access to technology in our society:

- Eighty percent of our largest high schools use computers for instruction; only 40 percent of our smaller, poorer schools are reporting such use.
- Thirteen-year-old students in the West are twice as likely to have access to computers as their counterparts in the Southeast.
- Only 12-16 percent of students in low socioeconomic groups have access to computers, compared with 31 percent in high socioeconomic groups.

208

- Low-income, white majority schools are twice as likely to teach programming and use computers creatively than low-income black majority schools, where the emphasis is on drill and practice and routinized low-level skills.

What could be a powerful instrument for stimulating thinking and learning and helping the nation achieve equality as well as excellence in education threatens to intensify already existing differences in access to learning materials. If technology enhances the quality of learning, action must be taken to equalize access of all citizens to its benefits. Here are some suggestions:

- Establish public computer centers.
- Involve industry and the military in making available critical services.
- Expand libraries to offer hardware and software for regular use by patrons.
- Establish special community schools tailored to the requirements of students of lower socioeconomic status.
- Develop home checkout programs for parents in the schools, similar to that sponsored by the Houston Independent Schools.

Educational research has documented that lack of access to books has a negative impact on learning by low socioeconomic status students. Unless action is taken soon with respect to computer availability, such disparities will be greatly intensified in our new information society.

In conclusion, let me emphasize that technology will add to our universal reservoir of tools and processes for enhancing individual thought, rather than replace existing resources. We will still need individuals who know subject matter. We will still need books for permanent storage and transmission of "the best that is known and thought in the world." As Barbara Tuchman has remarked, the new technology will not lead us to repackage Jane Austen or *Treasure Island.*

Perhaps the most dangerous problem is the tendency of some to regard development of computer literacy as a replacement for basic competence in reading, writing, and reasoning. As Joseph Weizenbaum reminds us, computer study offered no substitute for literature and history or basic subject learning. Overemphasis on computer literacy can waste resources and precious learning time. The evolution in technology is just that—an evolution that must build on the best of the past and the most pertinent of the present to prepare us for the promising yet demanding future just emerging.

James R. Squire

Bibliography

Bruce, Bertram, et al. "How Computers Can Change the Writing Process." *Language Arts* 62, no. 2 (February 1985): 143-49.

Braun, Ludwig. *Report on Educational Technology.* Long Island: New York Institute of Technology, 1983.

Hollifield, John H. "In Reality, High Tech Means Low Skills, Poor Pay." ERIC no. ED 241 816. Also in Southwest Regional Laboratory for Educational Research and Development, Los Alamitos, California, *Educational R and D Report* 6, no. 1 (Fall 1983): 2-5.

Landemann, Leanna. "The Education Market: Teacher Powered." *Computer Advertising News,* 1983.

Lewin, Henry, and Russell Rumberger. Report from the Center for Research in Educational Finance and Governance, School of Education, Stanford University, 1983.

Microcomputer Hardware and Software in the El-Hi Market, 1983-87. White Plains, N.Y.: Knowledge Industry Publications, 1983.

Papert, Seymour. *Mindstorms.* New York: Basic Books, 1980.

Sizer, Theodore. *Horace's Compromise.* Boston: Houghton Mifflin, 1984.

Withey, Margaret. "The Computer and Writing." *The English Journal* 72, no. 7 (November 1983): 24-31.

Zinsser, William. *Writing with a Word Processor.* New York: Harper & Row, 1983.

210

Increasingly, we recognize the value and importance of information in decision making, in productivity, and in improving the quality of life. The old cliché, "information is power," has taken on new meaning as we treat information products and services as valuable commodities to trade and protect, like gold or hog bellies.

TONI CARBO BEARMAN
Librarian and Information Scientist

15. The Paperless Society Revisited

F. Wilfrid Lancaster

F. Wilfrid Lancaster is one of the best-known proponents of a future in which information systems would become entirely paper-free. He is the author of *Toward Paperless Information Systems* (New York: Academic Press, 1978), which suggests how electronic systems may function in the place of the paper systems—involving books, journals, libraries, and mail—that still predominate. This chapter tells how some of the changes Lancaster envisioned around 1975 are taking place even faster than he expected.

Lancaster has been introduced as one of the Book in the Future project advisors. Chapter 17 below shows in more detail how he believes electronic systems will affect publishing and authorship.

Reprinted by permission of the American Library Association. F. W. Lancaster's "The Paperless Society Revisited," from *American Libraries,* September 1985, pp. 553-55. Copyright © 1985 the American Library Association.

Approximately ten years ago I gave my first talk on the replacement of print on paper by electronic publication. Since that time I have given many talks, as well as publishing two books and several journal articles more or less exhausting the subject. Recently, however, I was asked to reassess my various predictions in the light of what has actually taken place in the last decade. I propose to do that here; but before I proceed, it may be helpful if I summarize my earlier observations.

What I Predicted

In my early writings on the subject, I described a completely paperless communication system. With a hypothetical scientist as the user of this system, I outlined its general characteristics. The scientist would use a terminal to maintain electronic notebooks, compose reports for subsequent electronic publication, access sources of information in the form of databases, index and store information, and communicate with a geographically dispersed network of professional colleagues. Publications would be electronic. For example, a scientific report would be accepted into a database rather than printed in a journal, and all communications among authors, editors, and referees would be through electronic mail.

I expected such an electronic system to emerge, first because of opportunity—the fact that computer terminals of one kind or another would be commonplace in the office and home and would be used for a variety of purposes. Second, I pointed to the soaring costs of distributing information as physical artifacts—books printed on paper—and suggested that it would soon be economically impractical to continue this form of publication. Moreover, I contended that information was becoming less and less accessible in its print-on-paper form.

I also claimed that a fully electronic system might offer many advantages—improving accessibility, selectivity, and speed of dissemination. Finally, I pointed out that the movement from paper to electronics should be regarded as part of a normal and predictable evolutionary process. Just as the printed book replaced earlier written forms of communication, it could and would itself give way to something else.

The Stages of Change
As I thought further about this subject, I began to discern the various stages of an evolutionary process, one taking place within a number of interrelated facets. The sequence developments could be outlined as follows, under each facet.

Facet 1: Type of publication.
Various types are influenced by electronics in a logical sequence reflecting relative needs and perceived benefits.

Facet 2: Application of computers to publishing (in evolutionary order).
a. To print on paper.
b. To make available the electronic equivalent of a printed publication.
c. To generate new publications having no printed equivalent.
d. To introduce publication forms with completely new capabilities.
e. To cause the replacement of existing printed forms.

Facet 3: Amount stored.
a. Citations only.
b. Abstracts.
c. Complete text.

Facet 4: Type of information service affected.
a. Literature searching.
b. Question answering.
c. Document delivery.

Facet 5: Subject matter.
a. Science and technology.
b. Social sciences.
c. Humanities and popular literature.

Facet 6: Type of audience affected.
a. Institutional users.
b. Individuals.
or, in library terms:
a. Special libraries
b. Academic libraries.
c. Public libraries.

The Obsolete "Physical" Library
As we all know, computers have been applied to libraries in two rather distinct ways: (1) to automate internal record-keeping, and (2) to allow access to information sources not physically present in the library. The second is by far the more important. Indeed, it begins to change our entire concept of what constitutes a library, since one can visualize a vast store of information in intangible electronic form rather than in the form of tangible physical artifacts.

This concept led me to predict that the library as an institution housing physical collections would eventually become obsolete. This change would not necessarily mean that specialists in the organization and exploitation of information sources—i.e., the roles that librarians have been trained to perform—could also be dispensed with. Indeed, information professionals may be more important in the future, at least the near future, than they have been in the past.

To prepare today's librarians for their role in the next few years, however, will require some rather substantial changes in our professional education, with the focus shifting from the library as an institution to the librarian as a skilled information specialist and facilitator of communication, capable of performing in many different environments, say, as an integral member of a research team or operating in a freelance capacity.

Myth of the Immortal Book
The elements I've mentioned so far can be considered part of a larger scenario, and they are all things I have written about at some length. The ideas have not achieved universal acceptance. Indeed, one of my critics has spoken of the "myth of the paperless society." As far as I have been able to tell, however, rejection of electronic publishing is more often than not based on the rather vague feeling that the printed book is an indispensable element in our society and that it has been with us too long to be easily displaced.

This argument, of course, is complete nonsense. The printed book has lasted for only 500 years, which is a mere dot in the history of human communication, and many of its most common manifestations—the novel and the science journal, for example—have been around for a much shorter time. Some reasons given to me for the preservation of the book have been nothing less than amazing. For example, "I like to read on the beach." How long have people been reading on the beaches? I would suspect less than a hundred years. Or, "I like to read in the bathroom." How long have we had bathrooms, or bathrooms conducive to reading?

I don't propose to pursue such arguments any further. Instead, I would like to review the developments of the last ten years to see just how far we have moved toward a paperless society.

Where We Are
On the whole, I believe that the evolution is proceeding more rapidly than I expected a decade ago. Personal computers are becoming commonplace, and electronic mail is spreading into more and more communities of users. Videotex techniques are putting a variety of electronic information sources directly into at least some of our homes.

Developments in electronic publishing have been most impressive. Several hundred databases can now be accessed from a single terminal. Moreover, these databases embrace an astonishing variety of subjects, from the very general to the highly specific, including many of interest to the general public. The database industry is beginning to reach out to this general public by offering databases of interest at favorable rates, so that the owner of a personal computer has about the same level of access to electronic information resources that libraries had a decade ago.

More and more full text—newspapers, magazines, scholarly journals, encyclopedias—is becoming available online, making it increasingly easy to access an information source without actually owning it.

Completely new publications have emerged in the electronic environment, publications for which no print-on-paper equivalents exist. Such projects have been driven partly by economic aspects and partly by the enhanced capabilities that electronic publication can offer, such as in locating and manipulating information. Electronic publications are appearing in an increasing variety of forms or media, accessible through computer terminals or television sets or distributed as tapes or optical disks.

Electronics is also having some impact on authorship. Many authors now compose at a terminal rather than a typewriter, and some transmit their work to a publisher electronically. Through computer conferencing, collaborative authorship is becoming increasingly feasible. This has brought about a new type of publication, the knowledge base, a definitive summarization of knowledge on some subject arrived at through the consensus of a group of experts.

The Change in Libraries

These trends, of course, have had their effect on libraries. Many libraries are now offering for the first time a high level of literature searching support to their users. As more and more conventional and popular reference sources such as encyclopedias, dictionaries, and directories become accessible online, one can expect that more and more factual questions will be answered from electronic sources rather than from print on paper.

Document delivery has also been affected. Online union catalogs have greatly simplified the task of locating a needed item. Moreover, orders for documents from libraries or publishers can now be placed at a terminal. The ease with which full text can now be accessed, of course, suggests that document delivery—in the sense of physical reproduction and mailing—will eventually be bypassed. Text will be transmitted directly from an electronic store to the terminal of a user.

The idea of paperless communication now meets less resistance than it did a decade ago, hardly surprising in view of the rapid developments that have taken place. Nevertheless, some barriers to further acceptance still exist. The only real technographic barrier involves the high-quality transmission of graphic images, still a rather expensive proposition.

A more serious barrier is a psychological one. So far, computers seem not to have reduced the production of paper. Far from it. It appears that many people do not feel comfortable with records that exist only in electronic form. How long this dependence on paper will last remains to be seen. As it becomes easier and cheaper to store records in electronic form, through the medium of a personal computer, this situation may well change. Furthermore, a younger generation, growing up with a diet of computers and electronic games, may be less insistent on the need for paper copy.

Replacing the Book

That so much has taken place in the last ten years is all the more remarkable considering that very few true electronic publications exist as yet. Clearly, the printed book is not threatened by the types of publications now available in electronic form. How could it be, for most of the electronic products are merely printed books displayed electronically. An electronic encyclopedia could and should be much more than printed pages viewed on a terminal. The same must be said for the science journal. True electronic publication implies that authors would compose for a different medium and, in so doing, would no longer be constrained by the static limitations of the printed page.

When the true capabilities of electronics are employed to convey information or inspiration, we can expect that completely new communication forms will emerge. Such capabilities would include the use of sound, moving pictures, and electronic analog modeling. These capabilities may well lead to new forms of art and imaginative literature. Electronic painting and electronic poetry already exist, and, though it may now be hard to accept, there no real reason to expect that people will still be writing novels a hundred years from now.

What I am suggesting, then, is that the printed book will be replaced by something quite different from anything we have yet seen, and this will occur because the medium replacing it will be widely perceived to be better.

The replacement of print on paper is not inevitable. That is, society could presumably choose to reject the transition. However, we are so far along the road toward a paperless society that it is difficult to see what might occur that would permanently reverse the trend.

Let me conclude with a further point of clarification. The fact that I have written about an electronic future does not necessarily mean I endorse such a future or that I enthusiastically look forward to it. A new technology may improve an existing situation but bring with it its own set of problems. It can be used to benefit society or to impair it. The impact is determined by the qualities of the humans who exploit it, rather than by properties inherent in the technology itself.

V.
The Book
Professions:
Publishing

16. The Book in the Future A Publisher's Perspective

Simon Michael Bessie

Private reading is what defines the world of books, according to Simon Michael Bessie, and he argues that this activity cannot disappear, computers or no computers. While noting the hazards of prognostication, Bessie suggests that print-on-paper books are, in fact, with us for the near future. He also defends the contemporary publishing world against charges that it has become unwilling to support the publication of anything but the best-seller.

This essay was originally delivered as a lecture in the Engelhard series of lectures on the book at the Library of Congress, April 16, 1985.

Simon Michael Bessie, a widely experienced editor and publisher, is a Director of Harper & Row. He is Chairman of the Center for the Book's Executive Council and served as Chairman of its National Advisory Board from 1983 to 1985.

That forecaster's guide the Holy Bible offers some advice pertinent to the aim of this essay: "Of the making of many books there is no end" (Eccles. 12:12). In spite of this apparent endorsement, some have called the endurance of the book into question, and they have given reasons for doing so.

In considering the future of the book and the reasons for questioning it, I shall be concerned with something about which little can now be known with much certainty, and I—along with most others who deal with this subject—am far from expert. What I bring to it is a long experience as a publisher, and, since I plan to continue publishing books as long as I am allowed to do so, I have what might be described as a true concern with the future of the book.

So I write as a publisher of books—an activity viewed, with variant accuracy, as an art, a craft, a profession, a business, a game, a refuge for dilettantes, a scam. In any event, it is an occupation in which survival depends on an ability to predict what a few people will want to read, or at least buy. As a publisher, I have a record of prediction good enough to have survived for forty years. I am also the clear-eyed publisher who turned down *Lolita* and a dozen other books that made huge successes. In most of those cases, my second readings left me baffled that I had forecast so badly. I guess one is the slave not only of one's tastes but of one's moods. My guiding principle in this exploration of the future of the book will be: If you can't forecast confidently, forecast frequently.

First, we should try to get some sense of the subject: What is a book?

Webster (3d) says, "In general, a written or printed narrative, record, representation or a series of these....A collection of tablets of wood or ivory, sheets of paper, parchment or similar material, blank, written, or printed, strung or bound together."

The Oxford English Dictionary says, "The original meaning was 'writing tablet'....Generally: A collection of sheets of paper or other substance, blank, written, or printed, fastened together so as to form a material whole," and so forth.

I guess that does it all right for the past, but for the future—or even the changing present—it doesn't satisfy me. For example, if it is on microfilm and you read it with a viewer, is it not a book?

As I thought about it, I was reminded of Russell Lynes's definition of a *lady*, that "A lady is a woman who causes a man to behave like a gentleman." Which leads me to define a book less for what it *is* than what it *does*: A book is a durable object that contains words or pictures and that permits the act of reading. Improvements on this will be welcome, but for present purposes let us accept it as we approach the future by describing the present in the world of books and by trying to see what is happening.

First, some facts and a bit of interpretation. For purposes of comparison and trend-sniffing, I am going to line up 1983 with 1950, which I think it is fair to take as the beginning of the current era (and not only because it can claim to be Year One of TV time).

For 1983, the total of titles published was about 53,000. In 1950 it was 11,000. Does this mean a steady rise at the indicated rate? Not quite. At the moment it looks as though the number has peaked and is now stabilized, perhaps decreasing slightly. There is no question that there has been a feeling among publishers that too many books have been published. There was sympathetic enjoyment several years ago of a cartoon that mimicked an Alka Seltzer commercial—the one in which the unhappy man, the morning after, said, "I can't believe I ate the whole thing." The publishing version showed a man, knee-deep in books, saying, "I can't believe I published the whole thing." However, the recent decline is measured by one or two thousand, not by tens of thousands.

To my mind, the number of titles published depends less on the will of a few large publishers than on many other factors, such as the state of the economy; the money, especially governmental money, available for education and libraries; the number of publishers; and the impact of technologies.

Each of these factors—I shall try to persuade you—is capable of driving the numbers up as well as down. Furthermore, is the health of the book directly related to the number of titles published? Some observers today note a small decrease in overall numbers and put that together with the age-old complaint that it gets harder each year to publish books of quality, and they predict the demise of the literary novel or poetry or criticism. I believe, with Bernard De Voto, the American critic and editor, that the unpublished masterpiece is a myth. There are simply too many publishers and editors in passionate, nationwide competition, ferreting out scripts from coast to coast.

Is there anything to learn from a comparison of the *kinds* of books published in 1950 and 1983 (see table 1)?

What projectible trends can we find here? The biggest growth was in sociology and economics, and this at a time when both disciplines seemed to enjoy less confidence than some years ago. One of the largest declines was in religion, and this when the country is thought by some to be experiencing waves of religious revival and when publishers of religious books seem quite prosperous. Technology rises from tenth to sixth. But in a time when

Table 1

United States Book Publication, 1950 and 1983
Ten Most Published Categories, 1983[1]

Rank, 1983	Category	Titles, 1983	Titles, 1950	Rank, 1950
1	Sociology, Economics	8,470	515	9
2	Fiction	5,470	1,907	1
3	Medicine[2]	4,002	443	11
4	Science	3,620	705	4
5	Juveniles	3,197	1,059	2
6	Technology[3]	2,974	497	10
7	General Works[4]	2,767	345	14
8	Religion	2,433	727	3
9	History	2,296	516	8
10	Biography	2,135	603	5

[1] Sources: "American Book Publication—1950," *Publishers Weekly*, 20 January 1951, 240; and Chandler B. Grannis, "Title Output and Average Prices: 1984 Final Figures," *Publishers Weekly*, 23 August 1985, 41.
Several categories have changed in definition since 1950. These changes are indicated in the remaining notes.
[2] "Medicine and Hygiene" in 1950.
[3] "Technical and Military Books" in 1950.
[4] "Miscellaneous" in 1950.

technology seems to dominate, why only sixth? Fiction has declined *only* from first to second in a period when it is thought that more and more people are satisfying their appetite for story with movies and TV.

Please note that this list includes only the top ten of twenty-five categories and there have been considerable changes—up and down—in several others as well, such as business and sports.

Perhaps others can find hints of future change in these comparisons. Not I. I can observe that there has been a big growth in books on diet, but I can only wonder if it will continue. All I can predict with some confidence is that books will continue to reflect the broad range of our interests as they shift, or as they endure.

To round out the current scene in printed books we should look at the producers of books, the publishers; at the distributors, the wholesalers, retailers, and clubs; and at the consumers, libraries, and last, but most, readers.

It seems widely believed these days that book publishing, like other branches of American enterprise, has turned from smallness to bigness, from personal, privately held houses to large, corporate entities. Many are the examples: In 1950, Knopf, Pantheon, Viking, Holt Rinehart, Simon and Schuster, Morrow, Putnam, Random House, Dutton, Little Brown, and others were independent, relatively small, and managed by those who owned them. Today, they are owned by large corporations. No question about it: today, more books are being published by firms that are responsible to corporate bosses, boards of directors, and stockholders. More—but by no means all. Indeed, the notion that book publishing is now big business is true only of a small part of the industry.

Books in Print lists about 14,000 publishers. Of that number, about 400 could be called big or middle-sized—big meaning companies with proceeds of more than $30 million a year, middle-sized those with from $3 million to $30 million. That leaves 13,500 small publishers, many of them very small and specialized, but all of them capable of producing a printed book and making it available.

Since my publishing life has been almost evenly divided between a large firm—Harper—and a small-to-medium house—Atheneum —I have thought much about this aspect of publishing. I see no evidence that corporate ownership necessarily alters the nature or quality of a list. Random House has not been independent for many years, but I find no change in the kinds of books they produce. Much is made by some of the notion that corporate ownership with its focus on the bottom line *must* mean less experiment, fewer first novels, less poetry, a more commercial "product." Maybe it *should* mean that, and maybe it will, but so far the evidence is very thin. And even if the large firms moved in this direction, there is a heavy counterbalance in those hundreds, indeed thousands, of small firms with their immense diversity of tastes being exercised by people responsible only to themselves. Each year for some time now, there has been an emergence of new firms and an annual increase of 2.5 percent, net of mergers and failures, in the number of publishers.

And as big business, book publishing is somehow not quite there with such as oil and automobiles and foodstuffs. The whole book industry of the United States is smaller than the seventy-fifth individual firm in *Fortune*'s list. Even the largest of book publishers is still no IBM.

Another point about book publishing: It seems to have an intrinsic capacity to generate adaptations that mitigate the potential effect of bigness. For example, small, personal imprints within the large houses have proliferated in recent years and have, I believe, added much vitality.

The question about publishing, as an industry, of course, is: Can it adjust to the problems it now seems to face? One of these is this matter of corporate size and structure in an activity that places such value on individual taste and risk-taking. As I have indicated, I think it can and indeed is. But there are other problems, among which the principal ones seem to be rising costs, distribution miseries, technological rivals, and *readers*. And I propose to deal with them in that order.

It used to be said, at least in New York, that the price of a book should not exceed the price of a theater ticket. That was when both averaged five dollars. Well, if that rule holds, book prices are in good shape, being well below theater tickets. But book prices have risen faster than inflation in recent years, and many people think they are too high—with novels at fourteen to twenty dollars, nonfiction at fourteen to twenty-five dollars, and the average of all hardbound books at over thirty dollars.

The response, of course, is that you can find all the good reading you could desire in paperbacks, of which the mass-market ones now average just over three dollars and the bookstore ones just under twelve dollars. Another example of adjustment is found in this field of paperbacks, something I suppose can be seen as adaptation to the problems of price and of distribution. In the past thirty-five years paperbacks have grown to fill 60 percent of the entire adult book market, and in the past twelve years trade paperbacks have increased by 500 percent to become 40 percent of the total paperback market.

Still another adjustment lies in the enormous and growing discount market and the book clubs with their bargains. These two now account for a sizable proportion of trade book sales, and discounting has moved into the college market as well, in the form of a vast secondhand sale. Indeed, one wonders who buys books at full price, and why? Since I do less frequently than I used to, I know only that lots of people do, perhaps often as gifts. Whether or not they will continue to, I obviously don't know, and I do worry about the costs of books. Some people believe we can reduce them by better use of new production technologies in printing and binding, and efforts are being made in that direction. If there are any big breakthroughs there I don't see them. People are also trying to reduce distribution costs, which brings me to that part of the industry—and an important, confusing part it is.

The five legs on which book distribution rests are wholesalers, bookstores, book clubs, mail order, and, last but far from least, libraries. For a long time there has been a widespread conviction that book distribution is as antiquated and badly done as can be, that it is easier to buy almost anything at retail than a book. There is also a general certainty that the good bookstore is disappearing. Is this true?

Once again, numbers are not solid, but it looks as though there are about 19,000 bookstores, including about 5,500 general ones, 3,500 religious, 2,500 college, 1,100 department store, 700 paperback, and 600 secondhand. And it is held that there are 100,000 or more places where mass-market paperbacks are sold. Is this enough? Are they in the right places? Are they as good as some of them used to be? Are they solely concerned with best-sellers? Are there any clerks left who know a book from a buck?

The only answers I know to these questions are my own and those of friends in various parts of the country, and they vary widely. I am inclined to agree that few bookstores are as good as a few of them used to be. As far as I am concerned, neither are ice cream parlors, soda fountains, bars, groceries, butcher shops, or drugstores.

I still know a few good bookstores where you can find a reasonable selection of literature, old and new. I also know that anybody, anywhere in the United States, can get almost any book by mail—current ones from clubs and others from the several mail services. You can also get a Xerox copy of any book.

Indeed, the one thing I feel certain about in regard to distribution is the tremendous growth of the chains and of discounting in general. Walden has more than nine hundred stores, Dalton almost eight hundred, Crown about two hundred, and there are discounters all over the land. Is this good or bad for books? For publishers and full-price booksellers, it is a worry. For customers, it simply makes books like so many other things we buy, from cars to liquor. As far as I can see, America is now discount land, an occidental bazaar. And I see no reason to find this bad for books. Indeed, if I had my way, publishers would sell to wholesalers and retailers at a price necessary to cover their costs—including the author's earnings of course—and let retailers fix their own prices. But I do not expect to have my way.

There is both not much and a lot to say about the other channels of book distribution. The book clubs seem to have reached a fairly stable and prosperous level of activity. They claim to offer all good current books and a selection of classics and reference books. That's not entirely true, but they do offer a lot of good books to millions of people, many of whom might never reach a bookstore and probably would not otherwise get *The Discoverers* by Daniel Boorstin, Roget's *Thesaurus,* or Plato's *Dialogues*—to choose some examples that illustrate how one can load the dice in a friendly essay.

If I say little about wholesalers, it is simply because I find little to say. They are, I feel, more effective than they were thirty years ago. But when I consider the speed and efficiency of the computer and electronic communication, I wonder how much more effective they *could* be. Perhaps will be?

Of libraries, especially in this setting, there is a great deal to say. One cannot consider the future of books in the United States without trying to forecast the trends of libraries. The facts are at hand:

There are about 8,800 public library systems in the United States, and 1,300 of them have at least one branch beyond the main library. There are about 12,000 libraries in universities, colleges, government, armed forces, law institutions, and medical and religious places, and 4,000 of these are classed as special libraries.

If my observation is sound, none of these libraries has—or thinks it has—enough money to do the job as it could be done, and all of them worry that in the immediate future there may be less. I don't know how to foresee the particulars, but I suspect that any country that is working up a storm about the quality of its education will not be able to do much about it without feeding its libraries. And if libraries are starving, how can we explain the apparent steady growth in library circulation over the past forty years? Circulation has grown twice as much as has population.

I suppose the most colorful nightmare for book publishers is the bookless library. I first experienced it about twenty-five years ago at a great library school that was demonstrating some of the then-new hardware and software. And I came away with two convictions that I still hold. First, anything is now *possible,* including a country with one library and everything online. Second, that is most unlikely to happen, at least for as long as I can see ahead. And for two reasons. The cost is so far beyond the possible or the sane as to beggar the fantasies of the defense spenders. And the book, as Dan Boorstin has often said, is still the superior tool—perhaps not for the storage and retrieval of simple information, but certainly for conveying ideas, literature, and entertainment.

A related and perhaps equally important question is the future role of the book in education—a matter of much debate again now, just as it was twenty years ago. The fears of the sixties that the book would disappear from schools, as students were placed in electronic carrels for hours, have not proved sound. And the current experiments with education by TV, cable, and cassette seem to me to promise a very partial displacement of the book.

To summarize the situation within the book community:

Book publishing is changing—at least on the surface—but not very much. It continues to be an activity in which risks and decisions are made by individuals or small groups. It is still in major part a cottage industry, even if the cottage is computerized.

The products of the industry—books—are as varied, as numerous, as unpredictable in reception, and as essential to the lives of a modest but quite steady part of the population as ever they were—and probably more so.

Changes are happening in every part of the book world, but, from the inside, it looks as if the book—print on paper—is here to stay.

How does it look outside the castle? Is this another case of Maupassant's plague? Have we drawn the bridge over the moat and are we dancing while the pest rages outside?

Ever since it first appeared, the book has been subject to threats of extinction. In recent times, the bicycle, the automobile, movies, and radio have each been seen as the death of the book. My favorite example of the threat—if not so much to the book as to the book publisher—was the member of the Lippincott tribe who decided that the menace to his activity was the spread of the free public library. Since he couldn't oppose it as free or public he waged a campaign against it as a spreader of disease, as books passed from hand to hand.

Now, of course, the threat is found in television and the computer. Let's take TV first.

For these past few years I have been leading a double life. My essential activity continues to be the publishing of books. But I have also been increasingly involved in television as a trustee and member of the program committee of the public TV station in New York. This has given me some interesting insights into the world of the electronic genie which is thought, by some, to be out of the bottle and rampant. Before the insights, here are a few recent and fairly reliable facts.

In 1984 sales of books in the United States came to about $9 billion. In that year, Americans spent $14 billion on video recorders, disk players, game consoles, cable, video cameras, tapes, disks and cartridges; and I don't know how much more on the basic TV sets through which all this operates. Those sets were said to be on seven hours a day in the average household, and a peak audience could include more than 100 million people. Homes with TV totaled more than 83 million. This is not an American phenomenon. VCR populations in Japan, the United Kingdom, West Germany, the Netherlands, Australia, and Taiwan are all proportionately greater than in the United States.

The impact of TV on our lives and our culture has been almost endlessly examined for thirty years, producing enormous heat but not much light. And the same applies to its effect on books and reading. The obvious question is how can many people find much time for books if Americans are spending seven hours a day in front of a TV? To which our report of *Books in Our Future* answers that there is "elastic time" and quotes Theodore Caplow's finding, on his return to Middletown, fifty years after the Lynds studied Middletown for the first time. He says that people are viewing TV twenty-eight hours a week, but that the reading of books and newspapers and magazines has not decreased.[1] I like that finding, and I like Dan Boorstin's notion of elastic time. And I have a simpler suspicion: We may know that the TV is on twenty-eight hours a week or even seven hours a day in the average house, but do we really know how much it is watched? How much it simply makes background noise?

The children that my generation had were the earliest TV generation, and loud was the parental wailing. If these children were indeed lost to reading, how do we account for the considerable evidence that book sales have kept up with the population boom and library circulation has exceeded it?

What my experience with TV has shown me is that it may displace reading for some people at some periods of their life— perhaps forever for a certain number. But it also leads some to reading they might otherwise have missed. Programs like "Reading Rainbow" increase the sale of some children's books enormously, and series like "The Little House on the Prairie" can cause literally millions to buy copies of books that were published many years ago and half forgotten. Even adults seem capable of being stimulated by TV to read a book, as we have seen with the revived sales of classics following TV dramatizations.

One thing that technology seems to displace in the TV world is itself. When cable appeared, the broadcasters worried and fought it. But cable came on and stole time from broadcast. We are only a few years into the cable era and it now looks as though the video-cassette is displacing a certain amount of cable. *Books in Our Future* says, "Technology is not the problem. It is our opportunity."

The most recent goblin is the computer, which is seen by some as the end not only of reading but also of writing. The computer is certainly having an effect on books, but, so far, the principal one I see is to produce the largest increase of books in any category, namely computer books. It is also, of course, evoking other changes, principally in its database form, which is a superior way of storing and retrieving information for such lawyers, business-men, doctors, pharmacists, policemen, librarians, scientists, and others who need speedy access to data and fact.

Much study is now devoted among publishers to finding out what proportion of traditional print publishing is likely to move to electronic. The most confident guesses report that about 10 per-cent may go to database and cassette. For the report *Books in Our Future,* scores of scientists, publishers, printers, librarians, tech-nologists, writers, scholars, booksellers, and editors gave their judgment: "The consensus of the specialists in all the book fields is that in the near future, between the present and the end of the century, the printed book will remain the primary form of com-municating knowledge and experience and imagination."[2]

The specialists have been wrong before, as the stock market demonstrates regularly. But in this matter I find it notable that among those—comparatively few—who believe the day of the book is over, there is no real vision of what will take its place, just a sort of Buck Rogers notion that it will "all be electronic" on screens or tubes or something.

Suppose at some point in the future some books have moved to words on hand-held computer screens that are compact, fit in your pocket, and are easy to use in bed, in the plane, or on the beach. Big change? Yes, for printers. But those books will still be written by writers, selected by somebody who may as well be called a pub-lisher, and, most important, consumed by readers in the act of reading. Which brings me to our last matter for consideration in the future of the book—namely, readers.

Once again, much has been devoted to the question of reading and literacy. As far as I can see, these studies have led to little certainty but rather to an uneasy judgment that, recently, reading of books has declined slightly among sixteen- to twenty-year-olds and also among people over sixty-five. We do not know yet whether this is a trend or a blip. But we do know with greater certainty that illiteracy is astonishingly widespread in this home of free public education. It is reported by several studies that twenty-five million adult Americans are functionally illiterate, and adult illiterates are increasing by more than two million a year. And this is alarming whether you see the future book as print on paper or electronic. It is, obviously, the most serious threat to the future of the book. It is also the object of a large and growing campaign that may well develop into a crusade. That such an effort can succeed has been demonstrated in a number of places—for example, in Cuba, where a "war against illiteracy" twenty years ago succeeded immensely. The secret, of course, lies in a genuine communitywide effort such as is called for in *Books in Our Future.*

As against the worry of illiteracy and, as Dan Boorstin has labeled it, *a*literacy, let me remind us that our studies also show that "about half of all adult Americans read books and their number is not declining." This is surely a good base on which to build the future. As I contemplate the staying power of the book I remember these words: "The factor most likely to assure the survival of books is perhaps so obvious that it is easily overlooked: There is simply no experience in life that matches silent reading."

To conclude, let me remind you that I am speaking essentially as a publisher, as one who realized while in college that books would be the center of my activity—as writer or publisher, and certainly as reader. How do I see it fifty years later as I attempt to look ahead?

Ideas, information, and entertainment are now available in forms I did not anticipate half a century ago. These new forms play a growing role in my life and in some ways are supplying input I formerly found only in books. TV brings information and entertainment; databases offer facts and numbers; computers perform several valuable functions and will doubtless be taught to perform more. But this is all still minor compared to the capacity of the book —as I have defined it—for satisfying those needs. And I do not see *that* changing any more than I see conversation with other minds, or communion with animals and nature, or actively doing and making things giving way to passive or even interactive electronic simulation.

To end this effort at forecasting, let me offer another item from the Bible. This one is also from Ecclesiastes, but it may be less familiar: "Is there anything whereof it may be said: See, this is *new?* It hath been already of old time, which was before us" (1:10).

Notes

1. Library of Congress, *Books in Our Future: A Report from the Librarian of Congress to the Congress* (Washington: U.S. Government Printing Office, 1984), 8-9.
2. Charles A. Goodrum and Helen Dalrymple, "The Printed Book in a Digital Age," unpublished report to the Center for the Book in the Library of Congress, 7 September 1984, 28.

Implicit in all of this is that books are not and never will be products like other things in our mercantile society. Senior managements may annually reduce them to this, but we never should. We have all learned from the business techniques that exist outside of publishing, but if we look to a congruence, life in the corporate gestalt will be, as Thomas Hobbes saw man's life in the largest sense in 1651, "nasty, brutish, and short." And the world of books, which for us is finding, reading and publishing them, offers us all very much better.

PETER MAYER
Publisher

17. Electronic Publishing
Its Impact on the Distribution of Information
F. Wilfrid Lancaster

As electronic publishing comes into its own, it will affect not only the format in which we read what we want to know, but also the presentation, preparation, and even composition of that information, according to F. Wilfrid Lancaster. In this chapter, he sketches several stages in the shift from publishing on paper to electronic communication.

Lancaster, one of the Book in the Future project advisors, is also the author of chapter 15 above.

Reprinted by permission from *National Forum: The Phi Kappa Phi Journal,* vol. 63, no. 3, Summer 1983. Copyright The Honor Society of Phi Kappa Phi, 1983.

T he term "electronic publishing" refers to the application of computers and other electronic devices to publishing activities; an "electronic publication" is one that exists in some electronic format such as magnetic tape, disk, microchip, or optical disk. Because electronic publishing is often touted as the key to managing certain kinds of information in our time, here I would like to trace its development, to indicate the spread of its influence, and to predict its possible future course.

In the table accompanying this chapter, I have identified stages and substages in the evolution of electronic publishing, as well as several important facets of the spread of its influence. In the first stage, which is not yet complete, electronic technology is used either to produce conventional print on paper or to generate new electronic publications that virtually simulate print on paper (i.e., electronic technology is used to display an information source but has little effect on the way the information is organized or presented).

The first step of this initial stage in the evolution is the use of computers to photocompose, thus allowing printing on paper without conventional typesetting. The indexing and abstracting services were first to be significantly affected by this development, which is approximately twenty years old. Publications consisting of indexes and abstracts, by virtue of their size and cost, as well as the amount of data to be processed, had most to gain from automated production. Once publications such as *Index Medicus* and *Chemical Abstracts* were generated by computer, the machine-readable database used in the publication process became available in magnetic tape for other applications. Thus, in effect, each database was available in two versions: the conventional print on paper and the equivalent machine-readable form, the latter being the first real electronic publications.

The second step, almost as old as the first, was the emergence of completely new publications exclusively in electronic form. Initially, these were mostly collections of data—numerical, statistical, chemical, physical—but other types, including new indexing services and state-of-the-art compilations, emerged somewhat later. The new science journal in pure electronic form is just now emerging.[1]

The third step will presumably be the gradual replacement of existing print-on-paper publications by their electronic counterparts. This step has not been reached yet, although we may be on the threshold of it. There is already evidence of a "migration" from the use of paper publications to the use of electronic forms: some libraries have begun to cancel subscriptions to certain publications in favor of online access to the material in the publications on demand, while some other, newer libraries have bypassed the print-on-paper stage and moved exclusively to online access for those publications available in this way.

In the short history of electronic publication, it is possible to discern several dimensions of a rapid but orderly spread of use and influence. First of all, the various types of publications seem to go through the several steps of conversion to electronics in a logical sequence. The news media—newspapers and popular magazines—were affected after the indexing/abstracting services, with other forms, such as patents, standards, and technical reports, being influenced later. The scholarly journal has felt significant effects only recently, and certain types of publication, notably imaginative works, have hardly been influenced.

As different types of publication have been affected, so has the amount of information provided on each publication: bibliographic citations only, citations plus abstracts, data compilations, and, finally, complete text. The full text of large bodies of legal material has been available in machine-readable form for about twenty years. That of certain newspapers and popular magazines became accessible online somewhat later. Accessibility of the full text of scholarly journals online is a more recent development, and very few are so far available in this way. Nevertheless, plans are afoot to make many more such journals accessible in one electronic format or another.[2] A few reference books, such as directories and encyclopedias, are also accessible in full text form online.

As more types of publications became accessible in electronic form and as more information was stored, the type of information service affected by electronic publishing expanded accordingly. The first electronic publications, those provided by indexing and abstracting services, could be used for little else than retrospective literature searching on demand and for Selective Dissemination of Information (SDI) (using a computer to provide a current awareness service in which the interest profiles of individuals are matched against the characteristics of bibliographic items newly added to some database). When compilations of data and, more particularly, the content of conventional reference books were made available in electronic form, it became possible to use such sources to answer factual-type questions.

The impact on document delivery can itself be seen as falling into three stages.[3] In the first, electronic networks provide online access to union catalogs which allow copies of desired items to be located; the item itself is requested and delivered in a conventional

Increasing Impact of Electronic Publishing
Various dimensions of the spread of influence

Stages in implementation

1. Simulation of print on paper
   a) computer as printing device
   b) new publications in electronic form
   c) replacement of print on paper
2. Exploitation of full electronic capabilities. Impact on the way information is packaged and presented.

Type of publication affected

1. Indexing and abstracting services
2. Newspapers and magazines
3. Reference books
4. Scholarly journals
5. Other "information" items
6. Imaginative works

Amount stored

1. Bibliographic references
2. Abstracts
3. Full text

Subject matter

1. Science and technology
2. Social sciences. Business
3. Humanities
4. "General interest"

Mode of distribution

1. Magnetic tapes
2. Online access
   a) institutional terminals
   b) home computers
   c) two-way television
3. Other distributed forms
   a) tape cassettes
   b) videodisk
   c) other

Audience affected

1. Institutions
   a) special libraries
   b) academic libraries
   c) public libraries
2. The general public

Information service affected

1. Retrospective literature searching
2. Current awareness (SDI)
3. Question answering
4. Document delivery
   a) location
   b) ordering
   c) access and delivery

way. In the second, a request for a publication is generated at a terminal, causing the item to be supplied, again as conventional paper copy, by a publisher, library, or other agency. The final stage consists in the actual delivery of the document electronically. This might include online access to the full text, for example, a journal article, or it could involve the generation of a paper copy from an electronic source (for example, optical digital disk) with transmission of the text via conventional mail or via electronic communication. The accessibility of full text online allows the literature-searching and document-delivery functions to be combined, since it will usually be possible to search the text electronically (for example, looking for particular names or combinations of words/phrases) as well as reading it sequentially.

Another facet in the evolution to electronics is the spread of subject-related influence and the concomitant increase in the size of the audience affected. The first electronic publications were exclusively scientific and technical in nature, and they were used by individuals at only a small number of special libraries. As electronic publishing spread into the social sciences, into business, and into the humanities (the humanities are still not profoundly affected), the use and appeal extended to academic libraries of all types and sizes. Public librarians are only now beginning to witness the effect of the influence of electronic information management resulting from the more recent emergence of a wide range of "general interest" publications in electronic form: indexes to popular magazines, the text of newspapers and magazines, and conventional reference sources such as directories.

The final dimension of the table relates to the form in which the electronic publication is distributed or otherwise made accessible. At first, such publications were accessible only as magnetic tape to a rather small number of organizations who were owners of large mainframe computers. Since about 1970, the accessibility of electronic information sources has increased by orders of magnitude as more and more publications have been made available through online vendors.

But electronic publications have also become available in other forms and modes of distribution. In some places, two-way television (i.e., videotex) has put various types of electronic publications directly into the home. For use with home computers, a few are distributed in the form of tape cassettes while others (various types of training materials) are issued on some type of videodisk. Even the bilingual dictionaries available on hand-held microprocessors can be considered another form of electronic publication. No doubt further "forms" will emerge in the near future. It should be noted that some of these "electronic publications" are *distributed* as physical artifacts, while others, less tangible, are only *accessible* through a terminal like a domestic television set that provides the entry point to some telecommunications network.

The decreasing cost and increasing availability of home computers seems likely to provide the greatest impetus to the rapid spread of influence of electronic publications. I believe it to be highly significant that, in 1983, the owner of a home computer has about the same level of access to online information resources that only libraries had just a decade ago. Moreover, the vendors of online access have recognized the existence of this market and are offering favorable rates for use of these resources by the general public during off-peak hours.

All of this is past history. To look into the future presents more difficulty. It is my belief that we are evolving from a society whose formal communication patterns are based primarily on print on paper to one in which communication of all types will largely take place through electronic media.

There is no historical precedent for supposing that the book printed on paper will reign supreme forever. The printed book, no more than five hundred years old, occupies a small niche in the history of human communication. In point of fact, its period of supremacy will be much shorter than that of its ancestors. For materials distributed for their informational content, print on paper may be superseded more or less completely by the end of this century. For imaginative works it may take somewhat longer. Nevertheless, what reason does one have for supposing that people will still be writing novels a hundred years from now? The novel, in its true form, did not exist before the printing press. It is a form of artistic expression peculiarly suited to the medium of print on paper. Presumably, new forms of literary expression will be spawned by the electronic media.

Economic considerations seem clearly to favor electronic publishing. Technological progress will continue to reduce the cost of distributing information (including mail) electronically relative to the cost of distributing the same information in paper form.

It is true, of course, that there are many obstacles in the path of a complete transition to electronics. One such obstacle—lack of wide availability of terminals—seems likely to be overcome rather quickly through the rapid spread of home computers, of two-way television, of videodisk, and of other technologies.

A more significant obstacle is the fact that paper still acts as a type of crutch for most people. Up to now, computers have undoubtedly generated more paper than they have saved. One reason is that users have not had any convenient way of storing personal information except in paper form. As microcomputers become more pervasive, this situation will no longer exist.

My own children are much less reliant on paper than I am, and I suspect that this is not a phenomenon peculiar to my family. Their generation will be much less resistant than mine to the replacement of paper. The electronic game may be the single most effective bridge between the age of paper and the age of electronics.

In point of fact, resistance to the migration from paper may not be as strong or as widespread as one might suspect. At least, that is what the few studies addressing this issue seem to indicate. Seiler and Raben, for example, found rather little resistance to electronic publishing in the academic community, even in accepting the legitimacy of this form in considerations of promotion or tenure, where research and publication are so centrally important.[4]

The printed book, to be sure, does have many virtues: aesthetic appeal, reasonable portability, easy browsability, and the ability to be randomly accessed. Nevertheless, as a means of communicating information effectively, it is far from ideal. Its major limitation is that, in both text and illustrations, it is entirely static: it is not easily reorganized or updated. We seem to have reached the limits of what can be achieved with the printed book as a device for the transmission of information.

In contrast, electronic publishing is in no more than an embryonic stage of development: the simulation state as identified in the table. In fact, few, if any, "true" electronic publications yet exist. By "true" I mean "exploiting the full capabilities of the electronic medium." Most of the existing publications present information that was originally prepared for printing on paper.

In the longer term, we can expect that electronic publishing will have a profound impact on the way information is presented. Making an existing science journal or encyclopedia accessible online does not create a true electronic publication but merely displays a print-on-paper publication in a different way.

The true electronic journal will presumably be quite different from anything we now see in libraries. In the first place, the packaging and distribution would change significantly. In an electronic world, it would make no sense to subscribe to a single journal. Instead, a subscription would allow one's interest profile to be matched against the contributions accepted into a wide range of electronic databases. The way information is presented could also change, with less reliance placed on static illustrations and narrative text and more on electronic analog models (e.g., of experiments in applied mechanics).

Other publication forms would be affected in a similar way. The electronic textbook would be reorganizable by the individual instructor or student. Almost as many versions as there are users could thus exist. It, too, would incorporate dynamics and would be "interactive" rather than passive. Depending on the electronic medium adopted, the electronic encyclopedia could incorporate reorganizable text, moving pictures, and sound. All of these capabilities, of course, already exist, for example, in computer-based education,[5] although they have not yet been applied to what we normally think of as a "publication."

A considerable migration toward use of electronic forms of publication has already occurred in the past twenty years. This is somewhat remarkable considering how comparatively primitive these forms still remain. The replacement of print on paper will occur not because electronic publishing will present the printed book in an alternative format, but because it will lead to new and more effective ways of packaging and presenting information.

Elsewhere, I have written on the possible impact of these developments on libraries.[6] I will not go into this subject here, except to reaffirm my belief that the library as we now know it—a building housing physical artifacts—will cease to exist (in this prediction I differ from De Gennaro,[7]) although the need for the technical expertise of skilled information professionals may persist far beyond the time when the institution has outlived its value. Ironically, the library as an institution may crumble at exactly the time that the "librarian" assumes a key role as information consultant in a society heavily dependent on accessing and processing information.

Notes

1. W. J. Broad, "Journals: Fearing the Electronic Future." *Science* 216 (May 1982): 964-68.
2. Eugene Garfield, "Document-Delivery Systems in the Information Age," *National Forum*, 63, no. 3 (Summer 1983): 8-10.
3. Ibid.
4. L. H. Seiler and J. Raben. "The Electronic Journal." *Society* 18, no. 6 (1981): 76-83.
5. John H. Painter, "Approaching Computer-Based Education: How Will the University Respond?" *National Forum*, 63, no. 3 (Summer 1983): 20-22.
6. F. Wilfrid Lancaster. *Libraries and Librarians in an Age of Electronics* (Arlington, Va.: Information Resources Press, 1982).
7. Richard De Gennaro, "Libraries, Technology, and the Information Marketplace," *National Forum*, 63, no. 3 (Summer 1983): 30-31.

Looking at the panoply of new information media available, any dispassionate observer must conclude not that books will disappear, but that their claim on our attention and pocketbooks will diminish in the future. This does not mean that the book publishing industry will shrink in size; it will continue to grow, but will form a smaller part of the overall communications environment. Such a change is not new. It has been in progress for much of this century.

EFREM SIGEL
Editor

Of the computer we ask more. We ask not just about where we stand in nature, but about where we stand in the world of artifact. We search for a link between who we are and what we have made, between who we are and what we might create, between who we are and what, through our intimacy with our own creations, we might become.

SHERRY TURKLE
Professor

18. Spreading the Word

Morris Philipson

Publishers, not technology, will determine the success
or failure of publishing, according to Morris Philipson.
On one hand, he asserts, the arrival of computers has
not had the great effect sometimes claimed. On the
other hand, regardless of technological success, the
aims of the publisher, especially the publisher in the
humanities, are not turned toward information but
toward the judgment and comprehension to which such
information may, if and only if it is properly assessed,
contribute.

Morris Philipson, Director of the University of Chicago Press, was introduced above as one of the advisors
to the Book in the Future project.

This essay is adapted from a speech Philipson presented at the annual meeting of the Society for Scholarly Publishing in Washington, D.C., May 30, 1984.

From *Scholarly Publishing,* vol. 16, no. 2, January 1985. © University of Toronto
Press 1985. Reprinted by permission of University of Toronto Press.

A famous book in contemporary American philosophy is titled *Must We Mean What We Say?* The answer to that question is essentially yes, because, if we don't, we tear holes in the network of trust that makes human communication and cooperation possible.

Recently I was asked to speak at a meeting on the immediate and long-range future of publications, primarily those in the humanities. I was not aware until the printed program arrived, however, that my talk would be described in the following way: "How can publishers of scholarly books and journals marshal their forces and organize to best advantage to continue their important mission through the 1980s?" Does this mean what it says? The rhetoric is that of being embattled. "Marshalling forces" has as its model the warring image of enemy marshals arranging and deploying their military forces. Is the metaphor justified? If publishers are at war, who is the enemy?

This is not an isolated instance of such language being used where concern is expressed in trying to imagine how the future of scholarly publishing may change. I offer other examples. For the meeting called not long ago at the Library of Congress, under a congressional resolution to consider "the book of the future," such questions as these were put to the participants: "How are new technologies shaping the future of books, reading, and learning in America?" "What types of books (form or content) will be outmoded by new electronic technologies?" Some time after that I received a letter from an organization undertaking to prepare an exhibition for the Grolier Club in New York on "The Future of the Book." It requested responses to such questions as "What are the unique functions and services of the book which will be threatened by new electronic technologies?" And, again, "What changes do you visualize in the publishing industry before the end of the century? In the next 100 years? (Please feel free to direct your answer to any issue—literature, business practices, design, etc.)"

There are two classic tendencies at work here—both in the form of leading questions. One assumes that there is a hostile, antagonistic confrontation between the possibilities of electronic innovations on the one hand and the sluggish resistance of conservative publishers on the other. The second stems from assumptions about prophecy; one element of these is prehistoric and reflects the forgivable human wish to foresee the future, whether by reading signs or consulting oracles; the other, more recent, stems from the Age of Invention, and assumes that if something can be imagined as possible it will, necessarily, become actual, sooner or later.

Neither prophecy nor prediction is a science with any degree of certainty. The history of predictions has yet to be written, but each of us can instantly come up with a number of examples to show that, more often than not, what one generation has predicted as just around the corner, the next generation must retreat from as a blind alley.

Another explanation of the rhetoric of hostility—the choice of images of warfare—comes from the currently popular mind-set of journalism, namely, investigative reporting. It begins with the powerful assumption that the institution or organization or person being examined is either a liar or an incompetent, primarily concerned with obfuscating the truth in order to appear in the best light. Therefore such reporters ask questions like; "What mistake do you most regret having made?" Or "What has been your greatest disappointment?" Or "How would you have done things differently if you had known then what you know now?" That cast of mind is based on much experience of lying and incompetence; unfortunately having become all-pervasive, it no longer assumes a margin for truthfulness and competence. Let it be remembered that the phrase "a leading question" usually means "a misleading question."

Therefore, if one reads the question "How can publishers of scholarly books and journals marshal their forces and organize to best advantage to continue their important mission through the 1980s?" and accepts that it does mean what it says, we are to believe that there is hostile antagonism between such publishers and the inventors or purveyors of something generally classed under the phrase "the new technology" or "hi tech." There is also the possible implication that the conventional "forces" may somehow be unequal to that irresistible technological tidal wave and therefore, instead of accommodating to it, may well be pounded to death. Publishers of scholarship are portrayed as if we were button manufacturers while the news is breaking that the zipper has just been invented. Panic time!

I suggest that the only explanation for this melodramatic caricature is that Americans as a nation—and the people of other nations as well—have become completely politicized and are comfortable only with a sense of paranoia. Conspiracy as the father of historical progress. We are invited repeatedly not only to examine the present condition of scholarly publishing but to look ahead at "the challenges, opportunities, and hazards that lie in the future." The fact is that publishers are already doing this on a day-to-day basis. It is not dramatic. We do not go to work every day with the thought that the Great Database In the Sky will put us all out of business by five o'clock in the afternoon. If we are to spread the word that is rational, sensible, and within the realm of possibility, we have to acknowledge that different methods of composition and printing, distribution and storage are being developed, that certain substitutes for the printed word are possible and, in some cases, readily available, and that they do offer new opportunity. But to the extent that they are "challenges" and "hazards," we are victimized by the mistaken idea that they will transform scholarly publishing *whether we like it or not.*

No invention is going to transform publishing. There is no irresistible force at work here. Purveyors of hardware and software will not transform publishing. *Publishers* will or will not transform publishing. Experiments that we are willing to undertake will be controlled by our concern for many things in addition to technological innovations. We are concerned about the use of our financial and human resources; we are concerned about acceptance by our potential customers; we are wary of promises that cannot be fulfilled; we resist piracy and scorning of the responsibility to pay for use which matters mightily to both author and publisher. We are experimenting on an ad hoc basis—the only competent way to experiment—not by a panic psychology, an either/or approach of "convert to the new techniques or perish." The only competent way to experiment is critically.

For the publication of both books and journals, there is no new technology that can function without the prior existence of a conventional book or journal. So far, all electronic devices, especially for "information retrieval," depend on the prior existence of books or journals from which information is to be retrieved. There are three significant exceptions: current airline reservation information; current stock market reports; and the United Press International news wire. None of these has anything to do with scholarly publishing.

The current development—certainly that with which the University of Chicago Press has been involved for half a dozen years—has to do with the preparation of books or journal articles by authors in machine readable forms such as magnetic tapes or floppy disks at the one end and the use of those tapes or disks for photocomposition at the other end. Such innovations "promise" greater speed and lower costs. Those promises have yet to be kept. Where there is a saving in the costs of keyboarding it is eaten up by the costs of management invested in solving the problems of incompatibility on a variety of levels. We are told that the machinery is error-free, that errors are introduced by human beings. What we need are error-free human beings. That attitude of the rational mind leads to a preference for robots over human beings. Be that as it may, the innovations of current practical use to scholarly publishing are all in the service of preserving the appearance of conventional publishing.

In contrast to that, databases, mainly bibliographic, already in use for the physical and biological sciences and law, still remain to justify themselves financially. How expensive it will become to develop and to pay for the use of such sophisticated tools in other fields remains to be determined. To the extent that such experiments are subsidized by corporations or by government—rather than paid for by users—they are not in the "real world" and what the acceptable producer-consumer relationship will be is unknowable. But the point in time when the printed word will fade away and all research will be embodied in and made accessible through means of the computer is nowhere in sight. It is a fantasy of science fiction without any practical conception of what it will cost or whether it is a justifiable expense, to say nothing of whether the users would prefer it. What might emerge as a radical change in the future is absolutely unpredictable.

This is not because we cannot learn a new language. Even in the humanities we are doing that all the time. We not only know how to say but we know the meaning of such phrases as terminal keyboard, word processor, microcomputer, character recognition, digital scanner, digital facsimile, graphics software, graphics tablet; online storage and memory; verification systems, archiving systems, offline storage, retrieval systems. We even know phrases that are false, for there are people who talk of "the information industry" as if such a thing existed.

Now, all these words which are being spread—bandied about—are concerned with the *means* of communication rather than the *ends* to be served. I submit that all of us engaged in the operations of publishing would be much better served if we concentrated more concern on our purposes or the ends and the goals of what it is we are doing than on the means, let alone the new "challenges" to those means. I submit further that the quality of what is communicated for the purpose of advancing scholarly learning is infinitely more significant than the means by which it is "archived or retrieved." No proposition of the twentieth century is more false or self-destroying than McLuhan's silly idea that the medium is the message. The intellectual "challenge" of Plato's dialogues is the same whether preserved, and therefore available to be studied, on a scroll, in a codex, in a printed book, or on a video terminal.

There are some scholars who take great joy from considering the differences between the humanities on one hand and the natural sciences and mathematics on the other. But most scholarly publishers will acknowledge that the similarities are more important than the differences. Thought progresses by the experience of the uses it can be put to in both domains; and while choices of subject matter and method may appear to be radically different, in all the enterprises of the life of the mind movement goes from observation through generalization to hypotheses to theory and thus to application and practice. The word "information" may be the most elastic of all abstract terms, for it may mistakenly apply to every level from the simplest experience of observations to the most imaginative of abstract formulations. But in every realm—in every discipline of thought—the operation of judgment is crucial, and in this regard there is no difference between the humanities and the sciences. If as publishers we make the mistake of thinking that we are in the business of storing and distributing information only, then we are out of touch with what is essential to the human enterprise. Bear with me, if I spell out at some length the difference between information and judgment through an example examined by a commission of the United States Congress, subsequently made public.

The *New York Times* of Thursday, 29 December 1983, reported: "on the 23d of October 1983, a truck laden with the equivalent of over 12,000 pounds of TNT crashed through the perimeter of the compound of the U.S. contingent of the multinational force at Beirut International Airport, Beirut, Lebanon, penetrated the battalion landing team headquarters building, and detonated. The force of the explosion destroyed the building, resulting in the deaths of 241 U.S. military personnel. This report examines the circumstances of that terrorist attack and its immediate aftermath."

The commission was convened by the Secretary of Defense in November 1983 to conduct an independent inquiry into the terrorist attack, to examine the mission of the marines, the rules of engagement governing their conduct, the responsiveness of the chain of command, intelligence support, the security measures in place before and after the attack, the attack itself, and the adequacy of casualty handling procedures. It concluded that "significant attention must be given by the entire U.S. intelligence structure to purging and refining of masses of generalized information into intelligence analysis useful to small unit ground commanders." In the series of articles which appeared in the *New York Times,* the key words are strung together in the headline of an article that appeared on Sunday, 11 December 1983. It reads like an obituary: "Intelligence: Too Much Information, Too Little Evaluation."

The article continues:

The problem in Beirut was not insufficient intelligence, but insufficient evaluation, according to a variety of current and former military and intelligence officers familiar with the intelligence support provided to the Marines.

If anything, commanders up the line agreed, the Marines received too much raw intelligence about terrorism and were not trained to analyze it.

The right amount of evaluation would have been made possible by a judgment taking into account the observations reported as information, the interpretations of them in terms of probability depending on an understanding of the values, the belief systems of the human beings involved—what they believed they stood to lose or gain by what they might do—and the integration of that into the larger political picture with the assumptions not only of what U.S. forces were doing there in the short run but what is at stake in the long run. Such an operation of judgment based on observation, interpretation, and integration can take place only in a mature mind—the result of a liberal education where "liberal" means free of dogma and able to recognize as many of the elements at play which contribute to an enemy's way of life as those which contribute to one's own. It is the study of the humanities that best prepares such a mind. The study of the humanities matures the mind. Probability is a statistical concept; human understanding or comprehension is not. Dare I say what it is? It is in practice what wisdom is in theory.

If we forget that the cultivation of a mature mind is the goal of publishing in the humanities and place all our emphasis on the *means* by which so-called information might be more and more speedily communicated or retrieved, we will end up under the same condemnation, on our tombstone, as the conclusion of the commission previously cited: "Too much information, too little evaluation."

This is not a political speech, but there is nothing having to do with the life of the mind that cannot be made political to the extent that a nation determines who has power over what. To the extent that a nation has private as well as public institutions independently pursuing both the humanities and the sciences, it has been a free market in the realm of ideas. In a free market the national government alone will not determine whether some new technological innovation will overwhelm scholarly publishing or not. There is a free market of means as well as of goals. We would be very foolish indeed if we were to accept a sense of gloom from a belief that the conventional book and the journal *must* be replaced by images on a video terminal. We know for a fact that experiments in that direction have not yet saved money; we know that there is a very considerable amount of user resistance. In certain respects, the major advantage is that of speed. One can get certain information faster than used to be possible. But that is only information. It is not judgment. In some realms of human activity, greater speed is not desirable: for example, in being infused by a piece of music, or in savoring excellent food, or in making love. What's the hurry about information—more, available faster—if we haven't educated a class of people to make practical judgments that will keep us from being exploded to death?

The basic truth is that publishing is a business. There are good businesses and bad businesses. A profit-making business that makes a profit and a nonprofit business that breaks even are good businesses. A business operating with a deficit is a bad business because its bankruptcy will grind it to a halt or because subsidies from some other source that keep it alive do so only by an artificial support system. Still, good publishers concerned with the well-being of their operations want to satisfy many needs—not only financial but intellectual, contractual, psychological, and aesthetic as well.

The good word to be spread is that publishers are taking into account the variety of technical innovations that are currently available and are likely to watch for developments in the future. Actual development will depend on what compromises are made between dreams of the possible and experience of what works to satisfy—adequately—many different needs within the context of what we can reasonably afford to invest in a financial gamble. We must hedge our bets, because there is too much at stake to put all our eggs in any one basket. In scholarly publishing, as in other endeavors, the function of judgment is crucial. We cannot afford to ask —or answer—what differences will inescapably, inevitably, be made, in five years or ten years. We must protect ourselves from having our judgment distorted. The rhetoric of confrontation puts our thinking out of focus.

It is a measure of a mature mind not to demand answers to misleading questions.

19. The Book and Literature in the 1980s

Dan Lacy

The most important effects of technology on culture may not be the most direct ones, according to Dan Lacy. It may turn out to be far more important that the new technologies allow economical short press-run production of books than that some sort of video book may appear. Mr. Lacy reflects on the apparent rejection of the commonalities of mass culture by intellectuals. He also provides several examples of the interrelation of technology and culture in the recent past.

Mr. Lacy was introduced above at the beginning of chapter 9, his essay "Reading in an Audiovisual and Electronic Era."

Reprinted with permission from *Library Trends,* vol. 33, no. 2, Fall 1984, pp. 115-20.
© 1984 The Board of Trustees of the University of Illinois.

The technology of communication of course affects the forms of literature. Homer's Μῆνιν ἄειδε θεὰ[1] roars from the bard's throat; Virgil's *"Arma virumque cano"*[2] lies softly on the page. The spread of writing by Virgil's day had already made the epic poem an archaism, still beautiful as the Gothic spires of an American college campus may be beautiful, and still reflecting the grandeur but no longer the vitality of the original.

Similarly, the widening availability of print in the late eighteenth and especially the nineteenth century led to the dominance of the novel as a literary form, replacing drama. The further cheapening of print in the latter decades of the nineteenth century produced the dime novel as an alternative to live entertainment. Even an invention apparently so remote as the railroad had its effect on literature. By making possible the rise of prosperous, truly national magazines that were able to pay contributors well, the railroad fostered the development and the popularity of the short story.

In our own century the cinema and television have restored drama to its pre-eighteenth-century dominance as a literary form and have given it audiences beyond any earlier imagining. The new media have also affected the character of drama. The capacity to use both close-ups and sweeping out-of-doors scenes has given a powerful flexibility to cinema and television as compared with the constraints of the stage. The recent BBC productions of Shakespeare have offered a fresh and intensified perception of these magnificent works. Not only are traditional works transformed, but this new technology has made possible quite new dramatic compositions—new literary forms.

The revival of drama in its new forms now consumes the attention of audiences to an extent never before dreamed of for any form of literature, with television alone occupying an average of thirty to thirty-five hours a week. To a much lesser degree than might have been assumed, however, has this truly extraordinary development diminished the attention to printed literature. Far more books are sold and apparently read than before the advent of television. And success in one literary form appears to whet, not sate, the public desire to experience the work in another. Popular novels become popular films or television miniseries. A successful film or television series will reignite demand for the book on which it is based; and if the film or series is based on an original script, a novel may be concocted to meet the demand.

We now confront still another remarkable new development in information technology: the computer and related data communications technology, together with the capacity to record in compact digital form text, images, and sound. What effect, we inquire, will this powerful new capacity have on literature and on the book as an embodiment of literature?

I am inclined to believe that the effect will be less than is anticipated, certainly less than that of cinema or broadcast. The new technology will affect profoundly the ways in which literary works are reproduced, recorded, preserved, cataloged and bibliographically controlled. But it is not likely to create new literary forms. The capacity to store, search, manipulate, recall, and instantly convey bodies of individual data is a most important capacity; but I believe it does not, like cinema, provide a new medium for literary work, for new forms in which the human mind can present its considered perception of life.

True, there are two possible exceptions to this general statement. A digitized laser disk could record a variety of alternative scenarios, indeed could be programmed to create new scenarios, which would enable a reader, by inputting his choices, to have a part in shaping the outcome of the story, thus establishing a new sort of relationship between author and reader. This could be an interesting gimmick, but a gimmick nevertheless.

More important is the fact that the same digitized laser disk can record text, moving images, and sound. If one is prepared to read from a cathode ray tube—and that will become less vexing and inconvenient as the technology improves—it will be possible to have the text accompanied by sound and moving illustrations. This will provide a useful medium for travel books, natural history guides, and certain textbooks; but actually the technique is already available in less efficient form as videotapes or films. Like those earlier manifestations, this new technology is unlikely to generate significant new literary works.

We can conclude that the mediation of the human mind in giving meaning to experience that we call literature is unlikely to be affected in a major way by the new technology as a medium. There may, however, be indirect consequences of the new technology, as was the case in the relation of railways to magazines. Particularly may this be true in the impact of the technology on printing costs.

The developments in the field of printing during the 1940s and 1950s involved very high speed presses, special printing plates, and laminated paper adhesive bindings. The economies they produced were applicable only to very long runs, usually of at least 100,000 copies, and hence relatively few titles. They made possible the mass-market paperback, making books available at a nominal price within the reach of almost everyone. This sharp reduction in price made possible, and was reciprocally made possible by, the use of magazine patterns of distribution with newsstands and drugstores rather than bookstores as the ultimate point of sale.

These technological and marketing changes made it possible to reach enormous new audiences at great profit to the publishers and authors of books adapted to this format and method of distribution. But these rewards were available to only a small proportion of the titles published annually—a few hundred at most out of tens of thousands. Even at extremely low prices, only certain kinds of titles could find the enormous number of buyers necessary to make this form of publication practical. And the limited number of pockets in newsstand and drugstore racks in the 1950s, as well as limited channels of distribution, imposed a further restriction.

Books offered in the mass-market paperback format as it existed in the 1950s had to sell themselves without benefit of recent reviews or advertising or the assistance of clerks. Since only a few dozen titles were likely to be available at any given outlet, the newsstand rarely rewarded a buyer seeking a particular title. Rather it met the needs of one who wanted simply a detective story, a western, an adventure story, a sexy romance, or a book by a well-known author (such as Erle Stanley Gardner) whose name had the characteristics of a brand name, assuring the buyer that he was getting a book with the qualities he had enjoyed in the past one.

Of course many excellent books, especially readily recognized classics, appeared in the mass-market format; and their number greatly increased after the 1950s when paperbacks became widely used in schools and colleges and were sold in traditional bookstores. But the primary effect of this technology was to provide very large financial rewards for the writing and publishing of formula fiction crafted to meet the current demands of the mass market and for certain limited kinds of nonfiction works. This concentration of financial rewards was heightened by the increasingingly close interrelation of films, television, and best-sellers.

Probably the impact of this sort of best-seller fever on serious literary publishing was less than feared. The people who bought gothic novels and horror stories off the newsstands in the millions did not put aside Saul Bellow or John Updike to do so—and indeed writers of that quality themselves shared, if less extravagantly, in the mass-market income. Serious publishers were perhaps more aided in than distracted from their literary undertakings by their mass-market bonanzas. But without question the emphases of publishing were in some measure distored by these phenomena growing out of the developments of the 1940s and 1950s in printing technology.

The computer-related technology of the 1980s points the opposite way. It lowers the per-title or per-page cost of readying a book for publication rather than, as in the earlier decades, the per-copy cost of reproduction. It tends to make affordable not the production of a great many copies each of a very few titles but rather the production of a great many titles in a relatively few copies each. This will have two consequences. One is that it will be easier to publish works in small editions, perhaps of 2,000 or fewer copies. The other is that it will be more practical to do "demand" publishing, in which individual copies are reproduced from a master as needed (in the future more likely from a laser disk than, as in the past, from a microfilm negative). Each of these new or enlarged possibilities is likely to be more significant for the publishing of specialized scholarly and technical works than for literary publishing. But the publishing of small literary journals and experimental works may be facilitated. The bibliographical and heuristic power of the computer and the greater ease of sharing resources among libraries afforded by the new technology will also broaden access to less known and less widely held literary works.

In view of all these considerations it seems unlikely that the new technology, for all its vast importance in other ways, will have a major effect on literature, either as a medium creating new forms or as a more efficient means of reproducing and distributing old forms. Though the artifacts in which it is embodied may change, the literary text will remain.

There will be novels, short stories, poems, and essays, and with rare exceptions we will read them from printed pages and not from the cathode ray tube or the computer printout. The forces that will change literature in the decades immediately ahead are either societal ones affecting the universe of which literature is a part, or else forces internal to literature itself. They are unlikely to be generated by the technology of information or communication.

I am no critic of literature, and I feel diffident in suggesting what some of these societal and internal changes may be. But two trends over the last generation seem evident. One is that American, and indeed Western, society—or at least the intellectuals in those societies—feeling betrayed in earlier enthusiasms and suspicious of professions of noble sentiment, has forsworn magnificence, whether in literature, art, or music. It would be difficult to imagine anyone in our time even attempting to write a *War and Peace,* paint the ceiling of a Sistine Chapel, build a cathedral of Chartres, or compose a Ninth Symphony. No faith in religion, in patriotism, or in man would inspire it. We flee the fear of grandiloquence and pomposity to take refuge in minimalism and simplicity. Heroes yield to anti-heroes: Willie Loman replaces King Lear.

The other trend is a rejection by all the arts of a vocabulary worn smooth by use until it seems no longer able to express with precision the concepts of the creator. New tonal patterns, new forms of sculpture and painting, and new literary devices are sought. This has given a freshness and vitality to much of the creative work of our time. But a work of art is consummated in its perception. A book is actualized by being read, a picture by being viewed, a symphony by being heard—not through the mechanical acts of reading, looking, and listening, but through the audience being penetrated by the creator's work and achieving a new conception. To the extent that the creator abandons a vocabulary familiar to the potential audience—abandons it indeed precisely because he feels it has become overfamiliar—he forfeits the opportunity for that communion. He creates to express rather than to communicate.

Hence many of the most expressive creators of our time—a Pollock, a Cage, a Pynchon—to some degree fail in broad communication with a large and comprehending audience, while mass audiences are achieved by the exercise of meretricious skill with the opposite concern: with how many are reached rather than with what is expressed to them. To exaggerate the dichotomy: on the one hand those deeply concerned with creative expression, but not with achieving communication with a broad audience; on the other, those seeking to profit by a large audience and willing to shape their creation to whatever will draw the largest number.

This was not always so. Sophocles and Shakespeare were the most popular playwrights of their times. The giants of Victorian literature were also avidly read and some became public heroes of a sort. Even into the generation just past, Faulkner, Hemingway, and Eliot, among many others, wrote nobly and were read widely. And there are not lacking, even today, those—one thinks of Saul Bellow, John Updike, and Robert Penn Warren—who are profoundly committed with important ideas and are concerned to communicate as well as to express them, and who in consequence have achieved wide audiences as well as critical respect for both integrity and skill.

It is not the computer or the laser-read disk or the word processor, nor yet the changing economics of the publishing industry, that will determine with what themes literature will concern itself or whether a reunion of serious creator and broad audiences can be achieved. The instruments of literature will remain. The book will still be there, made easier by the new technology to produce and to distribute, but probably little changed in form or physical character. Authors and readers will determine how and to what end their potentials will be realized.

Notes

1. Opening words of Homer's *Iliad.*
2. Opening words of Virgil's *Aeneid.*

The greatest source of untapped, unfathomable riches is at hand—everyone's hand. The richest person in the world—in fact, all the riches in the world—couldn't provide you with anything like the endless, incredible loot available at your local library.... Our libraries are being eroded alarmingly by inflation. It behooves us—all of us—to stop the rot by the application of that prime preserver—money.

FORBES MAGAZINE

VI.
The Book
Professions:
Librarianship

20. Realities

Educational Reform in a Learning Society

Task Force on Excellence in Education,
American Library Association

Stimulated by the report *A Nation at Risk* (see chapter 1 above), a task force of the American Library Association exhibits the roles of libraries throughout the learning society. Libraries are important for preschoolers, for educational institutions, and for active adults both on the job and in the community. The task force argues that public support of libraries is sound investment in the community.

Reprinted from *Realities: Educational Reform in a Learning Society*. Chicago: Task Force on Excellence in Education, American Library Association, 1984.

The Four Realities

The way in which our American public schools are educating young people for a life of social and technological change is the focus of reports, recommendations, debate, political discussion, and public concern. In 1983, the National Commission on Excellence in Education reported its assessment and recommendations in the publication *A Nation at Risk: The Imperative for Educational Reform.* The 1984 political campaigns show that this concern is shared by people in every state and territory.

Much public attention is focused on recommendations for changes in elementary and secondary schools. Yet, as *A Nation at Risk* clearly states, proposals for educational reform must recognize the need for lifelong learning. Libraries are an essential part of lifelong learning. The autobiographies and reminiscences of public leaders and other achievers document the ways in which libraries have influenced their lives. All people in a learning society deserve access to good library service.

The vitality of libraries as educational agencies depends on wise actions by public decision makers and others who provide resources to educational institutions. The American Library Association identifies four realities for effective educational reform within a learning society. The four realities are:

1. Learning begins before schooling.
2. Good schools require good school libraries.
3. People in a learning society need libraries throughout their lives.
4. Public support of libraries is an investment in people and communities.

Reality 1: Learning Begins Before Schooling

The extent to which parents introduce their children to books, culture, and learning affects children throughout life. *A Nation at Risk* points out to parents:

As surely as you are your child's first and most influential teacher, your child's ideas about education and its significance begin with you. You must be a living example of what you expect your children to honor and emulate. Moreover, you bear a responsibility to participate actively in your child's education.

You should...nurture your child's curiosity, creativity and confidence....Above all, exhibit a commitment to continued learning in your own life.

Research shows that children who have been exposed to reading and other cultural experiences before they begin school have a better chance of success in formal learning than those who do not have this experience. Among the most important of the preschool experiences are the development of skills in listening, speaking, and looking that prepare for reading and form the basis for the enjoyment of learning. In our society, most parents work outside the home, so all members of the family and extended family (including grandparents and brothers and sisters) can play important educational roles. Family members set the stage for reading and other learning and provide models of behavior. This family influence in developing attitudes toward learning (often extended by collaboration with day care, preschool, and other community agencies) is important for the prevention of deficiencies in school and beyond. Libraries contribute to preschool learning in two ways: through the services, programs, and materials that help parents increase their skills and capabilities, and through programs that serve children directly.

Library service to parents and day care staff supports preschool learning in a variety of ways. Libraries provide books for adults to read aloud to children. Groups of children in child care and day care centers and in public libraries listen to stories and act them out. Children borrow books and records from libraries. Toddler programs that bring very small children and their parents to the library together provide a basis for later, more independent use of libraries by children as they grow older.

All these experiences for young children require action by motivated, enthusiastic adults—adults who will instill a love of reading. Parents, volunteers, and day care center staff learn from librarians how to select and use materials with children. Librarians have the skills, experience, and desire to conduct workshops for parents, older children, babysitters, early childhood specialists, teachers, and volunteers. The library has information to help parents face problems which they face daily. In some communities, multi-language collections for parents and preschoolers are essential. Through libraries, parents can learn how to use television and newer technology, such as computers, to nurture children's creativity and confidence.

Librarians also help create community coalitions of school personnel, public librarians, members of parent-teacher groups, and others concerned with preschool learning. Public library staff who provide information and referral services help parents develop effective partnerships with schools, preschools, day care centers, and other early childhood agencies.

Unfortunately, limited funds in many of our public libraries have caused cutbacks in children's services. Day-to-day realities of operating and staffing public libraries result in the lack of a full-time children's librarian in many libraries and branches. Because of limited library staff, parents and preschool children may wait months before being able to participate in a storyhour program.

To ensure that children and their parents have library services for effective preschool learning, public officials should

- appropriate funds for parent education and early childhood services in public libraries, particularly those which demonstrate outreach and which promote cooperation with other educational and community agencies, and
- establish state and federal regulations for preschool day care services which mandate book and library resources as part of the basic program requirements.

Reality 2: Good Schools Require Good School Libraries

Good schools enable students to acquire and use knowledge, to experience and enjoy discovery and learning, to understand themselves and other people, to develop lifelong learning skills, and to function productively in a democratic society. Libraries are essential to each of these tasks. In libraries, students learn how to locate, organize, and use information that will expand their horizons and raise their self-expectations. Librarians are teachers, and they serve both students and teachers.

As students develop library skills in finding information, they seek more information, compare and evaluate sources and opinions, and develop critical thinking. These skills, which should be part of every school's curriculum, can be learned in school libraries.

School libraries serve as learner-oriented laboratories which support, extend, and individualize the school's curriculum. A California research study demonstrated that students with library experience achieved higher level language skills than those without this experience. In Virginia, a study proved that students who combined independent study with extensive library use under a librarian's supervision attained higher verbal scholastic aptitude test scores than students who used libraries only incidentally.

A Nation at Risk points out the limitations of textbooks. Well-stocked school libraries offer a diversity of books and other materials for students of all abilities, including the most gifted. Librarians have an essential educational role in helping teachers and students choose materials for class work and independent study.

Today's libraries are adding access to computer databases to their information resources. School librarians should be involved in the development of these databases to assure that they will be appropriate for the maturity, interests, and ability levels of students. These new resources should be available to students in elementary schools as well as in high schools.

A Nation at Risk says that the elementary years "should foster an enthusiasm for learning and the development of the individual's gifts and talents." This describes what occurs when elementary school children develop early and lasting pleasures in using libraries. In Indiana, a study showed that reading skills, verbal expression, and library skills were significantly greater in an elementary school after library services were increased. Disadvantaged children in Boston increased their skills in verbal expression of ideas and their language ability after twelve weekly one-hour library programs with books and storytelling.

Access to a library for quick fact-finding and sustained work on a project should be among the rights of every child and young person. The student who encounters a librarian who is directly involved in teaching has access to a much wider world than that of a single classroom. The librarian, at successive grade levels, introduces literature and teaches research study skills. From the librarian a student learns how to locate, interpret, and present information. The librarian teaches classes as part of the instructional program, supplements classroom study with appropriate presentations on research, gives book talks, and instructs in computer use. When the school librarian helps design curriculum, both teachers and students benefit. In every school, therefore, librarians should be included as members of curriculum design and review committees. They should also be involved as planners, providers, and participants in in-service training programs for teachers.

Too many of the 105,000 schools in the United States have inadequate school libraries because they lack the staff, materials, space, and services required by students and their teachers. Even many of the schools that have library materials provide few library services because they lack professional librarians. Almost three million pupils (7 percent of the total) attend public schools without a school library. In 1982, our country had only one school librarian for every 954 students. This is the equivalent of an average of only twenty seconds a day for each student.

The lack of librarians is especially severe in elementary schools. For example, in Los Angeles, our country's second largest city, in only twenty of the city's 450 elementary schools is there a full-time librarian. Furthermore, in the last decade, the number of school library supervisory and consulting staff at state and district levels has declined sharply.

In *A Nation at Risk,* the National Commission on Excellence in Education recommends higher educational standards and expectations, increased time for learning, and increased attention to English, mathematics, science, social studies, computer science, and foreign languages. To achieve these requirements, school libraries must be stronger. Librarians, who are less bound by curriculum sequences than classroom teachers, can improve performance of students in every grade, in every subject, and at every level of ability.

To ensure that every child has access to the quality of school library service needed in a learning society, public officials should

- require that library research and information skills be taught as a new basic—providing instruction within the library program and in all subject areas at each level of elementary and secondary school;
- establish more specific state standards for school libraries;
- require school superintendents, boards, parents, teachers, and other interested people in every community to prepare a plan for developing school library resources, for using these resouces effectively, and for coordinating services with public libraries in the community;
- supply sufficient funds for school library programs so there are staff to coordinate the teaching of research and study skills in cooperation with teachers of English, social studies, science, mathematics, and other subjects;
- provide funds for sufficient library books, audiovisual materials, magazines, computer software, and other materials to support teaching and learning and to permit participation by school libraries in library networks for sharing of resources;
- earmark state educational funds for school library resources and program development;
- ensure that each state education department has skilled school library media supervisory staff to provide needed statewide professional leadership;
- require colleges and universities to provide future teachers with training in using libraries and library materials;
- require that education programs for school administrators and other education specialists include training in the administration and supervision of school libraries; and
- target federal education funds to specific school library resource development programs, including those that use the new technologies and those that demonstrate exemplary services.

Reality 3: People in a Learning Society Need Libraries throughout Their Lives

A learning society is committed to ongoing educational growth for everyone and provides each individual with a choice among formal and informal providers of education. Science has lengthened our life spans, but we need a learning society to allow each of us to benefit fully from the biological gain of years. Each person requires the challenge of new ideas and new concepts in order to grow and develop throughout adulthood.

Our society is characterized by a ceaseless search for solutions to the critical problems that threaten our survival in this age of continuing change. Our learning society is also an information-based society. Each person needs the means to cope with magnitude of data currently being generated.

Learning can take place in many settings. For millions of Americans, libraries are centers of learning. College and university libraries help learners of many ages who are enrolled in formal education. Educationally disadvantaged college students require remediation and library instruction so they can make the best use of library resources to develop their study skills. Corporate, government, and union libraries help people continue learning in a workplace setting. The public library is a learning center for all.

Through access to the ideas of the past and present, we gain the perspective essential for innovation. Inherent in the creation of all new knowledge and its application is the existence of a mechanism to collect, sift, organize, and distribute the products of a learning society. The mechanism that best responds to this need is the library. The library, therefore, must be free from restrictions which interfere with access to information.

New technology offers new formats for information and new ways of delivering information. Individuals must be technologically literate to participate fully in a learning society. *A Nation at Risk* states that twenty-three million American adults are functionally illiterate. For millions of Americans who have been left out or pushed out of formal education, the public library offers an optional, informal route to advancement. The library provides materials and programs that deal with both practical and cultural concerns, ranging from health information to modern philosophy. Literacy programs, materials for persons who are blind or disabled, and services for persons with limited proficiency in English help people of all ages. Library programs in correctional facilities, hospitals, nursing homes, and other institutions help residents understand themselves and gain a view of the outside world. Library programs also can contribute to the future productivity of those persons who return to the larger society.

The extent and quality of library resources and services vary greatly from community to community. In Colorado Springs, the public library extends services directly into more than a thousand homes equipped with microcomputers. In other communities the public library lacks a telephone. Some libraries offer services in modern, well-equipped new buildings. Others are housed in crowded, deteriorating buildings designed and built for an earlier age. Cooperation between libraries and literacy volunteers provides service for thousands of new readers, but demand exceeds capacity, and many wait months to participate. Some libraries offer valuable assistance to users in developing research and study skills, while in other libraries service is minimal.

New technologies offer opportunities for solving such problems as the disintegration of books, documents, and films and for sharing of information resources through computers. Libraries can cooperate to share resources if there is wise planning at local, state, and regional levels. This planning and cooperation depends upon the continuous collection and compilation of library statistics and other information by agencies of the states and the federal government. Sharing of library resources now is limited by inadequate staff, materials, and investments in technology. Constraints on sharing of services and of preserving valuable materials handicap us all.

To enable libraries to respond to these needs, public officials should

- fund public libraries so they can be easily accessible to all people and have the materials, staff, and buildings needed by people of all ages and all levels of schooling, whatever their interests or disabilities may be;
- ensure that public library services are available without charge and without violation of the reader's right to privacy;
- expand support for literacy training programs for adults;
- appropriate state and federal aid (which is often extended by private sector grants) to provide microcomputers in every public, academic, and school library as part of integrated, comprehensive programs of technologically sound library service;
- expand support for libraries and library services in hospitals, nursing homes, correctional facilities, and other institutions;
- target funds for the preservation and conservation of research resources needed by present and future generations; and
- expect teachers to help their students become better library users. Demand that every academic and school library have bibliographic, library use, and study skills instruction as an integral part of the institution's curriculum.

Reality 4: Public Support of Libraries Is an Investment in People and Communities

A democratic society depends upon the informed participation of its people. State and federal governments must ensure the right of all citizens to get information and resources for continued learning. Library services are important to the economy, the quality of life, the educational and intellectual activities, and the governments of our communities, our states, and our nation.

It is no coincidence that we are both a high technological society and a learning society. Information fuels economic development. Research and development depend upon access to information in many formats and locations. Few corporations can be self-sufficient in generating the information they need for development, but through their library staffs they can join in networks with other cooperating libraries and become both recipients and sharers of information. Libraries also provide men and women with the education and information they need to attain and hold jobs. Throughout their lives they can use library materials to improve and update their employment skills.

Library services also are important for sound government and the quality of community life. The library is objective in providing and stimulating a variety of opinions. It offers facts which stimulate ideas and ideas which encourage the public to discover new facts. In many communities the public library is the single cultural institution available to all people, irrespective of age, social condition, or educational attainment.

University, school, and public libraries are essential parts of our society's infrastructure. They support the work of scientists, professionals, and others engaged in research important for us all. The scholars who write texts for students need library resources to develop the ideas they wish to communicate. The atmosphere of open discussion which permeates many libraries provides people with space, opportunity, and time to present and test their ideas before the community.

Libraries share resources through the use of such new technologies as computerized databases and telecommunications. Escalating costs of telecommunications, however, are threatening the abilities of libraries to offer these benefits. Lower rates for library telecommunications are needed, following the pattern of United States library postal rates.

To ensure that libraries serve us all effectively, public officials should

- appropriate funds for library services targeted toward individual and community needs for job information, literacy, and development, as well as toward more general needs of library users;
- demand excellence in their academic, institution, public, school, and special libraries;
- supply each state library agency with the funds and staff needed to work with public officials and libraries of all types in planning services and sharing resources;
- mandate that state and federal government documents and the products of government-sponsored research be available to all through library networks;
- institute a library rate for telecommunications; and

- convene state and national conferences of library users, librarians, library policy makers, and public officials to assess the capacity of our libraries to serve the learning society, to measure the change which has taken place since the 1979 White House Conference on Library and Information Services, to encourage sound, long range, community-based planning for library services, and to initiate local, state, and federal action to improve library services.

Actions

The stake that we Americans have in our libraries matches today's public concern about education. *A Nation at Risk* and other reports have focused the nation's attention upon the imperative for educational reform. The four realities we have outlined make the following actions essential:

1. State aid for public libraries must be increased so that library services are available to all people in the learning society.

2. State support for resource sharing must be increased, and additional aid must be provided to school and academic libraries to enable them to meet basic service needs and participate effectively in resource sharing.

3. Federal funds for library services must be increased through new initiatives in aid for elementary and secondary school libraries and through appropriations for the federal Library Services and Construction Act and the several library programs in the Higher Education Act.

4. Federal responsibilities for library statistical data and planning information must be assumed by the National Center for Education Statistics in cooperation with the state library agencies, state departments of education, and national organizations.

5. Local, state, and federal agencies developing human services and education programs—such as those concerned with the aging, public television, literacy improvement, day care centers, and the arts and humanities—should strengthen their programs by including librarians and libraries in their planning and program development.

6. Librarians, library boards, friends of libraries, parents, and educators should consider the recommendations which resulted from the *Libraries and the Learning Society* seminars sponsored by the U.S. Department of Education, and they should implement those which are needed to reshape and improve library services.

Public response to *A Nation at Risk* indicates a nationwide concern and readiness for action to improve education. Within the last year more than half the state legislatures have increased state aid for schools, and over half have raised high school graduation requirements. States and communities have established uncounted commissions, committees, and task forces to examine and improve their schools. Attention to elementary and secondary schools constitutes an important beginning. With few exceptions, recognition of the value of libraries is missing from these educational reform efforts. Now it is essential to recognize these four realities of educational reform and act on them.

This change in the library's role from warehouse to supermarket, from a passive role of preserver to an active one of purveyor, has brought greater emphasis on service, identifying needs and communicating solutions, rather than on just the process of lending books.

ROBERT D. STUEART
Library Educator

21. Alliance for Excellence
Librarians Respond to A Nation at Risk

The Libraries and a Learning Society Project,
U.S. Department of Education

The recommendations of this project aim at strengthening public libraries and school library media centers. School library media centers should be professionally staffed, and their use integrated into the school curriculum. Public libraries are to adopt a learner's advisor role for all their patrons and to become even more strongly involved in adult education and adult literacy programs.

This report appeared at roughly the same time as *Realities* (chap. 20) and represents another response of the library community to *A Nation at Risk* (chap. 1). The excerpts reprinted here include the introduction and a gathering of the recommendations made throughout the project report.

Reprinted from *Alliance for Excellence: Librarians Respond to A Nation at Risk,* Recommendations and Strategies from the Libraries and a Learning Society Project. Center for Libraries and Education Improvement, Office of Educational Research and Improvement, U.S. Department of Education, July 1984. Washington: U.S. Government Printing Office, 1984.

Libraries and the Learning Society

The "information age" has swept around the world like a poorly forecast winter storm; its swirling blizzard of facts, figures, and data has been as bewildering as it has been challenging. This is the nature of the information age, but unlike the snows of February, it is here to stay. The necessity is for all of us to become acclimatized to it.

Much has happened since World War II to create this new era. The transistor has flipped electronics upside down, scientists have deftly rearranged genes, and human hearts have been transplanted. Americans bounded across the moon, and a laser beam from earth, 238,000 miles away, hit a target they left behind. As for the computer, fifth-generation models with artificial intelligence will soon be a reality.

Innovations such as these and so many more have churned up a tidal wave of new findings for us to absorb and master. Trying to stay afloat, the publishing industry has turned out more and more books—from 15,000 titles published in 1959, the mass grew to about 50,000 titles in 1983.

But this is only a part of what it is like to live in the information age. Satellites and TV have collapsed our horizons. In an instant we are spectators of World Cup soccer, or winter and summer Olympics; the next moment, we watch soldiers thousands of miles away probing broken buildings for bodies crushed in a terrorist attack. We live, in fact, in a global village, neighbors to all humanity.

As never before, issues pile up, spawned by awesome technology or by political and social ferment in every corner of the earth. These are issues without easy answers, and some of them may affect human survival. So they have to be understood; decisions must be made about them. To be responsible, rational citizens in this new time, we *must* chart a stable, persistent course through the waves of clues, tidbits, hard facts, and rumors.

This can be done, a *A Nation at Risk* eloquently urged, if we move aggressively to create a "learning society." To do so calls for forming an alliance among teachers, education administrators, parents and other citizens, and the nation's librarians. Through their united efforts, these men and women will be able to provide interrelated, lifelong educational experiences for people of all ages and in all walks of life. Only through this joint activity can a workable learning society be realized.

This is where the library comes in, whatever its type (school, public, special, or academic); it can and should play a full role in this process. It is an institution with extraordinary capacities. In it you will discover new ways of learning, find out how to plan an adventure into education, and then ascend to new levels of knowledge and understanding. The finest of libraries, you will discover, often are one-stop learning centers, the best buy you may ever have for your tax dollar.

Books and periodicals will continue to be vital resources in your learning activities at the library. But increasingly you will find the most modern informational and educational tools there. The computer, microfilm, and even the videocassette recorder and videodisk are being harnessed by librarians. Individuals can and do learn directly through these devices, which also handle administrative tasks, operate efficient links with other libraries both near and far, and store information.

So the library is a place where you will be able to learn by yourself at your own time and pace. Others benefit there from one-on-one instruction in reading, computation, basic study skills, or research.

The reality is that learning services are already available to people of any age at libraries from Alaska, to Maine, to Texas, north and south, east and west, and to the outlying U.S. territories. The preschooler can be readied for school at the public library; boys and girls pursue classroom assignments in their school library media center; the college student rounds out an independent paper at the college/university library on campus; professionals verify facts and challenge assumptions in medical, law, business, or other special libraries; the adult voter, consumer, parent-to-be, taxpayer, or curious citizen can learn at the public library.

Meanwhile, the senior citizen can find many resources at the library to enrich the more quiet years. Typically, a library in New York State, responding to requests, organized workshops on sign language and genealogy. In Pierce County, near Tacoma, Washington, librarians sponsored writing-discussion groups for people between their mid-fifties and nineties; twenty groups learned creative writing, then applied it in completing one hundred twenty different autobiographies.

One individual who has found library service of great value through seven decades has been Nobel Prize-winner Glenn Seaborg, a member of the National Commission on Excellence in Education. He fondly recalls growing up with libraries in Ishpeming, Michigan: "I remember going to the public library walking between snowdrifts over my head to get my favorite books before others found them." As a scientist of seventy-two, he remains "absolutely dependent" on the library to "provide me with access to the wide range of scientific journals which I must read to keep informed of advances in my field."

Libraries have been advancing in their range of services. No longer are you limited to the information resources in your town. Entire networks have been created so that one institution can call in materials from others in distant places. It has become routine for the library to belong to state, regional, and national systems; as a result, sharing is second nature for most librarians. A detailed book on the Colorado River Indian tribes might not exist in your community, but it will be on a shelf somewhere else. Through interlibrary loan, systems can make your library as big as the entire country. Wherever you are, the information of the nation can be brought to you.

Clearly, then, your library can be of real service in education at many levels. Clearly, too, it must have a full partnership in the learning society that will *have* to be brought to life if we are to be competent, knowledgeable citizens in the information age. Sustained by alliances among educators, parents, other citizens, and librarians, such a learning society can be developed and nurtured. Well-designed and well-maintained, this alliance will assure us that the whole will indeed be greater than the sum of its parts. A learning society offers unprecedented benefits to every individual.

To achieve their potential, libraries will have to be perceived in a new way. They must be accepted as an integral part of the overall education system in your community; the librarian must be considered an educator as well as a librarian. And your interest in libraries should be just as strong as your commitment to your local schools.

But to justify your commitment and support, library service in your community will have to be raised to the highest level of quality that community resources and energies can generate. To this end, and in response to *A Nation at Risk,* librarians, teachers, and others from across the nation have been deliberating. This report reflects their thinking and their priorities for achieving improved service in the American library.

On the pages that follow, you will find road signs for realizing what Elizabeth Stone, former president of the American Library Association, has called a "sound and persuasive vision of what the library of the near future can and should be." It is the report's view that an assessment of the nation's libraries should be conducted to determine their readiness to fulfill the vision of an "Alliance for Excellence."

These pages assert that in the learning society ahead, the library must play a central role as a learning center staffed with user-oriented professionals. Libraries everywhere—all types—should share their resources. Further, each school must have quality service of a high standard in its school library media center.

This report states with conviction that the library can be pivotal in the education renewal recommended so effectively by *A Nation at Risk,* a process intended to create an enduring learning society. Libraries cannot be tied to the past. Rather, libraries, newly energized, freshly chartered, can become centers of the learning society. This report details fresh directions for the library community which can benefit every citizen.

Recommendations

A. We recommend that the elementary and secondary school curriculum be strengthened by teaching the effective use of information resources, including libraries. Further:

1. Students should spend time in the school library media center to learn and practice information skills coordinated with classwork.
2. Students should be tested for competency in information skills in English, mathematics, science, social studies, and computer science.
3. Students in grades one through twelve should have guided reading, listening, and viewing experiences, for pleasure and fulfillment as well as for information and knowledge, to acquire skills and abiding interest in learning.

B. We recommend that every elementary and secondary school have quality library services and resources.

C. We recommend that libraries, associations, state educational and library agencies, and accrediting organizations adopt more rigorous and measurable standards for school library media services.

D. We recommend that school library media centers and public and academic libraries be open, to the fullest extent possible, to elementary and secondary school students and area residents. This policy would have the joint aims of expanding the time available for learning, while making more effective use of a community's library and information resources.

E. We recommend that school library media centers and public and academic libraries develop the collections needed to inform educators and librarians about developments in education and the library and information science field, and about new or expanded professional concepts and practices in those fields.

F. We recommend that candidates for the position of school library media specialist receive a broad general education that is geared to meet the challenge of the information age.

G. We recommend that school library media specialists be offered professionally competitive salaries and working conditions that are rewarding and satisfying.

H. We recommend that candidates for teacher or school administrator receive meaningful instruction in the role and activity of a school library media center.

I. We recommend that libraries accept their central role in the learning society as valid learning centers. Further, we recommend that these centers be staffed with user-oriented professionals who do not only understand community needs but also know learning resources. These learners' advisors would help patrons to gain the information and skills to function successfully in the learning society.

J. We recommend that libraries become active in adult literacy education programs at local, state, and national levels.

K. We recommend that the nation's school library media centers and public libraries be assessed for their ability to respond to the urgent proposals for excellence in education and lifelong learning. Further, we recommend that studies be conducted in such vital areas as

- defining information-seeking skills and behavior,
- fostering adult literacy,
- promoting adult learning,
- defining training and retraining, and
- developing a marketing strategy.

L. We recommend that librarians at local, state, and national levels develop and implement plans to share the resources and services of their institution in support of education and lifelong learning. We also recommend that at the national level, leadership should be exerted to endorse, assist, and support the states and local communitites in their efforts to share resources.

M. We recommend that library and information science educators reform and refine the recruitment, preparation, and continuing education of librarians and information scientists. Further, we recommend that the entire library community hold higher education responsible for providing high-quality education to equip professionals with special competencies to work effectively in libraries and information centers in the learning society.

22. Books, Publishing, Libraries in the Information Age

Ann Heidbreder Eastman

Ann Heidbreder Eastman admits that attention is due the electronic media in relation to contemporary librarianship and publishing. But in the end, books are what publishers and libraries are mostly about, and books are what the public identifies libraries with. Libraries, by seizing on book reading, promoting it, promoting literacy for its sake, and promoting the library as a place for books, will find allies among users and potential users and in publishing and education.

Ann Heidbreder Eastman, University Faculty Book Publishing Staff Officer of Virginia Polytechnic Institute and State University (Virginia Tech), has been an advisor to the Center for the Book in the Library of Congress since its founding. She is well known for her activities and publications in the area of library promotion. Eastman was one of the editors of the special issue of *Library Trends,* "The Quality of Trade Book Publishing in the 1980s," in which this article originally appeared.

Reprinted with permission from *Library Trends,* vol. 33, no. 2, Fall 1984, pp. 121-47. © 1984 The Board of Trustees of the University of Illinois.

Books, Publishing, Libraries: A 1984 Analysis

The State of Library/Publishing Cooperation

Three years ago an able editor from Knowledge Industry Publications who was concerned about changes in communication and cooperation among publishers and librarians proposed that I write or edit a book on the past and present of such ventures, but especially on their future. Since I worked for many years in publishing in the school and library market and since I had related responsibilities when I worked for Dan Lacy, then director of the American Book Publishers Council (now the Association of American Publishers), I sought his advice and participation.

Both of us were interested in the topic, and both of us talked with a number of leaders in the library field to determine whether there was a market for such a book. Regretfully, we had to confess that while we might do the writing, it seemed that few planned to do the reading, so we abandoned the project. (A personal note: Were I ever to write that or any other book about publishing, it would be dedicated to Dan Lacy. IIis capacity to think about the history of book publishing and libraries, to analyze ideas, and to pass them on to an audience has made thousands upon thousands of people aware of the continuing symbiotic relationship between these two professions [and as Mr. Lacy practices it, publishing *is* a profession]. One will not fly while the other stumbles and falls. The quality of his mind and the generosity of his spirit are attested to in virtually all serious publications about information, book publishing, and libraries. He seems able, always, to find the statesmanlike approach to a challenge.)

In the three intervening years, concern about the state of publishing and libraries has been considered in a number of books and articles. A sampling of those I turned to in writing this piece are: (1) *The Micro Millenium,* by Christopher Evans, (2) the anthology *Books, Libraries, and Electronics: Essays on the Future of Written Communications,* (3) *In Cold Type: Overcoming the Book Crisis,* by Leonard Shatzkin, (4) Part I, "The Impact of New Technologies," and Part II, "The Changing Role of Reading," of the Unesco study of the *Future of the Book,* (5) *The 1983 Consumer Research Study on Reading and Book Purchasing* of the Book Industry Study Group (see chapter 7 above for a summary), (6) "Reading: Old and New," the Winter 1983 issue of *Daedalus,* and (7) my notes from the March 1984 meeting of the Advisory Committee on the Book in the Future.[1]

Other than Mr. Bradbury's prophecy of bookless homes with huge television screens, what has prompted this attention to books and publishing and the interplay among the kinds of media in the library market? Concern everywhere about change, insecurity, and the disappearance of old lines of demarcation and the lack of new ones. While the number of dollars flowing into book publishing has increased dramatically, the number of units sold has not. While the amount of information being generated is growing at unbelievable rates, library materials budgets are not.

Both librarians and publishers have valid concerns about copyright legislation. Authors and other creators, as well as publishers, cannot work for free; yet, the public's right to know must be preserved. Lack of effective negotiation on copyright has done more harm to publisher/library communications and trust than any other single issue. Until that matter is resolved—until both parties agree to arrive at a sensible solution—probably some of the action I suggest in this article cannot be taken. Publishers and librarians agree on many more issues than they disagree on, but the present antagonistic posture of both parties is inhibiting a great deal of cooperative work.

The Effects of Automation on Publishing and Libraries
The use of the computer in publishing and libraries is a major reason both groups feel threatened, unprepared, and, yes, hopeful. One need not look far to find prophets of the death of the book—indeed, of all print. With every new technological development (film, other audiovisual material, microforms) and new leisure-time devices (bicycles, radio, television), the death of the book has been pronounced—prematurely.

I should confess that I don't agree that computers will be the final blow to books—for many reasons articulated in "Reading: Old and New" by Dan Lacy, Samuel S. Vaughan, Lewis Branscomb, William Goodman, and others. The book is uniquely portable, legible, unmechanical. The content of books is important to people, so the medium that brings the content is important too. After all, books have a tremendous head start on the newer media; perhaps some day mention of a computer program or an abstract will bring tears of joy to users' eyes, but I doubt it.

Like West Virginia, publishing is wild and wonderful. It is an intellectual, exciting, important business to work in. Good ideas and able people count. Publishing is changing, but those characteristics seem still to be there. Young people are drawn to the book industry because they are allowed to work hard, and, if they show potential for "thinking like a publisher," they move up from job to job, house to house. One thing is evident: it is not the *money* that keeps anyone in publishing. Salaries are roughly equivalent to those in academia. As an industry, publishing generates a profit just under what one can earn by investing in safe securities.

But publishing is more than people and books. It is—always has been and always will be—first and foremost a process or system without which the entire information community, and all its users, would quickly collapse. I am dumbfounded by much that I read about the computer's potential for instant distribution of all information to everyone in the world all the time. Surely intelligent information scientists and other computer experts realize that if every word written, each bit of scientific data processed, is made available, the wealth of dross would collapse the system. How could we survive if even every book manuscript were available? How could one find the books one wanted or needed to read in all that chaos? Why should library users pay, in one way or another—including taxes—to maintain a system that includes so much ill-conceived and ill-written work, work that doesn't deserve to be made public?

I am speaking of course of the function of the publisher as gatekeeper. By making a combined editorial/marketing decision, each publisher decides what to publish and at the same time what *not* to publish. Some magnitude of the problem is suggested in John H. Jenkins's statement: "A recent *New York Times* study indicates that the chances of an unsolicited manuscript being published is 15,000 to 1."[2] I have heard educators, librarians, and unpublished authors complain about how "unfair" the process is, about the tremendous numbers of important books that are not being published because publishers are looking only for "blockbusters" and tried-and-true formula books. That simply is not the case. Authors of publishable manuscripts who take the time to study publishers' lists to determine where their manuscripts might find likely homes and who submit them with informative cover letters will eventually find publishers. If there are great American novels moldering in desk drawers, the reason is that their authors did not sustain sufficient energy and nerve to find a publisher.

One problem today, in fact, is that more and more fiction is being written, in part as a result of its being taught in colleges and universities. Whether a publisher thinks he can publish (not edit, not print, not sell, but *publish*) it successfully is his decision. What Harper turns down Godine might well accept. Houses differ greatly, and the men (and a handful of women) who run them are individualistic. Like authors (and other people), they have egos, too. They publish to *their* vision of what their imprint should be, not someone else's vision. The successful book is that which generates excitement inside the house. It is this excitement that promotion and marketing people work to "bottle and sell" to the appropriate media outside: reviewers, other writers and publishers, newspapers, magazines, radio, and television. The worst thing that can happen to a manuscript is for the person who generated the excitement at the publishing house to lose that interest before the book is published or to move on to another position. The book can become an orphan; it can be "privatized," as William B. Decker, novelist and former managing editor at Viking, has said, not published.

I have passed over the third essential step in the publishing process—the production of the physical book—because Len Shatzkin has covered the topic so completely.[3] Suffice it to say that the computer is making change possible faster in this aspect of publishing than any other—and with potential for savings that will help to keep book prices down. (People who get hysterical about book prices should remember that publishing is a labor-intensive occupation, and that about 85 percent of the actual cost of any book is in *people* costs. As salaries have gone up in publishing, composition, printing, and binding—to say nothing of the rising cost of paper—and as publishers have had to pay higher rents and more for equipment and communication services, the cost of books has had to go up.)

In whatever form information is produced, it has to pass through these three steps of selection or editing, production, and promotion and marketing. Saying this implies that some party—I think it will be publishers—will continue to pay something to the author/creator to make his material public and that, in turn, customers will pay something to acquire the material or to use it. I don't think we should socialize publishing; I think the capitalistic system works quite well. Authors' and publishers' rights of ownership should be maintained.

Let us assume they are, and let us hypothesize that a publisher/producer of any kind of material needs to make a profit of $4,000 on one item. That can be done in several ways. He can produce 4,000 copies and add a dollar to the cost of each unit. He can produce 2,000 copies and add two dollars to each unit. Or, at the other end of the scale, he can produce one copy on a videodisk and charge $4,000 for it. Then libraries that want copies can pay the publisher—or a middle network—for the copies they want. The physical work of producing something still has to be done, and, what is most important in many ways, potential customers still need to know that the item exists. It still will need to be promoted and sold.

Much of what one reads in library literature about our future use of media implies that librarians at the point of purchase will have an option, that they will be able to decide whether they want a hardcover, paperback, or videodisk "copy" of *Duhem on Medieval Cosmology: Theories of Infinity, Place, Time, Void, and the Plurality of Worlds* by Roger Ariew (University of Chicago Press, 1985), for example. I don't think libraries always will have that option. I think the publishers at some point will have to decide in what form he can afford to make the title available, and, if librarians want to purchase it, they will have to be able to make it available to users in that form.

Application of the newer technologies in libraries and publishing raises the question of free versus fee information service. Will libraries use the arrival of new forms of communication to initiate fee-for-service systems, much as there are charges now for computer searches? Will patrons pay for and keep hard copies made from videodisks, rather than borrow a book? Librarians and other information scientists and library supporters are thinking through this issue now, because if access and the serendipitous discovery of books and other media cease to be a prime factor in information use—if patrons have to know exactly which item they want in order to get any item efficiently—then it will be difficult to promote to taxpayers the importance of libraries as places where materials are collected and made available. If the United States embraces the Public Lending Right at some future date, books will take their place as value-added items alongside computerized services on which a charge is placed.

Librarians, booksellers, and publishers are aware of the tremendous amount of book reading and book buying that goes on because people happen to find an idea or title that interests them. People browse through books and periodicals, as well as listening to radio and television, rather than turning to a particular medium for only one kind of information or reading experience. People come to the library for a magazine article and go home carrying several books on unrelated topics. Readers are serendipitous. In a recent study of library use at Virginia Polytechnic Institute and State University (Virginia Tech) entitled *The Landscape of Literatures,* Dr. Paul Metz suggests that

> while the present data replicate many findings from citation studies, they indicate important differences in the extent to which specialized literatures satisfy the needs of most disciplines. Generally, those fields which cite their own literatures most heavily also use a heavy concentration of library materials in their own literatures. The findings for the departments of mathematics and geography are in accord with the citation literature in showing, respectively, a very high and a very low degree of dependence on endogenous literatures. Although the difference between mathematicians' practices and those of geographers is in the same direction whether measured by citation counts or circulation records, in both cases the library data show a greater dependence on external literatures than citation counts reveal. This distinction is typical of most of the comparisons that could be made. The difference between library use within specialized literatures and citation of endogenous materials is found not only within the sciences and social sciences but

within the humanities as well; the circulation data show a wider use of literatures by historians and specialists in literature than was revealed by a citation study conducted for the National Enquiry [*Scholarly Communication: The Report of the National Enquiry.* Baltimore, Md.: The Johns Hopkins University Press, 1979, p. 46]....

The results of the study have a number of implications for the most basic aspects of library policy. By showing the degree to which use patterns depend on the disciplinary affiliation of library users, the study suggests that library use studies will be generalizable only to a limited degree and that an understanding of use must be based on the particular characteristics and missions of local institutions. By showing that specialists and nonspecialists use materials differently, the results call for a reexamination of fund allocation approaches to collection development. By demonstrating the extent and nature of cross-disciplinary use and the effects of decentralization, the results call into question the scattering of library collections and suggest lines of division which might best govern the structure of library systems. The high volume of cross-disciplinary use of library materials which the data have shown suggests that strong central libraries may be a powerful centripetal counterforce to the tendency of academic disciplines to break into noncommunicating specialties. Both the findings that specialists and nonspecialists approach literatures differently and that branch libraries appear to channel reading patterns provide a basis for arguing that, when library policies are set by client groups, the result may be private virtues which are public vices. Such an argument would support the role of professional librarians as the best trustees of collections and arbiters of conflicting interests within user communities.

The data from this study tend to indicate that the use of periodicals follows disciplinary lines more than does the use of monographs, though periodicals use is by no means totally predictable. Just how closely the use of periodicals follows disciplinary lines cannot be specified in this report, but it would be important to know this....

It appears that the less closely patron and material are related, the more likely materials are to be monographic; it may well be that even if an analysis is restricted to the use of monographs, the slowness of communications among fields would be such that older materials are used disproportionately by those from more remote fields.[4]

Not everything we read is something that we set out to find; the wealth of choices of all kinds of media and all kinds of ideas has been the strength of the American library system. The word "book" doesn't have to become pejorative just because librarians need to focus more attention (and funds) on acquiring automated data services. It is puzzling to hear informed, sophisticated librarians say, for instance, that accessing online information will threaten the library's policy of access to materials on all sides of an issue.

Surely libraries won't use one system as the sole source for all their materials, or to such an extent that the library would be harmed by biases built into systems produced by commercial entities. I should hazard a guess that never a book has been published without some bias, and that, while it sometimes doesn't turn out that way, most commercial publishers plan for (or hope for) a profit. Why do some librarians and scholars assume that anyone will be allowed to put anything in these massive and ubiquitous databases? Surely the scholars who create the databases will arrange in some way for their distribution and protection—with limited and authorized access to their content. Why are some librarians and other scholars so quick to assume that the *principles* of publishing will cease to exist because data will be delivered in an automated form?

While it is true that many academic libraries today are spending a larger percent of their materials acquisition budgets on serials than on books, the vast majority of items held by such libraries are books. Books still are the medium that draws most users to the library. Scholars of the humanities, literature, philosophy, religion, history, and the other liberal arts—like readers of drama, poetry, fiction, and nonfiction—will continue to seek book materials. Some readers are more interested in books published many years ago than they are in the latest research. Scholars and students in the sciences, engineering, and technology are the ones seeking up-to-the-minute information, and libraries are beginning to meet that need. But the needs of one group of disciplines have heretofore never dictated library policy for all the disciplines; nor has one group heretofore continually laid claim to the lion's share of the budget.

Until quite recently, the selection, acquiring, and lending of books (and other print materials) was thought to be part of a library's mission and service. Today, borrowing and lending books effectively sometimes is said to be less animated, duller, and more old-fashioned than acquiring and using automated information. I think that libraries are at the heart of the learning process in this country and that they will stay there. One reason is that in most places they are the only show in town, the only place where one can find older books; and libraries offer a rich collection of serious books, classics, and basic and seminal works in many, many fields from which to choose. Another is that libraries make possible our form of government. Where else is a "better-read, better-informed" America to turn?

Just as I don't imagine spending the rest of my life in my living room looking at a screen and pushing buttons, I cannot imagine not leaving the room for the library. There I will be able to find out what my information options are, and I will learn in such a way that I will respond and use the sources I need. I also expect to find people there who can help me. One finding of Chen's study of information sources needs emphasis: People said that their primary source of information was other *people*.[5] Libraries have taken giant steps *away* from readers' advisory services and making educated, informed librarians, who know ideas and books, available to users. Users can be taught to handle terminals and systems, but it is harder and harder to find people, especially out on the floor in public libraries, of whom you can ask your perhaps not-fully-formed question or make a general inquiry.

Signs of Distress in the Library Profession

Coupled with the coming of the computer in libraries have been other developments that are putting pressure on the library profession. The image of the librarian has not improved drastically across the years. Salaries have not improved in libraries at a great rate. It is difficult to recruit able students to the master's degree programs, and several universities have phased out their library schools or merged them with other programs: Rutgers University, the University of Denver, Case Western Reserve University, and University of Minnesota, to name four. The Office of Personnel Management of the federal government has attempted to reclassify librarians out of the professional series into a clerical series—to date, unsuccessfully. Several legal cases (most notably *Merwine* v. *the trustees of Mississippi State University)* have prompted librarians to defend the terminal degree, the Master of Library Science/Service/Library and Information Science/Services, as the definition of a professional, even though some of these programs are recognized as weak. Perhaps unfortunately—from a public relations point of view (because it sounds like vested self-interest) —the American Library Association (ALA) has announced that its next Executive Director must hold a library degree from a program accredited by the ALA.

After years of presenting itself as a humane profession with one or both feet solidly in the humanities (and thus knowing and caring about books and people, interested in reading books and talking about them), the profession seems to be moving toward the systems of science and technology, again perhaps because the challenge of automation is great and because librarians themselves are seeking information, knowledge, and influence.

Since blame for the nonproductive turmoil in some ALA Council meetings of late has to be placed somewhere, it all too easily gets directed at publishing. That policy-making and -monitoring body of the ALA has recently discussed and passed two empty resolutions—one on freight pass-through (which affected a few libraries briefly because clerical errors were made by wholesalers) and the other on trade book discounts. If ALA wants to write a policy statement for publishing, it should appoint a committee of librarians and publishers to try to do that. It is important to note that the ALA division that works most directly with publishers and wholesalers, the Resources and Technical Services Division, tried hard in both cases to keep these resolutions from coming to the ALA Council.

A handful of librarians seem to look down on commerce—especially the commerce indulged in by book publishers—not that of profit-making producers of furniture and other library supplies and equipment or of databases and other automated products, including library systems. The solution to this kind of problem lies where it always has: in educational programs and library school courses that help librarians more efficiently to select and purchase library materials. Earlier efforts (the 1969 and 1972 preconferences to ALA conferences, for example) proved very useful and successful. The CIP (cataloging-in-publication) program was regenerated as a direct result of the 1969 meeting.

Pressures on Scholars and Scholarly Publishers
While trade book publishers in general are examining the options automation offers them, one segment of the industry is being forced by the economics of specialized markets and short-run books to embrace automation, although there still is "less here than meets the eye," as Martin Levin has so aptly said.[6] University presses and other scholarly publishers more and more often are asking authors if their institution can provide camera-ready copy in the form of laser-printed or typeset pages. If the institution has the capacity to capture the author's keystrokes to drive photocomposition equipment, the publisher saves the cost of setting the book (or reimburses the institution for its lower-than-market costs).

Incompatibility of equipment has been a major problem for scholarly presses, which often find it cheaper to re-keystroke the manuscript than to convert it to the system used by the commercial photocompositor. If the press can accept the tape or disk, then either the editor has to make changes on that record or, more usually, the edited hard-copy manuscript is returned to the author, who makes the changes in the automated record. It is then the author's responsibility, too, to assume the publisher's responsibility for final proofreading and checking. While automated systems save money in some cases (which help to keep the prices of books down), faculty are keenly aware of the amount of time they are spending doing tasks formerly thought to be the publishers'.

Scholarly books live in that category of serious works that great numbers of people don't buy, and they are the kind of book in greatest jeopardy. Lola Szladits, curator of the Berg Collection of English and American Literature of the New York Public Library, said it well in the Winter 1983 issue of *Daedalus:*

Today, it is possibly true that the need for and interest in the humanities are on the wane. It cannot be quantified, but it is visible both in the quality and quantity of readers and their work. Fields tend to become narrower, restricted, as some studies are, to major authors or major trends. There is a marked tendency to turn out whatever work is required in the fastest possible time. An old-fashioned humanist has trouble understanding research today: instant answers to quick questions. Research—and it cannot be stressed sufficiently—is not identical with information and, in its long-term duration, includes contemplation and articulation.[7]

Libraries have been a primary market for scholarly books, especially academic and special libraries. Technically, it will be possible for a university library to order a copy of a title to be copied from the publisher's videodisk when a scholar requests it, but a great many of these serious books are meant to be read in toto. Many are not compilations of data to be consulted one section at a time, but cogent, developed, documented arguments that need to be followed from beginning to end. In short, the same principle that motivates people to read any work of fiction or nonfiction motivates them to read scholarly works. We cannot assume that because scholars use academic libraries, they are going to abandon pursuit of knowledge in books.

For library service, the special power of the computer, of course, is that it can scan vast quantities of machine-readable text or data to locate specific items quickly. The computer's major use will be as a locater or indexer of existing knowledge, wherever it is found. Once a researcher knows that what he seeks can be found in a particular book, he will want to read that book. Again, I am speaking of scholars working in the humanities and social sciences; those in engineering and the hard sciences seek more discrete information, which they often find in databases and journal articles.

The gatekeeping function of the publisher is essential to scholars, especially younger scholars. Should the day come when any research could be made available in any system simply because the author/creator put it in, scholars would lose the power of the referee. Most promotion-and-tenure committees insist on evidence of publication in vetted or refereed journals or in books from recognized scholarly publishers.

If academic libraries continue to cut back on their purchase of specialized scholarly books, if they begin to define the worth or value of an idea in terms of the number of times someone has sought access to it (rather than its importance in a total collection on a particular topic, which is what academic librarians have been good at judging), one could imagine the day when every university of any size would have its own "press," if only to handle requests for hard copies of materials.

In announcing the establishment of a new Office of Scholarly Communication and Technology, John William Ward, president of the American Council of Learned Societies, said: "The new technology is radically changing the environment in which scholars do their work. Without the participation of scholars, the system will evolve according to administrative, financial, and technical imperatives. The great danger is we will end with a system of scholarly communication which will be technically viable, but not intellectually desirable." This new office will

1. monitor change and disseminate information about important changes in the system of scholarly communication;
2. create closer relationships between major actors in the system (such as research libraries, learned journals, publishers, academic administrators, and corporate firms in the computer industry);
3. initiate studies on how well the system of scholarly communication is working; and
4. explore how technical change affects the way scholars think about their work, not simply how they do their work.

The director is Herbert C. Morton, former head of the publications program at the Brookings Institution and Resources for the Future, who contributed to the National Enquiry into Scholarly Communication.[8]

Another articulate spokesman for the state of university press publishers today is J. G. Goellner, director of the Johns Hopkins University Press. In 1978 Goellner made the following statement about financial support for university presses:

University press publishing is subsidized publishing, let there be no doubt about that. Even those few presses that receive no operating subsidies from their parent universities depend heavily on title subsidies to support the publication of individual books. It is simply not possible to publish the kinds of books that university presses exist to publish without financial assistance ....Many of the best, more important, most enduring scholarly books never sell enough copies to pay for their publication. The products of even the finest scholarship are not always snapped up eagerly in the marketplace....If somehow all financial support for university presses stopped totally tomorrow, most university presses would cease to exist, at least as we know them now, in short order—and the world of scholarship, higher education, and American culture would be much the poorer.[9]

Librarians and other educators and publishers and other vendors of information seem to be witnessing a fair amount of slippage currently of tasks, functions, and responsibilities among their fields. Some publishers seem inclined to tell educators and librarians how to do their business, and some librarians and information scientists seem to be interested in undertaking responsibilities traditionally thought of as belonging to the publisher. Lola Szladits describes one aspect of this situation: "What is missing from all discussions is a fact never questioned in the past few centuries—that we are masters of our future, not victims of machines nor the circumstances they may have created. Librarians can—and ought—to control their own computer programs, lest they sell out to businesses that would impose theirs." [10]

The Shared Responsibilities of the Book Community

Having attempted to outline some of the challenges faced by publishers and librarians in the next decade, I wish to identify a few areas in which we have had and continue to have shared responsibilities. Librarians, other educators, and publishers alike decry the fact that 27 million adults are functionally illiterate: these adults are unable to read simple instructions or to complete a simple job application. Another 45 million adults are only marginally literate, and each year the total number of illiterates grows by 2.25 million. Various surveys—the Book Industry Study Group 1983 survey, for instance—show that just under one-half of the adults in this country have read a book in the past year. But if half of the other half cannot read well enough to scan the evening newspaper, it is doubtful that they will make heavy use of libraries, even if talking computers become more available. One still needs to read the material being identified, as well as instructions for accessing it, whether the words are on paper or on a screen. Futurists who dismiss the literacy problem with a wave of the hand overlook many relevant facts, including the cost of serving an illiterate population.

Another area in which publishers and librarians have jointly done good and effective work in the past is what is called, for lack of a better term, "reading development" or "reading promotion." What is meant are projects, campaigns, and other efforts to bring more people to reading as a source of information, inspiration, ideas. Not far down this trail, one encounters some basic problems, one of which is that in working with librarians one veers soon into the area of library programming to stimulate reading, which is considered by some people to be an area publishers do not know much about. At the Association of American Publishers (AAP), we called it "reading development" when we seized every opportunity to mortise the habit of buying, borrowing, and reading books into every receptive organization, individual, or project that came our way. The book community needs a creative group to continue that kind of work. Conferences, research projects about book publishing and book use, published reports and papers, special booklists, and model projects in the selection and use of books and other materials and identifying and publicizing highly successful innovative or model book programs—these are some of the kind of things that have been successful and could be again.

Step One: Reaffirm the Importance of Reading

First, the book community needs to compile and analyze the evidence it has about the importance of reading and the impact it has on people's lives. Much reading research is carried out in structured school situations by educators who are primarily concerned with how reading is taught, rather than with the development of lifetime reading habits. Theoretically, every citizen of this country is taught to read when he passes through the public schools. But the instruction doesn't stick in many cases—60 million of them, it would seem. That's a lot of people to "miss." The major question is: What in the instructional process or what in the followup pattern of access to reading materials inhibits the ability to develop an enthusiasm for reading? Radio, then television, and now the computer have all been hailed as death-knells for books and reading, but these communication formats appear to stimulate reading. Readers who watch television often return to books to find more intellectually challenging, demanding ideas. We are not drowning in PBS (Public Broadcasting System) programs; we are drowning in the mundane, to which "tough," serious books are an antidote.

Mention of such books reminds me of a scholar who just turned ninety-four. She is in reasonable health in a retirement home to which she moved only last year. One of her major activities is reading (after ten years of making do with talking books, she decided to risk cataract surgery so she could read what she wanted to read). I asked her not long ago to what she attributed the fact that her mental capacities were not deteriorated, to which she replied: "I always am reading at least one very tough book." Perhaps challenge, not "entertainment," is the way to keep people sixty-five and over reading.

Step Two: Forsake the Either/Or Fallacy

Present debate about the advantages of the newer media and technologies are reminiscent of some of the early debates about the value of mass-market paperbacks. Was *Portrait of the Artist as a Young Man* worth less in the softcover than the hardcover edition? Is *A Distant Mirror* copied on paper from a videodisk more satisfying to a library patron than the current print edition? Although disks may solve major problems of space in libraries, if Mrs. Tuchman's book is reproduced verbatim on sheets of paper, is not the content of the same value (legibility, convenience for the reader, aesthetic pleasure aside)?

Lewis Branscomb's essay on "Video Disc Technology and the Book" in *Books, Libraries, and Electronics* opens the readers' eyes to the possibility of vastly increased indexing and access to materials, interactive media, and the combination of formats.[11] It is about the last of these I wish to comment. If text is to be "illustrated" with audiovisual complements, who will do the choosing? It seems essential that the same creative mind that produced the text of *A Distant Mirror,* for instance, that chose the ideas and the words to carry them, should also choose the music, art, and maps that seem to her faithfully to extend her meaning. People who speak of reading as a "passive activity" are not, I suspect, serious readers. Perhaps this comment reveals a basic problem: one cannot see the mind work (unless one is a medical researcher conducting tests). Somehow the computer seems to be the mind in action because it can go through some of the limited, first steps of information processing. But it is not; it is a machine. My dishwasher washing my dishes does not have the same "thoughts" or sensations that I would have doing those same dishes.

At the April 1984 meeting for the Center for the Book advisory board, Helen H. Lyman, former professor of library science at the University of Wisconsin and a literacy expert, made the following statement about the impact of mathematics and the computer on our use of language:

A strong divisive trend has been the separation of persons who use the language of mathematics from those who do not. A seeming correlate of this development has been the attempt to transfer to social and humanistic fields a seemingly scientific approach based on mathematics. More often than not this approach appears to result in a pseudo-scientific research and language rather than a verbal structure. A professional language (jargon) further obscures understanding outside of an informed elite. The use of words—the verbal aspects of the culture—has diminished and corrupted the language. A contributing factor has been the demands of a mass culture and mass communication. The dependence on words has lessened while audio and visual objects replace language. In writing, a similar simplicity has developed with limited vocabulary and simplistic sentences. Words become meaningless, lack precision, and euphemisms, acronyms, pseudo-false meanings—even common uses of syntax—are misleading. Politicians, scientists, media communications—yes, educators and librarians—misuse ordinary terms.[12]

In the September 1984 issue of *Scientific American,* Terry Winograd, associate professor of computer science and linguistics at Stanford University, shows why "no existing software deals with meaning over a significant subset of English."[13] He cites ambiguities of various kinds as the reason: lexical, structural, semantic, and pragmatic. These, coupled with problems of metaphor and poetic meaning, "make it impossible at present—and conceivably forever—to design computer programs that come close to full mimicry of human language understanding" (p. 142). "Hopes for a 'voice typewriter' that types text from dictation are just as dim as hopes for high-quality machine translation and language understanding" (p. 144). Winograd's findings suggest that computer translation of foreign-language materials and low-cost voice inputting of data are not in our immediate future.

While the computer does open many options for publishers and librarians, they should not get caught up in the either/or battle. For dozens of reasons, totally electronic libraries are not going to exist any day now. Neither are totally automated publishers. While in theory the technology exists to do many more jobs in libraries than are currently automated, in practice, in economic terms, libraries cannot put theory into practice. The book community has an important obligation to strengthen library use by promoting the availability of ideas in a wealth of kinds of materials and formats. Since books are what most people come to libraries to find, and since "book publishers have managed to maintain a degree of social responsibility thus far unmatched by any of the new electronic media,"[14] we should build on the strength of the past. By effectively promoting books and reading, all the concerned parties can promote libraries, information, and knowledge. We need to use a familiar, beloved medium to pave the way for all the rest. Now how can we do that?

Elements of a Successful Reading Campaign

The Attack on Illiteracy

It is difficult to find a group in the book/reading/library community which is not concerned about basic literacy; it is equally difficult to raise modest sums in some small towns and rural areas, for instance, to support local Literacy Volunteers of America (LVA) and related efforts to teach adults to read. The Center for the Book report on the book in the future is a report to Congress and is expected to recommend that Congress help to focus attention on the adult literacy problem and help resolve it, in part with dollars.[15]

Congress should adopt this recommendation and create a literacy program at the national level; this could begin by coordinating the various local programs and funneling to them a portion of the modest sums needed to keep them going each year (our local LVA in Blacksburg, Virginia needed the magnificent total of $1,700 for one year—and almost died of malnutrition). Regional, state, and local agencies and units of involved groups, including libraries, can work together to assess the need for literacy training in their areas and to allocate appropriate responsibilities to each group so that the programs are well promoted and supported.

Libraries need not wait for talking computers to reach out to the illiterate and newly literate. Selected collections of materials can be made available; those who cannot read at all can use tapes, films, filmstrips, and illustrated books. Past efforts to convince publishers of trade books that they should have limited vocabulary/high interest manuscripts written and published for the new adult reader have not been successful because it has been impossible to describe the locus and size of the market to publishers. It is impossible to find out which agencies currently are buying such materials or would buy more if they existed. Should the federal government launch and fund an adult literacy program, publishers could anticipate a market, and some would publish for it.

Sad to report, a proposal from the Association of American Publishers that President Reagan establish a "Business Committee for Literacy" went unheeded, so no publisher support was generated through the trade association. A year later, Harold McGraw, former president of McGraw-Hill, and several colleagues, including Dan Lacy, established the Business Council for Effective Literacy, which will maintain a small professional staff to interact with adult literacy groups in the field and with the corporate community. It will regularly assess literacy activities and needs and be of help to corporations in more effectively targeting their funds and taking part in national, state, and local literacy planning. The Business Council for Effective Literacy will issue research reports, literacy and corporate program profiles, topical pamphlets, and other publications for business and industry. It will provide professional advice and technical assistance and sponsor meetings and seminars. As a relatively small operating foundation, the council will focus on facilitating corporate funding and involvement rather than making large or frequent grants itself. The council hopes to become involved in the reading and writing problems of children in due course, but its immediate and central priority is *adult functional illiteracy*. The council's seven primary objectives are to

1. attract corporate financial support to strengthen and expand existing programs of tutor training and tutoring;
2. encourage corporate support for the development of new approaches to tutoring and tutor training;
3. encourage the business community to become involved in planning and policy-making;
4. help advance research on adult literacy;
5. develop and disseminate general information;
6. increase general public awareness and understanding about the scale and nature of the illiteracy problem; and
7. foster improved communication.

With ten other related organizations, ALA has established the Coalition for Literacy, which is raising funds for a broad campaign approved by the Advertising Council of America. Some of this support will be provided by the Business Council for Effective Literacy. Launched in 1984, the campaign's goal is to attack the literacy problem on the national level by (1) recruiting volunteers for existing local literacy programs and (2) appealing to the business community to make its members aware of the nation's literacy problems and of their stake in helping to reach and teach adult illiterates. An 800 number (1-800-228-8813) has been established to put potential students and tutors in touch with appropriate local programs. By participating in the Coalition for Literacy, the American Library Association has helped local libraries to achieve a leadership role in their communities. [16]

The Purpose and Structure of a National Campaign

The time is right for the major book, reading, and library groups to mount a clearly articulated national campaign to promote books and reading. This effort should be guided by a board or council on which all the major groups are represented. Its purpose should be to inform the public about the importance of and pleasures in books and reading. Its staff should be drawn from the fields of public information (PI) and advertising, and it should be housed in its own quarters and should spend funds raised for its use alone.

One of the problems in the book community is that so many groups exist to which book and library people can belong and which they can support. Not many are adequately staffed and funded, and almost none has the wide dissemination (outside libraries) of public information about books and reading as its primary mission.

It is interesting that, at the end of the line for the White House Conference on Library and Information Services (1979), at the conclusion of the Library of Congress meeting on the Book in the Future (1984), and at the close of many articles and books on aspects of publishing and librarianship, the final recommendation is that the "thing we truly need" is a public information campaign. In one way, public information becomes an "out," an easy solution to difficult problems. It is assumed to be the one thing everyone understands, everyone is equipped to critique, and everyone can do with little thought, planning, or research. None of these assumptions is correct. Perhaps discussions—oral and written—conclude that public information is the answer because, having talked through divisive problems, the group wants to feel that it has found common ground and consensus in one area at least. If the "doing" of a PI program is the only activity about which the group can agree, it is unlikely that an effective PI program will be generated. People mean such different things when they use the terms "public information," "public relations," and "promotion" that one needs to work hard to make oneself clear.

National/Regional/State Articulation of
Public Information Goals and Programs

At the same time the committee and staff are planning for a national reading promotion effort, regional, state, and local units of the participating organizations should be determining (1) how they can contribute ideas—content—to the national campaign and

(2) how they can develop an appropriate vehicle within their organizations and with their constituents to accomplish the national goals and goals of their own which relate to the larger campaign.

Using an exemplary project that I know well may reveal how these several levels of involvement can work together: the Books That Made the Difference project of the Center for the Book in the Library of Congress.[17] Phase one was conducted jointly with the College of Arts and Sciences at Virginia Tech. That phase was comprised of interviews with almost fourteen hundred Americans, who were asked two questions: What book made the greatest difference in your life? and What was that difference? Two writer/scholars, Patricia Sabine and Gordon Sabine, met or talked with people in forty-four states to ask these questions. Some of the responses were taped, and many subjects were photographed.

The Sabines have presented numerous audiovisual programs drawn from their materials, and just over two hundred of the respondents are included in the book about the project, *Books That Made the Difference: What People Told Us,* which was published in 1983. In addition to the first 128 pages—the interview section—which was offered gratis by the Book-of-the-Month Club to almost a million people in January 1985, the book includes a selection of statements about the importance of reading and libraries and almost forty pages of ideas for local Books Make a Difference projects.

For one year, the National Book Awards picked up the Books Make a Difference slogan, as did the American Booksellers Association, but other than individual responses to requests for help, neither the center nor Virginia Tech could undertake a public information campaign to support the concept of regional, state, and local projects.

What kinds of books made a difference? All kinds—from *The Adventures of Huckleberry Finn* to *Escape From Freedom* to *How To Win Friends and Influence People* to *The Sensuous Woman* to *Wuthering Heights.* Only five books (including the Bible and dictionaries) were mentioned by more than three persons: there was a tremendous spread of reading interest. The Sabines found that "the book is very much alive....[This] project dramatizes the fact that people need to do more than just *get* information; they have to be able to give it meaning for themselves and use it to make a difference for themselves. There is a hunger for books."[18]

A review of the titles selected by the fourteen hundred subjects left one with the impression that not many classics or best-sellers strongly influenced people, that self-help books loomed large, that serious fiction did not stand out. Yet when the Sabines read and reread statements to cull the best—the most interesting, the best-said, the most thoughtful—they discovered that the effective statements were made, in general, about serious books—many in the humanities—those that have lasted, those that are still in demand and still in print.

The Books Make a Difference idea is endlessly flexible and tailor-made for both national and local promotion campaigns. I cite it here because it is the kind of idea that a national organization that existed to bring word about books/reading/libraries to a mass audience of readers and potential readers, library users and potential users, could have picked up and seeded right across the country. I am not suggesting that a new organization would necessarily reach back for this idea.

The Center for the Book, in fact, intended to "place" the Books Make a Difference concept with an appropriate organization, but we were unsuccessful. One reason we failed is that we encountered "turf problems." While admitting that it was a good concept—simple but exciting, interesting but not too complicated or expensive for even the smallest library to undertake—a few groups said they could not take it up because it was not their idea or because they would not get "credit" or visibility for devising Books Make a Difference projects. We on the Center's board thought we had performed a service for libraries—in a time of tight budgets, staff layoffs, and library closings—by devising a trial run to be sure our idea truly worked. Our efforts to donate an idea (which could easily have been adapted to a parent group's focus) and a good bit of preliminary work failed. Hence my earlier statement that a new agency or organization has to be adequately funded and staffed independently, which is *not* to say that the pattern of cooperation seen in the Books Make a Difference project should not be replicated.

How might a national program work, and why couldn't the Center for the Book and my College of Arts and Sciences launch it? Money, in a word. Only the interview portion of the project was even partially funded, so we were able to create a national promotion to which local projects could attach themselves. What would an ideal scenario have been?

We needed to create visible promotion materials that could be distributed free or at modest cost to locales: posters, brochures, buttons, bookmarks, camera-ready art, ad mats, and "canned" releases that local librarians could adapt for their own use. We should have published a series of how-to-do-it pamphlets to get people started in planning and doing projects. One might have dealt with generating interest among the local media, working cooperatively with them, and getting the interviewer or interesting subjects on radio and television programs (especially call-in shows). Another might have suggested kinds and locations of exhibits around the community, not just in the library. A third might have shown libraries how to get major industries and groups to conduct their own in-house Books Make a Difference projects. We might have provided camera-ready art and complete ads (to which local dates and places for interviews, programs, exhibits could have been added so local projects could be easily advertised).

Perhaps the most important ingredient in such a campaign are professional promotion and program staff members who can go from place to place to help local people start projects and to assist states and regions in coordinating and promoting the results of projects. In one place, the Friends of the Library might be the project sponsor; in another it might be the Rotary Club; in a third it could be the local literacy group. Staff members need to be able to work with such groups and to put them in touch with one another.

Professionals don't "do" Books Make a Difference projects—or National Library Week or Banned Books Week or Children's Book Week—for the sake of the event. They use such vehicles to promote books, reading, and libraries. The whole point of the Books Make a Difference project is that it is a library promotion venture. Why? Because the library is *the* community resource where all those titles and many, many more can be found. Local interviewers could make this point, which would be reinforced if they handed out information about the library to every subject.

Two responses from librarians with whom I talked in setting up the original project made me aware of the project's potential. One was the typical reaction: "We're delighted to participate in such an upbeat, positive effort related to ideas. These are tough times in libraries. We don't have many opportunities to go to our taxpayers with a positive message." (Many librarians who made this kind of statement were watching City Hall hack their budgets to death while they contemplated bond issues and branch closings.) The other point was related: "This project gives us an opportunity to offer the media here something fresh, interesting, and noncontroversial; we can give, not take."

In a Books Make a Difference campaign, while some members of the national staff were helping start state, regional, and local projects, others could be interviewing "famous" subjects and taping and photographing them. These interviews would be fed out to the states a few at a time—or grouped by areas such as sports, film, theater, music, political life, and the like—so local project directors would have a constant feed of fresh books and differences from famous people, those to whom local people would pay attention, to whom they would respond. Packaging such interviews on tape and film for distribution to radio and television stations would be effective. Broadcasters could use them as spot announcements with a message from the library or about the local project.

There isn't space here to spell out all the administrative and working relationships that need to be developed to create an effective national network of people dedicated to the promotion of books and reading. I mean to suggest only that it can be done and that a professionally conceived and developed continuing PI effort could provide essential aid to states and locales. Many, many different agencies do effective one-shot PI programs, which are in part wasted because there is no followup, no analysis. In conducting Books Make a Difference projects, for instance, libraries could learn a great deal about what the public knows and does not know and thinks and does not think about the library itself. Projects could be one vehicle (among several) to assess user needs.

From the myriad of education and library organizations that promote libraries and library causes, one stands out—the American Library Association. Nothing I have said here should be construed as negative comment about its communications program. Indeed, the newly enlarged vision for National Library Week is based on establishing a network of concerned, involved organizations whose members also care about the contribution libraries make in our society. But the whole burden of book/reading/library promotion is not ALA's alone. The book community is larger than just teachers or just librarians or just publishers. We need most an effective mechanism to integrate the PI goals of all appropriate groups and, at least annually, to conduct a national reading promotion campaign that most groups can adopt and play off of through their units across the country. We need a catalyst, which might be called the National Reading Council.

Why don't we have such an organization? For two primary reasons:

1. Book publishers, likely beneficiaries who are proficient at promoting and selling their own titles, see the need for a general promotion effort but they appear to be unwilling to support it financially.
2. Librarians, also likely beneficiaries, are not generally proficient at PI; as libraries have spent more and more money on nonbook materials and services, many library managers, at least, have turned their backs on books and reading as promotion vehicles for the library.

In the book industry, effective directors of promotion, publicity, advertising, and sales departments usually are members of the management team who participate in major decisions about many aspects of book publishing and who usually are respected and quite well paid. In libraries, PI people generally have low visibility, are rarely members of the management team, and often do PI work in addition to other major assignments.

Readers of *Publishers Weekly* and other trade journals are aware that the Association of American Publishers has cut back staff support of its projects that help people to develop lifetime reading habits. Readers of *American Libraries* and other library media know that there are a large number of subgroups in the library community trying to promote library causes effectively but not enjoying the success they should.

Many library administrators think library PI is what they read about: releases, social events, spot announcements for radio and television, brochures and other publications, posters, etc. That is not the case. Those items are the frosting on the cake. The thinking and planning, the strategy and work that produce such items is public information. Because, however, the visible bits and pieces of a PI effort are what can be promoted, PI is viewed as itsy, bitsy—and confused, diffuse, and consisting of minutiae. Launching an effective national campaign could help to educate and motivate those library managers who seem to need the exposure, those who don't fully appreciate the importance of quality library promotion.

If a national umbrella organization—a National Reading Council—were created, individual librarians would have to understand the need for focus on some characteristic of libraries that is also common to other cooperating groups, and that can be isolated and used to promote library service. Another reason library PI is viewed as diffuse and ineffectual is that libraries send contradictory messages to the public; one talks about its automated catalog, another promotes programs for children, and a third tries to raise money for a new branch. The image of libraries has dimmed as library promoters have tried to keep librarians *inside* happy, rather than sending messages that users *outside* can respond to.

Those who use libraries today know that all kinds of materials can be found there—print, nonprint, automated—and rejoice in that fact, especially when they find what they seek. In an attempt, however, to escape the "libraries are merely storehouses of books" notion, librarians have confused the public, which has not helped the image of librarians. Any successful PI effort finds a tool, a hook, a symbol that will work in a variety of different situations, formats, times, and places. That symbol, I think, is reading and the book. Libraries should consider returning to what has been a successful tool to promote libraries.

Using books as the promotion tool, libraries can find allies with money and enthusiasm for a national campaign. Literacy is on everyone's mind. Reading is done in many places in addition to the library, but millions of people get what they read from the library. Further, the concept of books and reading enjoys the support of numerous nonbook nonlibrary organizations; some aspect of their national programs links up to books. It is books and reading that form the common denominator. If library groups solicited publisher support and treated publishers like true partners, they would respond. One doesn't hear of library furniture producers promoting furniture in general or database producers stimulating interest in any but the products they market. Librarians should not overlook the support they have had from publishers in the past—support they could have again.

Just as some librarians view the newer media and technologies as more important than books, so some library promoters view using radio and television to promote libraries as, somehow, more important than print. The result is that the quality of promotional writing about libraries has decreased in the past fifteen years.

Efforts to produce films, filmstrips, spot announcements, and slide/tape shows that don't start with a script never are successful because the cohesion, the editorial point of view, the thought process one wants an audience to go through is missing. Libraries may have taken a route in promoting their services which makes less of an impression on the user than does a brochure or release. For one thing, it takes longer to read something than to watch it briefly on television or listen to it on the radio; people remember more of what they read than of what they are told. Furthermore, a large percentage of Americans do their listening and viewing while they are doing something else. It is almost impossible to read something attentively and do anything else, so one's attention is more focused while reading. As W. Russell Neuman, codirector of the MIT Program on Communication Policy, has said:

To understand how media are really used in the home, consider the Least Objectionable Program Theory. Television executive Paul Klein's notion is that the average viewer does not watch a program per se, but rather watches "television." The viewer plops down in front of the set, spins the dial, examines the programs available, and selects the least objectionable. Surveys repeatedly confirm that most viewers report watching "whatever is on...."

According to the latest Nielsen data, the average viewer watches about 4.5 hours of television a day. Women over fifty-five years of age average about six hours a day. The set is on seven hours a day. Television is a tremendously successful commerical medium. The audience, on the whole, is quite happy with it. But people are not using this quintessential mass medium for information retrieval.

Television, as well as the magazines in the bathroom and the radio in the kitchen, become part of the environment of the house. They are conveniently available and part of the ambience. They are not sought out purposefully for information retrieval; they are part of the media habit. Much of the time they are used while other activities are ongoing. Viewers focus on the television only 65 percent of the time. Thirty-three to 55 percent of the time, television shares their attention with other household activities. The percentages are even higher for radio. Users consume our media in a casual and passive way. Only 3 percent even bother to change the channel when a commercial comes on in the middle of a program.[19]

Conclusion

In times of stress when people feel threatened, they naturally respond by pulling back, by doing only the essential things, by attending first to their own needs and those of others for whom they are responsible. Both publishers and librarians have lived through periods of stress in the last decade. Now is the time for these two groups to plan to work together again. Self-service is at times a necessary short-range goal, but in the book community it can quickly become counterproductive. Because the symbiotic relationship between publishers and librarians, producers and users of materials, is so strong, each group makes much more progress if it moves in concert with the other.

Maybe we should have written that book, Dan. Maybe....

Notes

1. Christopher R. Evans, *The Micro Millenium* (New York: Viking Press, 1979); *Books, Libraries, and Electronics: Essays on the Future of Written Communications,* ed. Efrem Sigel et al. (White Plains, N.Y.: Knowledge Industry Publications, 1982): Leonard Shatzkin, *In Cold Type: Overcoming the Book Crisis* (Boston: Houghton Mifflin, 1982); *The Future of the Book,* Part I, *The Impact of New Technologies,* ed. Priscilla Oakeshott and Clive Bradley, Studies on Books and Reading, no. 8 (Paris: Unesco, 1982); Michel Gault, *The Future of the Book,* Part II, *The Changing Role of Reading,* Studies on Books and Reading, no. 9 (Paris: Unesco, 1982); *The 1983 Consumer Research Study on Reading and Book Purchasing* (New York: Book Industry Study Group, 1984); and *Daedalus,* vol. 112, no. 1 (Winter 1983), whose theme was "Reading Old and New."
2. John H. Jenkins, *The Future of Books* (Austin, Tex., 1982), 7.
3. Leonard Shatzkin, "The Production of Books," *Library Trends* 33 (1984): 181-94.
4. Paul Metz, *The Landscape of Literatures: Use of Subject Collections in a University Library* (Chicago: American Library Association, 1983), 64-65, 108-11.
5. Ching-chih Chen, "Citizen Information Needs—A Regional Investigation," in *Information Needs of the 80's,* ed. Robert D. Stueart (Greenwich, Conn.: JAI Press, 1982), 77-94, 107-13.
6. Martin Levin, personal communication to the Center for the Book, 7 March 1984.
7. Lola L. Szladits, "Answers and Questions," *Daedalus* 112, no. 1 (Winter 1983): 22.
8. See *Scholarly Communication: The Report of the National Enquiry* (Baltimore: Johns Hopkins University Press, 1979). For a description of the Office of Scholarly Communication, see *The Community of the Book: A Directory of Selected Organizations and Programs,* comp. Carren O. Kaston (Washington: Library of Congress, 1986), 29.
9. J. G. Goellner, "The Future of University Presses," *Library Journal* 103 (1978): 1699.
10. Szladits, "Answers and Questions," 25.
11. Lewis Branscomb, "Video Disc Technology and the Book," in *Books, Libraries, and Electronics,* ed. Sigel et al., 117-33.
12. Helen H. Lyman, statement at a meeting of the Center for the Book Advisory Board, Library of Congress, 12 April 1984.
13. Terry Winograd, "Computer Software for Working with Language," *Scientific American,* September 1984, 130-45, 136.

14. Branscomb, "Video Disc and the Book," 120.
15. Such recommendations appear in the full report *Books in Our Future* (Washington: Library of Congress, 1984), 43-49.
16. For descriptions of these and other literacy programs, see *The Community of the Book,* comp. Kaston.
17. Gordon Sabine and Patricia Sabine, *Books That Made the Difference: What People Told Us* (Hamden, Conn.: Shoe String Press, 1983).
18. Ibid., 5.
19. W. Russell Neuman, "The Media Habit" (Paper delivered at the Washington Program in Communications Policy Studies of the Annenberg School of Communications, Washington, D.C., 1984).

23. Beyond Bibliography

Frederick G. Kilgour

Librarians embracing technology will be able to serve users more personally and more thoroughly while operating from smaller physical bases, according to Frederick Kilgour. Knowledge information-processing systems, intelligent systems that will become possible with the development of "fifth-generation" computers, will give rise to libraries that can gather, assess, and organize information into a worldwide, electronically distributed base.

Kilgour, Founder Trustee of OCLC Online Computer Library Center, which is known for its national shared cataloging network, was introduced above as an advisor to the Book in the Future project.

Beyond Bibliography was delivered as the third British Library Annual Research Lecture in 1984 and published by the British Library in 1985. It is reprinted with permission. Copyright © 1985 The British Library Board.

As the 1980s have brought forth the rapid enlargement of information technology, I have been increasingly stimulated by the new prospects for users of information and for libraries. I hope to communicate my excitement to you, and I must get swiftly off the mark, rather like a California jack rabbit surprised while lunching, for this essay must travel a long road—a road that stretches from the Middle Ages to the very threshold of the twenty-first century.

At that threshold we will find the second computer revolution, which will certainly be more momentous than the first. Its base will be fifth-generation computer systems, which will have emerged from new concepts and new technologies, and which will perform functions hitherto impossible. The supremacy of these machines over their predecessors will lie not in their enormously greater power to process, but in their power to reason. Their major characteristic will be symbol manipulation, not the arithmetic processing that has been the basic computer operation from the first-generation, vacuum tube machines of the 1950s to the fourth-generation, very large-scale integrated-circuit supercomputers of the 1980s.

Fifth-generation computer systems will acquire, interpret, update, retrieve, package, and store huge amounts of information. Users will communicate with them in everyday language, professional and technical jargon, or even graphically and will receive from them knowledge in packages created for their specific needs. These personal, reasoning machines will take us far out beyond the familiar realm of bibliography that has served us so well for so long.

Fifth-Generation Computer Systems

T. Moto-oka, keynote speaker at the International Conference on Fifth Generation Computer Systems in 1981, stated, "Fifth generation computer systems will be required to have an extremely wide variety of sophisticated functions to solve the numerous problems which today's computers have and to meet the social needs of the 1990s, during which decade computerization is expected to find many more applications than nowadays."[1] Moto-oka described the functions, some of which are: (1) functions that enable inputting and outputting of information via speech or voice, graphics, images, and documents; (2) the ability to process information conversationally using everyday language; (3) the ability to put stored knowledge to practical use, and (4) the functions of learning, associating, and inferring.[2]

Fifth-generation computer systems will be knowledge information-processing systems (KIPS) with processing intelligence approaching that of humans. Man-machine interfaces will also approach verbal intercourse. In short, they will be extremely powerful systems.

Artificial intelligence will be basic to the design and operation of fifth-generation computers. In *The Fifth Generation,* E. A. Feigenbaum and Pamela McCorduck have written, "If we can imagine an artifact that can collect, assemble, choose among, understand, perceive, and know, then we have an artificial intelligence."[3] Seemingly endless fruitless discussions have debated the question, "Can machines think as do human beings?" It is the wrong question. Machines will certainly be able to carry out thought-like processes, but there will be many human attributes missing. For example, a machine may "think" its way to the solution of a problem more accurately and swiftly than a human being, but it will not have the human's realization as to what it is doing.

A flying machine is analogous to a thinking machine. Man has wanted to fly like a bird at least since the time of the mythical architect and sculptor, Daedalus. You will recall that Daedalus fashioned wings of wax and feathers so that he and his son Icarus could fly to Sicily to escape the wrath of Minos, King of Crete. Icarus disobeyed his father by flying very high, causing his wax wings to be melted by the sun and plunging him to his death in the sea, but Daedalus did indeed fly to Sicily. The kerosene queen that brought me over the sea from North America also flew, but not like a bird, and not with cognizance of its flight.

Expert systems—or knowledge-based systems, as you say in England—are artificial-intelligence programs. They have been defined as computer programs that perform at the level, or beyond the level, of expert human capabilities. The knowledge of knowledge-based systems is of two types. The first is conceptual and factual knowledge that pervades library materials of all kinds. The second is knowledge that may be unique to a single individual; it can be thought of as intuition, rule of thumb, and effective guessing. These two types of knowledge, in combination with programs for simple problem-solving logic and application of common-sense reasoning, comprise knowledge-based systems.

Two powerful expert systems are already in operation. One is Dendral, which solves chemical structure problems from mass spectographic data with an ability that exceeds human capabilities. Another is Caduceus, a medical system designed for physicians, in which the knowledge base is some 500 diseases and 4,000 symptoms. One of its authors feels that Caduceus knows four times as much as any physician.

Ann Clarke, of the British Library Research and Development Department, and her colleague, Blaise Cronin, of the Aslib Research and Consultancy Division, have described a simple knowledge-based system, PaperChase, that retrieves bibliographic citations to medical journals at Beth Israel Hospital in Boston, Massachusetts. PaperChase monitors the progress of a user's search, and when the search fails or is in imminent danger of failing, the program suggests other names of subjects to be searched that may yield a more fruitful result.[4] According to the authors of the PaperChase system, "The program encourages the user to type whatever seems natural, and...the program matches what is typed to items in the database, not by anticipating possible variations, but by applying methods similar to those that a person would use."[5]

Two major types of artificial-intelligence programs will make computers easy to use: the expert systems just described and man-machine interfaces. For the most part the expert systems will be transparent to the user, but man-machine interfaces will be very evident. Indeed, the ease or lack of ease in the exchange can make or break any system. Ease is absolutely fundamental. It is hoped that man-machine interfaces of the future will lead to the demise of the terms "user hostile" and "user friendly."

Fifth-generation man-machine interfaces—or natural-language systems, as they are called in the United States—will allow a person to communicate with a machine using his own language, whatever that may be, or by some other means of expression. Examples are jargon, professional and otherwise; mathematical and musical notation; graphs and two- or three-dimensional designs; and every manner of sound, both musical and unmusical. In general one can say that communication will be in words, either written or sounded, or will represent the non-verbal thinking of the engineer or sculptor in the form of designs, charts, and graphs.

The man-machine interface must be so designed that the machine can understand that different phrases may have the same meaning. To use an example from the preceding paragraph, it must be able to understand that "man-machine interface" is the equivalent of "natural-language systems."

Information-processing systems as I have described them may seem not just beyond the realm of bibliography but even beyond the realm of reality. They are not. In fact they will come into being in the 1990s.

Four major research and development projects with schedules ranging up to ten years are currently pursuing the fifth generation: (1) the Japanese KIPS group (1981); (2) the Alvey Programme (1982); (3) the European Strategic Programme for Research in Information Technology (ESPRIT, 1982); and (4) the Microelectronics and Computer Technology Corporation (MCC, 1982) in the United States.

The Japanese fifth-generation project was the first. It was exceedingly well designed as an integrated system, starting with the user of information and proceeding to powerful hardware. Its four main areas of investigation are (1) man-machine interfaces, (2) software engineering, (3) very large-scale integrated circuits and (4) knowledge-based systems. The Japanese project's target is affordable, reliable microcomputers and large stores of machine-readable information by the 1990s.

The Alvey Programme, or Alvey Directorate for Advanced Information Technology, is located in the United Kingdom's Department of Industry. Its principal research and development projects are (1) software engineering, (2) very large-scale integrated circuits, (3) man-machine interfaces, and (4) intelligent knowledge-based systems. These are comparable to the four Japanese KIPS projects. The schedule for their completion is a decade, with an initial cost of £350 million for the first five years.

The Commission of the European Community established ESPRIT in 1982. ESPRIT will rely on the research and development capabilities of universities and public research units. Major areas of research and development will be (1) advanced microelectronics, (2) advanced information processing, (3) software technology, (4) office automation, and (5) computer-integrated flexible manufacturing. ESPRIT is not as precisely targeted on the development of fifth-generation computers as are the programs of the Japanese and British.

The American entry in the fifth-generation race is the MCC, a consortium of American computer companies. MCC's research program includes (1) advanced computer architectures for knowledge-based systems and artificial-intelligence applications, (2) microelectronics packaging, (3) software engineering, and (4) computer-assisted design and computer-assisted manufacture.

With these four research projects under way—and others will follow—librarians, publishers, and other information providers find themselves in the situation which Alfred North Whitehead described a half-century ago when he wrote, "Professionalism has now been mated with progress. The world is faced with a self-evolving system, which it cannot stop."[6] Progress toward the second computer revolution cannot be halted. What this fact means for libraries is discussed in the remainder of this lecture.

The Future Active Library

As has been said, fifth-generation computers will certainly generate the second computer revolution, much more significant for librarians than the first, for they will also generate what I like to call the first library revolution. Intelligent machines offering each user the opportunity to ask for information specific to his needs, in his own terms, and at his own convenience and permitting him to tap large stores of information will transform the traditional library, hitherto as inflexible and passive as the books and journals it contains, into the active, revolutionized library of the future.

The large traditional library is a monolithic arrangement of volumes and catalog entries, as inhuman as any other monolith. It does not change one whit when I enter. It does not recognize me as Fred Kilgour nor differentiate me from any other user. Studies have shown that it fails to produce the information I want from 40 percent to 60 percent of the time. Once inside a library building I can consult a reference librarian when I cannot find what I want, which is all too often, but much of the time I don't. I go without, as apparently do my fellow users, for from occasional statistics that have become available to me it seems that less than 5 percent of the users seek out reference librarians.

The active library of the future is foreshadowed, however, in many small libraries, where the single librarian or small staff have a thorough knowledge of the collection and know what is of interest to individual borrowers. They can exercise initiative in making information available to specific individuals, even information that the individuals may not know that they need. Expert systems of the future active library will perform these functions and greatly enhance them.

In the active library all librarians will be taking responsibility for the information they disseminate, for much of that information will come from non-published sources. There is already an immense output from word processors in machine-readable form flowing over telephone circuitry all over the world. Presently much of the knowledge it purveys is generally unavailable, but when KIPS become operational some of it will become widely accessible. In the future, libraries will be technically capable of assessing the knowledge that goes directly from word processors to end users. Their expert systems will not only collect and select such knowledge, but also organize it for use, probably in the form of relational files.

Expert systems will undoubtedly carry out searches using the techniques of associative searching long used by information scientists in their laboratories. An associative search of a relational file can efficiently yield special individualized packages of information for each individual searcher. The maintenance of such files and the processing of such searches require immense computer power, which the fifth-generation computers will possess.

Users will become their own reference librarians by accessing these files as well as files in machine-readable form from more traditional sources, such as books and journals. The small files will reside in their personal KIPS machines, the huge files in central sites, interconnected in grids. Retrieval from these files will involve interaction of the personal machine with the inquirer to define with exactitude the information needed. As a former reference librarian, I can envisage a couple of examples of such improved definition. A typical searcher's request might be, "Does the library have *The Economist?*" If the library has only a partial file, the answer is both yes and no, and it is only with the redefinition of the question in terms of the actual issue wanted that the question can be answered. Similarly, the question, "What books do you have about blacks in the United States?" can be redefined to produce one book or one narrow topic concerning blacks in the United States. It is this kind of redefinition of requests that expert systems will carry out.

To be active participants in the development of the revolutionized library I have been describing, librarians should concern themselves with developing statements of the societal benefits of libraries as they exist today and as they will be in the future. If they do not come forth with such statements of benefit, library development will wander more or less aimlessly, as indeed it does today. Librarianship sorely needs a target expressed in societal terms. As Murray Laver has said, "it is always useful to be as clear as you can before you start about where you want to go." [7]

Librarians must be more willing not just to accept change, but to become its agents. It was not until the implementation of computerized networks beginning a dozen years ago that librarians were exposed to doing old things in new ways. I have had personal experience with the reception of changes introduced by computerized networks, and I have been both proud and pleased with the way many of my library colleagues entered into change, but at the same time distressed by others who seemed to feel that the ways of doing things in the coming century would be the same as during the past century. The deterrent to progress presented by this attitude was recognized in an award which the American Library Association made to me several years ago, wherein were listed several of my characteristics, the last being that "he had skin a foot thick, which was fortunate indeed because we fought him every step of the way en route to his Promised Land."

With very few exceptions librarians have not been innovators. During the century preceding 1970 the single major library innovation, namely the user-operated photocopier that first appeared in libraries in 1960, was developed outside. Because library innovation did not seem to be required, innovators were selected out of librarianship. As a result, library innovators are in excessively short supply just when they are most sorely needed, as the next two sections will reveal.

EIDOS

The first measurable revolutionary step toward the active library of the 1990s is the Electronic Information Delivery Online System (EIDOS), which three of us at the Online Computer Library Center (OCLC) are in the early stages of developing. A prototype system is currently running, but much more development and research are still required to bring EIDOS through the innovation stage and into full operation. The principal assumption underlying EIDOS is that the major use of text is the consultation or analytical examination of relatively short sections. My professional experience suggests that these may constitute three-fifths to three-quarters of the use of monographs.

Two technological events that occurred almost simultaneously motivated the development of EIDOS at this time, namely the distribution of millions of affordable microcomputers and the advent of electronic publishing. Recently there were 14 million micros in the United States, of which 14 percent possessed telecommunication possibilities. In the United Kingdom there were more micros per family than in the United States.

I shall discuss the second technological event at greater length, because electronic publications are the source of the information in EIDOS. Electronic publishing is evolving in four phases: (1) preparation of text in machine-readable form for the production of paper copies, with subsequent discard of the machine-readable version; (2) publication in paper copies and in a machine-readable version; (3) publication in machine-readable form only; and (4) publication of information in machine-readable form in an encyclopedia-like database. Each of these four phases exists today, with the fourth being confined almost entirely to numerical databases. Phases 2 and 3, wherein publication is in machine-readable form, with or without a paper version, are the main concern of this lecture.

Machine-readable editions have interesting analogies in production and distribution with medieval manuscripts. A medieval scribe probably never made two copies of a text exactly alike, for to err is human, and he must have made different errors of commission and omission in each text he produced. Such errors are frequent in medieval manuscripts. Similarly, electronically published copies are not necessarily exactly alike or exactly like the printed version. We have found lines that are on one page in the electronic version to be on the previous page in the printed text. A printed left-hand square bracket may be a virgule in the electronic version. Why, we don't yet know.

The economic aspects of electronic publication are also interestingly similar to those of the Middle Ages. Up until the twelfth century, publishing was entirely a retail trade, with one copy being produced at a time. From the twelfth to the fifteenth centuries, it was both a retail and wholesale trade, but with wholesale production rarely exceeding ten to fifteen copies. Beginning with the Gutenberg era in the fifteenth century and up until the advent of the electronic era, publishing has been a wholesale business requiring the stocking of an inventory. With electronic publishing, it is now possible for the publisher to operate simultaneously a retail and wholesale business, in that he will have to stock only one copy of an electronic text and produce copies on demand.

Frederick G. Kilgour

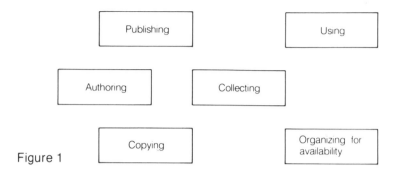

Figure 1

He can also produce parts of a text separately, as was often done in the Middle Ages. It is likely, for example, that more manuscript copies of individual Canterbury tales were produced than of all the tales collected in a single volume. Similarly, electronic publishing permits a publisher to produce economically one, ten, or a thousand copies of one chapter of a book to meet a special demand. The capability of matching supply to demand enhances a publisher's revenue in a manner impossible with Gutenberg technology.

Electronic publishing makes possible for the first time in millennia an integrated design of a generalized information system. There are six components in such a system (fig. 1): (1) writing (or authoring); (2) publishing; (3) copying; (4) collecting; (5) making available for use; and (6) using.

During the Middle Ages collecting and making available for use were combined (fig. 2). In medieval monastery libraries a librarian collected the manuscripts and made them available for use by listing them and arranging them on a shelf or in a cupboard. These two components remained combined in Gutenberg era and right up to and including the present time.

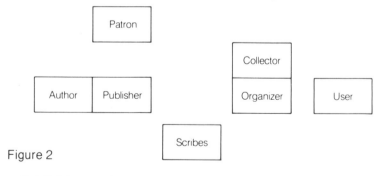

Figure 2

Publishing and copying were combined beginning in the fifteenth century, for printers were also the publishers, unlike medieval scribes (fig. 3). Today the most frequent arrangement is for material to go from the publisher to the printer to be copied,

310

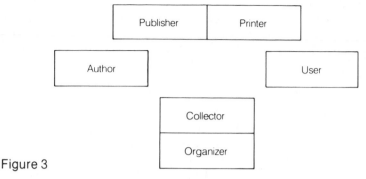

Figure 3

with the copies going back to the publisher. The two functions are still intimately associated.

In electronic publishing, the author, the publisher, or the printer may produce the text in machine-readable form. When the author produces the text on his word processor, the manuscript in digitized form goes to the publisher, where it is reviewed and, if accepted, edited in machine-readable form (fig. 4). Next the edited

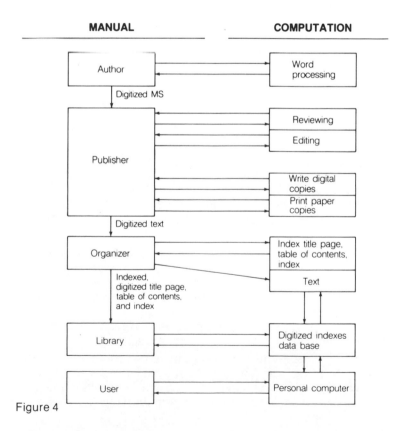

Figure 4

version goes to the printer if paper copies are to be produced. When printing is completed, the digitized manuscript is returned to the publisher, then is passed to a group that processes it so that the title, table of contents, and indexes are set up for libraries to include in their local online catalogs; here collecting and making available for use are unlocked for the first time since the Middle Ages, with making available for use preceding collecting.

We anticipate that for some years to come the material entering EIDOS will be books in the machine-readable version of printed books as submitted to composition machines. How does EIDOS process these machine-readable texts? First the system removes the mark-up symbols required for composition. Next delimiters are manually inserted in the text to identify components such as title page, table of contents, index, and main body of text. Special tags and delimiters are manually inserted in what is the equivalent of the title page to identify title, author, place, publisher, and date for machine conversion to the equivalent of a catalog entry. Human intervention is also necessary to construct a profile of the entire text that includes such information as the number of indexes, the placement of page numbers, and the maximum number of lines on a page.

A program then processes the tagged and delimited text to produce retrievable data that are stored in seven files. One file contains the descriptive catalog records, composed of author, title, place, publisher, etc. A second file contains tables of contents; a third, index pages; and a fourth, main texts. There are also a component directory file, a page number file, and a file containing the tagged and delimited title page equivalents described in the previous paragraph.

To enable user access, a separate program processes the descriptive catalog records to produce search keys. At present these keys are derived from author, title, and combined author-title information, then stored in the corresponding index files. Future keys will use names of subjects to approach directly the tables of contents and indexes.

Sitting at his personal computer and using the foregoing search keys, the user will retrieve the title of the monograph that he hopes contains the information he needs. Employing a simple command, he will next retrieve the table of contents, or the index, or a page of text directly. Having identified a page containing the information desired, he can call up that page by number. He may also browse preceding and following pages to extend his search.

Although transparent to the user and of no concern to him, the records containing title, table of contents, and index will be in local library catalogs. Copies of the entire texts will be stored at a central site, because storage locally would be prohibitively expensive.

Lack of knowledge about the use of information is the major deterrent to the full development of EIDOS and similar online full-text systems. Appropriate research investigations are discussed in the last section of this chapter. There are other and more immediately definable problems. For example, the fact that there are almost no standards for electronic publishing adds complexities to such products as EIDOS. Fortunately mark-up standards for machine-readable manuscripts are coming into being in the United Kingdom and the United States, and wide acceptance of such standards will facilitate the preparation of text for EIDOS processing.

In general a document that has no table of contents, no index, and no headings is useless for EIDOS processing; however, EIDOS will include novels, children's books, and poetry. A generalized effective indexer not requiring human intervention does not appear to exist, although it is anticipated that the use of knowledge-based or expert system techniques can produce effective automatic indexes for alphabetical languages and probably for Chinese, Japanese, and Korean. Development of such an indexer is a challenging prospect.

Scholarly citations to digital documents present problems when there are no page numbers in the document. Brian Shackel of Loughborough University of Technology, who is the principal investigator of the Birmingham Loughborough Electronic Network Development (BLEND) project, has a file of journal articles produced on word processors and entered into his file before publication. For citation purposes Professor Shackel numbers consecutively the paragraphs in each article. Applying his solution to a pageless monograph having headings would mean numbering the paragraphs following each heading and automatically constructing a directory of headings. This solution reminds one of the technique used in the Middle Ages for making citations to manuscript text, an example being "Galen. de usu part i.6.c. 10." Actually such citations are used currently, most familiarly in the book, chapter, and verse references to the Bible. There are similar legal references such as "Friendly Societies Act 1896, 5.9 (1)." Classical references also use a non-paginated scheme, for example Cicero *De officiis* 1. 133, 140, which refers to sections 133 and 140 in book 1. The general solution to the citation problem seems to be an adaptation of medieval citation systems.

EIDOS not only looks backwards to the Middle Ages for inspiration but also forward for targets. The table relates the major components of EIDOS with components of an active library operating in a future KIPS environment. As can be seen, the components are strikingly analogous, but they are in no way equivalent. EIDOS contains no artificial intelligence, whereas the active library is *nothing but* artificial intelligence. The figure does reveal that there can be paths, albeit long and arduous, for evolution from

EIDOS into the future. These evolutionary paths will not material-
ize until many extensive research projects have been carried out.

EIDOS	KIPS Library
Personal computers	Affordable fifth-generation computers
Machine-readable databases— local and central	Machine-readable central knowledge bases
Human indexing	Expert systems for knowledge organization and retrieval
Derived keys	Man-machine interfaces

Needed Research

The last section of this essay will not attempt a catalog of every
research area that could be fruitfully investigated today, but
answers, or at least partial answers, to the following questions are
urgently needed for continued development of document and
information delivery systems. Research on the first three should
begin at once.

What is the end use of information, and who are the end users?
There are almost no firm answers to this two-pronged question.
For example, it is not at all clear who the end users may be of the
information in a book purchased by a teacher or borrowed from a
library. Students are the likely end users, but not much is known
about their immediate and future use of the information. The
rapidly growing number of students possessing personal computers means that many students will have direct and easy access to
information in such systems as EIDOS. For effective initial development of EIDOS it is important to know more about these student
end users, and every other type of end user as well.

*What is the information that is consulted or used intensively in
books and journals?* The answer to this question will make it
possible to select for inclusion in document-delivery systems materials that will yield a high percentage of needed information in
reply to requests and obviate the inclusion of little-used material.
Striving for multiple duplicative responses is not justified, but at
the present time it is impossible to establish a pragmatically effective target.

*How many texts or journals are required for a valid field test and
how many for a mature system?* One can only guess at each of these
figures today. It is likely that a field test need not include documents in all subject areas and need not strive for the same target of
useful replies as would be set for a mature system.

If research is not undertaken soon to answer these three questions, information and document delivery systems will wander forward slowly and expensively, acquiring data empirically that might make it possible to add small enhancements to the system. The rapid and efficient way to make major advances is through the technique of research that has been well known since the sixteenth century.

Finally, two questions that are longer-range. The first is, *How can knowledge-based systems improve user access to online information?* Techniques for constructing tables of contents and indexes were discussed in the previous section, but the major aid to untrained searchers for information will come from the construction of knowledge-based systems. These systems will result from a combination of knowledge produced (1) by investigations designed to answer the questions about users and the information they consult and (2) from heuristic information obtained from highly trained information seekers such as reference librarians. One would hope that such a knowledge-based system could approach the comprehensiveness of Caduceus, which was described above.

Is it possible to construct in the near future a man-machine interface that will enable users to seek information using their own language and jargon? One should view the man-machine interface as the transliteration of a seeker's question into the language of the knowledge-based system to ensure that the seeker receives the information needed.

The paths ahead are cluttered with unknown knowledge almost begging to be discovered, and there is no greater intellectual exhilaration than that which comes with discovery.

Notes

1. T. Moto-oka et al., "Challenge for Knowledge Information Processing Systems," in *Fifth-Generation Computer Systems: Proceedings of the International Conference on Fifth-Generation Computer Systems, Tokyo, Japan, October 19-22, 1981,* ed. T. Moto-oka (Amsterdam: North-Holland Publishing Co., 1982), 5.
2. Ibid., 5-6.
3. E. A. Feigenbaum and Pamela McCorduck, *The Fifth Generation: Artificial Intelligence and Japan's Computer Challenge to the World* (Reading, Mass.: Addison-Wesley), 36.
4. Ann Clarke and Blaise Cronin, "Expert Systems and Library/Information Work," *Journal of Librarianship* 15 (1983): 286-87.
5. G. L. Horowitz and H. L. Bleich, "PaperChase: A Computer Program to Search Medical Literature," *New England Journal of Medicine* 305 (1981): 928.

Frederick G. Kilgour

6. Alfred North Whitehead, *Science and the Modern World* (New York: Macmillan, 1931), 290-91.
7. Murray Laver, *Information, Technology, and Libraries* (London: British Library, 1983), 2.

It is true that the library is a storehouse of information, but so is a data bank of any kind. What the library's retrieval system does is provide a human intermediary between the store and the user, who responds to each user's needs specifically, and adjusts the access and interprets the store accordingly.

LESTER ASHEIM
Library Educator

24. New Wine, New Bottles

Warren J. Haas

Academic libraries in the "information age" have already faced, since World War II, the growth of universities and the overwhelming growth of scholarly literature. Now they face continuing growth in literature, the emergence of electronic resources for scholars, and futures that are uncertain both financially and in regard to their integration into the organization of their universities. The new experience requires new research into how libraries can be organized for research according to the contemporary needs of scholars faced with old and new resources.

Warren J. Haas, introduced above as an advisor to the Book in the Future project, is President of the Council on Library Resources, a foundation that encourages and assists research about libraries, focusing on problems faced by academic and research libraries.

From *International Librarianship Today and Tomorrow: A Festschrift for William J. Welsh*. New York: K. G. Saur, 1985. Reprinted with permission of K. G. Saur, Inc., © 1985.

This paper is concerned with the future of academic research libraries. More specifically, it considers some management issues that must be attended to if those libraries are to have a future. Not only because of past contributions of libraries to scholarship, but also because their performance is a matter of present concern to faculty, students, and university financial officers, the subject of research library management is worth consideration.

During the next decade, library administrators will have to find ways to shift their attention from libraries per se, often seen as organizations with responsibilities fixed by their institutional settings, to the management of what might be best described as a set of dynamic functions unbounded by established structures. The transformation stems from at least three powerful forces: (1) adjustments in the configuration of activities related to the generation, production, supply, and use of information; (2) modifications, made possible by information technology, in the nature and methodology of much research; and (3) recasting of the outlook and priorities of foundations, government, and business that will, in turn, tend to integrate further the academic disciplines and, possibly, even affect the long-established boundaries of universities themselves. The projected change in the task of library management is prompted as much by new realities and intellectual necessity as it is by aspirations for efficiency.

Library management, as a matter for special attention, came into its own only after research library operations expanded along with the rest of higher education following World War II. Librarians, being a responsible lot, usually have sought to run a tight ship, but before 1945 their attention was, in large part, concentrated on service routines and on internal technical operations. The extension of higher education to a much larger portion of the population and the transformation of wartime research capabilities, essentially undiminished in volume, to a peacetime setting combined during the 1950s and 1960s to recast research libraries: they "globalized" current acquisitions, creating a new level of linguistic and operating complexities; they rebuilt their facilities to accommodate expanding student bodies and collections; they began to experiment with photographic and, subsequently, early computer technologies; and their budgets increased in step with those of all other university components. Library after library was surveyed by external consultants, not so much to test managerial performance as to determine library adequacy in the light of projected demands. In general, the dominant goal for management was to expand fast enough to keep even with the rate of institutional growth. The method, by and large, was to rely on established ways of doing things rather than to seek fundamental change in operating methods. New managerial layers were established, reflecting growing staff size and dispersed operations, and additional units were added to meet specific needs, for example, the language and subject specialists to support area studies.

About 1970, the surge of growth came to an end, and since then a gradual retrenchment to more sustainable levels has been under way. The transition has been uneven, affecting some institutions more severely than others, but, in general, a mix of relative austerity and a sense of administrative responsibility (both inherent and induced) has for the past fifteen years directed attention to the processes of library management as never before. Professional associations, foundations, schools of library science, consulting organizations, and libraries themselves have sponsored or undertaken analytical studies and training programs of many kinds. Initially, special attention was given to the organization and staffing of research libraries in the context of operating obligations and the realities of budget limitations. Large numbers of librarians were offered opportunities to develop supervisory skills and the personal qualifications required for expanding their participation in management. More recently, attention has been directed to refining operating performance in preservation, collection development, and user services.

The most important library development of recent years is the extensive application of computers to technical operations. Besides controlling the cost of cataloging and related activities, the development of cooperative databases has greatly increased bibliographic and location information. The influence of computers on internal operations has opened new organizational prospects for consideration by library administrators and has set the stage for the future changes that are the subject of this paper.

The Council on Library Resources (CLR) has made a special effort to bring scholars and university administrators into closer communication with librarians to talk about the fundamental changes under way in all aspects of creating, producing, organizing, protecting, and using information—changes that will affect the ways scholars work, the methods of publishing, the manner in which universities are organized, and, most dramatically perhaps, the future form and functions of libraries. The scope of this change, its effects, and the costs implicit in it call for the attention of all concerned. There is a great gap between our understanding of the characteristics and use of information and the requirements of the "information society" that are now being shaped by many factors and interests.

It is also clear that as "information systems" promise more they also grow more complex and costly, additional reasons why attention must be paid to topics that are now largely unexplored and an effort must be made to articulate the interests and requirements of universities and scholars. Too little is known (and not enough is made of what is known) about such matters as the relationship between information availability and economic progress, the implications for society of constraints on access to information, the social role and functions of library and other information agencies, the quality and validity of information maintained in computer-based systems, or the relationship between format and usefulness. Information, in all of its forms, is the product of much human effort, but too little thought is given to the process of putting that product to full use.

The council's program has always included a research component but, by and large, such work has been linked directly to specific CLR goals. It is now evident that the range of important issues has expanded well beyond these limits; many library-related issues are also of interest to organizations and individuals other than libraries and librarians. In response, CLR expects to expand its research capacity beyond established program areas to include topics pertinent to not only libraries and their users, but all other components of the system of scholarly communication. This research will help promote productive new links between CLR and other organizations and will encourage comprehensive approaches to addressing information system questions by universities themselves, publishers, computer and other technology-based groups, and the academic disciplines. The hope is that the new research will stimulate wide discussion and, ultimately, encourage complementary action on many fronts.

The intent is not to concentrate research activity in one place. Rather, it is to encourage skillful people from many universities and academic disciplines to undertake work along lines they themselves determine in the context of a set of related topics. A sense of cohesion will be achieved by bringing participants together with some frequency and in a variety of settings to review progress, to test each other's work, and, over time, to establish the dynamic spirit that is characteristic of colleagues engaged in a common endeavor. Building and maintaining a high level of activity should help advance several interrelated objectives important to librarianship and professional education:

1. From concentration on the most important issues, a reasonably complete understanding of the issues involved will be achieved, and specific findings will gain the attention of those who are responsible for the development of future information systems.

2. From encouragement of participation in the research program by faculty in a number of pertinent disciplines, links between leading library schools and other academic departments should be strengthened.

3. The number of individuals who are exceptionally well trained in the substantive aspects of library and information service should be expanded, thus strengthening the base for further work.

4. From the giving of visibility to research of high quality, all who contribute to or use the system of scholarly communication will become better informed about the implications of the information revolution for teaching and scholarship.

While these are specific objectives, they do not fully convey the underlying reason for the council's interest in mounting a major research enterprise. Simply put, the time has come to acknowledge that the capacities of recently developed technologies are such that important aspects of teaching and research now can be fundamentally transformed and improved for the benefit of students, individual scholars, and society. Libraries have a unique and inescapable role to play in this transformation. They only need to find the way.

The Research Program

While broad areas of research will be determined finally by the CLR board and its advisors, and while specific projects in the context of the general program will be developed by many individuals as they prepare proposals, it is necessary to speculate about possible subjects for investigation in order to stimulate interest, establish funding requirements, and set procedures. A series of discussions with faculty and administrators from several universities has identified many important topics. Those that are listed below are only examples, but, taken together, they provide some sense of the matters that are on the minds of individuals from many academic disciplines.

The research process in the new information setting.

1. What is the "natural history" of information systems for various disciplines? Are they all at various stages on the same path, or are they quite different in fundamentally important ways?
2. Can we learn more that is useful from a planning point of view about the relationship between the characteristics and performance of technology-based systems and their acceptance by users?
3. How can the integration of information, rather than its further segmentation, best be advanced in the future course of system evolution?

4. How can the interface between technology and scholarship be studied and monitored on a continuing basis?
5. How is "high technology" really serving people, and whom is it serving?
6. Should (and can) the library be redefined as a center of ideas and values, as well as of information and documents?
7. Do technological systems reduce research skills?
8. How do scholars actually work? How will their way of working change in response to each new technology?
9. New systems should not be an impediment to those with established ways of working. How can scholars have a role in determining the process of transition?
10. Can new software systems be devised that will enable scholars to "write in the margin" and readily develop refinements as necessary for their own needs?

User needs, resources, and access.

1. How can universities influence technological development so that the way is opened to a democracy of learning?
2. Acquisitions vs. access—what are the implications for users?
3. How can the effect of prospective technologies on publishing be assessed in the light of scholarly needs and interests?
4. How can libraries become more effective as a point of guidance? Are there ways to develop more effective communications between libraries and scholars? Librarians may need to help scholars organize their work.
5. How can users have more of a voice in planning databases?
6. Is there reason to hold on to a book culture?
7. To what extent can librarians be experts on the quality of information or publications?
8. How can the conflict between the need for serendipitous browsing and collection storage efficiency be resolved? Are there technological solutions?

Bibliographic control.

1. Computer technology offers new access paths to information; therefore indexing is of special importance. In an operational sense, how can academic subject specialists be more effectively involved?
2. Can ways be found to encourage careful scholarly assessments, on a periodic basis, of the literature of disciplines (narrowly defined), as a useful means for control of the literature?
3. Which information needs of scholars are not now met in bibliographic databases, and how can refinements be made?
4. How do bibliographic requirements vary by discipline? How can the national bibliographic structure accommodate supplementary components for specific purposes?

5. Can experiments be devised and conducted to test alternate bibliographic systems that might be envisioned more in the context of new technological capabilities, and less as a reflection of historical precedents (e.g., inclusion of items regardless of format, etc.)?

These examples suggest that there is a need to bridge the gap between some of the basic research in information science and the equally important applications-driven work that has dominated most library organizations, including CLR. In brief, the new research emphasis will be on developing further the background of facts and building sufficient understanding among those who must participate in setting the information policies and forming the necessary management systems, with particular attention to the long-term interests of scholarship, universities, research libraries, and the society of which all are a part.

New Management Approaches for New Obligations

The once uncomplicated and essentially independent activities of writing, publishing, and managing libraries are all being transformed. The volume of worldwide publishing grows with economic and technical advances and growth in the population itself. Computer, telecommunications, and text storage systems open the way for fragmentation of activity and responsibility, as well as for increased speed and capacity. Some information has monetary value, and there is great competition to establish and control markets by commercial and nonprofit organizations alike. But there is no simple correlation between the value of information and its economic worth, a matter of growing importance that might, if unattended, provoke serious discontinuities in system performance and unacceptable inequalities of access. This fundamental transformation in the information system is essentially one of new capabilities. Changes made in the system of scholarly communication will affect every aspect of society. Libraries have been the keystone of the system in the past, but it is now clear that the shape of that keystone must change if it is to function in a new structure. Despite many claims and assertions, the information structure of the future has not yet taken shape, but the pace of change is such that it is now imperative that "architects" of great skill, individuals who are concerned with the well-being of universities, scholarship, and libraries, go to work with some degree of coordination, before what may be unsatisfactory structures are imposed by default.

There are many matters that need attention. Among the most complex is the general subject of collection management, where fundamental change in both intent and practice seems inevitable.

In general, the largest portion of library expenditures can be traced to the number of annual acquisitions and the size of accumulated collections, For the most part, these expenditures have been made in anticipation of need. Given present and projected technologies for information storage and distribution, it is certain that costs will increase for the *use* of information as that information is needed, rather than for the purchase and ownership of a book or journal filled with information. Unless there are fundamental changes in the expectations of users and the habits of bibliographers, this new demand on funds will, for the foreseeable future, be in addition to, not in place of, most annual acquisition costs. It seems unlikely that incremental funding in the amounts required will be available. Without a careful revision of collection management practices, erosion of collections rather than enhancement of service is a real risk. At root, the key question is whether library managers can develop a collection strategy that makes effective use of existing and anticipated options, including storage alternatives, reliance on machine-stored records rather than printed sources, and cooperative collecting and access plans. Can costs be controlled without creating unacceptable handicaps for users? To accomplish this assignment, a better understanding is needed of the relationship between the format of information and its utility. The information needs of individual disciplines and the research methods of individual scholars need careful investigation. It is absolutely essential that scholars themselves join librarians in the search for answers, in order that new directions for collection management may be acceptable as well as efficient.

A second primary topic for attention concerns the organization of information activities in research universities. A few institutions have acknowledged that library operations and services are increasingly linked to computer and telecommunication services, and questions have been raised concerning operating overlaps, cost control, and planning responsibility. How can the decentralized character of a university be accommodated while the parts are brought into constructive collaboration? What are the long-range economic implications for universities of technology-driven information systems? What is the role of the commercial information sector in the light of university goals and scholarly needs? These and many other questions need attention. The answers may well influence the organizational structure, not only of libraries but of universities themselves.

The third matter for concentrated attention deals with the accommodation within institutions of new transinstitutional relationships. Information, like light and air, permeates our lives. It is generated in an infinite number of places and is used in innumerable ways. The sheer quantity of information and shortcomings in the traditional ways of organizing it are combining to establish an information system that is at once much expanded and further segmented, transcending the capacities of any single institution. The need to live simultaneously in two (or more) worlds is perhaps the most difficult management challenge. There are many aspects to be considered: economics, system performance, and operating controls are all topics that need careful investigation. Strategic planning in this arena is in its infancy. For example, annual budgeting processes are essentially inconsistent with the requirement for assured continuity in multi-institutional efforts. Without such continuity, individual libraries are reluctant to change their own operations for fear that their own performance in delivering services from external sources will be jeopardized. There is much to learn about the organizational forms that cooperative undertakings might best take to accomplish specified tasks, and there is obviously a need to explore control mechanisms designed to keep cooperative ventures contained by their mandates.

These notes only suggest the character of the demanding and complex period that lies ahead for research libraries, their universities, and their users. Technology and its cost are the driving force, but it is the opportunity to achieve new levels of library performance that argues for enthusiastic and unqualified participation in the exploration of new frontiers by the library profession. Success will bring to the profession the respect of the widening circle of society that lives at the hub of the new information age. The following statement will show how that success may be defined.

Scholarship, Research, and Access to Information: A Statement from the Council on Library Resources

Those who are concerned with libraries and books have long recognized and often strongly asserted the need for unconstrained access to information as a condition essential to every democratic society. The computer, telecommunications, and text storage technologies that now play a prominent and at times dominant role in many aspects of library service and information systems have created a very different and complicated new environment. The established structure is changing, and powerful economic forces are having a profound influence on all aspects of scholarly communication, libraries, and information services generally. While technology is powerful and brings a promise of unmatched opportunities, it is essential to remember that ready access to information is not automatically assured. That goal must be constantly and aggressively pursued. The statement that follows, from the board of directors of the Council on Library Resources, is simply a reassertion of an old principle, one that now seems to need special attention.

For twenty-eight years the board of the Council on Library Resources has concerned itself with the development and performance of academic and research libraries. In terms of collections and service obligations, those libraries have grown greatly during that time. Teachers, scholars, and research faculty are more dependent on them than ever before. During those same years, libraries have also become more complex organizations than they once were. Computer applications have transformed operations, opening the way to development of many specialized services and sophisticated methods of management and control. Economic realities have encouraged and telecommunications (linked with computing) have made possible new affiliations among libraries and, also, the rapid growth of business concentrating on the organization and distribution of information to customers of all kinds, worldwide.

These changing patterns of organization and recent technical innovations bring, along with promise, some potential problems affecting access to information that must be resolved if full benefits are to be realized. The first concerns certain restrictive practices of a few of the growing number of commercial and nonprofit database producers and suppliers, especially as they promote their products and services to the academic research community. Simply put, there are conditions for doing business in universities. For vendors of services and information to be useful, even acceptable, participants, those conditions need to be upheld and met. The need for high quality and reliability is obvious. Even more important, research and scholarship require unconstrained access to information. Scholarship is personal, but its results are not private. To judge the validity of scholarly work, the records of past and present research must be open to scrutiny. This is the only way the intellectual audit trail that is at the heart of discovery can be maintained. Limited or conditional access to bibliographic records (or information about information in any form) is of particular concern. Universities, their members, and all of society must keep bibliographic channels open and accessible. In a real sense, the index to the accumulated record of mankind is the hallmark of a democratic and open society.

Second, ways must be found to assure continuing attention for those aspects of culture and learning that are important but, in a commercial sense, not necessarily in fashion. In financial terms, the capital investment and operating costs of new, technology-based information systems are great, and funding plans of many kinds are necessary. But there is too often a tendency to assume exact correlation between the economic value of information and its intrinsic worth. Uncritical adherence to the concept of information as a commodity will distort the agendas of institutions and disciplines alike. In order that the concerns of libraries and the needs of scholars might be expressed and met, better ways must be found to build responsible partnerships among all elements of the system of scholarly communication—public and private, commercial and not-for-profit, personal and institutional. Public interest in the principle of open access must appropriately influence the structure of the information system and its components. It is certain that the information needs of society cannot be defined by the marketplace alone.

Finally, the new and deeper affiliations now taking shape among libraries and their parent institutions carry both responsibilities and dependencies that affect access. Cooperative collecting and preservation activities, for example, imply an end to institutional parochialism because extended access is a corollary of cooperation. As individual libraries become, to varying degrees, components of "the nation's library," the nation's scholars become their users. That fact needs to be explicitly acknowledged and accepted, for, in the long term, if present trends continue, it will reshape the goals and methods of research libraries.

Even this incomplete list of matters needing attention if open access is to be achieved gives some hint of the difficulties ahead. There are no simple answers or absolute prescriptions. Success is not so much a matter of balancing interests and seeking an appropriate response as it is one of providing many responses that, in the final analysis, are themselves balanced and thus meet reasonable expectations. All information is not the same; the uncritical homogenization of the term is probably a source of much difficulty. Publishing, producing, and distributing information involves costs that must somehow be met. The value of information often changes with use, time, and form. Unconstrained access does not imply cost-free information any more than free information assures accessibility. The information society is in part a state of mind, characterized by shifting needs and methods. Increasingly, it is also becoming a set of established systems that bring risks of constraints along with promises of efficiency. For this very reason, there is a great need to establish the principles and set the conditions under which information will be made accessible. It is the shaping of those principles, both the process and the substance, that is at the heart of our problem.

As did the development of moveable-type printing more than five hundred years ago, today's computing, communications, and storage technology can profoundly affect civilization by accelerating the rate of change and reducing the isolation of segments of society. Whether change will be improvement as well and whether further social integration will lead to a fuller sharing of the benefits of technical progress are matters for wide discussion and thoughtful action. Our universities, collectively, are an important forum for this discussion, and, inescapably, they are leaders in setting the course for action as well. Libraries, as central components of universities traditionally charged with responsibility for accumulating, organizing, preserving, and promoting the use of the accumulated record, must rise to this challenge of unsurpassed importance.

For its part, the Council on Library Resources will keep this topic at the forefront of its program. With others who support the cause, we will work to make a powerful, unambiguous case underscoring the public's expectations for accessible and expansive information services, and we will take all appropriate steps to help assure that libraries continue to fill their established role as the source for the full record of the past and as the indispensable base for information services in the future.

Board of Directors, Council on Library Resources

25. The Library Business and the Future

William J. Welsh

Librarianship has performed the same functions since its beginnings, according to William J. Welsh. But economic, legal, and social problems confront librarianship as it attempts to maintain its place in the information business and the arts and entertainment business, which are changing with the development of communication and storage technologies. Librarians must work now to ensure that they can deliver their traditional services to patrons in the future.

William J. Welsh is Deputy Librarian of Congress. For many years he has been deeply involved in the application of new technologies at the Library of Congress and throughout librarianship. This chapter is adapted from remarks he made at the Thirtieth Anniversary Program of the Resources and Technical Services Division of the American Library Association, held in New York at the association's annual conference in June 1986.

There are the long future and the short future. The long future is the mid-twenty-first century with a technology that will surprise everyone. Here is my version: In the kitchen, the *Joy of Cooking* is online. Nearby, a small computer-driven device dispenses martinis mixed to individual tastes. A wireless device in the car in the driveway has enabled the driver to move a frozen dinner from the freezer to the microwave to be ready to eat upon arrival. In the workshop, the manual on how to repair an "electric spoon" is online. In the family room, income tax questions are being answered online by a service from the IRS. In the bathroom a member of the family who has severe abdominal pain gets an online diagnosis from the National Institutes of Health database: ingrown toenail. In the bedroom, a large screen on the ceiling displays (online, of course) *Out of Africa* or *Murphy's Romance.*

Down the road in the library, robots are acquiring, cataloging, and preserving data files for home use. (The only human being in evidence is a white-haired consultant—he looks something like a university chancellor—asking what happened to Module VI.) Back at home, we find the "Dynabook," a portable, paperback-sized monitor/receiver that gives access to virtually all recorded culture.

The long future will surprise everyone, especially those of us audacious enough to offer thoughts about what our libraries will be like in the year 2056. Even now, however, we have a great number of databases available—900 source files for federal numeric and textual data alone. I have begun to wonder, when I travel by airplane, which airline will be the first to substitute magazines on disks or tapes for hard copy—a small video screen would fit easily in the space above the tray table. I don't think it is too early to believe that optical disk technology will bring about a major change.

Needless to say, all this will move and shake librarianship in significant ways. Librarians must create new structures and organizations to house the data files and textual records. But the library will probably be with us well into the next century. There may, in fact, be fewer changes than we expect—maybe the general public will be unable to afford many of the heralded new services made possible by the personal computer.

Rather than talk further about what we can only vaguely envision, let me discuss the short future, the library business over the next twenty years. That is much more clear, though still obscure and challenging enough. Just what is the library business? The first library we know much about, that of Ashurbanipal, twenty-six centuries ago, performed much the same functions as our libraries provide today. Publication formats have changed since then, from clay to floppy disks, and clienteles have changed as literacy expanded. But the library of Ashurbanipal collected works, classified them, and made them available for use.

The fundamental role of the library has, then, remained remarkably persistent, an important point to keep in mind as we look toward the future. Let me now discuss two aspects of the library's role in the short future, the information business and the arts and entertainment business.

The Information Business

This is the hot business of the moment, the one we are perhaps first inclined to think of in connection with libraries. It is the one with a large market and thus a large and flourishing industry to serve it. In the old days—before computers—the information side of librarianship was a cottage industry. There were reference librarians with a handy-sized collection of reference books to which they directed their patrons or which they scoured themselves for facts and figures as needed. The client varied by type of library, but the basic process was, so far as any great art can be, unvaried. There were the reference librarian and the reference collection—paid for, touchable, finite in size, and, to a large degree, standard in format—and the customer—citizen, company researcher, student, or whoever.

Now, of course, we have changed all that. Some libraries do work in the older mode, especially smaller public and college libraries, but many others work at least partly in a new mode. Some, working entirely in the new mode, tend to be special, indeed very special, libraries which are almost bookless, though machine-packed. The reference "collection" is spread across the continent at the end of various utility wires, and that collection may be supplemented by computerized files purchased to be stored, manipulated, and read locally and by files produced in-house. The cost of the "collection" is by no means fixed or predictable, because each "visit" to a distant utility has its own cost.

Still other libraries, probably a majority of larger libraries, now work in a mixed mode. The librarians and patrons exploit the fixed-cost, standard-format collection when practical and resort to online services (or, perhaps, patrons are referred to a search service) in some instances to save the user's time, to avoid certain searching blocks, or to get the most current information.

What is the "information" that squirts out the end of the wire or rises from the grooves of the compact disk? Mostly it is plain facts and figures, many of them, of course, bibliographic facts. They are the items venerated by Thomas Gradgrind in Charles Dickens's novel *Hard Times:* "In this life," Gradgrind says, "we want nothing but facts, sir; nothing but facts."

Hot and Cold Facts in the Marketplace and the Library

We may categorize our facts a little further. We may break them down into hot facts, lukewarm facts, and ice-cold facts. Each probably has a different future in the marketplace and in libraries.

Hot facts are those relating to hot topics, those of greatest general interest, those, in brief, that can be sold at profit. Such facts will increasingly become a problem for libraries because of their very salability. The information industry—formerly known as publishers—will look more to marketing factors than to social need in deciding what facts to make available. Paying customers will want the speed and power of searching that is possible only in online access. Producers/packagers of the data will wish to fulfill those desires and will also wish to be able to charge for each use, a practice the technology permits. Libraries that wish to deal in hot facts will have to play the new game. Barring large-scale adoption of new kinds of billing or subscription-type billing, libraries will have to pay according to use.

Many commentators have plowed and picked over this field, discussing pay-per-use versus costs of traditional subscriptions, as well as whether users should receive free access or "fee access." These issues are important but have been well thrashed out in the literature. Let me add merely my own statement of conviction. I believe that decent library service for the American people requires that what has traditionally been free should continue to be free in the equivalent electronic form, unless the traditional alternative remains readily available. Even where the traditional alternative exists, the speed and power of online access to data should be reasonably available to the general public at a cost that is not exorbitant. I could analyze the words *reasonable* and *exorbitant* at length, but I will simply say that we as responsible librarians must ensure that access to such information as is required by an alert and aware citizenry must be no less available to the American people at the end of our careers than it was at the beginning. If necessary, we should establish literacy stamps analogous to food stamps for the poor. Or we might, as Peter Briscoe and his colleagues have suggested, require by law that "copies of electronic publications derived from databases, or the databases themselves," be deposited "in regional library consortia or library utilities, as well as the Library of Congress" to ensure database integrity, physical preservation, and the public right of access.[1]

Since we have established that electronic data will be available in libraries, we need next to ask librarian-type questions: What about bibliograhic access? What becomes of retired data?

Bibliographic access. What does bibliographic access mean in the online environment? It can mean something as "simple" as what we mean now by bibliographic access to books, that is, a simple listing of what is available for our patrons' use. For example, it could consist of brief descriptions of our optical disks or of online files such as *Chemical Abstracts.* More elaborately, it could mean whatever catalogers, indexers, or bibliographers could come up with to help patrons through the swamp of electronic services. An arrangement of online files that would permit automatic selection by subject of both online files themselves and the citations and facts within the files is not implausible. Indeed, one could envision a kind of access to such files and their data that could be easily mastered by junior high school students, or even senior faculty at a university.

Retired data. As long ago as 1976, Hugh Cline of the Education Testing Service was urging us to explore the "question of libraries serving as depositories of ... research data files." He observed that "collecting, cleaning, documenting, and disseminating such data files is, indeed, very similar to the activities of many libraries in maintaining their holdings."[2] The problem of orphan data files has become much more acute since Cline wrote those words. Some institutions, such as the University of Michigan, Princeton University, and the National Archives, have begun to archive data files, but most data files face, at best, an uncertain future and create major new challenges for libraries. For example, how shall we deal with the "coral reef" phenomenon in data files, in which tiny facts add or subtract themselves to a file one by one or in little clumps until they make an immense reef, but one that is never fixed in shape or extent? What is it we should save? The accumulation of certain days? Or should all additions find a home? If so, how do we acquire them, preserve them, and make them accessible? What is happening to data files whose hot facts have become cold and, therefore, unprofitable? Do libraries not have fundamental obligations to collect and preserve hot facts for twenty-first-century scholars and their heirs? If we do not collect and save, who will?

These are two sets of issues surrounding the hottest of facts, those available through the online services, and they need to be studied seriously by the profession. I have proposed that the Resources and Technical Services Division of the American Library Association establish a joint task force with its Reference and Adult Services Division to recommend what cooperative action we must take to preserve the new machine-readable heritage of America.

The problems are perhaps simpler for some media for hot facts than others. CD-ROMs and other disks suited for storage of hot facts are actual physical objects, but the varieties of "merchandise" provided by the national networks are spectral entities. The disks at least, being objects, can enter the traditional processing stream by being described, labeled, and stored, and their descriptions can then be sent out to the world. The descriptions provide what we might call "meta-access," which is, if the reader will excuse my saying so, the boring kind of access.

A more interesting issue concerns access to the actual data recorded on the disk. This issue is analogous to the issue of indexing a book. In books, there is little standardization among indexes. Some are excellent, some are almost worthless. Let us hope that a degree of standardization will emerge in retrieval systems for data on disks and that the quality will generally exceed that of indexes for books. I am not sure what we can do to promote this end, except to purchase disks and services judiciously. Possibly the American Library Association could set up a *Consumer Reports* kind of testing service for disk systems. Certainly more journals could publish columns like the one regularly featured in *RQ* in which "electronic" publications are reviewed as carefully and seriously as our traditional reference sources have been.

In brief, libraries, as sources of hot facts, are in a new world, in which they must deal with new issues, establish new systems and procedures, and pay—or have patrons pay—new costs.

Lukewarm facts are in a different situation. They include the information lying in wait in the stacks of libraries everywhere, the journeyman facts, the workaday facts at rest in original documents, ancient manifestos, yellowed newspapers. They are the facts sought by today's scholarly researchers, who, assisted by librarians and a mixture of research tools, are even now excavating them, shaping them, breathing an informing shape into them, and issuing them as scholarly articles and monographs. Some of these facts are the disinherited hot facts of yesteryear (which is why librarians have to be concerned about today's hot facts). Like faded movie stars, these are the facts that very few will now pay to see. Having no commercial market, they may be happily given over by the commercial world to the non-profit institutions: the libraries and archives of the world.

Libraries and archives may of course choose to retain lukewarm facts in traditional form, generally on paper. If so, however, they must also make certain that that paper lasts as long as the (very unpredictable) need for the information it contains. That is why the Library of Congress is planning to open a $12 million mass deacidification plant in Fort Detrick, Maryland. Using diethyl zinc, we expect to give at least a half-million books a year a paper lifetime of five hundred years, a truly happy ending for the no-longer-hot facts of the world.

To save space, preserve items, or, most importantly, speed and ensure access to items, libraries may alternatively convert old materials to one of the new media, such as optical disks. The Library of Congress has in progress an optical disk pilot program, of which I will say no more here than that the system continues to look most promising. We believe this technology will enable research libraries like the Library of Congress to continue to fulfill their historic role as collectors and disseminators of recorded knowledge without succumbing to the economic pressures created by the need for ever-larger facilities.

In developing an optical disk program, however, we have had to confront problems other than technological ones. An example is the area of works "of a certain age." These works are old and perhaps mediocre enough to have slight commercial value, but recent enough to be under copyright protection. It is my hope to be able to negotiate from the creative community the authority for libraries to preserve such items without having to expend excessive effort at securing licenses to do so, let alone pay royalties. I hope to be able to establish that our hearts are pure, that our only wish is to preserve forever for scholarly use the less valuable titles that are still under copyright protection. Our success in coming to such understandings will determine whether or not significant quantities of the published literature and other arts of the twentieth century survive for use by researchers in the twenty-first.

Ice-cold facts are the least interesting of all. They are the low-use, low-interest items, generally in the public domain, awaiting some possible future scholarly interest. They fill the books that cover thousands of shelves in large research libraries. They are the precipitation statistics for Tasmania in 1927 and the railroad timetable for Needles, California, at the turn of the century. Slowly these books are being converted to a permanent archival form. This effort should and must continue, and we are in the happy position here of moving, generally, without copyright concerns. Our only constraints are money and technology. Given money, we can disk materials in image or digital form, microfilm them, or do whatever else might serve the world of scholarship best.

The Arts and Entertainment Business

Libraries are in the arts and entertainment business when they acquire the products of the human imagination, for example, novels, poetry, plays, or commercial motion pictures (nowadays usually on videotape). Here again, we have serious problems. Entertainment in this land of ours is a big business. Libraries have been able to acquire the latest Ngaio Marsh mystery or Louis L'Amour western and lend it to patrons without payment of royalty. This has been so despite the interest of publishers in selling the maximum number of copies or, more precisely, in maximizing profits. There are many reasons for this—historical, philosophical, political, and economic. The philosophical reason is based on the belief that libraries, like our schools, benefit the entire nation and therefore merit public support. Libraries help keep aflame the blaze of literacy, and librarians are zealous missionaries for the book.

Moreover, one consequence of this library activity may, in fact, be increased book sales overall. Many librarians also argue that there is another economic benefit to publishers from our strong free library tradition, which is that any money libraries may cause to be lost through lower sales of popular books is more than made good by their purchase of "serious" books that are not best-sellers.

But we may be sure that all such arguments will receive close scrutiny in the future. In areas of publishing where there is no firm tradition of free lending from libraries like the tradition that does exist for books, publishers will press for royalties. We see this happening now in the case of software. Some libraries now treat online fact services on this basis. Indeed, even where firm tradition exists, we see agitation for payment, as in efforts to establish a public lending right for books in the United States. This is just the beginning.

The American Library Association, in contrast, asserts that "the charging of fees and levies for information services, including those services utilizing the latest information technology, is discriminatory in publicly supported institutions providing library and information services."[3] This policy will not remain the consensus of our profession in 2006 unless we librarians remember our tradition *now* and exert every effort necessary to ensure that the future holds no contraction in essential library services for the American people. Publishers are right to protect their legitimate interests, and these are guaranteed well in the present copyright law. We all profit from a publishing industry that flourishes. A profitable publishing industry brings more incentive and opportunity to authors and a wider, deeper, and more various literature to readers. But we must be vigilant in ensuring that the riches that the copyright law fosters are shared by all, even the poorest, through nondiscriminatory public libraries.

The two great challenges of contemporary librarianship are, first, to preserve mankind's recorded patrimony and, second, to make it available to all. The second, making recorded culture available to all, is the more fundamental and the more urgent of these two imperatives—it is the reason for the first. Of what value is the preserved word if it is never read by those who most need it? We must join with our colleagues in publishing and the rest of the creative community to ensure that *everyone* benefits in the rich new world which technology is shaping: publishers, librarians, and readers of every sort.

Notes

1. Peter Brisco, Alice Bodtke-Roberts, Nancy Douglas, Michele Heinold, Nancy Koller, and Roberta Peirce, "Ashurbanipal's Enduring Archetype: Thoughts on the Library's Role in the Future," *College & Research Libraries* 47 (1986): 125.
2. Hugh F. Cline, "Appendix: The Library of Congress as a Depository for Basic Data of the Social Sciences," part of Appendix C, "Advisory Group Reports," in *The Library of Congress in Perspective: A Volume Based on the Reports of the 1976 Librarians's Task Force and Advisory Groups,* ed. John Y. Cole (New York: R. R. Bowker, 1978), 259.
3. American Library Association Policy Manual, sec. 50.4, "Free Access to Information," published in the annual *ALA Handbook of Organization* (Chicago: American Library Association).

VII.
Books Present
and Future

26. Freedom and Equality of Access to Information

Summary and Conclusions

Commission on Freedom and Equality of Access
to Information, American Library Association

This report to the American Library Association has
aroused great controversy in that organization.
Addressing the question of how Americans can really
be equal in a situation in which information, unequally
distributed, grows in importance, this commission
report supports, with careful qualifications, some
deregulation of the media, such as broadcast media and
telecommunications. The qualifications assert the need
to attend specially to the "information poor." Many
members of the American Library Association oppose
such deregulation.

This commission was chaired by Dan Lacy, author of
chapters 9 and 19 above.

Reprinted by permission of the American Library Association. "Summary and
Conclusions," from *Freedom and Equality of Access to Information: A Report to the
American Library Association,* by the Commission on Freedom and Equality of
Access to Information, Dan Lacy, Chair. Copyright © 1986 American Library
Association.

K nowledge is power. We have known that from the beginning. How freely and how equally citizens have access to knowledge determines how freely and how equally they can share in the governing of our society and in the work and rewards of our economy. Questions of access to knowledge, and to the information on which knowledge is based, have an especial importance today. Decade by decade and year by year the problems our government faces grow both more urgent and more complex, requiring more knowledge to comprehend and respond to them. And ever more sophisticated skills are needed to be able to participate effectively in the economy.

As our need for knowledge grows, our dependence on complex sets of institutions and mechanisms to supply it becomes greater. The printed page, the television screen, and the computer terminal all supply the information we once got by word of mouth or from personal experience. And all of these media of information are managed by large institutions and controlled by elaborate laws and regulations. Anyone who would understand how information reaches us must understand several industries, a number of complex technologies, and a network of uncoordinated and sometimes contradictory public policies.

This nation's basic policies and institutions for disseminating information were formed in the era of print dominance. Freedom of information was defined as freedom of the press. Print literacy was the key skill for acquiring information. Copyright was related to the making of printed copies. Information flowed through the physical distribution of books, pamphlets, newspapers, and magazines. Public access was offered through the sale of books, magazines, and other publications and the collection of printed works in libraries.

The coming of the audiovisual media—films, records, radio, and television—achieving their major impact in the 1920s and thereafter, radically altered the technological, institutional, and policy framework for the dissemination of information. And now we have yet another powerful force—the computer, along with advanced telecommunications—offering enormous new opportunities, altering institutional frameworks, and demanding new policies. These latest technologies do not only provide new and very powerful

341

media for communicating information. They also affect, in important ways, our access to older media. The technology of print has been changed in ways that permit small editions and even publishing on demand; new possibilities for the extremely compact storage of printed texts in reproducible form are provided; and far more powerful bibliographical tools provide a new level of access to print. Similarly, the new technology multiplies the ways in which audiovisual materials can reach us and creates new opportunities for access to them.

In many ways we operate in a new world of information and communication. We need to look again at the institutions and policies created in the past in our attempt to make print-borne information available widely and to all. We need to reexamine the policies developed to deal with films and radio and television when those media were created. How well do they fit the era of the computer, the satellite, and the laser disk? Do we need to change old institutions and policies? Do we need to create new ones?

In our special concern for the consequences of the new information and communications technology, we need to remember that print still bears a major, and in many ways the most important, burden of communication. We need to assure that it remains accessible to all and that the institutions and policies that guarantee freedom and equality of access are sustained. Old questions need to be asked again. What are the threats of censorship today? Does the postal system encourage the distribution of publications? In a time of multimillion-dollar suits has the libel law become not only a protection of individuals but a chilling threat to robust debate? Does copyright stimulate or restrict the flow of information? Does the government, as the greatest repository and source of information, seek to enlarge or restrict its dissemination? Is the guiding thrust of public policy toward the widest accessibility of information or toward limitations and constraints?

The goal of freedom in information and communication is a double one, with its two aspects inseparably complementary: for all who wish to speak or write to be free to do so, and for all who wish to hear or read them to have that opportunity. It is in terms of their relation to that dual goal that we have tried to view technological, legal, and policy developments.

At the founding of the republic, when communication was oral or through scattered, small, independent presses, only the government had the power to suppress speech or printing. The constitutions of most of the new states forbade their legislatures to deny freedom of speech or of the press, and the First Amendment of the federal Constitution similarly enjoined the Congress.

But with the coming of highly organized publishing industries in the latter part of the nineteenth century, freedom became more complex. Freedom to express one's views effectively required not only freedom from government suppression, but also opportunity of access to the media that had become the gateways to reach the people. This dependence on freedom of access to the media became far more important with the coming of films and broadcasting. And questions of access are now being redefined by the still newer media of the computer, the videocassette and videodisk, and new means of telecommunications.

In considering freedom of access to the newer media that have come to dominate communications in our time, we have to view at least five aspects:

1. Have *public authorities*—federal, state, and local—themselves attempted to deny or limit access?
2. Does the *technology* of the newer media tend to broaden or to narrow access?
3. Does the *economic organization* of the newer media give private owners, as gatekeepers, a power to deny or limit access?
4. Are there *significant barriers that limit the access of individuals* to the information they need, even though it is available through the media?
5. Who should pay the *costs* of communication, and how does that affect access?

Government Censorship

Although the mere presence in the Constitution of the First Amendment had no doubt inhibited public authorities from most censorship of print, until the 1950s it was rarely called upon in court to invalidate restrictive laws and police actions. Up to that time federal, state, and local authorities felt free to deny the right to publish or disseminate books and magazines, and especially films, on grounds that they were obscene. Even overt political censorship was by no means unknown, especially in customs offices. In a series of landmark decisions in the 1950s, the Supreme Court narrowed to a very thin edge indeed the permissible grounds for prosecuting the publisher of a printed work or the producer of a film on grounds of obscenity and denied any right of prior restraint. In consequence, printed works and films as exhibited in theaters are now almost entirely free of restraint. Remaining censorship activity is aimed rather at the purchase of such materials by libraries or their use as textbooks. Though there is constant pressure on both these fronts, in our judgment it does little or nothing to limit realistic access to titles which, though perhaps barred from an occasional school library, are likely to be made the more available on the newsstand. Textbook pressures from both right and left and from religious, ethnic, and other specially concerned groups are a greater problem, requiring continuing vigilance, but one on the whole successfully confronted.

Such an application of the First Amendment to the newer media is far less clear. The Supreme Court has held in the *Pacifica* case that broadcasts reach so easily to children and others in the home that the Federal Communications Commission (FCC) may forbid the use of "indecent" words even though they are by no means "obscene" by the standards set down for print and films. As a result of this legal position and even more as a result of the sensitivity of advertising-supported broadcasts, many films shown freely in theaters can be televised only in bowdlerized form if at all. Cable, certainly for the premium pay channels, has been equated with theatrical rather than broadcast standards. Hence a film viewable only in expurgated form, if at all, on a broadcast channel may be seen in its original uncensored candor on the adjacent HBO channel.

As broadcast channels, through teletext and other means, are increasingly used to distribute text as well as images, a crucial question will be whether the textual messages will be controlled by the FCC under broadcast standards or will have the freedom of print. So far the trend has fortunately been the latter.

Except for the federal government's efforts to control the dissemination of information it itself generates or collects—a serious problem indeed, dealt with below—governmental censorship, we believe, is now a much less serious limitation on freedom of access than factors arising from the technology and organization of the newer media and the ability of the public to use them.

Technology and Access

Some technologies of communication tend to make the flow of information available to very wide audiences, usually at the price of narrowing the opportunities for the input of information in the media and hence narrowing the choices available to audiences. Other technologies make input easy from a wide variety of sources, but usually at cost of limiting audiences. Some technologies must flow through limited channels that make practicable public or private censorship or control. Others utilize so wide a variety of channels that control is almost impossible. Some require of the user little cost and no special skills; others may be expensive or difficult to use.

The technologies that have come, one after another, to change the flow of information in this century have had widely varied characteristics. The audiovisual media—films, radio, and television—enormously broadened access and made it cheaper and less demanding of skills, but forced it through controllable channels (theaters, broadcasting stations, and networks) and narrowed the opportunities for input. The technology of broadcasting in particular, and of television even more than radio, required the granting of monopolies over the control of designated sectors of the electromagnetic spectrum. Until recent years, printing technologies required high investment in plant and hence presented a barrier to entry into newspaper publishing. At the same time technology made books, magazines, and newspapers much cheaper and hence available to much larger audiences. But some of the changes, like those that made possible mass market paperbacks, tended toward greatly increasing the number of copies per title, but for a very limited number of titles.

The newest technologies, with which we are specially concerned, have had a number of effects. When computers were first introduced, their cost made them available only to government agencies and very large corporations, who gained a power over information not enjoyed by others. The development of the technology of personal computers has greatly widened access to information, but still at a cost in terms of money and specialized skills much higher than is required for access to the traditional media.

These new technologies have also, through cable television, videocassettes and videodisks, and the promise of direct satellite-to-home broadcasting, multiplied the opportunities to enter the audiovisual media.

In general, the most recent developments in the technology of communication have all moved toward freedom and diversity of input, whether in printed, audiovisual, or digital form, but in some instances have made access by users more expensive or difficult.

Organization of the Communications Industries and Access

An area of special concern must be the degree to which the organization of the newer media gives a "gatekeeper" power to deny or limit access by speakers or writers. Throughout the century there has been an overall tendency toward more powerful gatekeepers due to the technological or competitive advantage of large communications firms. Local, and until recently long distance, telephone service was set up as a franchised monopoly because the technology was believed to make such an arrangement natural, even inevitable. Radio and television stations were necessarily given a monopoly over the use of particular sectors of the electromagnetic spectrum in a particular geographic area. Economies of scale and FCC allocations decisions concentrated national programming into three networks. Pressures of competition and similar economies of scale dramatically reduced the number of newspapers in almost every city. For a large part of the history of the film industry, the control by large film producers of theater chains and distribution networks severely limited the number and increased the power of movie "gatekeepers."

To the degree that the technology and economic organization of any medium give a few persons or companies the power to control or deny access to the most effective ways to reach an intended audience, private agencies have a power denied to the government by the First Amendment. Public concern has responded to this unacceptable situation in various ways. When monopoly seems inescapable or technologically desirable, as in the case of the telephone services, the response has been to make the medium a franchised common carrier, required to make its facilities available to all who wish to communicate and to do so without discrimination, usually at rates fixed by a regulatory body. The opposite approach is to use the antitrust laws and regulatory authority to break up monopolistic and oligopolistic controls. This was done, for example, in forcing film producers to divest theater chains and to abandon the use of practices like "block booking." Similarly FCC regulations limit the number of broadcasting stations under a single ownership. The FCC has also limited "cross ownership" of broadcasting stations by a newspaper or cable system in the same community.

Where completely free and vigorous competition cannot be realized and common-carrier arrangements are impractical, there have been both public and private responses. The private response has been in the growing power and pervasiveness of professional journalistic ethics enjoining fairness and objectivity in reporting the news and the granting of opportunity for opposing views to be expressed, as by columnists or letters to the editor. The public response has been a variety of regulations, most notably the equal-time and fairness doctrine applicable to broadcasts and the public access and leased-channel provisions affecting cable TV.

During the last few years there has been a strong movement away from the common-carrier and the regulatory concepts toward a reliance on competition and professionalism to assure an adequate breadth of access to the media. Intercity telephone traffic has been opened to almost completely free competition save for transitional restraints on AT&T. Broadcast companies, with support from many civil libertarians and from journalists in other media, have been pressing for the end of fairness doctrine and equal-time requirements. Cable systems have been relieved of must-carry requirements and seek relief from other regulatory provisions like mandatory access.

This movement has aroused deep concerns. Many fear that doing away with the fairness and equal-time provisions of broadcast regulations would permit the foreclosure of minority views from the air and that elimination of must-carry and public access and leased-channel requirements would have the same effect for cable. Indeed they believe that more stringent requirements for public service broadcasting should be placed on stations as public trustees of extremely valuable rights to the exclusive use of designated channels. Companies providing information through electronic channels have feared that the growing trend to deregulate telephone companies and the failure to impose common-carrier obligations on cable companies may open the possibility of all these companies becoming information providers themselves and giving their own undertakings preferential status for the use of their networks.

Limitations on Access by Users

The limits on access by users of information, as distinguished from access by providers of information, arise from problems of physical access, from cost, and, perhaps most of all, from lack of ability to make use of opportunities.

To have adequate physical access to printed materials means not only to be able to get currently issued books, magazines, and newspapers but also the opportunity to use accumulated stores of publications. A unique value of print is that it lends itself to collection of materials from present and past, on all subjects, from this and other countries, putting the user in command of the accumulated knowledge and creativity of the entire race, as can no other medium. But this opportunity depends on a strong system of libraries interlinked to complement each others' strengths, on a powerful bibliographical apparatus that makes it possible to locate individual items within the total mass of resources, and on physical availability of those libraries to all sectors of the population.

Physical access to the newer media requires access to the appropriate instruments and network connections. Radio and television receivers are now nearly universal; telephone instruments have been so, but their universality may be threatened by potentially sharp increases in costs. Access to cable systems, however, though it will be increasingly important, is still foreclosed to a substantial percentage of the population. In many areas, even in some large cities, no cable system is available; and the expense of cable, especially of premium service, makes it beyond the reach of much of the population. The situation is even more difficult with respect to access through computers or computer terminals to electronic databases. Personal computers have become far cheaper and far more common, but they are still beyond the reach of most Americans and, at present at least, probably beyond their everyday need. Adequate access to the resources they can provide will require institutional arrangements to give the public access to terminals.

Having the means to buy books and theater tickets, to subscribe to magazines and newspapers, to own radios and television sets, and to pay tuition to schools and colleges has, of course, been a key determinant of access to information. A commitment to equality of access to needed information has attempted to diminish the discriminatory impact of such costs through the free public library, free or inexpensive government publications, free public schools, and low-cost public colleges and universities. One of the most urgent public policy problems is to encourage an equity of access to information, regardless of the user's means, in the face of sharp budget pressures and new and expensive technologies. This will be dealt with further below in a more general discussion of the allocation of costs of communication.

But the principal barrier to access is, as it has always been, lack of skill in using the media. It has been estimated that more than 25 million adult Americans do not read well enough to meet the demands of everyday life. The use of newspapers, magazines, books, and government pamphlets is foreclosed to them as a means of gaining information they need. This problem is now compounded by the need for skills in using computers. Many fear the already painful gap between "information haves" and "information have-nots" will be gravely widened by the lack of computer skills among the already less-privileged.

The lack of skill is not only in reading itself, or in using a computer terminal. A more common lack is the unawareness of information resources, and lack of familiarity with how to use or gain access to them. Probably a majority of Americans never use a public library or enter a bookstore. And unfortunately this is most true among those groups in society that most need information to deal with their problems: the poor, the ill-educated, the elderly, the unemployed.

Who Should Pay the Cost of Information?

A question that runs through all of the issues we have listed is who will pay for information and cultural experience. It may be the user, like the buyer of books and the audience at plays and cinema theaters. It may be the one providing the information, as in free government publications or material issued by churches, businesses, labor unions, and political parties to persuade readers to their views and, most important of all, as in free public schools with free textbooks.

But in fact the cost of most information flow is shared. Advertisers pay all the cost of disseminating their own messages in newspapers, magazines, and broadcasts; and in order to draw readers or viewers to the media in which their messages are included, they also pay all the costs of the program content in broadcasts and a major part of the cost of the editorial content of magazines and newspapers. In this way, such publications are available to their subscribers at much less than their actual cost.

Governments—federal, state, and local—intervene in many ways to lower the cost of information to their recipients. Free elementary and high schools are provided, usually with free textbooks, and a major share of the cost of higher education is publicly provided. Free public libraries provide access to publications without cost. Government publications are sold at prices reflecting only the cost of overrun printing and distribution, with the cost of authorship, editing, typesetting, and platemaking and an initial press run borne by the taxpayer. Some electronic information services, like those of the Department of Agriculture and the National Library of Medicine, are offered directly by the government, without charge to most users. The cost to users of other machine-readable databases is reduced by offering tapes of the data to competing vendors at reproduction cost. Public appropriations meet much of the cost of public radio and television and subsidize much of the production of performing arts and of scholarly publication, as well as of the research on which much information depends. Indeed, most serious information flow—as distinguished from entertainment—takes place only with governmental or advertiser support. Users are able and willing to bear only a small part of the cost of the flow of information on which our society and economy depends. This is as true of highly educated professionals as of the poor and marginally literate.

To have the government or those interested in providing information bear all or most of the cost so that it is free or inexpensive to the user obviously enlarges the flow of information. And it is especially important in providing that equality in access to information essential to equality of economic and political opportunity. In many areas public support of information dissemination should be greatly increased.

But this is not the whole answer. It should be remembered that he who pays the piper calls the tune. This is clearly the case in advertiser-financed communication. The day is no doubt past when a large advertiser could command favorable editorial treatment of his own firm or product in a reputable newspaper or magazine. But advertisers will support only those editorial services that will appeal to customers of their products and in general provide an appropriate context for their ads. They are not likely, for example, to support the publication of material to meet the needs of the poor and marginally literate. Even the affluent are likely to be well-served by advertising-supported publications only when their interests draw them together as a coherent market. Advertisers will readily support magazines for antique collectors, tennis players, or yachtsmen, who form coherent markets for groups of expensive products, but not for poetry or short-story lovers, who do not. Nor are advertisers likely to sponsor controversial programs for fear the animosity generated in viewers or readers may be deflected to their products.

When government pays the cost it, too, will tend to call the tune. Every federal department has a public information staff and budget. They perform an essential service in making information available; but it is regularly presented in the light most favorable to the department, and much of the effort of those staffs is in fact devoted to preventing the release of information. Only the existence of a vigorous and inquisitive press representing the public's interest in fuller disclosure prevents government domination of the news of government activity.

In general, the federal government has shown a greater concern for the provision of information to powerful and affluent sectors of the economy than to those made powerless by their lack of information. Through the activities of such agencies as the Departments of Agriculture and Commerce, for example, and such bibliographic services as the National Technical Information Service the government has gone to commendable lengths to provide information to American industry and agribusiness. But the *Miranda* decision of the Supreme Court, requiring police to give those arrested information as to their legal rights, has been roundly criticized by some conservative political leaders, and the Reagan administration has made vigorous efforts to eliminate or reduce programs of the Legal Services Corporation intended to inform those who cannot afford private counsel of their legal rights.

Even public support of broadcasting is not without similar problems. Public broadcasting's programming is heavily oriented toward those already well provided with informational and cultural resources, not toward the needs of the poor, the elderly, or the marginally literate, who suffer most from lack of information that would help them improve their situation. For it is the culturally affluent who are most able to influence public appropriations, most likely to contribute financially to the support of public broadcasting, and most attractive as an audience to the corporations that sponsor much public broadcast programming.

There can be no doubt that when users pay for information themselves they are better served. They get what *they* want and need. And they get it much more efficiently when it is provided by market-driven private suppliers highly motivated to ascertain customers' needs and devise products carefully designed to meet them. Particularly is this true of the new information technology, where much of the accessibility and usefulness of information depends on the user-oriented software through which it is made available.

The problem is that the needs of much of the population cannot be expressed as a demand in the marketplace that will evoke the information services needed. They cannot be so expressed because millions of those made relatively powerless in our society by the lack of education, of knowledge and skills—those most in need of information—have neither the sophistication to seek it out nor the means to pay for it. Schools and libraries should have resources to act as their surrogates, expressing their needs as marketplace demands.

Recent Policy

We are given deep concern by recent thrusts of public policy in relation to the situation described in this report:

1. In telecommunications and broadcasting there is a strong movement to substitute competition for regulation as a means of assuring fair access to the media. Intercity telephone service has been opened to competition, and AT&T has been almost entirely freed from the limitations formerly imposed on its entering unregulated businesses. Strong sentiment has been expressed for substantial deregulation of both radio and television, strengthening the presumption that licenses will be renewed, eliminating competing applications at renewal, and removing fairness and equal-time requirements. There has also been an effort, partially realized, to remove cable systems from control by local franchising authorities.

2. There is, however, little effort to invigorate the competition on which reliance is placed. Limitations on the multiple ownership of broadcasting stations have been substantially relaxed, and there is little disposition to promote effectively public or leased-access requirements for cable. Further, in a competitive environment, subsidies supporting universal telephone service at reasonable rates are being phased out, and substitute policies assuring lifeline services, particularly for the elderly and poor, are not fully in place.

3. There has been a determined effort to limit and control the flow of information from the federal government. This has included reductions in the support of federal statistical and information-gathering programs, decreases in government publications, stricter and broader programs for classification of government documents, requirements that government employees sign contracts allowing the government to censor whatever they may write for publication for the rest of their lives, limitations on contacts with the press, and narrowing of the Freedom of Information Act.

4. There has been pressure for a curtailment or withdrawal of federal support for programs and institutions to increase access to information. This has included removal from the budgets submitted to Congress of all provision for the support of libraries other than those of the government itself and for the support of the National Commission on Libraries and Information Science; reduction in support for public broadcasting; reduction in postal subsidies for the distribution of books, magazines, newspapers, and library materials; and reduction—in constant dollars—of federal funds for education. Notable is a specific attack on funds for legal aid to inform and assist the poor as to their legal rights.

5. Perhaps even more significant than the efforts to curtail existing programs has been the inaction in response to emerging publicized recognition of the serious literacy problem, in terms of both better teaching of basic skills in the schools and instruction for the twenty-five million or more functionally illiterate adults, but this recognition has been accompanied by no concrete action to deal with the problem at either level. There has been active recog-

nition of the problems presented by the massive increase in the number of immigrants, legal and illegal, who are illiterate in English, but again almost no measures to deal with them; indeed support of bilingual education programs has been decreased. There has not even been recognition of the important problems and enormous opportunities to broaden the flow of information to everyone through the new technology, and of course no comprehensive program to address those problems and opportunities.

It should be emphasized that these policies that give us concern are by no means peculiar to the Reagan administration. There is always tension between the press and the administration in power as to the release of government information. Every recent administration has sought to reduce federal library support; none has moved imaginatively to use the newer media for public enlightenment. But proposals to lessen support for the dissemination of information and to impose a variety of restraints have been far more intensively pursued in the Reagan administration, reversing many earlier policies.

What Should Be Public Information Policy?

What do we believe should be the principal thrusts of public policy with respect to information? These have been stated in some detail in the full report of this commission, but in broad summary our views are:

1. On balance we believe the deregulation of broadcasting and telecommunications is generally desirable. As we let in more and more competitive channels and media, we should correspondingly let *go*, especially with regard to content regulation. Existing regulations, like the equal-time and fairness provisions as now implemented, may in fact have been counterproductive in obtaining the goal of robust wide-open debate.

2. However, as regulations governing how broadcasting licenses are to discharge their public trustee responsibility are relaxed or removed, we believe that there should be recognition of the inadequacies of the existing system. The failure of both commercial and public broadcasting to serve the needs of the elderly, the poor, and the marginally literate and of commercial broadcasting to serve children—all groups which broadcasting is specially fitted to serve—is a major failure in our society. That failure must be remedied. Accordingly, we believe that there should be a larger support of public television, but that increased support should be made on condition of a larger service to those sectors of society now ill-served by print and by both commercial and public television, including the elderly, the poor, those not adequately literate in English, and children.

3. We believe also that deregulation should be accompanied by measures to assure the continuation of universal telephone service at reasonable cost set forth as an objective of the Federal Communications Act and to assure equitable and nondiscriminatory access to deregulated telephone service and to cable.

4. The federal government should recognize more clearly the dependence of the economy and society as a whole on the statistical and other information it collects and should maintain the adequacy and professional integrity of those services.

5. It is especially important that the consistent and disturbing pressure toward restricting the availability to the public of government information be checked and reversed. The Freedom of Information Act should be preserved and strengthened, not diminished. Control of scientific and technical information should be very narrowly limited to confidential or secret information of specific military value. Security classification should be limited to significant areas of national security. The obnoxious requirement of contracts requiring federal employees to submit any writings to official censorship before publication, even after leaving federal employment, should be done away with, and present contracts voided. Criminal penalties for the revelation of information that is actually secret and significant to the national security is a sufficient sanction.

6. A variety of channels should be kept open and encouraged to maximize the availability and utility of government information to the public. Private writers, reporters, publishers, broadcasters, and electronic data disseminators should be encouraged to acquire, add value to, and distribute information derived from the government. The government should not use tax-subsidized services to compete directly with private-sector publishers and information companies that are effectively meeting public needs so long as this does not result in reduced citizen access. Nor should the Government Printing Office so centralize the publishing of government materials as to restrict executive agencies in using the most efficient means of reaching those needing their materials. But it is even more important that there be effective government publishing programs, including appropriate electronic programs, when they are necessary to bring information from government services to those who need it.

7. The increasing use of libel actions by public officials, often seeking extremely large punitive damages, threatens to become a dangerous limitation on robust political debate and aggressive investigative reporting. While continuing to allow officeholders and other public figures to protect themselves against intentional or reckless falsehood through the right of demanding retraction or actual damages, the libel law should not be allowed to serve as an instrument of intimidation of critics of public officials or figures.

8. One of our principal recommendations is a general one relat-

ing to the whole area of electronic information dissemination using the newer computer and telecommunications technology. We are impressed with the fact that the availability of printed materials to the American public does not depend on the technology of print alone. It requires an enormous, complex, and interrelated institutional structure, including authors, publishers, magazine and newspaper distributors, book wholesalers and booksellers, book clubs, mail order services, and libraries. These are linked by impressive cataloging and bibliographical services and interlibrary loan and cooperative practices that have been built up over decades. They permit an inquirer—at least the skilled and persistent inquirer—to identify, locate, and usually gain access to any text desired from among the tens of millions that exist. If we are to be able to take similar advantage of the powerful new technologies becoming available to us, we will need to create a comparable institutional structure, linked by comparable bibliographical standards and comparable cooperative practices. This is an enormous task, and will require imaginative leadership, wide cooperation, including international cooperation, and public support. It is an endeavor, stretching over years, that should be a major objective of the American Library Association and the National Commission on Libraries and Information Science, with enlarged public funding for NCLIS.

9. Another principal recommendation relates to the role of institutions that can serve in an intermediary capacity in bringing information to those who need it. Libraries are the key institutions performing this function, but there are many others that have specific roles, such as social service agencies, health centers, legal aid offices, agricultural extension agencies, and community centers. It seems clear to us that by far the greatest impediments in the way of individuals gaining access to information that would broaden their lives and help them meet their personal and social needs lie within individuals themselves: lack of awareness of what information exists and how it could help them, lack of needed skills including an adequate level of literacy, lack of motivation. This impediment is compounded by the new technology—adding to the skills needed, bringing more unfamiliarity and even mystery. This condition goes to the very heart of the problem of equality of access to information. For those most in need of information are likely to be those most lacking in the skills to seek and use it. But all of these improvements in training will not remove the need for institutions that can assist the information seeker in gaining access to the sources of information he or she needs. Though this need may be greater in the case of those with limited education or economic needs, it is one we all experience at one level or another.

Libraries now serve reasonably well the needs of that minority of the population habituated to their use, and with notable exceptions they tend to be at least minimally supported in that function by state and local governments. But libraries are far from having the resources or capacity to serve as well as they would like the needs of those who have remained outside the library circle. This includes many of limited education and means and perhaps of limited literacy in English, precisely those whose need for information may be the greatest and most urgent. There is a basic need for large federal support to enable libraries to serve as information intermediaries to those deprived sectors of the population.

This need is becoming greater with the new technology. Libraries will be indispensable intermediaries to make information from electronic databases generally available, not merely to deprived groups but to society generally. To perform this function they need equipment and training. And the profession will need to establish the networks, bibliographic standards, and cooperative arrangements referred to earlier. This too will take large and continuing public support. And it will need to be at the national level, for the indispensable infrastructure of networks, standards, and bibliographic controls is necessarily national.

We recognize fully that in a time of budgetary stringency like the present, it is unrealistic to expect large new funding, especially for objectives only generally defined. The immediate need is for the library profession in conjunction with other concerned groups to develop concrete and realistic programs to meet the most acute needs and to lay a careful basis for a successful request for appropriations. We have proposed several priority agenda items for libraries in the full report.

We realize that all of these broad proposals and that the more specific recommendations in the main body of the report are difficult to achieve and will require a multitude of individual concrete actions over a long period. What is perhaps more important than any specific recommendation is to have always before us guiding aims of public policy that can be the basis of individual policy decisions. Those aims, we believe, should include

1. maintaining a free communications system that does not restrict or bias communication to conform to the prescription of public authorities or, overall, of the authority of private owners of media facilities;
2. encouraging and supporting a structure of the media that makes them sensitively responsive to demands for information of the enormous variety of people and institutions that make up our society, including dissident and minority groups and views; and
3. supplying the resources that will enable major social needs for information to be expressed as effective demands in the mar-

ketplace, so that the communications system will be able to respond to the needs of the powerless and information-poor as well as to those of the powerful and sophisticated.

It is impossible to separate the communications system of a society from its general goals. Any society will adopt means that fit its ends. If the goals of a society envision structured and repressive authority, with power restricted to an elite, it will see that the distribution of information is controlled to serve those ends.

And if the goals we envision are ones of freedom and equality, in which all share the benefits of a culturally rich, productive society, the communications system we create will be dedicated to freedom and equality. The choice is ours.

Finally, we believe that the National Commission on Libraries and Information Science and the American Library Association and its allies should set up a means to give steady and continuing attention to the development and achievement of public policies in light of the goals we have tried to state.

Strike down the bony hands of our high priests of pseudo-security who would save the book by placing it within impregnable vaults. Let us take our stand with John Milton on the side of free ideas, a free intellect, and the faith in the truth to conquer any false doctrine.

HARRISON E. SALISBURY
Journalist

27. Books in Our Future

Librarian of Congress Daniel J. Boorstin

Books in Our Future strongly asserts that the book is not obsolescent and suggests measures that will ensure the access to books that citizens of a democratic culture require. *Books in Our Future* is a report to Congress, made in 1984, on the state of the culture of the book in the United States. It treats the concerns that have been raised over literacy, actual reading, education, the media, and various features of computerization from the perspective of the Librarian of Congress.

Reprinted here is Boorstin's analysis of the future of the book. The full publication also includes information on particular programs, some already under way, others required in the future, along with information on the Book in the Future project.

Books in Our Lives

We Americans have a habit of writing premature obituaries. Our love of novelty and our speedy pace of change tempt us to imagine that the new technology buries the old. A century ago some predicted that the telegraph and the telephone would spell the end of the postal system. Television of course brought prophecies of the demise of radio. In this century more than once we have heard enthusiasts for a new technology predict the demise of the book. When the automobile first became popular some actually said that few Americans would stay home reading when they could be riding the countryside in their flivvers. The rise of photography, phonography, and the movies led others to foresee the disappearance of the book from the classroom. It would be displaced, they said, by the latest "audiovisual aids." But today textbooks still dominate the classroom.

The Culture of the Book

Meanwhile, books in their traditional form encompass us in a thousand ways. Each of our major religions is a religion of the book, with sacred texts that are the source and the vehicle of theology, morality, and hopes for the future. Our education has been built around books. The structure of our political life rests on our books of law, history, geography, and biography. Books are the main source of our knowledge, our reservoir of faith, memory, wisdom, morality, poetry, philosophy, history, and science.

The book-stored wisdom of the Bible, Locke, Burke, Blackstone, and the great authors of the European liberal tradition was the foundation for the grand experiment of our Founding Fathers. They put the free access to printed matter, along with freedom of religion, among the first items of the first article in the Bill of Rights of our Constitution. "I cannot live without books," declared Thomas Jefferson after his books were shipped from Monticello to become the foundation of the renewed Library of Congress in 1815. And at once he began building a new personal library. Without books we might be tempted to believe that our civilization was born yesterday—or when the latest newsmagazine went to press. The very omnipresence of books leads us to underestimate their power and influence. One measure of their meaning to mankind is the

359

desperate hunger of people in unfree societies to read everything that is not government-authorized pap.

It is no accident that people everywhere have considered books sacred and have made them the source and the vehicle of their religious faith. For the power of the book has been uncanny, mysterious, inestimable, overpowering, and infinite—just as the activity of reading has a unique individuality, intimacy, and privacy.

Our civilization is a product of the "culture of the book." Of course, the book itself—the printed, bound volume—is a triumph of technology. But when we speculate on the future of the traditional book we are not thinking about a single product of technology. Never since the discovery of fire and the invention of the wheel has any other innovation had so pervasive and so enduring an influence on ways of thinking, feeling, worshiping, teaching, governing, and discovering. The revolution since Gutenberg is without precedent. Its consequences are yet to be seen in much of the world. This effect, in Thomas Carlyle's familiar words, was "disbanding hired armies, and cashiering most kings and senates, and creating a whole new democratic world."

We all have an enormous vested interest in the book. The Library of Congress possesses some 20 million volumes, accumulated over two centuries at a cost of hundreds of millions of dollars. In the United States today there are more than 100,000 libraries—federal, state, and city, public, special, school, and institutional—which house at least a billion volumes, constantly increasing. The Library of Congress alone receives 1,000 new volumes from all over the world every day.

We see books everywhere, of every conceivable variety, in homes and schools, in offices and workshops. Not only Bibles, prayer books, dictionaries, encyclopedias, and textbooks, but also novels, books of mystery, romance, travel, nature, and adventure, and children's books, along with how-to-do-it books on sewing, car repair, home maintenance, computers, gardening, athletics, and health, not to mention telephone books, mail-order catalogs, and company directories. Books are everyday fixtures of our lives, guides and measures of our civilization. To try to extract the book from our lives would be fatal, but luckily this is impossible.

Our long investment in books is only one reason to expect the book to remain a fertile resource in the America of the next decades. The proverbial convenience, accessibility, and individuality of the book are unrivaled now or by any new technology in sight. The book is independent of outside power sources, and offers unique opportunities for freedom of choice. "One reads at one's own speed," Vincent Canby reminds us, "in short snatches on the subway or in long, voluptuous withdrawals from the world. One proceeds through a big, complex novel, say *War and Peace* or *Crime and Punishment,* like an exceptionally well-heeled tourist in a foreign landscape, going slowly or fast depending on the roads, on one's own mood, and on the attractions along the way. If one loses something, one can always go back to pick it up." For all these reasons, books are messengers of freedom. They can be hidden under a mattress or smuggled into slave nations.

We Americans have never been inclined to underestimate new technologies, nor have we held on sentimentally to the ways of our grandparents. Our faith in obsolescence comes from the amazingly speedy changes in our ways of life. Naturally, then, we enjoy science-fiction fantasies of a world of microchips, where our library-store of books has become obsolete and our personal book-shelves unnecessary. For we eagerly discard the old if there seems a newer, more interesting—even if more complicated—way of doing the same task. Rube Goldberg gave us an eloquent slogan for our national way of life: "Do It the Hard Way!"

A Nation of Readers?

Before we try to assess the effect of new technology on the book in the future, we must ask some elementary questions. Today, what is the state of book publishing, bookselling, and libraries? How many Americans are reading books? Who are they? Is their number increasing or decreasing?

The very qualities that are the unique delight and glory of the book—privacy, intimacy, individuality, variety, and endless inter-stitial opportunities for use and enjoyment—make a nation's read-ing difficult to put in statistics. And when people are asked they seldom underestimate their reading.

Book Publishing and Bookselling
Still, there are copious facts about the publishing and sale of books. As this report goes to press, statistics from *Book Industry Trends 1984,* the *Bowker Annual of Library and Book Trade Information,* and *Publishers Weekly* indicate that the book publishing industry is healthy.

Domestic expenditures on books, which showed an average annual increase of 10.3 percent in dollars from 1979 to 1983, are projected by industry statisticians to show an average annual increase of 13 percent in dollars from 1983 to 1988. Sales for the industry rose from $3,177,200,000 in 1972 to $8,821,700,000 in 1983. The number of U.S. book titles published has been increasing moderately in most years for the last decade—from 38,053 in 1972 to 53,380 in 1983. Fiction as well as nonfiction titles (biography, history, political science, sociology, economics, and science and technology) have increased.

The amount of money spent for buying books is increasing, and this trend is expected to continue. U.S. expenditures on books rose by 47.8 percent, from $7,304,500,000 in 1979 to $10,798,300,000 in 1983. The number of bookstores has increased significantly, from

11,786 in 1973 to 19,580 in 1984. At the same time that outlets for books have been increasing in number, they have been becoming more conspicuous and more accessible.

Books have become visible in drugstores, supermarkets, and airports. Discount book chains find locations in shopping malls and at traffic centers downtown. These outlets have further democratized book buying—reaching not only the traditional "book lover" but also the broad base of non-book-oriented shoppers. Critics have suggested that these large new market opportunities have persuaded some publishers to limit their lists to titles that they can expect to be featured by the chains, leaving some new, radically innovative authors and narrow-interest books unpublished. But these discount chains have attracted new book-buyers and encouraged more imaginative, more energetic, and more competitive marketing of books.

According to the Bureau of the Census, the number of book publishers in the United States has increased from 1,250 in 1972 to 2,128 in 1982. "Niche" publishing and marketing has created new, narrow channels for the sale of books. Some publishers and booksellers with the help of the computer have begun targeting a small list of titles to specialized audiences. The capacity of the computer to analyze the proliferating mailing lists—from credit card and catalog purchases, club and association memberships, and subscription lists of special interest magazines—has helped focus the making and selling of books in a way that reduces waste and maximizes profits. Now a publisher can produce books on World War II airplanes or mushroom raising or steam railroads with a newly reliable estimate of potential customers. With specialized book publishing have come specialized bookstores focusing on a single audience—for regional books, hobbies, mysteries, science fiction, health, or the environment.

The general bookstore with a large stock of older as well as current books has become harder to find. Some of us miss the informed friendly advice and personal service of a well-read bookseller. And we miss the delights of browsing in the miscellaneous stock of a secondhand bookstore. These have tended to become "antiquarian" bookstores, putting out-of-print books beyond the pocketbook of the casual reader.

The Active Reader

Questions about book *reading,* as distinct from book *selling* and book *buying,* are, of course, more difficult to answer. For "reading" a book can mean many different things—from browsing to careful note-taking. How many Americans, beyond the reach of the "required reading" of the schoolroom, are reading books? How many books are they reading? What is the effect on book reading of the competition of new leisure activities and new technologies?

Recent studies by the industry and sociologists give us some helpful clues. The first national survey of reading habits by the Book Industry Study Group (BISG) was released at the Library of Congress in 1978. Based on 1,450 in-depth interviews of a representative sample of the population by Yankelovich, Skelly and White, the study provided some data on the personality profile of the American book reader. The results of a second BISG survey, made in 1983, confirmed the findings of the first.[1] According to the two surveys, about one-half of the American public can be called book readers, that is, they have read one or more books in the last six months.

Popular stereotypes of readers, it seems, are misleading us. The 1978 BISG survey suggests that the "bookworm," the nearsighted recluse who seeks asylum from the world, is a figment of our imagination. He is not typical of our heaviest readers today. Active people are book readers, and book readers are generally active people. The heaviest readers of books, the study showed, take part in their church, their political party, sports, and community affairs. The study found that retired people, who are also less active in other ways, read less than other people, and not necessarily because of physical problems. Americans over the age of sixty-five read much less than younger Americans. The 1983 BISG survey confirmed these findings and added more evidence that we must think of book reading not as a passive condition but as an engaging *activity*.

The spread of television, with its new forms of passivity, brings a new, and even more urgent significance to reading. Our dictionaries define activity as "energetic action; liveliness, alertness"— certainly desirable in citizens of a free republic. The more constructively active people are, the more likely they are to be readers of books. Readers of books are likely to be alert citizens. When we help people improve their reading skills, and motivate them to read books, we are not merely opening their avenues to culture and enlarging the audience for literature. We are giving them a technique that will enrich the community.

Elastic Time
Another hasty assumption is that time given to new forms of leisure activity is necessarily subtracted from that given to older forms. In 1976, sociologist Theodore Caplow and his colleagues returned to "Middletown" (Muncie, Indiana), the scene of the 1929 and 1937 landmark studies of American daily life by Robert and Helen Lynd. Of course, television was hardly known when the earlier studies were made. But in 1977 Caplow, as reported in *Middletown Families: Fifty Years of Change and Continuity* (Minneapolis, 1982), found the median time for viewing television was about twenty-eight hours per week. Though some of this "viewing" was "so passive as not to interfere with conversation, study, or housework," most viewers could recall the programs they said

they had watched. The average workweek in Middletown at this time was thirty-eight hours and the average schoolweek about thirty-two hours. This meant that for adults and young people television was engaging nearly as much time as their main daytime occupation.

"What other activities were displaced by television?" Professor Caplow asked. Surprisingly, his findings indicated that other communication media were not displaced at all. Newspaper circulation had kept pace with the population. Radio listening had not declined. Motion picture attendance, though it had temporarily declined, was now rising to the level of the 1920s. Parents at Middletown dinner tables were complaining that television had driven out books. But there was solid evidence to the contrary. Per capita circulation of public library books was no less than in 1925, and now there was a greater ratio of nonfiction to fiction. In the meantime, new sources of books had appeared. While in 1925 there were no bookstores in Middletown, in 1977 there were thirteen, and books were being sold, too, in many other retail outlets. Per capita circulation of national magazines had also increased. Every participant sport (except billiards) found in Middletown in 1925 had relatively more per capita participants in 1977, and dozens of new sports had been taken up. In 1977 Middletown had seven bowling centers, five golf courses, and a thousand home swimming pools.

Where had all the extra hours come from? At least in that typical American community, time given to television was not taken from time give to reading. The sociologists had to invent the notion of a "leisure explosion." People are not necessarily reading books less because they are doing other things they were not doing before. Productivity of leisure hours seems to have increased as much as productivity of work hours. In our technological society, time seems to have become uncannily elastic. People do more these days.

The Twin Menaces: Illiteracy and Aliteracy

New technologies are new allies in our national effort to inform and educate Americans. We must enlist the new technologies with cautious enthusiasm. The threat to a knowledgeable citizenry is not from new technology. But there is a threat from our hasty readiness to exaggerate or misconceive the promise of new technologies, which carries the assumption that the culture of the book is a thing of the past. Today we are failing to do all we should do to qualify young Americans to read and so draw on the main storehouse of our civilization. We are failing to provide enough access to books. And we can do much more to increase the motivation to read.

We must face and defeat the twin menaces of illiteracy and aliteracy—the inability to read and lack of the will to read—if our citizens are to remain free and qualified to govern themselves. We must aim to abolish illiteracy in the United States by 1989.

Illiterates: Americans Who Can't Read

Our whole society—our public and private institutions and our families—must take responsibility for helping our citizens learn to read. The evidence suggests that our nation as a whole is not doing a good job. According to *A Nation at Risk,* the report of the National Commission on Excellence in Education, at least 23 million adults are functionally illiterate by the simplest tests of everyday reading, writing, and comprehension.[2] And the pool of adult illiterates is growing by about 2.3 million persons each year (including school dropouts, immigrants, and refugees). Some 40 percent of our seventeen-year-olds cannot draw inferences from written material, and only one-fifth can write a persuasive essay. The 1983 BISG survey reports that since 1978 the reading of books has declined among sixteen- to twenty-one-year-olds. And as we have noted, the reading of books has declined also among Americans over the age of sixty-five, only 29 percent of whom reported reading a book in the last six months.

Most disturbing is the widely noted decline in emphasis on reading and writing in our elementary and secondary schools. With this has come a decline in the reading of the classics of the English language. These are displaced by textbooks and other teaching materials that do not develop and stretch reading skills in the early stages of education. Instead of more "difficult" works that extend the vocabulary and increase the reader's confidence, pupils read current and "newsworthy" items that often prove of only transient interest. Every textbook should be an aid to literacy.

Many school libraries have been neglected or abolished. In few school libraries have the expenditures kept up with the level necessary to maintain a basic book collection. In 1983, in the country as a whole, the *School Library Journal* reports that the average annual rate of expenditures for books for school libraries was $4.58 and the median was $3.71 per pupil, less than half the cost of one new or replacement hardcover book. While the prices of children's books have risen 30 percent and adult nonfiction and reference books have risen in price even more since 1978, the average per-pupil expenditure for books in this period has increased only 33 cents or about 7 percent. School library budgets for the next years are not expected to rise significantly. As school funds are curtailed, school libraries are among the first targets, especially in elementary schools.

For adults, too, our publicly supported institutions that encourage the reading of books have too often declined or disappeared. Some once-strong urban public library systems, like that in

Detroit, have been withering for lack of funds. The Detroit Public Library now has new hope, thanks to a tax increase approved by the citizens of Detroit in mid-1984, but the problem persists there and in other cities. Chicago, for example, has been struggling to find support for an adequate public library facility. But what happened in Detroit and the recent spectacular renaissance of the New York Public Library, with the aid of private funds, have set examples for other metropolitan libraries and show what can be done by energetic leadership and an awakened citizenry.

Libraries are too often given a low funding priority—below sewage, street maintenance, and police. In the very neighborhoods where people most need constructive leisure and self-improvement activities, libraries often cease to be accessible, though they could serve as avenues to upward mobility, as antidotes to juvenile delinquency, and as the most open of universities. While our national budget for defense increases and while the weapons of defense become ever more sophisticated, requiring literate citizens to operate them, the facilities to help Americans become literate and remain literate do not keep pace.

Aliterates: Americans Who Don't Read
An *aliterate* is a person who can read but who does not, or who reads only under compulsion. In the United States today aliteracy is widespread. Although the total number of book readers (those who have read one or more books in a six-month period) has increased in the last five years by about 8 million, this reflects an increase in population and the advance of the postwar baby boom generation into the prime reading years (thirty- to thirty-nine-year-old group). The percentage of adult Americans who could read a book but do not has remained constant at about 44 percent. The BISG survey reports that in the last five years the proportion of "heavy book readers" (those who have read twenty-six or more books in the previous six months) has increased from 18 percent to 28 percent of all book readers.[3] But book reading in the under-twenty-one age group appears to have declined in these years from 75 percent to 62 percent, and, as we have seen, at the same time book reading in the sixty-five and older age group has also declined. Women, it appears, read more than men, whites read more than other Americans, and single adults read more than married ones. White collar workers read about a third more than blue collar workers. Young adults read much more than older adults. In summary, only about half of all Americans read some books each year.

Reading Begins at Home
The best way to motivate people to read is to encourage reading at home and early in life. The 1983 BISG survey confirmed that book reading is greatest among children whose parents or guardians value reading both for pleasure and as a key to achievement. Children who read a great deal were regularly read to by their parents, grandparents, or older brothers and sisters. As outlined in

a special, thirty-six-page summary of the 1983 BISG survey released at the Library of Congress on April 11, 1984, 83 percent of the parents of children who were classified as heavy readers said they encouraged their children to read and appreciate books as compared to only 57 percent of the parents of light readers.[4] More children would be reading—and would themselves become avid readers—if their parents were readers, talked about what they had read, and encouraged the family to read at home.

Senior Aliterates

Another group of aliterates— Americans who could and should be reading more books—offers some more puzzling problems. According to the Census Bureau, today 11.2 percent of the U.S. population is sixty-five or older, and it is estimated that the percentage will be over 13 percent by the year 2000 and nearly 20 percent by the year 2025. These aging Americans read less than the population as a whole. As we have indicated, of those over sixty-five, only some 29 percent are book readers, compared with 50 percent of the whole population. Physical disabilities are one reason, but apparently not the crucial one. Older non-book readers appear to suffer from lack of motivation to read. Why? Books offer companionship and keep people alert and active. We need to discover the causes and find ways for books to enrich the lives of our senior citizens.

Prisoner Illiterates

A special group who suffer both from illiteracy and aliteracy are Americans in prison. At the present time there are over half a million prisoners in federal and state prisons, of whom about 95 percent will be released eventually. According to the Correctional Education Association, at least 60 percent of the prisoners are functionally illiterate—they cannot read, write, or compute at the third-grade level. Courts have held that the Constitution requires prisons to have a law library for the benefit of prisoners. These libraries vary widely in quality. But most prison libraries are meager, and far too little attention is given to helping our prison population acquire or improve reading skills. Yet no other single skill would be as important in helping prisoners find a productive place in society after their release. The three-year Books for Prisoners project of the Association of American Publishers (1974–77) provided evidence that prisoners like books, care for them, and hunger for more. We must strengthen literacy training and education programs in our nation's correctional system.

Combining Technologies: The Adaptable Book

The culture of the book will continue to be enriched by new technologies. The traditional book, of course, lacks the novelty, commercial hype, and futuristic romance that surround more recent technologies of communication. While exploding newer

367

technologies have excited popular attention and the interest of the newspaper and magazine press, interest in reading, enthusiasm for books, and the prosperity of the book-publishing industry have remained relatively stable. Today about half of all adult Americans read books, and their number is not declining. Of these, more than a third are heavy readers of books, and that proportion is increasing. The staying power of the traditional book is astonishing.

Until the twentieth century the advances of media technology aimed mainly at wider, speedier, and more economical diffusion of printed words and images. The technology of recent decades has added new and complementary dimensions to our experience. Photography has enlivened books by authentic pictures and portraits. The phonograph has preserved and diffused the voices of statesmen, singers, and poets and the virtuoso performances of musicians. Motion pictures have kept alive images of the past and have translated books into newly vivid moving, talking images. Radio has widened the audience beyond time and space and added new opportunities for entertainment, suspense, information, news, and instruction. Television, which some said would mark the demise of opera, has instead given opera a new life and vast new audiences. And, of course, television has made every home a theater, a showcase, a museum, a newsroom, and classroom. Optical disk technology promises to help us combine earlier technologies to open new vistas to scholars and citizens.

New Technologies Bring More Readers
Each of these technologies has created new inducements to read books. The plays of Shakespeare, Chekhov, Ibsen, Shaw, Arthur Miller, and Tennessee Williams, the novels of Dickens, Dumas, Hugo, Flaubert, Tolstoy, Hardy, Orwell, and Mann enjoy revival in libraries and bookstores with their reappearance in movies or on the television screen. Popular screenplays or series written for television themselves become a new raw material for mass-market paperbacks. Publishers' records show that the television series based on Alex Haley's *Roots* and Herman Wouk's *Winds of War* attracted thousands of new buyers and readers of these books. Evelyn Waugh's *Brideshead Revisited,* first published in 1945, had a renaissance in American bookstores in 1983 when it became a television series. "Reading Rainbow," a television series funded by the Corporation for Public Broadcasting and the Kellogg Company to encourage reading among children of ages 5–9, has sold hundreds of thousands of copies of books on which the programs were based. Books on cassettes can entice new readers. The computer itself has provided a popular subject matter for books. R. R. Bowker's new *Retailers' Microcomputer Market Place* will list over six thousand books and five hundred periodicals about computers.

New Technologies Serve Scholarship and Humanistic Culture
New technology plays new scholarly roles. For decades, micro-filming projects have preserved texts of books, journals, and newspapers and made research collections widely available. Scientists at the Crocker Nuclear Laboratory at the University of California at Davis are using a cyclotron to analyze the ink on a fifteenth-century Bible. Scholars at the Clark Library of the University of California at Los Angeles are developing micro-computer programs for textual criticism and editing. The latest and by far the best concordance to Shakespeare has been made by computer. The capture of the 60 million words of the monumental *Oxford English Dictionary* by computer will make the production of all future editions faster, more economical, and more up to date. Our leading American dictionaries and encyclopedias now use computer technology to ease revision, to make new words, novel meanings, and new articles readily available to the public.

Each new technology changes the environment for the culture of the book. Multiplying media have deprived the printed word of its traditional monopoly on access to knowledge, information, and the masterpieces of civilization. For at least a century, speedily innovating technology has multiplied enticing distractions and increased competition for the time and energy and money once devoted to buying and reading books. The telephone, phonograph, radio, and television and their portable, wearable forms have made the silence that facilitates reading harder than ever to find. But they have also made the boundless choices and personalized experience of the book more welcome and more necessary.

The Mirage of "Computer Literacy"
Meanwhile, the American enthusiasm for the newest is betrayed in our everyday vocabulary. People never spoke of movie literacy, radio literacy, or television literacy. *Literacy,* "the ability to read and write," was assumed to be the prime requisite for a free people. It carried with it the capacity and the opportunity to select one's own sources of knowledge and to enjoy a private, individualized experience of pleasure and self-instruction. Now we hear pleas for "computer literacy"! Here is a telltale clue to the continuing kudos of the book as the main avenue to knowledge. This expression also shows how we fuzz over our culture with fashionable ambiguities. Our enthusiasm for "computer literacy"—the ability to manipulate the latest model of this latest device—seems about to over-shadow our concern for book literacy. But mastering a machine is no substitute for the ability to read, and computer competence itself depends on the ability to read. Schools and summer camps and correspondence courses aim to make "computer literates" out of people who remain ill at ease in the world of books.

To keep our thinking straight and our culture alive and our people free we must keep our definition of literacy sharp and clear.

To use computers effectively requires a familiarity with books and a friendliness to books. We have yet to find a feasible alternative to the ability to learn from the printed word and enjoy the boundless treasures. The book is always "user friendly." We must aim to make all Americans book friendly.

The Alliance of Technologies

The same human ingenuity that produced the book has produced later technologies, and they are all allies. Our task is to recognize and promote their alliance. We must see the role which the computer is already playing and that which it is likely to play. Then we will not underestimate or abandon book literacy. The enemy of the book is not technology but the illusion that we could or would abolish the culture of the book.

There is no end to our hopes for devices to spread the benefits and pleasures (and frustrations) of technology to our whole nation, including our children in school. While people in older worlds, confronted with a new technology, have been inclined to ask "Why?" we Americans have usually asked "Why not?" Our false prophets have been those who declared that something was impossible. The telegraph, telephone, phonograph, radio, television, nuclear energy—and now the computer—all violated the confident "impossibilities" of the experts. Therefore as we speculate about the book in the future we must not dare to prophesy that *anything* will be impossible here. The miracles of the computer will be supplemented by others more astonishing. Yet we must not allow our innovating hopes and enthusiasm to dazzle us. We must do our fallible best to suggest the extent and the limits of the roles of the new computer technology.

Special Services of the Computer

We can already see that for some purposes the newest technology can provide services superior to those of the traditional book.

First, services of information, where data change frequently and where speedy access is essential. This includes current facts for lawmakers, government and business managers, doctors, hospital administrators, pharmacists, journalists, law enforcement officers, merchants, and dealers in commercial markets.

Second, services of access, to bibliographies and other information about the sources of knowledge or information. The Library of Congress has pioneered in this area. The Library's Congressional Research Service provides for members of Congress and their staffs instant access through the automated "Scorpio" system to the current status of the ten to twenty thousand bills submitted by members of each Congress. In 1968, the Library began storing its current English-language cataloging (available at that time only on printed catalog cards or in book catalogs) on computer tapes, available to other libraries through its MARC Distribution Service.

Libraries have formed networks like OCLC and the Research Libraries Group (RLG) that have used these records and records from member libraries to speed cataloging and interlibrary loan work while saving large sums of money. Through the widely acclaimed CJK (Chinese-Japanese-Korean) project, the RLG, in cooperation with the Library, has developed a remarkable machine that uses a single keyboard for cataloging books in these three languages.

Third, services of storage, retrieval, and preservation, combined with a new flexibility of access. In 1983 the Library began experimenting with the analog videodisk for storage and retrieval of graphic and photographic materials in color. Today researchers are using this system for speedy, nondestructive access to our most precious and most fragile visual materials. In collaboration with the publishing industry, we have also been experimenting with optical digital disks that store print material in unprecedented compactness and with high resolution to preserve the material and make periodicals, music, maps, and manuscripts more conveniently accessible.

The Computer in the Publishing Process
The computer greatly facilitates the process of bringing out a book. When an author types on a word processor, the text can be transferred to a computerized photocomposition device without rekeyboarding. The printer has cameras, scanners, and presses that are controlled in part by microprocessors. Finally, the publisher can keep sales, royalty, and other records on a computer and use the computer as an aid in producing frequent catalogs that bring newly published books to the attention of potential readers.

Books and Parts of Books "On Demand"
The computer makes it possible to print books in formats other than the familiar ink-on-paper octavo-sized volumes. When the full text of a book is held in digital form by the copyright licensee, the publisher, or a wholesaler, it can be called up from the corporate main computer. On request from a bookstore, a library, or a reader, the book or its parts could be printed out in the manner of the present high-speed reprographic machine. Within the next decade we may be seeing even smaller machines using lasers for this purpose. These printers could conceivably be tied to home telephone or television cables. Perhaps such machines might be offered "free" to subscribers to new kinds of book clubs or newspaper services.

New "print-on-demand" systems could vastly enlarge the stock of books currently available for purchase. Perhaps marginal titles that do not repay the printing on paper in large runs now required by book production technology could be published in this way. Storage costs would be minimal. And book buyers would less often

371

have to be told that a favorite title had gone out of print and had to be sought in the secondhand market. Today a manuscript must be of a certain length to be worth publishing as a book. On-demand printing might make it economic to publish shorter manuscripts or to offer single chapters as the reader requires.

Textbooks and Technical Books Combine Technologies

Already in some engineering, medical, and other technical books a pocket in the back of the cover holds plastic magnetic disks ("floppy disks"). The mathematical and statistical data recorded on them can be revised and updated more economically and more speedily than if they were in the printed texts. Some kinds of information—legal opinions, new legislation, pharmaceutical data, census and economic figures—are now issued first on speedily available tapes or disks, to be followed later by print-on-paper bound books. Just as audiovisual aids have assisted teachers of biology, medicine, geography, geology, history, art, music, and countless other subjects, so now magnetic disks further increase the student's access to data, words, and images.

Learning Aids

Mixture of formats provides new opportunities for tailoring the learning process to the needs and capacities of the individual student. Along with convenient inexpensive means for repetitive drill come new forms of interactive learning with the student responding and receiving immediate feedback of correction or praise. Computer aids seem to work especially well for students with learning or physical disabilities and learners who have passed the normal age for the usual textbooks. The main peril of these systems is the risk of undervaluing the human teacher.

Computer Alternatives to Print on Paper

For some purposes, the traditional paper formats have already been displaced by images on the cathode ray tube. In the future these and other paper-format materials may be created on thin sheets of glass or plastic from data stored on laser cards or microchips. The size of the letters to be viewed could then be adjusted for any reader's eyesight. It is conceivable that plastic cards the size of credit cards could carry all the words of a short book. The new CJK keyboard and other terminals are already taking advantage of computer-stored images to reduce the obstacles to reproducing the complex Asian ideographic characters for cataloging purposes. The optical disk, now in experimental use at the Library of Congress, stores about three hundred printed volumes per disk. When this technology is perfected, it might be possible for several hundred twelve-inch two-sided disks, requiring less than ten feet of shelf space, to hold the quarter-million books and documents added to a typical research library each year. And new technology will provide newly simplified finding and retrieval systems for the compacted data.

Unexplored Opportunities

But we need not await future technologies to find new opportunities for enriching the culture of the book. During World War II a standard format was used for printing the Armed Services Editions —little oblong paperback reprints, of which nearly 123 million copies were distributed free. These 1,322 titles were produced in wartime at a cost of about six cents each. The project required the cooperation not only of the armed services but of the War Production Board, seventy publishing firms, a dozen printing houses and composition firms, paper suppliers, and scores of authors. Millions of readers in uniform found enlightenment and good cheer from a menu that included Katherine Anne Porter, Robert Benchley, Lytton Strachey, Max Brand, E. B. White, Leo Rosten, Herman Wouk, Budd Schulberg, and Graham Greene and in moods that range from *The Education of Henry Adams* to *McSorley's Wonderful Saloon*. The Armed Services Editions proved to be one of the greatest cultural bonanzas in American history. They stirred the reading appetites of millions who would never lose their taste for books. They required a minimum of technological innovation and a maximum of imagination and organizing talent. It is not surprising that a vast new market for paperback books appeared after the war.

If so grand an enterprise could be accomplished under the constraints of a wartime economy, surely we today are capable of enterprises of comparable grandeur. Many opportunities come from our fantastically multiplying media. Television, which so thoroughly reaches into every American home, offers unprecedented means to whet appetites for reading among Americans of all ages. A few projects, Like "Reading Rainbow" and the "Read More About It" project of the Library of Congress and CBS, with its slogan "linking the pleasure, power, and excitement of books and television," have begun to use television to invigorate the culture of the book. Still, such projects are too few. We need many more of them to keep our citizens in touch with our whole human heritage and so fulfill anew the hopes for enlightenment on which our nation was founded.

When printing from movable type was first invented in Europe it was praised as *Ars artium omnium conservatrix* ("the art preservative of all the arts"). In our age, we can reap the harvest of a half-millennium of the printed word. We must not forget that for us reading books is "the activity which enriches all others." There is no business, work, sport, skill, entertainment, art, or science that cannot be improved by reading and whose rewards cannot be increased by books. The reading of books, as we have seen, is not a passive, marginal social fact but a major national activity. We must use all our technologies to make the most of our inheritance, to move toward an American renaissance of the culture of the book.

Notes

1. For a summary of this report, see chapter 7 above.
2. For excerpts from *A Nation at Risk,* see chapter 1 above.
3. See chapter 7 above for changes in some of these figures discovered in final analysis of the BISG data.
4. These parents said that the following statement described them "very well"— that is, at the highest level of a four-level scale—"I have encouraged my child to read and appreciate books." Eighty-three percent of the parents of heavy readers describe themselves this way, and only 57 percent of the parents of light readers. *1983 Consumer Research Study on Reading and Book Purchasing: Focus on Juveniles* (New York: Book Industry Study Group, 1984), 33.

Bibliography
prepared by Joseph F. Brinley, Jr.

The works cited in this bibliography provide further expositions of the trends and proposals described in the chapters above. The bibliography includes many of the titles mentioned in the chapters, additional commission reports, and other publications that are articulate but not highly technical or narrowly professional.

The bibliography is divided into five sections: Reading and Learning; Reading and Society; Technology and the Future of the Book; The Book Professions—Publishing; and The Book Professions —Librarianship.

Reading and Learning

Becoming a Nation of Readers: The Report of the Commission on Reading, prepared by Richard C. Anderson, Elfrieda H. Hiebert, Judith A. Scott, and Ian A. G. Wilkinson, with contributions from members of the Commission on Reading. Pittsburgh: National Academy of Education; Washington: National Institute of Education, U.S. Department of Education; Urbana, Ill.: Center for the Study of Reading, 1985.

For an introduction and excerpts, see chapter 3 above.

Ernest L. Boyer. *High School: A Report on Secondary Education in America*. New York: Harper & Row, 1983.

High School, prepared for the Carnegie Foundation for the Advancement of Teaching, is a comprehensive treatment of public high schools in the United States. The book situates high schools and their teachers, students, principals, parents, and communities in relation to the roles America sets for the high school. *High School* presents statistical information about high school performance and public moods about high schools, but most of the book is based on twenty-day observations of fifteen high schools. Recommendations stress setting educational goals and core curricula, attention to anticipated employment of graduates, and attention to teachers' working conditions and incentives. *High School* also proposes universal community service by students.

Jeanne S. Chall. *Learning to Read: The Great Debate*. Updated ed. New York: McGraw-Hill, 1983.

A classic study of learning to read in the primary grades, *Learning to Read* in 1967 asserted the superiority of phonics instruction for at least first and second grade and suggested that increased emphasis on reading for meaning is appropriate after that. The updated edition reproduces the 1967 study and adds an introductory essay describing research since 1967 and refinements Chall would make in her own theory today.

375

The Great School Debate: Which Way for American Education?
Edited by Beatrice and Ronald Gross. New York: Simon & Schuster, 1985.

The Great School Debate is a sourcebook on the controversy raised by *A Nation at Risk*. The editors have gathered commission reports, commission reports against those reports, essays critical of the notion of commissions making reports at all, educational proposals from various partisans, and commentary—64 articles in all. Appendixes describe people, organizations, and the key documents.

Carman St. John Hunter and David Harman. *Adult Illiteracy in the United States*. A Report to the Ford Foundation. New York: McGraw-Hill, 1979.

This influential study covers definitions of functional illiteracy, its extent in different parts of the population, and the efforts that have not yet successfully approached the problem. The recommendations stress the need for "community-based" literacy programs, in which local communities would set the standards, the contents, and the criteria for instruction. Annotated bibliography.

Irwin S. Kirsch and Ann Jungeblut. *Literacy: Profiles of America's Young Adults*. Princeton, N.J.: Educational Testing Service, 1986.

Literacy reports the results of a very large and important study, conducted by the National Assessment of Educational Progress, of literacy among 21- to 25-year-old Americans. In the study, the development of the evaluation instrument is itself of great interest, because it is able to assess literacy at a great variety of levels. The instrument also treated literacy as involving more than one skill by dividing literacy into reading prose ("prose literacy"), working with documents such as job applications and schedules ("documentary literacy"), and being able to make further calculations on the basis of quantitative information in texts ("quantitative literacy"). The researchers gathered a great deal of information about the backgrounds of the study group and gave them a standard multiple-choice reading test so that the results measured with the new assessments could be compared to the results of the standard one. Among the results: (1) Americans are overwhelmingly able to perform easy tasks that require reading. (2) The ability to accomplish more difficult tasks is strongly associated with higher levels of education, with higher levels of parents' education, and with being white rather than Hispanic or black. Hispanics tend to fall in between whites and blacks. (3) The 22- to 25-year-olds studied performed better than younger people still in school, suggesting perhaps that literacy continues to improve after the end of formal schooling. In general, few of those studied were able to accomplish moderately complex tasks. *Literacy* gives many examples of the tasks the young adults found easy and difficult.

376

Jonathan Kozol. *Illiterate America*. Garden City, N.Y.: Anchor/ Doubleday, 1985.

Kozol recounts the dependency and disenfranchisement to which the illiterate is subject. He critically assesses various governmental and institutional studies of illiteracy and programs of assistance. Kozol's conclusion is that illiterate Americans themselves and those who live near them must create literacy organizations: community-based organizations will shape literacy for the sake of empowering people.

A Nation at Risk: The Imperative for Educational Reform. A Report to the Nation and the Secretary of Education, United States Department of Education, by the National Commission on Excellence in Education. Washington: U.S. Government Printing Office, 1983.

For an introduction and excerpts, see chapter 1 above.

A Nation Prepared: Teachers for the 21st Century. The Report of the Task Force on Teaching as a Profession of the Carnegie Forum on Education and the Economy. Washington: the Forum, 1985.

A Nation Prepared asserts that American competitiveness in the all-important knowledge sector of the world economy requires a work force educated for innovation, not mass production. Only a teaching profession with the characteristics of autonomy associated with a profession—self-certification, adequate income, adequate support staff, promotion on the basis of competence, high standards for entry, etc.—can give this. The task force recommends abolition of undergraduate degrees in education and institution of new Master of Teaching programs.

The Nation Responds: Recent Efforts to Improve Education. U.S. Department of Education. Washington: U.S. Government Printing Office, 1984.

The Nation Responds provides many examples of efforts towards educational excellence at all levels throughout the United States. An overview of programs, debates, and research by public and private organizations and professional associations is followed by descriptions of the initiatives of states and examples of programs of municipalities, professional associations, and private corporations and grant-making organizations.

Robert M. Rosenzweig and Barbara Turlington. *The Research Universities and Their Patrons*. Prepared under the auspices of the Association of American Universities. Berkeley: University of California Press, 1982.

The advisory committee for this report included university presidents and foundation and corporate executives. The report advocates the retention of the teaching university as a basic research institution, with support from government but also with a closer relationship to the corporate world. One chapter focuses on libraries, particularly with regard to automation, preservation of materials, and remedies to the information explosion.

What Works: Research about Teaching and Learning. U.S. Department of Education. Washington: the Department, 1986.

What Works summarizes, in one page each, about forty-five practically applicable findings of research into preschool, elementary, and secondary education. The suggestions are directed to parents, supervisors and administrators, and, mostly, teachers. Recommendations cover reading, writing, mathematics, science, discipline, expectations, and many other areas. References to reports of research are given.

Reading and Society

Mortimer J. Adler. *The Paideia Proposal: An Educational Manifesto.* New York: Macmillan, 1982.

Written on behalf of the Paideia Group, a group of scholars and educators, *The Paideia Proposal* outlines a system of elementary and secondary schooling aimed at making all Americans—and so all citizens—self-motivated lifelong learners and competent participants in democracy. Such childhood education involves (1) a single curriculum that covers for all children the foundations of the liberal arts and sciences, (2) extensive employment of coaching and discussion along with more traditional classroom instruction, and (3) remedial teaching to enable underprivileged children to participate fully in this education.

Books in Our Future: A Report from the Librarian of Congress to the Congress. Washington: Joint Committee on the Library, Congress of the United States, 1984. Available from the U.S. Government Printing Office.

For an introduction and most of the text, see chapter 27 above.

Eva T. H. Brann. *Paradoxes of Education in a Republic.* Chicago: University of Chicago Press, 1979.

Seeking the deepest causes of the recurrent problems of American education, Brann finds paradoxes in the notions of educational utility, cultural tradition, and training for individual rationality. For example, American culture is founded upon the Western tradition but conceives itself as breaking away from it. Brann suggests that at the collegiate level an education based on inquiry into the books of the Western tradition and aimed at contemplation provides a genuinely educational reconciliation of the paradoxes for the student.

The Community of the Book: A Directory of Selected Organizations and Programs. Compiled by Carren O. Kaston. Edited by John Y. Cole. Washington: Library of Congress, 1986.

The Community of the Book describes 89 organizations that

promote books and reading, administer literacy projects, and encourage the study of books. Expanding on the brief list of organizations in *Books in Our Future,* the directory describes important professional associations of booksellers, publishers, librarians, book researchers, scholars, teachers, and writers and other organizations interested in literacy, the book industry, books and technology, books and the media, censorship, the history of books, and the international role of the book.

Freedom and Equality of Access to Information: A Report to the American Library Association. Commission on Freedom and Equality of Access to Information, Dan M. Lacy, Chair. Chicago: American Library Association, 1986.

For an introduction and excerpts, see chapter 26 above.

Paulo Freire. *Pedagogy of the Oppressed.* Translated by Myra Bergman Ramos. New York: Herder and Herder, 1972.

Pedagogy of the Oppressed argues that an education toward self-motivation requires that learners identify and act against oppressive social structures—true learning and growth in freedom do not happen independently of each other. Freire draws on modern, especially Marxist, philosophy to make his case, and he is immersed in the conditions of Latin America. Nevertheless, his direction toward self-motivation shares some aspects with Mortimer Adler's classically based scheme. Freire's learning groups suggest a model for the community-founded literacy groups proposed by Kozol and by Hunter and Harman (see above under "Reading and Learning").

The Future of Literacy. Edited by Robert Disch. Englewood Cliffs, N.J.: Prentice-Hall, 1973.

In this collection of reprinted articles and excerpts, a variety of eminent literary and scholarly figures, among them, Claude Levi-Strauss, Herbert Marcuse, Marshall McLuhan, and Eugene Ionesco, assess the meaning and future of literacy. Some essays are profoundly philosophical, addressing how words mean anything at all and how society shapes meaning through traditions and revolutions of words and structures of communication. Others turn toward the development and, perhaps, demise of the modern culture that has been shaped by the influence of printed books.

The Humanities in American Life. Report of the Commission on the Humanities. Berkeley: University of California Press, 1980.

The recommendations of this report aim at strengthening the role of the humanities both in education and in American culture as a whole. The commission, sponsored by the Rockefeller Foundation, included notable scholars; business executives; politicians; and executives in public broadcasting, research librarianship, and other fields. Education beyond the basics is needed for participation in a democracy, and the commission's recommendations stress this requirement. The humanities in public culture should include not only a national culture but also local interests, such as local history and preservation. Much of the report addresses responsibilities for funding.

The 1983 Consumer Research Study on Reading and Book Purchasing. Conducted by Market Facts, interpreted by Research & Forecasts, prepared for the Book Industry Study Group. 3 vols. New York: Book Industry Study Group, 1984.

For an introduction and summary, see chapter 7 above.

Reading in America 1978. Edited by John Y. Cole and Carol S. Gold. Washington: Library of Congress, 1979.

The centerpiece of this book is a summary of the *1978 Consumer Research Study on Reading and Book Purchasing,* the predecessor of the 1983 study summarized above in chapter 7. The book includes commentary on the 1978 survey and on reading in America at that time by Martin P. Levin, Barbara Tuchman, W. Thomas Johnson, and Charles B. Weinberg and a summary of a symposium organized by the Center for the Book in the Library of Congress.

"Reading: Old and New." *Daedalus,* vol. 112, no. 1, Winter 1983.

The "Reading: Old and New" issue of *Daedalus* contains seventeen essays on reading in our culture. Among areas of concern are the division between academic and public culture, the financial and organizational conditions of book publishing and distribution, reading in the electronic future, and what reading means in the light of literary theories that argue against a stability of meaning in the text. Contributors include writers, publishers, and scholars. Chapters 9 and 10 above were drawn from "Reading: Old and New." The issue was reprinted with one more essay as *Reading in the 1980s* (New York: R. R. Bowker, 1983).

Gordon and Patricia Sabine. *Books that Made the Difference: What People Told Us.* Hamden, Conn.: Shoe String Press, Library Professional Publications, 1983.

This book encapsulates 200 responses to the questions, "What book made the greatest difference in your life? What was that difference?" Traveling across the United States in 1980 and 1981, the Sabines interviewed almost 1,400 Americans. The titles named show great variety—not just religion and philosophy, but biography, history, a great deal of fiction, Dr. Spock's *Baby and Child Care,* and even a calorie-counter book were named.

Charles Wegener. *Liberal Education and the Modern University.* Chicago: University of Chicago Press, 1978.

Liberal Education and the Modern University relates the research university, professional education, and the sort of education that befits a free citizen. Wegener's investigation is grounded in the late-nineteenth-century histories of the American research universities, when not only laboratories but also libraries first became important components of educational institutions. Wegener sees education as going beyond the transmission of subject matter, or even transmission of a tradition of educational methods, to an area of pure activity, and he studies the problems of institutionalizing such activity.

Technology and the Future of the Book

Ben H. Bagdikian. *The Information Machines: Their Impact on Men and the Media.* New York: Harper & Row, 1971.

The Information Machines examines the effect of electronic communications on contemporary society. Radio, television, and computerization all affect the speed with which we know things and the quality of what we know, sometimes for the better and sometimes for the worse. The expenses of production, too, affect who can afford to provide what kinds of information, affecting in turn the selection of the content actually delivered. Bagdikian focuses, though not exclusively, on changes in news reporting.

David Burnham. *The Rise of the Computer State.* New York: Random House, 1983.

The Rise of the Computer State details the threats to personal freedom posed by the new abilities to transfer vast amounts of information about individuals. The substitution of electronic fund transfer for the use of money will allow a government or another institution to track an individual's movements throughout the day. Political polling via two-way cable television may substitute hasty emotional reaction to issues for more considered action. Burnham is particularly fearful that increasing authoritarianism in American society could become an eager ally of invasive technology.

Communications and the Future: Prospects, Promises, and Problems. Edited by Howard F. Didsbury, Jr. Bethesda, Md.: World Future Society, 1982.

Forty-six papers or excerpted papers, prepared for the 1982 General Assembly of the World Future Society, address a great range of topics on the future of communications in this volume. Computerization, communications, a shift from written to oral culture by way of video, librarianship, and psychology are discussed in the light of projected improvements in information technologies and their expected implementation throughout the world in all levels of society.

Christopher Evans. *The Micro Millenium.* New York: Pocket Books, Washington Square Press, 1980.

The Micro Millenium is a futuristic account of computers and their influence on society. Evans describes the history of computers, their current effects, and their immediate future, particularly in terms of networks of computerized information. He goes on to defend the notion of artificial intelligence and describes the social consequences of worldwide information flow and the effects on human development of the arrival of a new class of intelligent beings.

Edward A. Feigenbaum and Pamela McCorduck. *The Fifth Generation: Artificial Intelligence and Japan's Computer Challenge to the World.* Reading, Mass.: Addison-Wesley, 1983.
The Fifth Generation examines efforts toward the manufacture of artificial intelligence and the relation of those efforts to the world economic order projected for the end of the twentieth century. Feigenbaum and McCorduck describe the projects that aim at linking ever-faster logical processing with flexible computerized knowledge bases; the national backing for those quests of not only the Japanese but also the French and English; and the failure of major American institutions to provide competitive support.

F. W. Lancaster. *Toward Paperless Information Systems.* New York: Academic Press, 1978.
Toward Paperless Information Systems provides a scenario for future online systems for nonrecreational information. Lancaster examines, first, a paperless information system developed for the CIA and, then, the tendencies in modern scholarly communication and in technology that may make paperless systems for scientific information feasible. Such systems may, Lancaster believes, supersede scholarly journals and monographs for many purposes.

Ithiel de Sola Pool. *Technologies of Freedom.* Cambridge, Mass.: Harvard University Press, Belknap Press, 1983.
Technologies of Freedom treats the relationship of communications to the law and to regulation. Different regulatory systems have arisen for print, common carriers such as telephone and telegraph, and mass broadcasting. Each system ensures different kinds of access and rewards different kinds of ownership. Pool describes the histories of these media and the law and assesses the future as the media convergently offer what formerly seemed the others' unique modes of communication.

William Saffady. *Video-based Information Systems: A Guide for Educational, Business, Library, and Home Use.* Chicago: American Library Association, 1985.
Video-based Information Systems describes current and soon-expected systems that display information on cathode ray tubes or liquid crystal displays—television, videocassette, videodisk, cable, videotext, telefacsimile, videoconferencing, and computer data display. Saffady's book gives a good consumer's description of how each works and its technical limitations. Information, rather than entertainment, applications are described. Each chapter has a bibliography identifying articles on particular business or institutional uses.

Sherry Turkle. *The Second Self: Computers and the Human Spirit.*
New York: Simon and Schuster, 1984.

The Second Self tells how working with computers, from playing
with games to designing programs at high levels of research,
affects the thought and emotions of people. Turkle conducted an
anthropological investigation of those immersed in the world of
computers. Her interests range from whether children think the
toys that teach them to spell words are alive to the assertion by
artificial intelligence researchers that no personal identity is
necessary for thinking to take place. Turkle concludes by asking
what happens to our sense of responsibility when we cannot distinguish computers' processing from our own.

The Book Professions—Publishing

American Books Abroad: Toward a National Policy. Edited by William A. Childs and Donald E. McNeil. Washington: The Helen
Dwight Reid Educational Foundation, 1986.

American Books Abroad examines the difficulties of American
books in foreign markets. This work by the Reid Foundation for
the U.S. Information Agency Task Force on American Books
Abroad, presented with the task force's recommendations, was
stimulated by the perception that the United States is losing the
"war of ideas" with the Soviet Union, partly because of a great deal
of heavily subsidized Soviet publication for export. American problems include high prices, piracy, publishing traditions, currency
problems, and a lack of public funding. *American Books Abroad*
recommends various private and government actions to improve
the worldwide position of American publications and ideas.

Benjamin Compaine, Christopher H. Sterling, Thomas Guback,
and J. Kendrick Noble, Jr. *Who Owns the Media? Concentration of
Ownership in the Mass Communications Industry.* 2d ed. White
Plains, N.Y.: Knowledge Industry Publications, 1982.

Who Owns the Media? addresses concentration in the newspaper, television, radio, magazine, movie, book, and cable and pay
television industries. Concentration within each industry, by mul-
timedia conglomerates, and by holding companies whose primary
business is not in the media are areas of concern. The examination
is primarily economic, but literary content and freedom of access
are also considered.

Lewis A. Coser, Charles Kadushin, and Walter W. Powell. *Books:
The Culture and Commerce of Publishing.* New York: Basic Books,
1982.

Three sociologists examine trade, scholarly, and college textbook presses. *Books* studies the process of publishing from its
beginning—how an author gets his or her work into the system—
to the end—the effectiveness of book reviewing. Much of the work
profiles people who work at various levels of the industry. Among
the conclusions are that activity is utterly different in the worlds of

small scholarly presses, publishers of "serious" trade books, and publishers aiming at the large markets of blockbusters and that the importance of different professionals in them varies accordingly. The authors fear homogenization of the few books that will be brought to large audiences.

The Future of the Book. Part 1: *The Impact of New Technologies.* Edited by Priscilla Oakeshott and Clive Bradley. Studies on Books and Reading, no. 8. Paris: Unesco, 1982.

The Impact of New Technologies is a thorough overview of the current and expected effects of the new technologies on books. A major portion treats educational books, both for developed and less developed countries. In the latter, there are great problems with basic literacy, some of which may be addressed with the help of television and video technologies, while at higher educational levels the simple procurement of textbooks is often a difficulty. *The Impact of New Technologies* also treats general books, informational books, technology in book writing, publishing, printing, distribution, and use, and its effect on the book professions.

The Future of the Book. Part 2: *The Changing Role of Reading.* Prepared by Michel Gault for the French National Commission for Unesco. Studies on Books and Reading, no. 9. Paris: Unesco, 1982.

The Changing Role of Reading assesses the status of book reading and the role of reading worldwide, but mostly in Western Europe. There are important differences in literacy and book use within Europe. Gault's report stresses the importance of easily accessible libraries, especially for small children. *The Changing Role of Reading* shows that there are fears in Europe, too, of concentration of publishing in the hands of a few companies intent on quick profits through publishing fast-selling books.

"The Quality of Trade Book Publishing in the 1980s." Edited by Walter C. Allen, Eleanor Blum, and Ann Heidbreder Eastman. *Library Trends,* vol. 33, no. 2, Fall 1984.

This issue of *Library Trends* assesses the quality trade book— "serious" fiction or nonfiction for the "general reader"—and its place in the world of publishing. Contributors include scholars, publishers, and publishing consultants. Contributions by two literary agents, A. L. Hart and Richard Curtis, provide a rare look at this part of the industry. Book production, marketing, and promotion are treated, as well as editorial activity. Two essays from this issue were reprinted above in chapters 19 and 22.

Scholarly Communication: The Report of the National Enquiry. Baltimore: Johns Hopkins University Press, 1979.

This volume finds that the system of scholarly communication for the humanities and social sciences, involving both publishing and librarianship, has a number of problems but is not in serious danger. Its outstanding recommendations are for the formation of an online national bibliographic system and in support of national institutions for periodicals and for a library system in general. It urges that journals be allowed to suffer some attrition and that the publication of monographs be more strongly supported. *Scholarly Communication* is the report of the National Enquiry into Scholarly Communication sponsored by the American Council of Learned Societies.

Leonard Shatzkin. *In Cold Type: Overcoming the Book Crisis.* Boston: Houghton Mifflin, 1982.

Leonard Shatzkin sees two trends in the trade book industry leading to a crisis: books are too expensive, and publishing is not profitable enough. Shatzkin traces these problems and others in a survey of the entire trade publishing process. Shatzkin believes that the crisis can be averted if a different book distribution system is instituted, one that gives publishers responsibility for selecting titles to be displayed in local bookstores and allows the booksellers, in turn, to hold publishers responsible for their books' performance.

The Book Professions—Librarianship

Alliance for Excellence: Librarians Respond to A Nation at Risk. The Libraries and a Learning Society Project, U.S. Department of Education.

For an introduction and excerpts, see chapter 21 above.

The Changing Role of Public Libraries: Background Papers from the White House Conference. Compiled by Whitney North Seymour, Jr. Metuchen, N.J.: Scarecrow Press, 1980.

Six papers advocate new services for ordinary and disadvantaged citizens and describe the resources that will be required to support them. Neighborhood information service, for example, links people to local social services, government agencies, and other services. Attentive and flexible service for the disadvantaged is valuable in both urban and rural settings. Career information centers, continuing education services, new technology, and the preparation of librarians for these sorts of services are other focuses. The papers were prepared for the 1979 White House Conference on Library and Information Services. Seymour provides similar information, in the context of the history of public libraries, in *For the People: Fighting for Public Libraries* (Garden City, N.Y.: Doubleday, 1979), which he wrote with Elizabeth N. Layne.

Martin M. Cummings. *The Economics of Research Libraries.* Washington: Council on Library Resources, 1986.

The Economics of Research Libraries reviews the economic relations of research libraries to their universities and the internal economics of the libraries themselves. It also tries to situate libraries in the expected future of higher education. Research libraries have responded to the information explosion, new technology, and declines in student populations with changes of staffing patterns and materials acquisitions, the development of interlibrary cooperation, and generally better informed management. They must also respond to the prospect of the "wired" campus, in which students and faculty have microcomputer-based access to large databases, both on campus and off campus.

Kenneth E. Dowlin. *The Electronic Library: The Promise and the Process.* New York: Neal-Schuman Publishers, 1984.
For an introduction and excerpt, see chapter 13 above.

Michael H. Harris. *The Role of the Public Library in American Life.* Graduate School of Library Science Occasional Papers, no. 117. Champaign, Ill.: University of Illinois Graduate School of Library Science, 1975.
The Role of the Public Library in American Life is a brief revisionist history of public libraries in America to about 1950. Harris asserts, with ample documentation, that public libraries were founded not for the intellectual perfection of the common man, but rather as elitist institutions which, it was hoped, would restrain some of the evil impulses of the lower classes. Even the changed emphasis toward protecting the public's right to know, which libraries adopted in response to pre-World War II fascist book burnings in Europe, allowed librarians to remain passive servants of an intellectual elite.

An Information Agenda for the 1980s. Edited by Carlton C. Rochell. Chicago: American Library Association, 1981.
This volume projects the impact of technological and social change on the storage and transfer of information. *Information Agenda* includes papers prepared for a colloquium convened by the American Library Association in 1980 and papers reflecting on that colloquium. Issues include the use of information as a marketable commodity, the effects on society of too much unassimilated information, and the proper role of government, all in the context of such expected developments as ever-cheaper computerization, widespread videotext, and continuing financial restrictions on libraries.

International Librarianship Today and Tomorrow: A Festschrift for William J. Welsh. Compiled by Joseph W. Price and Mary S. Price. New York: K. G. Saur, 1985.
Fifteen essays assess the activities of librarianship across national borders. Some describe a nation's library development and structure, providing a picture of the system to which international efforts will have to join up. Others treat international developments themselves. Bibliographic control and use of new tech-

nologies in bibliography are important subjects. Funding, both within nations and for international efforts, is a pervasive interest. Specifically treated are the United States, Australia, Norway, the Federal Republic of Germany, the Soviet Union, Denmark, Kenya, Canada, and Great Britain.

F. W. Lancaster. *Libraries and Librarians in an Age of Electronics.* Arlington, Va.: Information Resources Press, 1982.

Lancaster studies the prospects of librarianship in an age to be dominated by paperless information systems, in which, of course, the library's role as a warehouse of publications would be curtailed or eliminated. He believes that the librarian will have an important role acting as a skilled and informed guide to electronic resources for information seekers. Lancaster reviews the uses of computers in publication and the current economics of online information provision in order to show a trend toward electronic publication.

Barbara B. Moran. *Academic Libraries: The Changing Knowledge Centers of Colleges and Universities.* ASHE-ERIC Higher Education Research Report no. 8. Washington: Association for the Study of Higher Education, 1984.

Academic Libraries describes the most important issues facing academic libraries in four areas: the new technologies, management, personnel issues, and library collections. Moran sketches the history of each topic and describes likely changes and responses. *Academic Libraries* reports extensively on interlibrary cooperation in computerized shared cataloging systems and other functions of bibliographic utilities, acquisitions, and the failure to implement a national periodicals center. Personnel issues include shared responsibility and librarian status in the university.

Theodore Schuchat. *The Library Book.* Seattle: Madrona Publishers, 1985.

The Library Book tells about the workings of the modern public library. Schuchat takes as his model the Enoch Pratt Free Library in Baltimore. He describes in nontechnical terms its history and services, including not only the collections and reference services but also technical services, especially acquisitions, services for special groups such as young adults, telephone reference services, and the governance of the library and its relation to funding authorities. A final chapter examines how electronics is changing library service.

Efrem Sigel, Erik Barnouw, Anthony Smith, Dan Lacy, Robert D. Stueart, and Lewis M. Branscomb. *Books, Libraries, and Electronics: Essays on the Future of Written Communication.* White Plains, N.Y.: Knowledge Industry Publications, 1982.

The essays in *Books, Libraries, and Electronics* describe the effects of new communications technologies on the transmission of text and on the social and economic organization on which that transmission depends. Topics include the future of the book; video, especially television, in relation to text; changes in authorship; publishing; and videodisk technology. Stueart's essay on libraries shows how libraries are shifting from being oriented toward collection of materials and maintenance to being oriented toward service and describes the implications of this change for library functions.

Lawrence J. White. *The Public Library in the 1980s: The Problems of Choice.* Lexington Mass.: Lexington Books, 1983.

An economist's review of the situation of public libraries in America, *The Public Library in the 1980s* analyzes who benefits from and who pays for public libraries. Reaffirming the common result—about a quarter of adults, heavily middle class, are users, but everybody pays—White goes on to show that the public library doesn't really fit the economist's definition of a public good, a good in which adding a beneficiary brings no added cost. But the library approaches this model in providing children's services, and it should shift its emphasis to this area.

Index